Inclusive Innovation in the Age of AI and Big Data

Inclusive Innovation in the Age of AI and Big Data

Edited by

DARYL LIM
H. Laddie Montague Jr. Chair in Law
Penn State Dickinson Law, USA

PETER K. YU
University Distinguished Professor and Regents Professor of Law and Communication
Texas A&M University School of Law, USA

OXFORD
UNIVERSITY PRESS

OXFORD
UNIVERSITY PRESS

Oxford University Press is a department of the University of Oxford. It furthers the University's objective of excellence in research, scholarship, and education by publishing worldwide. Oxford is a registered trade mark of Oxford University Press in the UK and in certain other countries.

Published in the United States of America by Oxford University Press
198 Madison Avenue, New York, NY 10016, United States of America.

Library of Congress Cataloging-in-Publication Data
Names: Lim, Daryl editor | Yu, Peter K. editor
Title: Inclusive innovation in the age of AI and big data / [edited by] Daryl Lim, Peter K. Yu.
Description: New York : Oxford University Press, 2026. | Includes bibliographical references.
Identifiers: LCCN 2026002467 (print) | LCCN 2026002468 (ebook) | ISBN 9780197799413 hardback | ISBN 9780197799437 updf| ISBN 9780197799420 epub | ISBN 9780197799444 online
Subjects: LCSH: Technological innovations—Law and legislation | Technological innovations—Economic aspects | Technological innovations—Social aspects | Artificial intelligence—Law and legislation | Big data—Law and legislation
Classification: LCC K487.T4 I52 2026 (print) | LCC K487.T4 (ebook)
LC record available at https://lccn.loc.gov/2026002467
LC ebook record available at https://lccn.loc.gov/2026002468

DOI: 10.1093/9780197799444.001.0001

Printed by Integrated Books International, United States of America

The manufacturer's authorized representative in the EU for product safety is Oxford University Press España S.A. of Parque Empresarial San Fernando de Henares, Avenida de Castilla, 2–28830 Madrid (www.oup.es/en or product.safety@oup.com). OUP España S.A. also acts as importer into Spain of products made by the manufacturer.

Contents

III. INITIATIVES TO PROMOTE INCLUSIVE INNOVATION

IV. AI TECHNOLOGY AND EQUITABLE DEVELOPMENT

V. AI-DRIVEN INNOVATION AND GLOBAL CHALLENGES

Foreword

Innovation constitutes a critical element in our ability to tackle the myriad and complex challenges facing today's world. It enables us to find new ways to fix old problems and generate novel approaches to new ones. A diverse, broad-based intellectual property ecosystem that taps the creativity of everyone strengthens society's ability to deal successfully with difficult problems, drives economic growth, and improve lives. Tapping the full range of human potential is not merely a matter of equity; it is essential to advancing technological leadership, economic resilience, and societal well-being. The hard fact is that women are significantly underrepresented in this ecosystem, and there is vast untapped potential.

Throughout history, women have made invaluable contributions in many fields. It is essential that we recognize their contributions and provide them with the support and opportunities they need to thrive. When we all take responsibility to enhance women creators' use of the intellectual property system, we help close the diversity gap. To do so, however, requires an in-depth understanding of the demographics and relevant metrics, as well as the tools—legal, technological, and other—to promote inclusivity. This is not an easy task.

The research represented in the chapters to follow underscores the importance of tapping into inventor diversity to promote inclusive innovation. The authors will share with you their experience of how to discover and analyze the data needed to understand the diversity gap among inventors. Such data not only illuminates disparities but also provides an empirical foundation for evidence-based policy reforms and institutional accountability.

Patent data, for example, provide an excellent measure of women's innovative activities. Research indicates that patents provide crucial advantages for businesses, especially small enterprises and startups, by enhancing access to capital, attracting customers, and spurring job creation. The contributions will deepen our understanding of inclusive innovation.

Additionally, we will learn which industries tend to favor women inventors and which do not. The chapters conclude with concrete policy recommendations and institutional strategies to narrow the diversity gap and promote inclusive innovation through legal, technological, and organizational levers.

Making innovation ecosystems more inclusive is essential for progress. This volume will explore practical strategies of how we can open doors for women and other underrepresented groups. By doing so, we are not only leveling the playing field but also unlocking a wealth of fresh perspectives and ideas. Let us not forget that innovation thrives on diversity.

Lisa Jorgenson
Deputy Director General, Patents and Technology
World Intellectual Property Organization

Acknowledgments

This volume grew from a shared commitment to advancing conversations on inclusive innovation in the age of artificial intelligence and big data. The initial seeds were planted at a symposium jointly organized by the Institute for Computational and Data Sciences (ICDS) at Penn State University and Penn State Dickinson Law in August 2023. We are deeply grateful to both institutions for their generous co-funding and institutional support, which made possible the event and the open-access publication of this volume.

We are especially indebted to Dean Danielle Conway of Penn State Dickinson Law and the late Professor Jenni Evans, Director of ICDS, for their vision, leadership, and unwavering support in bringing together policymakers, scholars, and practitioners from around the world. Their shared commitment to fostering inclusive, interdisciplinary dialogues was instrumental in shaping the intellectual foundation of this book. Jenni's untimely passing is an immeasurable loss to the global scientific community and everyone who has collaborated with her. Her legacy endures in the scholars she mentored, the communities she built, and the countless lives she touched through her work. We honor her memory with this volume and remain inspired by her example of integrity, curiosity, and compassion.

We also extend our heartfelt thanks to Lisa Jorgenson, Deputy Director General, Patents and Technology at the World Intellectual Property Organization (WIPO), for contributing a thoughtful and inspiring foreword to this volume. Her leadership in advancing inclusive innovation at the intersection of law, policy, and technology—at WIPO and before—has provided invaluable guidance to the global community.

In addition, we are grateful to the contributors to this volume for their rich insights and practical recommendations and to the many colleagues and participants who offered feedback at the symposium and beyond. The thoughtful engagement with all of these individuals and their diverse perspectives have greatly enriched the conversations relating to this project. We hope that this book will advance efforts to build more inclusive, equitable, and dynamic innovation ecosystems around the world.

Finally, we thank Peter Daniell, Charlotte Kershaw, Getsy Deva Kirubai, and other editors at Oxford University Press and Newgen Knowledge Works. It has been a pleasure working with them. We also express our deep appreciation for the supportive and innovative research environments provided by our home institutions, Penn State Dickinson Law and Texas A&M University School of Law.

About the Editors

Daryl Lim is H. Laddie Montague Jr. Chair in Law and Associate Dean for Research and Strategic Partnerships at Penn State Dickinson Law, where he founded its Intellectual Property Law and Innovation Initiative. He holds university affiliations with the Institute of Computational and Data Sciences and the Center for Socially Responsible Artificial Intelligence. A globally recognized expert in intellectual property and antitrust law, he consults internationally and serves on several influential advisory bodies. His work has been cited by U.S. agencies, featured in top law journals, and covered by major media outlets. He is a member of the American Law Institute.

Peter K. Yu is University Distinguished Professor, Regents Professor of Law and Communication, and the Director of the Center for Law and Intellectual Property at Texas A&M University. Born and raised in Hong Kong, he held the Kern Family Chair in Intellectual Property Law at Drake University and was Wenlan Scholar Chair Professor at Zhongnan University of Economics and Law in Wuhan, China. He served as a Visiting Professor of Law at Bocconi University, Hanken School of Economics, Hokkaido University, Tel Aviv University, the University of Haifa, the University of Helsinki, the University of Hong Kong, and the University of Strasbourg. He has served as the general editor of *The WIPO Journal* published by the World Intellectual Property Organization and sits on the Scientific Advisory Board of Max Planck Institute for Innovation and Competition.

About the Contributors

Margo A. Bagley is Asa Griggs Candler Professor of Law at Emory University School of Law and held the Hardy Cross Dillard Chair at University of Virginia School of Law. She was Hieken Visiting Professor in Patent Law at Harvard Law School in 2022. She is an elected member of the American Law Institute and a faculty lecturer with the Munich Intellectual Property Law Center at Max Planck Institute for Innovation and Competition. She has published numerous articles, book chapters, and monographs as well as two coauthored books, with a third on the way. A registered patent attorney and an inventor, she is an expert advisor to the African Union and a Co-Director of the Innovator Diversity Pilots Initiative and the Harvard Global Access in Action Program. She has served on two National Academies committees on intellectual property matters and has been a consultant to several UN organizations.

Paola Cecchi-Dimeglio is a leading authority on helping senior leaders make more inclusive decisions for themselves and their organizations, having advised some of the world's largest for-profit and non-profit companies. An award-winning expert on behavioral and data science, big data and artificial intelligence (AI), race and gender, and leadership strategy, she holds dual appointments at Harvard Kennedy School of Government and Harvard Law School, where she serves as the faculty chair of the Executive Leadership Research Initiative for Women and Minority Attorneys. At Harvard Law School, she is also a Senior Research Fellow at the Center for the Legal Profession. She is the CEO of People Culture Drive Consulting Group, a strategic data-driven and behavioral-science consulting firm with offices in the European Union, the United Kingdom, and the United States. She earned a JD, LLM, a Magistère DJCE degree in common and civil law, a PhD in social sciences, *summa cum laude*, while studying at universities in France, Belgium, and the United States.

Colleen V. Chien is Professor of Law at UC Berkeley School of Law, where she teaches, mentors students, and conducts empirical research on intellectual property, innovation, AI, and the criminal justice system. Her work focuses on how technology and data can advance social benefit. She is a Faculty Co-Director of the Berkeley Center for Law and Technology and has served in the Obama White House as a Senior Advisor, Intellectual Property and Innovation, and more recently in the Biden Administration in the Department of Commerce and at the United States Patent and Trademark Office. She founded the Innovator Diversity Pilots Initiative to boost participation in innovation and the Paper Prisons Initiative to narrow the second-chance gap between eligibility and delivery of second-chance relief in the criminal justice system. She is a recipient of the Early Career Medal of the American Law

Institute and is a graduate of Stanford University (Engineering) and UC Berkeley School of Law.

Martin Correa is the Senior Counsellor for the Future of Intellectual Property at the World Intellectual Property Organization (WIPO). He holds a master's degree in international law from Heidelberg University. Specializing in innovation, intellectual property, and trade, he led key multilateral negotiations on behalf of Chile—including at the World Trade Organization, WIPO, the UN Conference on Trade and Development, the Asia-Pacific Economic Cooperation Forum, and the Pacific Alliance. Prior to joining WIPO, he served for twelve years in the Intellectual Property Division of the Ministry of Foreign Affairs and Trade of Chile, leading intellectual property negotiations in free trade agreements, such as the Trans-Pacific Partnership and the Comprehensive and Progressive Agreement for Trans-Pacific Partnership.

Christopher L. Dancy is Associate Professor of Industrial and Manufacturing Engineering, Computer Science and Engineering, and African American Studies at Penn State University. He directs The Human in Computing and Cognition Lab and is a Co-Director of the Center for Black Digital Research. His research explores human cognition, computational systems, and social structures, with a current focus on AI and racialized systems. A recipient of the National Science Foundation's NSF CAREER award, he co-leads the Computational Representation of Human Decision Processes research area at the NSF AI Institute for Societal Decision Making, where he studies how racialization shapes decision-making in disaster response and recovery.

Deborah R. Gerhardt is Paul B. Eaton Distinguished Professor of Law at the University of North Carolina School of Law, where she teaches art law, copyright, intellectual property, and trademark law. Her scholarship explores the intersection of law and creativity, with recent work on arts leadership, public memory, copyright protection for AI-generated works, and nontraditional trademarks. From 2022 to 2025, she served on the Trademark Public Advisory Committee for the United States Patent and Trademark Office. In 2018, she received the University of North Carolina's Distinguished Teaching Award for Post-Baccalaureate Instruction.

Jordana Goodman is Assistant Professor of Law at Chicago-Kent College of Law at Illinois Institute of Technology and an innovator-in-residence at the Massachusetts Institute of Technology. Her research explores the intersection of diversity, equity, and inclusion and intellectual property law, focusing on race and gender inequality issues. Before working as a professor, she worked as a patent prosecutor for six years, writing patent applications to develop portfolios for a variety of clients in Boston. She was awarded her JD, *cum laude*, from Boston University School of Law in 2015 and her MS in chemical engineering from Worcester Polytechnic Institute in 2020. She earned her BS, *magna cum laude*, in chemistry and anthropology from Brandeis University.

Suzanne Harrison is an author, a patent futurist, and an economist. She works with companies, large and small, to help them utilize patent data to make more informed decisions and realize the true value of their intellectual property. She just completed a three-year term on the Patent Public Advisory Committee for the United States Patent and Trademark Office. She is also the founder and principal of Percipience LLC, a board-level advisory group focused on intellectual property and innovation strategy, management, and quantifying and mitigating intellectual property risk. Since 1995, she has led a group called the ICM Gathering, an invitation-only group of twenty companies that meet regularly to define, create, benchmark, and test best practices in intellectual property management. Her books draw on her work with this group and feature success stories of companies leading the way in innovative intellectual property management. She holds an undergraduate degree in economics from the University of California, Davis and an MBA from the University of Chicago.

Bowman Heiden is the Executive Director of the Tusher Strategic Initiative for Technology Leadership at UC Berkeley. He is also a Co-Director of the Center for Intellectual Property at the University of Gothenburg and a Co-Chair of the Technology, Innovation, and Intellectual Property Program at the Classical Liberal Institute at New York University School of Law. He is the co-founder of the Berkeley Deep Tech Innovation Lab, the Dynamic Competition Initiative, and ICM Global. Over the past twenty years, he has managed over 200 innovation projects with industry, university research institutes, healthcare providers, and startup ventures. He holds degrees in engineering, technology management, and economics. His research is at the interdisciplinary interface of economics, law, and innovation—in particular, intellectual property, innovation economics, competition policy, and geopolitics in knowledge-intensive sectors. Before turning his focus to the fields of innovation strategy and policy, he played professional basketball in several European countries.

David R. Hunter is Emeritus Professor of Statistics at Penn State University, where he was a faculty member from 1999 to 2025. He served as Head of the Department of Statistics from 2012 to 2018 and has been heavily involved in developing data science programs at the university. He is a fellow of both the American Statistical Association and the Institute for Mathematical Statistics. He is best known for work in three areas: statistical algorithms (most notably, the class known as MM algorithms), statistical modeling of networks, and mixture models (particularly finite mixtures in which the component distributions are not parametrically specified).

Jessica C. Lai is Professor of Commercial Law at Victoria University of Wellington in New Zealand, specializing in patent law, the protection of mātauranga Māori, and feminist perspectives of intellectual property. She is the author of three books, including *Patent Law and Women* (Routledge 2022) and *Indigenous Cultural Heritage and Intellectual Property Rights* (Springer 2014), and the co-editor of *A Research Agenda for Intellectual Property Law and Gender* (Edward Elgar 2024). She is a Te Apārangi Royal Society of New Zealand Rutherford Discovery Fellow and a former

Swiss National Science Foundation postdoctoral fellow. She holds a Doctorate from the University of Lucerne in Switzerland and multiple degrees from Victoria University of Wellington.

Jyh-An Lee is Professor and the founding Executive Director of the Centre for Legal Innovation and Digital Society at the Faculty of Law of Chinese University of Hong Kong. He oversees the New Ventures Legal Team, a clinical support group that collaborates with the university's Pre-Incubation Centre to assist startup companies. Holding a JSD from Stanford Law School and an LLM from Harvard Law School, he has published on various facets of intellectual property and digital technology law. Since 2016, he has also served as a panelist for the Asian Domain Name Dispute Resolution Centre.

Yan Li is a JD candidate at Chicago-Kent College of Law with a unique interdisciplinary background spanning technology and legal studies. He holds a degree in computational mathematics and brings over fifteen years of software engineering experience, with specialized expertise in cybersecurity and cryptography. He is passionate about the intersection of AI and legal practice, exploring how emerging AI technologies can transform and enhance legal services. His diverse background offers valuable insights into the evolving relationship between technology and legal practice.

Jingwen Liu is a research fellow at the Centre for Legal Innovation and Digital Society at the Faculty of Law of Chinese University of Hong Kong. Her research interests include intellectual property law, competition policy, data governance, and comparative legal study. Her publications have appeared in various academic journals, including *Columbia Journal of Law & the Arts*, *American Business Law Journal*, *European Intellectual Property Review*, and *Journal of Intellectual Property Law & Practice*. She has been listed as a WIPO ADR Young Member since 2023. Prior to commencing her PhD study, she was a practicing lawyer in the People's Republic of China, specializing in trademark and brand protection. She also held a visiting position at Singapore Management University Yong Pung How School of Law in 2021.

Brent Lutes is an applied economist, currently serving as the Chief Economist for the United States Copyright Office, where he advises the Register of Copyrights and other policymakers on the economic impacts of programs and policies related to copyright systems and on how domestic and foreign policy may affect the underlying economic objectives of intellectual property systems. His responsibilities include evaluating these impacts on the Office, creators and other copyright stakeholders, and the general public, as well as developing internal and external research to support policy determinations and operational decisions. His research focuses on creative industries, the creative economy, and intellectual property institutions.

Miriam Marcowitz-Bitton is Professor of Law at Bar-Ilan University Faculty of Law in Israel and holds the Raul Wallenberg Chair for Human Rights. She received her LLB and LLM degrees from Bar-Ilan University School of Law, as well as another

LLM and an SJD from University of Michigan School of Law. She was a visiting assistant professor of law at DePaul University College of Law, Miami University School of Law, and Ohio State University School of Law. She was also a Microsoft Research Fellow at UC Berkeley School of Law and a Visiting Fellow at George Washington University Law School. She writes and teaches in the fields of intellectual property law, law and technology, and property. Her current research agenda focuses on gender and innovation, exploring the gender gap in patenting and trademark prosecution in Israel and the United States.

Regan Murphy is Associate Attorney at Brennan Burtker LLC. She is a graduate of Chicago-Kent College of Law with a certificate in intellectual property. She obtained her BS in agriculture and consumer economics, with a concentration in public policy and law and a minor in business, from the University of Illinois Urbana-Champaign in 2021.

Carlotta Nani is a Postdoctoral Research Fellow in the Innovation Economy Section at the Department of Economics and Data Analytics at WIPO. Her research agenda focuses on the structural drivers of gender inequality and its impact on economic development. She holds a PhD in development economics from the Geneva Graduate Institute. In her doctoral research, she implemented two projects in Bangladesh to examine how gender stereotypes and social norms shape household decision-making and influence labor market outcomes. Prior to joining WIPO, she held research positions at the Centre for Finance and Development, the World Trade Organization, the International Labor Organization, and the German Institute for Economic Research (DIW Berlin).

Michael Palmedo is a statistician in the Office of the Chief Economist of the United States Copyright Office. His research applies data from copyright registrations to questions about the location and characteristics of consumers and producers of creative works in the United States. He has also advised the Office on the registration activities by people and firms in specific states and countries. Prior to 2023, he directed legal-economic research on international and comparative copyright laws at the intellectual property program at American University Washington College of Law. He holds a PhD in economics and an MA in international affairs.

Khamal Patterson is Executive Board Vice President of the nonprofit STEM Education and Innovation Center in Fredericksburg, Virginia. He is an attorney, a research consultant, and a contractor in Maryland and Washington, DC. His scholarship focuses on original research that illustrates the complex connections between culture, commerce, and intellectual property. He also advocates strengthening safeguards to protect the integrity of the market in developed countries and prevent the exploitation of vulnerable source communities. He has a particular interest in understanding the demand for illicit cultural goods and has published in an anthology on the subject. He recently served as the senior program officer on the Cultural Antiquities Task Force within the United States Department of State's Cultural

Heritage Center, where he assisted law enforcement in identifying and repatriating cultural objects illegally imported into the United States. His work on cultural heritage, intellectual property, ethics, and their interplay has been recognized. It has also inspired proposals that led to recent procedural changes at the United States Patent and Trademark Office.

Julio Raffo is Head of the Innovation Economy Section at the Department of Economics and Data Analytics of WIPO. Before joining WIPO, he conducted research at the École Polytechnique Fédérale de Lausanne in Switzerland, the Institut Français des Relations Internationales in France, the Pan-American Health Organization, and the Red Iberoamericana/Interamericana de Indicadores de Ciencia y Tecnología. He holds an economics degree from the Universidad de Buenos Aires and a master's degree in industrial organization, innovations, and international strategy and a PhD in economics from the Université de Paris Nord. His main research interests are the economics and metrics of innovation and intellectual property, with a particular focus on their intersection with socioeconomic development.

W. Keith Robinson is Professor of Law at Wake Forest University School of Law. He is an expert in patent law and the intersection of AI and legal institutions. His research explores how legal frameworks govern emerging technologies, focusing on the legal and ethical implications of AI in legal processes. He has commented on intellectual property issues in various media outlets and has delivered over seventy presentations worldwide on patent law. His work aims to ensure transparency, fairness, and security in governmental functions by developing regulatory frameworks and best practices for deploying AI applications.

Ryan Safner is an economist in the Office of the Chief Economist of the United States Copyright Office. In his current role, he uses copyright registrations data to better understand the impact of copyright on creative industries and individuals. He was Associate Professor of Economics at Hood College. His research broadly explores the economic history and political economy of innovation and expression. He holds a PhD and MA in economics from George Mason University.

Michelle Saksena is Senior Research Economist in the United States Patent and Trademark Office's Office of the Chief Economist, where she leads research that informs intellectual property policy and advances understanding of innovation dynamics. Her work focuses on analyzing large-scale patent data to address critical issues in innovation, including diversity, inclusion, and the functioning of the patent system. A recent co-authored publication in *Nature Biotechnology* on gender disparities in patent citations highlights her contributions to equity-focused research. She has also authored influential government reports such as "Progress and Potential" and the "National Strategy for Inclusive Innovation," developed public data resources (including the PatentsView series), and presented findings at major conferences to advance the field of innovation economics.

W. Michael Schuster is Associate Professor of Legal Studies at the Terry College of Business at the University of Georgia. His research focuses on intellectual property and empirical legal studies. It has appeared in a variety of academic journals, including the *Southern California Law Review*, *Alabama Law Review*, *UC Davis Law Review*, and *American Business Law Journal*. He has held prior academic positions at the University of Michigan and Oklahoma State University. Before entering academia, he was an attorney at the law firm of Vinson & Elkins LLP in Houston, Texas, where he specialized in intellectual property.

Gauri Subramani is Assistant Professor in the Management Department at the College of Business at Lehigh University. Her research focuses on inequalities in innovation contexts, including the U.S. patent system, scientific research, and digital platforms. She studies gender and resource inequalities and the mechanisms by which these inequalities arise, along with opportunities for interventions to reduce performance gaps. Her work has been published in *Harvard Business Review*, *Management Science*, *Nature Biotechnology*, and *The Review of Economics and Statistics*. She holds a PhD from Haas School of Business at UC Berkeley and a BA from Wellesley College. She has worked as a political appointee in the Office of Economic Policy at the United States Department of the Treasury.

Deja Workman is a PhD candidate in informatics in the College of Information Sciences and Technology at Penn State University. They have been a graduate research assistant in the Human in Computing in Cognition Lab since 2022 and a graduate researcher at the Center for Black Digital Research. Their current research interests include carceral algorithms and their effects on Black narratives, cognitive science for modeling anti-Blackness, feature engineering, and accessibility of Black digital archives. Their dissertation focuses on the holistic connections between AI and Blackness. They earned a BS in information sciences and technology, with a minor in sociology and a certificate in diversity studies, from Penn State University.

Introduction

Daryl Lim and Peter K. Yu

The Emerging Debate on Inclusive Innovation

Three Core Questions

Innovation is often celebrated as a catalyst for progress and prosperity, but it may also perpetuate exclusion.[1] In the age of artificial intelligence (AI) and big data, where technological change occurs at an unprecedented pace and scale, there is a high risk that the disparities caused by exclusion will be further entrenched and globalized. To fulfill its social promise and full potential, innovation must advance inclusion, equity, and justice. Structural reforms and other policy interventions may, therefore, be needed to ensure that these ecosystems distribute benefits equitably without reinforcing inequalities they might otherwise help overcome. Law, policy, governance framework, and institutional design should also be evaluated, and at times reimagined, to enable underrepresented individuals and communities to participate in innovation. In doing so, these individuals and communities will be able to enjoy the fruits of creative and inventive endeavors—whether theirs or others'.

Although the debate on inclusive innovation began to garner growing attention in the mid-2000s, it dates back to the 1960s,[2] when developing countries demanded reforms to make the international intellectual property system more balanced and equitable.[3] The debate on inclusive innovation centers on three core questions: Innovation by whom? Innovation for whom? And innovation to what end?[4]

[1] Colleen V. Chien, *The Inequalities of Innovation*, 72 Emory L.J. 1 (2022).

[2] Robyn Klingler-Vidra, Alex Glennie & Courtney Savie Lawrence, Inclusive Innovation 1 (2022). Commentators trace this debate back to the appropriate technologies movement.

[3] Peter K. Yu, *A Tale of Two Development Agendas*, 35 Ohio N.U. L. Rev. 465, 468–511 (2009).

[4] On inclusive innovation, see Handbook of Inclusive Innovation: The Role of Organizations, Markets and Communities in Social Innovation (Gerard George, Ted

Daryl Lim and Peter K. Yu, *Introduction* In: *Inclusive Innovation in the Age of AI and Big Data*.
Edited by: Daryl Lim and Peter K. Yu, Oxford University Press.
DOI: 10.1093/9780197799444.001.0001

Innovation by whom is the question most often explored in academic and policy debates. Although much extant research on inclusive innovation has focused on gender disparities, the research has now expanded to tackle inequalities attributed to other socioeconomic factors, such as race, age, wealth, education, occupation, and workplace location. Answering this question is important because it helps us understand how to strengthen innovation ecosystems while ensuring that they benefit all of humanity. The question also enables us to locate legal, policy, and institutional reforms that would maximize participation in these ecosystems. For instance, when people have been excluded from an innovation ecosystem, policymakers need to know whether the exclusion was caused by faulty institutional designs, a lack of innovative capacity, inadequate complementary measures (such as education, infrastructure, or business support), or some other factors.

The second question pertains to innovation for whom. Instead of the production end, this question focuses on the consumption end. Even if innovation ecosystems can maximize participation, we still need to evaluate whether the fruits of innovation have been distributed equitably—at the local, regional, and global levels. This question has been historically contentious due to the longstanding North-South divide, which has limited the benefits of innovation to a small segment of the world's population, most often in the Global North. Although the arrival of increasingly powerful emerging economies—such as China, Brazil, and India—has challenged this binary division,[5] many developing countries and their nationals and firms, sadly, remain left behind. Moreover, in today's globalized economy, inequality *within* countries is just as problematic as inequality *among* countries. It is, therefore, no surprise that Goal 10 of the UN Sustainable Development Goals, adopted by all UN member states in September 2015, specifically calls for reducing "inequality within and among countries."[6] To a large extent, the

Baker, Paul Tracey & Havovi Joshi eds., 2020) [hereinafter HANDBOOK OF INCLUSIVE INNOVATION]; KLINGLER-VIDRA ET AL., *supra* note 2; NEW MODELS OF INCLUSIVE INNOVATION FOR DEVELOPMENT (Richard Heeks, Christopher Foster & Yanuar Nugroho eds., 2017); THEO PAPAIOANNOU, INCLUSIVE INNOVATION FOR DEVELOPMENT: MEETING THE DEMANDS OF JUSTICE THROUGH PUBLIC ACTION (2018); RESEARCH HANDBOOK ON INTELLECTUAL PROPERTY RIGHTS AND INCLUSIVITY (Cristiana Sappa ed., 2024).

[5] Peter K. Yu, *The Middle Intellectual Property Powers*, *in* LAW AND DEVELOPMENT OF MIDDLE-INCOME COUNTRIES: AVOIDING THE MIDDLE-INCOME TRAP 84 (Randall Peerenboom & Tom Ginsburg eds., 2014); Peter K. Yu, *Three Megatrends in the International Intellectual Property Regime*, 41 CARDOZO ARTS & ENT. L.J. 457, 458–66 (2023).

[6] G.A. Res. 70/1, Transforming Our World: The 2030 Agenda for Sustainable Development, at 14 (Sept. 25, 2015).

debate on inclusive innovation can be linked to the debate on innovation and economic inequality, which has also begun to gain wider policy and scholarly attention in recent years.[7]

The third, and least explored, question relates to innovation to what end. Disparate individuals, firms, and governments are likely to come to different conclusions on the justifications and objectives of an innovation ecosystem. Indeed, when the international community deliberated on the creation of the human right to enjoy the benefits of scientific progress and its applications in the run-up to the adoption of the Universal Declaration of Human Rights shortly after the Second World War, it intentionally refrained from identifying the specific purposes for this fundamental right.[8] At that time, the delegates feared that some countries might misuse the designated purposes to stifle the freedom of scientific research and "legitim[ize] political restrictions on science."[9] As far as innovation policy is concerned, those viewing scientific and technological advancement through a nationalist lens will align the innovation ecosystem with efforts to promote national security and global competitiveness. By contrast, those using a human-centered or cosmopolitan lens will emphasize product safety, sustainable development, and overall benefits to humanity. In addition, some observers will lie somewhere in between, while others may use more than one lens to view the innovation ecosystem.

In sum, the debate on inclusive innovation is rich, complex, and diverse. It covers many different actors, institutions, economic sectors, and academic disciplines. Although the chapters in this volume focus more narrowly on issues relating to intellectual property protection and advances in AI and big data analytics, innovation can be defined broadly to cover all forms of technological advancements that benefits (or harms) humanity. In view of the more limited scope of this book project, this introductory chapter and the remaining contributions focus on innovation as it relates to the intellectual property system, AI technology, and big data analytics.

[7] Peter K. Yu, *Intellectual Property, Global Inequality, and Subnational Policy Variations*, *in* INTELLECTUAL PROPERTY, INNOVATION AND ECONOMIC INEQUALITY 81, 101 (Daniel Benoliel, Peter K. Yu, Francis Gurry & Keun Lee eds., 2024) [hereinafter INNOVATION AND ECONOMIC INEQUALITY].

[8] Peter K. Yu, *The Complex Interplay Between Intellectual Property and the Right to Science*, 105 B.U. L. REV. 705, 714 (2025).

[9] Richard Pierre Claude, *Scientists' Rights and the Human Right to the Benefits of Science*, *in* CORE OBLIGATIONS: BUILDING A FRAMEWORK FOR ECONOMIC, SOCIAL AND CULTURAL RIGHTS 247, 254 (Audrey Chapman & Sage Russell eds., 2002).

Inclusive Innovation and Intellectual Property

Although the intellectual property system, broadly defined, is a quintessential part of the innovation ecosystem, it is only one of the ecosystem's many components.[10] Historically, the development of intellectual property law and policy has aligned with Western industrial and commercial paradigms. It has privileged certain forms of knowledge and creativity—most notably, copyright, trademarks, patents, and industrial designs. Because the intellectual property system tends to prioritize formalized, documentable outputs over communal and iterative innovation processes, it leaves behind other forms of innovation and creativity, such as indigenous knowledge, creations based on oral traditions, and community-driven innovations.[11]

In addition, over the past centuries, the intellectual property system has favored certain creative and inventive activity at the expense of others. Even though reforms have emerged, especially in more recent decades, the existing system still discounts the contributions of many otherwise productive members of society—in particular, women, minorities, and other underrepresented and marginalized communities. The debate on inclusive innovation targets these deficiencies in intellectual property law and policy.

In the past decade, there has been a growing concerted effort to make the intellectual property system more inclusive and equitable. Immediately coming to mind are the studies and other activities conducted by national intellectual property offices and the World Intellectual Property Organization (WIPO). For example, in 2016, the UK Intellectual Property Office published two pioneering studies on gender profiles in patenting—one on the United Kingdom and the other on the entire world.[12] An update of the worldwide study appeared three years later.[13] In November 2022, the European Patent Office drew on its patent data to produce a report on women's participation

[10] Daniel J. Gervais, *TRIPS and Development*, *in* Intellectual Property, Trade and Development: Strategies to Optimize Economic Development in a TRIPS-Plus Era 3, 4 (Daniel J. Gervais ed., 1st ed. 2007); Peter K. Yu, *Intellectual Property and the Information Ecosystem*, 2005 Mich. St. L. Rev. 1, 15. Broadly defined, the intellectual property system should cover not only affirmative rights but also limitations and exceptions as well as the many negative spaces relevant to this system.

[11] Daryl Lim, *AI, Equity, and the IP Gap*, 75 SMU L. Rev. 815, 843–44 (2022); Peter K. Yu, *Cultural Relics, Intellectual Property, and Intangible Heritage*, 81 Temp. L. Rev. 433, 466–67 (2008).

[12] U.K. Intell. Prop. Off., Gender Profiles in UK Patenting: An Analysis of Female Inventorship (2016); U.K. Intell. Prop. Off., Gender Profiles in Worldwide Patenting: An Analysis of Female Inventorship (2016).

[13] U.K. Intell. Prop. Off., Gender Profiles in Worldwide Patenting: An Analysis of Female Inventorship (2019).

in inventive activity.[14] The European Intellectual Property Office issued a similar report regarding women's participation in industrial designs.[15]

Across the Atlantic, the Office of the Chief Economist of the United States Patent and Trademark Office (USPTO) published a pioneering study entitled "Progress and Potential: A Profile of Women Inventors on U.S. Patents" in February 2019.[16] That study was followed by a quick update a year later.[17] In June 2022, the Office of the Chief Economist of the United States Copyright Office also released a study analyzing the contributions of women authors in the copyright arena, drawing on data from U.S. copyright registrations from 1978 to 2020.[18]

At WIPO, research staff have actively engaged with the debate on inclusive innovation.[19] Not only did they release studies, working papers, and other publications,[20] but the organization also convened, in November 2024, an unprecedented Global Research Experts Meeting on Improving Gender and Diversity in Intellectual Property and Innovation. Offering "insights into new research, data, and policy solutions aimed at building a more inclusive global [intellectual property] landscape," this event had its second edition in November 2025.[21]

In academia, commentators have actively explored whether the existing intellectual property system privileges some forms of knowledge and creativity over others. To name a few, Jessica Lai provides a book-length critique

[14] Eur. Pat. Off., Women's Participation in Inventive Activity: Evidence from EPO Data (2022).

[15] Eur. Union Intell. Prop. Off., Women in Design (2023).

[16] U.S. Pat. & Trademark Off., Off. of the Chief Economist, *Progress and Potential: A Profile of Women Inventors on U.S. Patents* (U.S. Patent & Trademark Off., Off. of the Chief Economist, IP Data Highlights No. 2, 2019).

[17] U.S. Pat. & Trademark Off., Off. of the Chief Economist, *Progress and Potential: 2020 Update on U.S. Women Inventor-Patentees* (U.S. Patent & Trademark Off., Off. of the Chief Economist, IP Data Highlights No. 4, 2020).

[18] U.S. Copyright Off., Women in the Copyright System: An Analysis of Women Authors in Copyright Registrations from 1978 to 2020 (2022).

[19] *Intellectual Property, Gender, and Diversity*, World Intell. Prop. Org., https://www.wipo.int/en/web/gender/ (last visited July 23, 2025).

[20] *See, e.g.*, Élodie Carpentier & Julio Raffo, The Global Gender Gap in Innovation and Creativity: An International Comparison of the Gender Gap in Global Patenting over Two Decades (2023); Élodie Carpentier, Jennifer Brant, Utsav Bahl & Aikaterini Kanellia, *Closing Innovation and Intellectual Property Diversity Gaps: A Global Literature Review* (World Intell. Prop. Org., Econ. Rsch. Working Paper No. 86, 2024); Gema Lax Martinez, Julio Raffo & Kaori Saito, *Identifying the Gender of PCT Inventors* (World Intell. Prop. Org., Econ. Rsch. Working Paper No. 33, 2016).

[21] *WIPO's First Global Research Experts Meeting on Improving Gender and Diversity in Intellectual Property and Innovation*, World Intell. Prop. Org. (Nov. 12, 2024), https://www.wipo.int/en/web/women/w/news/2024/wipo-s-first-global-research-experts-meeting-on-improving-gender-and-diversity-in-intellectual-property-and-innovation.

of the gendered nature of patent law and the knowledge governance system it supports.[22] Robert Brauneis and Dotan Oliar have published an empirical study of copyright registrations in relation to race, ethnicity, gender, and age.[23] Colleen Chien discusses the inequalities of innovation based on income, opportunity, and access while offering legal and administrative solutions to address these inequalities.[24] Paul Gugliuzza and Rachel Rebouché study the lack of gender diversity in patent litigation.[25] Alenka Guzmán and Flor Brown examine gender-related variations in innovative activities, with a focus on Brazil, India, and Mexico.[26] Building on his earlier study, Dotan Oliar and his coauthor Marliese Dalton document the gender gap in copyright registrations.[27] And Sean Tu, Paul Gugliuzza, and Amy Semet analyze the gender gap in patent practice in the pharmaceutical field.[28]

Although most of the empirical studies listed above focus on gender disparities, new research, including some chapters in this volume, explore the impact of race and other socioeconomic factors on innovation and the intellectual property system. Regarding race and culture specifically, Anjali Vats provides a theoretical book-length study on how intellectual property laws can be viewed as "discursive formations" shaped by culture, identity, and power.[29] In the past decade, she and Deidré Keller have collaborated on the Race + IP Conference series, which recently celebrated its fifth anniversary and helped launch a new strand of scholarship known as "critical race intellectual property."[30] Tabrez Ebrahim and Rafeel Wasif discuss how Asian Americans, when compared with other ethnic groups, are overrepresented

[22] Jessica C. Lai, Patent Law and Women: Tackling Gender Bias in Knowledge Governance (2022).

[23] Robert Brauneis & Dotan Oliar, *An Empirical Study of the Race, Ethnicity, Gender, and Age of Copyright Registrants*, 86 Geo. Wash. L. Rev. 46 (2018).

[24] Chien, *supra* note 1.

[25] Paul R. Gugliuzza & Rachel Rebouché, *Gender Inequality in Patent Litigation*, 100 N.C. L. Rev. 1683 (2022); *see also* Jordana R. Goodman, Paul R. Gugliuzza & Rachel Rebouché, *Inequality on Appeal: The Intersection of Race and Gender in Patent Litigation*, 58 U.C. Davis L. Rev. 829 (2024).

[26] Alenka Guzmán & Flor Brown, *Building Innovation Skills to Overcome Gender Inequality: Mexico, India, and Brazil*, *in* Innovation and Economic Inequality, *supra* note 7, at 177.

[27] Dotan Oliar & Marliese Dalton, *Are Men and Women Creating Equal? Contextualizing Copyright and Gender in the United States*, *in* Innovation and Economic Inequality, *supra* note 7, at 145.

[28] S. Sean Tu, Paul R. Gugliuzza & Amy Semet, *Overqualified and Underrepresented: Gender Inequality in Pharmaceutical Patent Law*, 48 BYU L. Rev. 137 (2022).

[29] Anjali Vats, The Color of Creatorship: Intellectual Property, Race, and the Making of Americans (2020).

[30] Anjali Vats & Deidre A. Keller, *Critical Race IP*, 36 Cardozo Arts & Ent. L.J. 735 (2018); *see also* Peter K. Yu, *Reshaping Intellectual Property Scholarship from Within*, 85 U. Pitt. L. Rev. 857, 875–89 (2024).

as inventors on U.S. patents but underrepresented as technology startup founders.[31] Xuan-Thao Nguyen writes about how Asian American women innovators are now disrupting the oft-unwritten code of conduct in the high-tech sector.[32] In addition, one cannot overlook the important pioneering contributions made by legal scholars, such as the late Keith Aoki, K.J. Greene, and Lateef Mtima.[33] Rooted in the tradition of critical race theory, these scholars expose the systemic biases against Black authors and inventors in the U.S. intellectual property system.

AI-Driven Innovation and New Equitable Concerns

With the arrival of ChatGPT, Copilot, Dall-E, Midjourney, Stable Diffusion, and other generative AI tools, questions raised by this new technology have received unprecedented scholarly and policy attention. In the context of inclusive innovation, AI has added a new and complex, yet largely underexplored layer of challenge to an already rather difficult law and policy debate. Tackling this layer is a key goal of this volume.

AI systems are often perceived as neutral, but they reflect the data and values they encode. Even when the underlying training data have been collected carefully, they frequently replicate historical patterns of exclusion in society and through institutional processes.[34] AI systems and other algorithmically enhanced or AI-driven technological products and services—which will be referred to later by the shorthand "AI-driven innovation"—also come with bugs, biases, and other flaws that have been built into the systems, often unintentionally. Among the widely reported controversies are those relating to the propensity of the COMPAS algorithm to assess African

[31] Tabrez Y. Ebrahim & Rafeel Wasif, *Innovation Originators*, 31 Mich. Tech. L. Rev. 1 (2024).

[32] Xuan-Thao Nguyen, *#MeToo Innovators: Disrupting the Race and Gender Code by Asian Americans in the Tech Industry*, 28 Asian Am. L.J. 17 (2021).

[33] *See, e.g.*, Intellectual Property, Entrepreneurship and Social Justice: From Swords to Ploughshares (Lateef Mtima ed., 2015); The Cambridge Handbook of Intellectual Property and Social Justice (Steven D. Jamar & Lateef Mtima eds., 2024); Keith Aoki, *Distributive and Syncretic Motives in Intellectual Property Law (With Special Reference to Coercion, Agency, and Development)*, 40 U.C. Davis L. Rev. 717 (2007); K.J. Greene, *Copyright, Culture & Black Music: A Legacy of Unequal Protection*, 21 Hastings Commc'ns & Ent. L.J. 339 (1999); Kevin J. Greene, *Thieves in the Temple: The Scandal of Copyright Registration and African-American Artists*, 49 Pepp. L. Rev. 615 (2022).

[34] Lim, *supra* note 11, at 831–32. See also Deja Workman and Christopher Dancy's chapter in this volume.

Americans a higher recidivism score in the criminal justice context,[35] the misidentification of racial minorities by facial or object recognition technology,[36] and the sexist, racist, and Holocaust-denying messages spitted out by now-discontinued chatbots.[37] These controversies reveal how AI-driven innovation can systematically misrepresent or devalue the experiences and inventions of underrepresented and marginalized individuals and communities.[38]

Worse still, the challenges posed by AI technology and big data analytics to inclusive innovation are not limited to national contexts. At the global level, AI systems are likely to continue their inequitable distribution of benefits while reinforcing power asymmetries, unless they are properly designed in a process that take existing socioeconomic inequalities into consideration. Thus, inclusive innovation must be understood as not only a domestic equity concern but also a global justice issue.

Although the many challenges AI technology has posed to national and global inclusivity call for an urgent policy response, inherent tensions exist over the need to balance inclusion with technological advancement. For instance, demands for rapid AI deployment may sideline equity considerations, while well-intentioned inclusion initiatives risk becoming performative when unaccompanied by systemic reforms.[39] As AI capabilities continue to grow, recognizing these tensions will be critical to advancing a more candid, more reflexive, and ultimately more effective agenda for inclusive innovation.[40]

Moreover, the intensifying arms race between leading AI powers, such as China, the European Union, and the United States, has highlighted the need for inclusive innovation strategies at the global level. These strategies should be attentive to geopolitical dynamics, the calls for data sovereignty, and the distributive impacts of technology. They should also take account of the wide disparities in data infrastructure and other local conditions that have

[35] Julia Angwin, Jeff Larson, Surya Mattu & Lauren Kirchner, *Machine Bias*, ProPublica (May 23, 2016), https://www.propublica.org/article/machine-bias-risk-assessments-in-criminal-sentencing.

[36] Jana Kasperkevic, *Google Says Sorry for Racist Auto-Tag in Photo App*, Guardian (July 1, 2015), https://www.theguardian.com/technology/2015/jul/01/google-sorry-racist-auto-tag-photo-app.

[37] *Microsoft "Deeply Sorry" for Racist and Sexist Tweets by AI Chatbot*, Guardian (Mar. 26, 2016), https://www.theguardian.com/technology/2016/mar/26/microsoft-deeply-sorry-for-offensive-tweets-by-ai-chatbot.

[38] Lim, *supra* note 11, at 831–32. See also Jordana Goodman, Li Yan, Regan Murphy, and Khamal Patterson's chapter in this volume.

[39] Lim, *supra* note 11, at 830–31.

[40] See Daryl Lim's chapter in this volume.

constrained the ability of researchers and entrepreneurs in developing countries to participate in frontier AI development, such as limited access to computational power, human talents, and training data.[41] These disparities risk entrenching dependency on AI models, platforms, and policies shaped by a few dominant economies (and their firms). Such dependency will further marginalize underrepresented voices in global innovation governance.[42]

Pathways to Inclusive Innovation

In view of the lack of inclusivity in the existing intellectual property system and the new challenges posed by AI technology and big data analytics, policymakers and commentators have called for reforms to improve innovation ecosystems. These reforms require attention to who innovates, what forms of innovation are recognized, and where innovation occurs.

Innovation is not monolithic. It encompasses various economic sectors, including both formal (such as pharmaceuticals, computer software, semiconductors, telecommunications, and machine tools) and informal (like community-driven innovations in agriculture and caregiving).[43] Innovation policy must, therefore, move beyond traditional subject matter and geographies to be truly inclusive. Regulatory frameworks should particularly target structural barriers at the local, regional, and global levels.

Thus far, the demographics of innovators remain significantly skewed. Whether in patenting, grant funding, or other innovation-related activity, women, racial and ethnic minorities, and individuals from lower-income households and underrepresented communities consistently participate at disproportionately low rates.[44] To recognize the contributions of these otherwise productive members of society, legal frameworks must evolve to better protect diverse forms of innovation and creativity, especially those that have

[41] U.N. Conf. on Trade & Dev. [UNCTAD], Technology and Innovation Report 2025: Inclusive Artificial Intelligence for Development 79 (2025). See also Peter Yu's chapter in this volume.

[42] Peter K. Yu, *Artificial Intelligence, Intellectual Property, and Sustainable Development*, *in* Intellectual Property, Ethical Innovation and Sustainability: Towards a New Social Contract for the Digital Economy? (Christophe Geiger ed., forthcoming 2026).

[43] Franco Malerba, *Sectoral Systems: How and Why Innovation Differs Across Sectors*, *in* The Oxford Handbook of Innovation 380, 380 (Jan Fagerberg, David C. Mowery & Richard R. Nelson eds., 2006).

[44] Jessica Milli, Emma Williams-Baron, Meika Berlan, Jenny Xia & Barbara Gault, Equity in Innovation: Women Inventors and Patents (2016), https://iwpr.org/equity-in-innovation-women-inventors-and-patents/.

historically remained outside the reach of conventional intellectual property regimes, such as collaborative, non-market, or culturally embedded innovations.

At the institutional level, universities, corporations, and funders should reassess incentive frameworks and internal structures that shape who is encouraged to innovate, whose contributions are valued, and how resources and recognition are distributed. Aiming to create working environments in which diverse talents can thrive and be recognized, such reassessment and follow-up reforms could include invention disclosures, commercialization pipelines, and adjustments to hiring, promotion, and tenure criteria.[45]

In parallel, public policy should adopt a more expansive view of innovation that incorporates social and distributive goals alongside economic growth. Governments and intergovernmental bodies should assume leadership in investing in underserved communities, developing inclusive metrics, and embedding equity into innovation strategies (including those related to AI development). These reforms can help reconfigure innovation ecosystems to ensure broad-based participation, equitable outcomes, and meaningful contribution to shared human advancement.

Finally, inclusion efforts must embrace alternative knowledge systems, community-driven innovations, and creative expressions that extend beyond conventional intellectual property regimes and corporate research-and-development pipelines. Alternative models that intergovernmental bodies, policymakers, and commentators have highlighted include bottom-up, frugal, grassroots, and rural innovation.[46]

In sum, inclusive innovation is both a moral imperative and a strategic necessity. By centering on underrepresented voices, challenging dominant paradigms, and reimagining innovation architectures, we can build innovation ecosystems that are more just, resilient, creative, and responsive to societal needs. This effort will require spaces for critical reflection, an interdisciplinary dialogue, and bold experimentation to expose exclusionary mechanisms while charting diverse and equitable paths forward. With the new challenges posed by AI technology and big data analytics and the high

[45] See Michael Schuster, Miriam Marcowitz-Bitton, and Deborah Gerhardt's chapter in this volume.

[46] Klingler-Vidra et al., *supra* note 2, at 4–5; Papaioannou, *supra* note 4, at 57–63; World Intell. Prop. Org., 2011 World Intellectual Property Report: The Changing Face of Innovation 40 (2011); Yasser Bhatti & Jaideep Prabhu, *Frugal Innovation and Social Innovation: Linked Paths to Achieving Inclusion Sustainably*, *in* Handbook of Inclusive Innovation, *supra* note 4, at 354.

stakes involved, finding appropriate pathways to advance will become even more urgent and important.

Structure of This Volume

This volume brings together policymakers, commentators, and practitioners from around the world to offer a comprehensive and interdisciplinary roadmap for understanding and advancing inclusive innovation. Featuring participants from four continents, the fifteen chapters in the remainder of this volume provide normative critiques, empirical insights, interdisciplinary perspectives, and practical recommendations to facilitate the development of innovation and intellectual property ecosystems that reflect the full diversity of human knowledge and creativity and that serve the broader goals of justice and shared prosperity.

The chapters glean insights from a wide range of academic disciplines, including communication, critical race theory, data science, economics, innovation policy, international relations, law, science and technology studies, sociology, and statistics. This approach reflects the inherently interdisciplinary and multidisciplinary nature of the debate on inclusive innovation and the diverse expertise needed to understand and address related challenges. The chapters expose how demographic disparities, law and policy, governance frameworks, gatekeeping practices, and data and technological infrastructure foster and reinforce inequalities while offering practical interventions to build more inclusive innovation ecosystems. This book aims to equip policymakers, commentators, and industry leaders with the tools needed to design innovation ecosystems that are inclusive, equitable, and responsive to the complexity and diversity of contemporary society. It seeks to reframe innovation as a collective endeavor rooted in justice, participation, and shared prosperity.[47]

[47] This reframing aligns with the evolving human rights framework for intellectual property, which emphasizes the important, complementary roles played by the right to take part in cultural life, the right to enjoy the benefits of scientific progress and its applications, and the right to the protection of interests resulting from intellectual productions, as articulated in the Universal Declaration of Human Rights, the International Covenant on Economic, Social and Cultural Rights, and other international and regional human rights treaties and related interpretive documents. Yu, *supra* note 8. For prior discussion of this framework by one of the volume's editors, see Peter K. Yu, *Intellectual Property and Human Rights in the Nonmultilateral Era*, 64 Fla. L. Rev. 1045 (2012); Peter K. Yu, *Reconceptualizing Intellectual Property Interests in a Human Rights Framework*, 40 U.C. Davis L. Rev. 1039 (2007); Peter K. Yu, *The Anatomy of the Human Rights Framework for Intellectual Property*, 69 SMU L. Rev. 37 (2016).

This volume is organized into five thematic parts: (1) innovation gaps and demographics; (2) disparities in the patent system; (3) initiatives to promote inclusive innovation; (4) AI technology and equitable development; and (5) AI-driven innovation and global challenges. These parts address different aspects of inclusive innovation, both in general and more specifically about AI and big data. Although some contributions have focused more on AI than big data analytics, due in large part to the fast-growing scholarly and policy attention on the former, one should not lose sight of the interconnectedness between AI, machine learning, and big data analytics. As the United Nations Conference on Trade and Development (UNCTAD) rightly observes in *Technology and Innovation Report 2025*: "There is a strong synergy between AI and big data. AI can improve data analysis and pattern recognition, while big data can be used in training models."[48]

Innovation Gaps and Demographics

The first part provides the empirical and conceptual foundation for this volume. It examines who participates in innovation, how demographics and institutional gatekeepers shape the patterns of innovation, and the systemic barriers plaguing underrepresented and marginalized groups. Utilizing empirical data in both the United States and abroad, the chapters show how gender, race, education, occupation, and other socioeconomic factors influence participation in innovation ecosystems.

Opening this part is a chapter by Brent Lutes, Michael Palmedo, and Ryan Safner from the Office of the Chief Economist of the U.S. Copyright Office. Chapter 1, "The State of Inclusivity in Copyright and Creative Ecosystems" reveals persistent disparities in those ecosystems along gender, racial, and other socioeconomic lines. The authors demonstrate how underrepresentation in authorship reflects static inequities while reinforcing systemic biases that shape societal narratives and perpetuate exclusion. Drawing on original data and recent studies, the chapter finds that women remain underrepresented in most creative sectors despite incremental gains. It further shows that the COVID-19 pandemic has disproportionately affected the output of women creators, particularly those independent or in early career. The authors point out that socioeconomic factors, such as education,

[48] UNCTAD, *supra* note 41, at 17.

age, and urban location, strongly predict creative output. They also remind us that broader socioeconomic inequities largely drive racial disparities in copyright registrations, even though distinct patterns have emerged across different types of creative works. This chapter underscores the complex, compounding, and inefficient nature of demographic gaps in copyright and creative ecosystems. It calls for more granular data, nuanced policy interventions, and greater scholarly and policy attention to the overlapping structural barriers confronting underrepresented creators.

In Chapter 2, "Understanding Demographics in Patent Data," Michelle Saksena and Gauri Subramani critically examine how researchers often analyze the relationship between inventive activity and demographics, particularly gender, by inference using U.S. patent data. This chapter shows that women remain significantly underrepresented among U.S. inventors, with slow progress toward parity. It discusses how gender gaps in patent application conversion rates have compounded such underrepresentation, as women are less likely than men to see their applications granted. The authors remind us that reliance on granted patents alone disproportionately obscures women's inventive activities. Using data from PatentsView, a public platform hosting and disseminating USPTO data, the chapter further explains how name-based disambiguation and gender attribution, though widely used in empirical research, have inherent limitations, especially for women due to name changes and the binary assumptions in existing algorithms. The chapter calls for more nuanced understanding of the opportunities and limitations of patent data to allow researchers to better understand and address demographic disparities in the innovation system.

Complementing the previous two U.S.-focused studies, Carlotta Nani, Martin Correa, and Julio Raffo from WIPO broaden our perspective through Chapter 3, "Gender Differences in Intellectual Property Awareness: Evidence from a Global Survey." Utilizing survey data from 25,000 individuals across fifty countries, this chapter examines global gender disparities in intellectual property awareness. It finds that women consistently report lower familiarity with patents and trademarks but demonstrate higher awareness of copyrights and industrial designs. These findings reflect patterns of occupational specialization and barriers within the innovation system. The authors further highlight the confidence gaps that may compound participation barriers, noting that women often underestimate their intellectual property knowledge despite performing well in certain areas. To realize women's potential in innovation and intellectual property systems, this chapter underscores the need for targeted awareness campaigns, institutional reforms, and support mechanisms that address knowledge gaps and structural barriers.

Disparities in the Patent System

The second part of this volume zeroes in on a single but dominant form of intellectual property right: patents. This part draws empirical insights from data on patenting activity and observations on professional practices from around the world. Featuring intellectual property scholars from Israel, New Zealand, and the United States, the three chapters in this part provide a deep dive into how gender, race, and other socioeconomic factors influence participation in the patent system. Two of these chapters underscore the important yet oft-overlooked roles played by patent attorneys.

This part begins with Chapter 4, "The Gender Gap in Academic Patenting." Written by Michael Schuster, Miriam Marcowitz-Bitton, and Deborah Gerhardt, this chapter examines the persistent gender gap in academic patenting. It reveals that, despite growth, women remain underrepresented as inventors and in commercialized university research. Using comprehensive patent data concerning leading research institutions in the United States, this chapter finds that women are significantly less likely to appear as inventors, their patents granted at lower rates, and their patents cited less often than those of their male counterparts. The chapter further states that women are more likely to patent alone, while men dominate larger, collaborative inventor teams, exacerbating disparities in network access and professional opportunities. The authors argue that these gaps diminish women's participation in knowledge transfer and have tangible financial implications, contributing to broader gender inequalities in academia and innovation. To address systemic barriers, they propose a range of legal, institutional, and cultural reforms, including blind patent reviews, improved data collection, mentorship programs, greater incentives for commercialization, and changing hiring, promotion, and tenure practices.

In Chapter 5, "Patent Attorneys and the Increasing Use of Artificial Intelligence: A 'Thought Experiment' on Our Human and Technological Gatekeepers," Jessica Lai highlights how patent attorneys can actively construct notions of inventors and inventions through gendered and racialized lenses. Frequently overlooked in discussions of innovation inequality, patent attorneys influence patenting outcomes and commercialization strategies.

The author warns that the growing use of generative AI in patent practice risks reinforcing these biases, given the technology's reliance on historically skewed data and faulty assumptions. This chapter expands the discourse on inclusive innovation by examining how professional practices, algorithmic systems, and data governance structures mediate access to innovation opportunities, raising urgent questions about how sociotechnical gatekeepers can be reformed to foster more equitable and inclusive innovation ecosystems.

In Chapter 6, "Inventing Fairness: Exploring AI's Role in Patent Reform," Jordana Goodman, Li Yan, Regan Murphy, and Khamal Patterson explore the interrelationship between inventors, patent attorneys, and patent examiners. This chapter examines how racial and cultural contexts shape the experiences of the various actors within the U.S. patent system. Using a case study on the NuDred hair sponge, the authors illustrate how cultural misalignment and communication breakdowns between Black inventors and (often non-Black) patent examiners result in misclassifications, flawed prior art assessments, and barriers to patent protection. They argue that these inequities are embedded in interpersonal interactions and broader institutional practices and norms. The chapter explores the potential for generative AI tools to serve as a corrective mechanism, offering greater clarity in terminology, reducing misunderstandings, and addressing hermeneutic gaps that disadvantage minority inventors. While acknowledging the promise of these technologies, the authors emphasize that AI alone cannot remedy systemic exclusion. Instead, they advocate for integrating AI with deeper structural reforms to legal education, examiner training, and patent evaluation processes. By combining technological interventions with cultural competency and institutional accountability, this chapter offers a multidimensional strategy for making the patent system more inclusive, responsive, and fair.

Initiatives to Promote Inclusive Innovation

The third part of this volume explores how organizations can foster inclusive innovation environments through initiatives such as redesigned processes, targeted mentorship, and leadership engagement. This part also presents innovation metrics that go beyond conventional measures of inventorship to capture latent potential and structural barriers. The chapters in this part pay particular attention to how AI can reinforce or help mitigate exclusion, depending on how the technology is deployed.

Opening this part is Chapter 7, "Inclusive Innovation in an Age of AI: Insights from the Innovator Diversity Pilots Initiative." Written by Margo Bagley and Colleen Chien—two patent scholars one of whom has worked in the U.S. administration—this chapter presents insights from the Innovator Diversity Pilots Initiative they direct. It highlights why inclusive innovation is critical for economic growth, national competitiveness, and societal impact, particularly in the age of AI and big data. The authors document how barriers to participation in inventive activities and the legal profession persist across the innovation lifecycle, from ideation to commercialization. They further identify frictions such as social dynamics, institutional opacity, and systemic bias that disproportionately impact women and underrepresented minorities. Through case studies and pilots, this chapter showcases how education, mentorship, institutional process redesign, and public-private policy leadership can foster inclusivity. The chapter illustrates how AI can serve as a supportive tool to amplify these interventions by bridging social gaps and enhancing evaluation fairness. The authors nonetheless caution that human relationships and institutional commitment remain central and emphasize that AI should augment, not replace, the human and systemic changes needed to build inclusive innovation ecosystems.

In Chapter 8, "Improving Diversity and Inclusivity Measurements in Inventorship: A Competitiveness Perspective," Suzanne Harrison and Bowman Heiden argue that enhancing diversity and inclusivity in inventorship is a matter of equity and a strategic imperative for national competitiveness, technological leadership, and economic growth. Linking inventorship to GDP growth, they emphasize the need to expand and fully utilize the existing innovation and inventorship pool by addressing underrepresentation among women and other demographic groups. The chapter critiques the limitations of using patents as a proxy for inventive activity and proposes more nuanced metrics that distinguish between diversity (representation) and inclusivity (actual participation versus potential). Using examples and data from the Diversity Pledge Program, the authors advocate for an "inclusivity first" approach, which prioritizes activating latent inventorship within organizations to foster sustainable diversity, improve innovation output, and achieve positive-sum growth. This chapter encourages firms to look beyond nominal metrics and adopt tailored interventions that remove barriers to participation, thereby ensuring the development of more equitable and productive innovation ecosystems.

Paola Cecchi-Dimeglio emphasizes organizational interventions in Chapter 9, "Bridging the Gender Gap in Innovation: A Behavioral Approach to Inclusivity." She presents a behavioral approach to closing the gender gap in innovation, arguing that organizational structures and communication practices play critical roles in fostering or impeding inclusivity. Through five large-scale experiments conducted within major corporations, she demonstrates how participation and diversity in innovation activities can significantly increase through leadership engagement, simplified patent submission processes, dedicated online platforms with regular email nudges, storytelling videos, and the adoption of inclusive language. The author finds that these interventions enhance both the quantity and quality of idea submissions from women and other underrepresented groups and reshape organizational cultures. This chapter emphasizes that fostering inclusive innovation requires simultaneous efforts in addressing structural and behavioral barriers and combining leadership support, process redesign, and intentional communication strategies to create environments in which all employees feel empowered to contribute.

AI Technology and Equitable Development

The fourth part of this volume turns to new challenges and concerns posed by advances in AI technology—and, to some extent, also big data analytics. Continuing with an inclusive innovation lens, the first two chapters interrogate the structural and epistemic dimensions of exclusion, drawing attention to how racism, sexism, and other socioeconomic inequalities are reproduced through data collection, technical design, and statistical modeling. The chapters call for more rigorous, justice-oriented approaches to evaluating inclusivity while cautioning against overreliance on flawed proxies or incomplete metrics. The next two chapters move from technical to prescriptive, examining how AI regulation, patent law, and transnational governance frameworks can influence the distribution of resources, opportunities, and risks within innovation ecosystems. By comparing national approaches and identifying reforms that embed accountability and transparency, these chapters highlight the potential of law, policy, and governance frameworks to promote equitable participation on a global scale.

This part begins with Chapter 10, "Identifying Potential Inlets of the Biocentric Man in the Artificial Intelligence Development Process." Written by Deja Workman and Christopher Dancy, this chapter critically analyzes how AI engineering processes—from problem identification to dataset development and data processing to integration and monitoring—are structurally shaped by what Sylvia Wynter terms the "biocentric Man," a construct centering on whiteness, maleness, and Western norms while excluding and harming Black communities. By deconstructing the standard AI development process, the authors reveal how antiblackness and systemic oppression are perpetuated through not only biased data and algorithms but also organizational decisions, resource management, and development workflows that normalize extractive practices, invisibilize labor, and prioritize corporate efficiency over social equity. This chapter calls for a foundational reimagining of the AI development process that explicitly centers on underrepresented communities, questions the necessity of select AI systems, and embeds critical reflection at every step of this process to disrupt the reinforcement of racial hierarchies. The chapter advocates for a shift from reactive bias mitigation to proactive, justice-centered design that confronts the legacy of technocolonialism and the ongoing reproduction of racialized harms in AI systems.

In Chapter 11, "Taking Stock: What Statistics Can and Cannot Do," David Hunter provides three vignettes to illustrate how statistical thinking, grounded in common sense, can help illuminate but also obscure issues of inclusivity and diversity. Through his experience developing a model for undergraduate admissions at the University of Michigan—a model that eventually became the focus of the U.S. Supreme Court case of *Gratz v. Bollinger*[49]—the author shows that interpretable models can foster transparency and dialogue even at the expense of predictive power. The author then examines the use of blind auditions in orchestras, highlighting the difficulty of inferring causation from observable data while admonishing against overstating what statistical models can prove. The chapter then critiques efforts to measure sexism in academic science. It suggests that even rigorous data analyses may fail to capture structural biases due to limitations in what can be measured, a phenomenon the author links to the oft-mentioned "streetlight effect"—the tendency to look under a streetlight for lost keys that have been dropped elsewhere. Together, these three vignettes urge caution in

[49] 539 U.S. 244 (2003).

interpreting statistical findings about inclusivity and reinforce the need for humility and skepticism when drawing conclusions from data.

The next two chapters turn to what remedies can be put in place, preemptively or otherwise, to address the emerging challenges to inclusive innovation posed by AI development. In Chapter 12, "Equitable Progress and the Regulation of AI," one of us (Lim) proposes "equitable progress" as a guiding principle for AI regulation, emphasizing that AI governance must prioritize fairness, inclusivity, and accountability to ensure that technological advancement aligns with human dignity and benefits underrepresented communities. Using a crossdisciplinary framework that builds on Rawlsian justice, participatory governance, and the capability approach, this chapter explores the complex trade-offs between innovation and equity, transparency and performance, accountability and liability, and economic growth and workforce displacement. The chapter compares regulatory models from the United States, the European Union, China, and Singapore, advocating for harmonized global standards that balance innovation with social justice while recognizing the dual role of AI in amplifying and disrupting creativity and innovation. This chapter emphasizes that embedding ethical imperatives into AI governance is both a technical necessity and a moral obligation to reduce systemic disparities and foster global equity.

This part ends with Chapter 13, "Responsibility, Transparency, and Accountability in AI Patents," in which Keith Robinson calls for the adoption of a framework based on principles of responsibility, transparency, and accountability to ensure that the U.S. patent system better promotes ethical AI innovation. The author argues that, while existing patent law doctrines and mechanisms—such as inventor oaths, disclosure requirements, and public access to patent records—incorporate some elements of this framework, these arrangements insufficiently address the societal risks posed by AI technology, particularly regarding bias, opacity, and disproportionate impacts on underrepresented groups. To make inventors and patent owners more accountable for the downstream effects of their AI innovations, this chapter proposes specific reforms such as mandatory algorithmic impact assessments, enhanced disclosure requirements for AI inventions, and patent marking of AI methods. The chapter contends that the USPTO, with its history of mission-driven policy experimentation, is well positioned to implement reforms that align AI's benefits with societal values and ensure the more equitable distribution of these benefits.

AI-Driven Innovation and Global Challenges

The final part of this volume explores the global challenges confronting the future of AI-driven innovation and the feasibility of developing globally inclusive AI. This part focuses on two developments of which mainstream media have provided considerable coverage: first, the technological rivalry between China, the European Union, and the United States in the AI arena and, then, the fast-expanding gap in AI adoption and development between the Global North and the Global South. Juxtaposing these two developments, the two chapters highlight the drastically different challenges confronting developed and large emerging countries on the one hand and low-income and lower-middle-income countries on the other.

In Chapter 14, "Navigating Turbulence: The Challenge of Inclusive Innovation in the U.S.–China AI Race," Lee Jyh-An and Liu Jingwen analyze how legal frameworks in the United States and China shape the intensifying AI arms race, focusing on data privacy, intellectual property rights, and export controls. They highlight how China's centralized, government-driven approach accelerates AI innovation by providing local AI firms with unparalleled access to vast datasets and a favorable stance on the copyrightability of AI-generated works. The authors compare the Chinese approach with the U.S. decentralized, market-driven approach. The latter offers strengths in venture capital, technological leadership, and export controls over semiconductor chips and AI models, but it faces growing pressures from privacy reforms and legal uncertainties around AI training data. This chapter argues that, while China's legal infrastructure may enable rapid AI advancement, the United States' strategic use of export restrictions could hinder China's access to critical technologies. The authors nonetheless point out that the long-term outcomes of these rival strategies remain uncertain and that the dynamics involved illuminate how divergent legal systems and policy choices shape the competitive trajectories of the world's two AI superpowers.

This volume concludes with Chapter 15, "Bridging the Global Artificial Intelligence Divide," written by one of us (Yu). This chapter covers an increasingly important yet still underexplored challenge in the AI arena: the need to bridge the inequitable AI gap between the Global North and the Global South. In the past few years, this gap has received considerable attention within the United Nations, including in the two reports released by the UN Secretary-General's High-Level Advisory Body on Artificial

Intelligence[50] and the *Technology and Innovation Report 2025* published by UNCTAD.[51] Lamenting how research on AI-driven innovation thus far have focused primarily on developed countries, this chapter outlines the challenges confronting AI development in the Global South. It then identifies six policy options that developed countries could adopt to boost local AI development and adoption and, in turn, bridge the global AI divide: (1) intellectual property reforms; (2) international technology transfer obligations; (3) the Global Fund for AI; (4) AI resource pools; (5) open innovation and datasets; and (6) indigenous innovation. This chapter concludes by offering three key takeaways from the discussion of national, regional, and international efforts to bridge the global AI divide.

[50] U.N. Sec'y-Gen.'s High-Level Advisory Body on A.I., *Governing AI for Humanity: Final Report* (Sept. 2024); U.N. Sec'y-Gen.'s High-Level Advisory Body on A.I., *Governing AI for Humanity: Interim Report* (Dec. 2023).

[51] UNCTAD, *supra* note 41.

I.

INNOVATION GAPS AND DEMOGRAPHICS

1

The State of Inclusivity in Copyright and Creative Ecosystems

Brent Lutes, Michael Palmedo, and Ryan Safner

Introduction

Art, literature, news media, entertainment, and other creative works simultaneously reflect and influence social norms. For example, American television entertainment reflects current American society (albeit sometimes in an abstract or idealized way), and many real-world social interactions are modeled on ideals and expectations that derive from that same content. It is a self-reinforcing process of cultural and social evolution. Thus, it is possible, perhaps even common, for systematic biases or underrepresentation in creative works to translate into social perceptions—and for those perceptions to be further reflected in creative works, thereby reinforcing the biases and underrepresentation.

For those reasons, underrepresenting some segments of society in creative ecosystems not only can be inequitable in a static sense but may also have important dynamic, compounding implications. In particular, the underrepresentation of one group gives outsized weight to the views and norms of other groups as reflected in creative works, which in turn can bias collective social perceptions, leading to more biases in creative works, and so on, in a reinforcing cycle. These biases can impose direct—and, in some cases, measurable—economic costs separate from the inherent inequities they represent. Knowing where biases and disparities exist is a necessary step toward addressing them and potentially redirecting the endogenous cycle.

To that end, this chapter examines the state of inclusivity in the copyright system. It draws on recently published research in this area and presents novel results relating to the effects of COVID-19 on gender disparities in

Brent Lutes, Michael Palmedo, and Ryan Safner, *The State of Inclusivity in Copyright and Creative Ecosystems*
In: *Inclusive Innovation in the Age of AI and Big Data*. Edited by: Daryl Lim and Peter K. Yu, Oxford University Press.
 DOI: 10.1093/9780197799444.003.0002

creative production as well as the socioeconomic and demographic characteristics of creators. The chapter is divided into three main sections to address inclusivity of (1) gender; (2) socioeconomic characteristics; and (3) race/ethnicity.

Gender of Authors

Although research into the demographic aspects of the copyright system is relatively sparse, the work that has been done predominantly focuses on gender. Understanding gender disparities is important and warrants the attention of researchers. Nonetheless, the nearly exclusive focus on gender, as opposed to other demographic characteristics, is largely due to the fact that the gender of participants in creative ecosystems can be readily and reliably identified using straightforward statistical techniques.[1] These techniques assign gender probabilities to individuals based on the relative number of males and females with their names in a relevant population.

There are limits to this approach and, thus, corollary limits on our understanding of gender issues in creative ecosystems. For one, the approach is not well suited for determining the gender of any single individual. Rather, it is best aimed at measuring the proportion of males and females within a large group of individuals. Additionally, the validity of this method can be culturally dependent, as it relies on given names being strongly and consistently gendered (which is not the case in all cultures or languages). Also, the method creates ambiguity between gender and biological sex.[2]

These challenges notwithstanding, direct information about creators' gender is rarely available. Thus, name-based gendering remains the most consistent and credible approach for conducting gender analyses in this context. In the remainder of this section, we discuss existing and ongoing research into the gender attributes of creative ecosystems, all of which, including our own novel analyses, rely on name-based gendering.

[1] *See, e.g.*, Guillermo L. Martinez, Julio Raffo & Kenta Saito, *Identifying the Gender of PCT Inventors* (World Intell. Prop. Org., Econ. Rsch. Working Paper No. 33, 2016), https://ssrn.com/abstract=4434107.

[2] This ambiguity results because, depending on the context, reported names may either be legal names or preferred names. Legal names given at birth may correlate better with biological sex than do preferred names. Further complicating the matter, legal names can be changed after birth and may no longer correspond to biological sex. Consequently, our use of the term "gender" is meant as a heuristic, noting that the analysis cannot distinguish "gender" from "sex."

Table 1.1. Author share by gender and the type of work (1978–2012)

(1)	(2)	(3)
Type of Work	**Female Author Share (%)**	**Male Author Share (%)**
Artwork	45.7	54.3
Nondramatic literary work	42.6	57.5
Dramatic work	30.0	70.0
Music	24.0	76.0
Motion picture or filmstrip	21.8	78.2
Machine-readable work or computer program	11.8	88.2

Note: Brauneis and Oliar use slightly different shorthand terms to demark categories of work. Here we convert their terminology to the Census Bureau terminology for consistency. The "music" category is a combination of musical works and sound recordings.

We begin with the work of Robert Brauneis and Dotan Oliar, who examined the gender of authors listed in U.S. copyright registrations between 1978 and 2012. They find that, averaging across all types of creative works, women constituted about 36 percent of registrations in 2012.[3] This is six percentage points higher than the same measure in 1978. Comparing these numbers to women's share of the labor force reveals two informative facts. First, between 1978 and 2012, women's share of copyright registrations grew at about 1.5 times faster than women's share of the labor force.[4] Second, women's share of copyright registrations in 2012 lagged significantly behind women's share of the labor force (36 percent compared with 47 percent).

Brauneis and Oliar further find that the gender gap in registrations is highly variable depending on the type of work being registered. Table 1.1 reports women's share of registrations by the type of work, with artwork being the least male-dominated between 1978 and 2012 and machine-readable work (e.g., software or databases) the most male-dominated during the same period.[5]

[3] Robert Brauneis & Dotan Oliar, *An Empirical Study of the Race, Ethnicity, Gender, and Age of Copyright Registrants*, 86 Geo. Wash. L. Rev. 46 (2016).

[4] A compound annual growth rate (CAGR) of 0.54 percent for the former compared with 0.35 percent for the latter.

[5] For further information on the types of works categorized by the United States Copyright Office, see U.S. Copyright Off., Library of Congress Copyright Data as Distributed in MARC 21 Format 18–20 (2008), https://www.copyright.gov/policy/women-in-copyright-system/LOC-Copyright-Data-as-Distributed-in-the-MARC%2021-Format.pdf.

Brauneis and Oliar also note that machine-readable works, despite having the largest gender gap of all types of works, show one of the greatest gains in female authorship since 1978, with a total increase of about 12 percentage points (as opposed to the 6 percentage point overall average increase). Women's share of registrations of nondramatic literary works (e.g., books) saw similar gains, increasing by about 12 percentage points.

Separate from the gender gap, Brauneis and Oliar's work also reveals interesting patterns regarding collaborative gender preferences. They find that, when a work has more than one author, the coauthors tend to be of the same gender. That is, men have a propensity to collaborate with other men, and women have a propensity to collaborate with other women. In fact, the first author of a work being a woman increases the likelihood of the second author of that work being a woman by more than 40 percent. Similarly, the first author being a man increases the likelihood of the second author being a man by 25 percent.[6]

Brauneis and Oliar also find that, conditional on the type of work, female authors tend to be younger than male authors, and the works they register have a greater tendency to be unpublished. For example, within nondramatic literary works (the category containing the most registrations by female authors), the average age of female authors was about forty-five compared with forty-seven for men. Within that same category, 61 percent of registrations from women were for published works, whereas 66 percent of registrations from men were for published works.

In 2022, the United States Copyright Office published its report on women in the copyright system.[7] The report found that meaningful progress had been made regarding gender parity in copyright registrations. The pace of progress had increased since the work of Brauneis and Oliar, but a gender gap persisted. Overall, the report finds that, in 2020, 38.5 percent of copyright registrations were for works by female authors (compared with 36 percent in 2012). This equates to a 0.84 percent compound annual growth rate (CAGR) between 2012 and 2020, compared with a 0.54 percent CAGR between 1978 and 2012 (a 56-percent increase in the growth rate). This

[6] In 2012, the unconditional probability of an author being a woman (man) was about 36 percent (64 percent), whereas the probability of a second author being a woman (man) conditional on the first author being a woman (man) was about 51 percent (80 percent).

[7] This report was based on the work done by Joel Waldfogel, who served as Kaminstein Scholar at the United States Copyright Office from 2021 to 2022. U.S. Copyright Off., Women in the Copyright System: An Analysis of Women Authors in Copyright Registrations from 1978 to 2020 (2022).

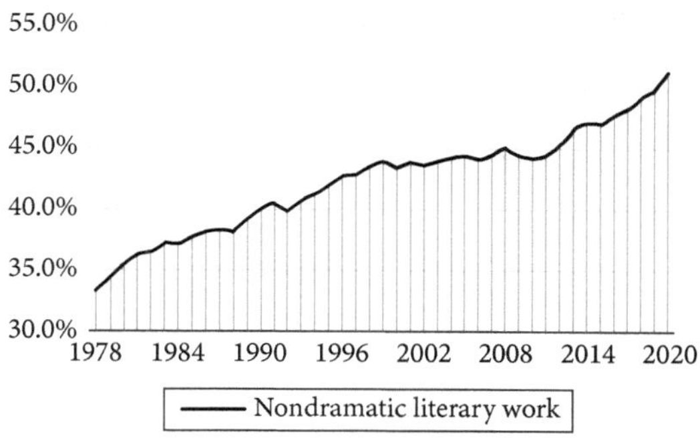

Figure 1.1. Female authors' share of registrations for nondramatic literary works
Source: U.S. Copyright Office, *supra* note 7.

can be seen in Figure 1.1, which depicts the growth of female authorship in nondramatic literary works.

The research also shows that progress and the residual gender gap remain highly varied between types of works (as illustrated in Figure 1.2). In fact, if one uses women's share of the U.S. population as a parity benchmark, female authors have more than closed the gap in nondramatic literary works, accounting for slightly more than 51 percent of registrations. At the other end of the spectrum, the gender gap remains quite high in registrations for machine-readable works and sound recordings, with women accounting for only 20 and 22 percent, respectively. Nevertheless, registrations for machine-readable works also demonstrated the highest growth rate in female author share, increasing by 172 percent in the forty-two years between 1978 and 2020 and by 73 percent in the last eight years of that range alone.

A useful innovation of this work is the construction of occupation-specific gender shares as an alternative benchmark for gender parity in copyright registrations. These comparisons are depicted in Figure 1.3. Points below the diagonal indicate that women's share of registrations for a particular type of work is lower than that of related occupations. Points above the diagonal indicate the converse. All but one type of work (architectural drawings) fall below the line. Even nondramatic literary works, where women's share of registrations matches their share of the U.S. population, fall short of this alternative parity benchmark. Indeed, women's 60-percent share of occupations related to literary publishing suggests that we might expect to see significantly more than 51 percent of registrations coming from female authors.

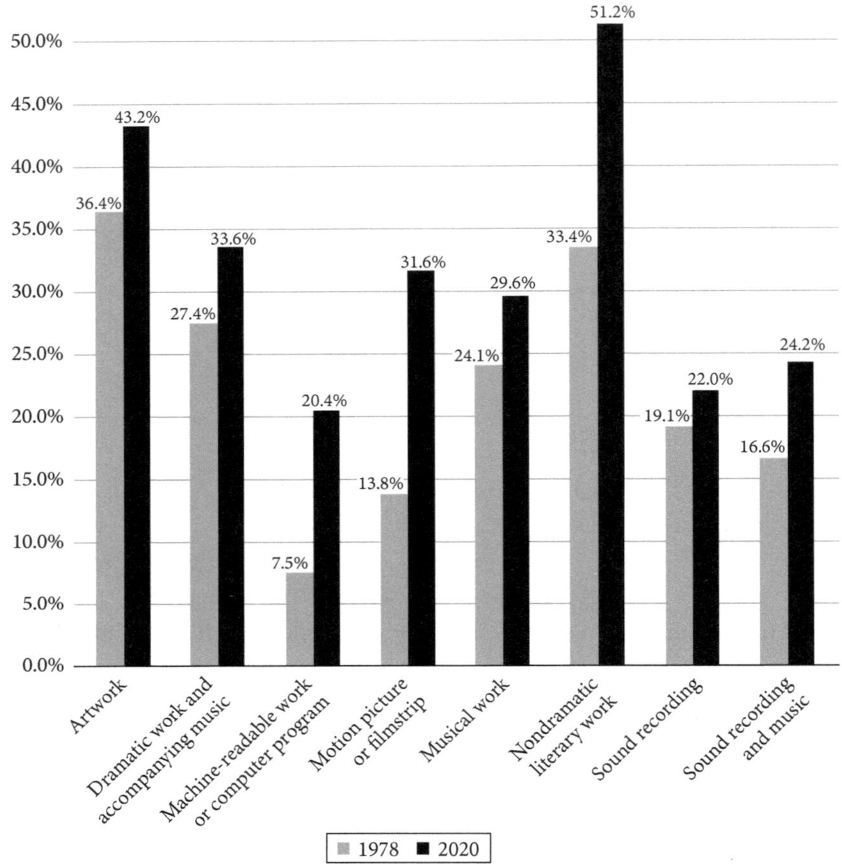

Figure 1.2. Share of female authors in copyright registrations 1978 vs. 2020
Source: U.S. Copyright Office, *supra* note 7.

Overall, these findings suggest that barriers to gender parity are complex. On the one hand, some of the gender gap in registrations is simply a reflection of the labor gender gap in relevant creative fields (aside from literary and artworks, women have a less than 50-percent share of relevant occupations). On the other hand, the results suggest that women in those occupations are not producing as many creative works as their male colleagues, they have a lower propensity to register their works, or both. These sources of disparity implicate different policy interventions. Thus, further research into the channels of gender disparity in creative ecosystems can help policymakers better target remedies.

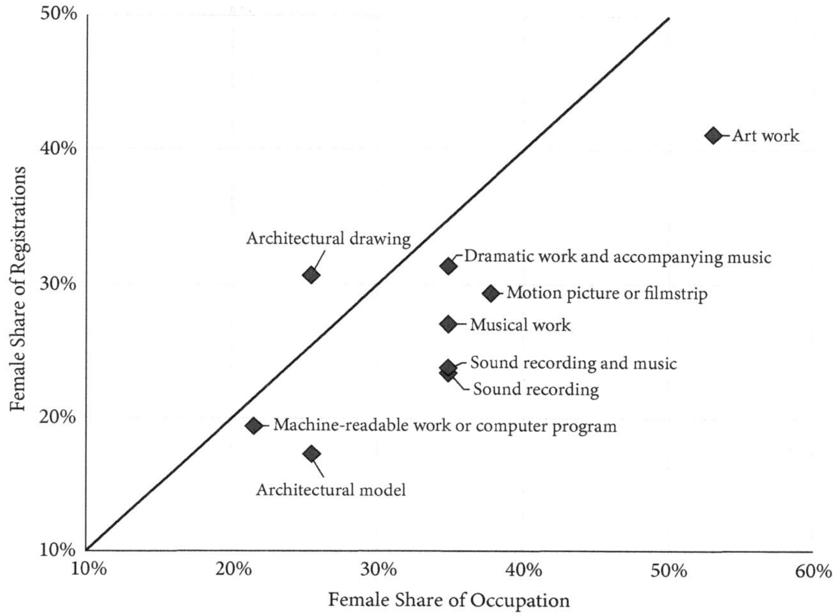

Figure 1.3. Female occupation participation rates vs. copyright registration rates (2011–2020)

Source: U.S. Copyright Office, *supra* note 7.

Note: The diagonal line represents the expected registration rate by female authors if gender representation rates were equal in occupation data and registration data.

To that end, the COVID-19 pandemic can offer some useful clues. Substantial evidence suggests that the pandemic disproportionately affected women in labor markets.[8] Employment losses in general were, at their peak, about 19 percent greater for women than for men.[9] However, much of this gap can be explained by pre-pandemic sorting across occupations and industries that vary significantly in their sensitivity to disruption by the pandemic.

[8] *See, e.g.*, Jörg Bluedorn, Francesca Caselli, Niels-Jakob Hansen, Ippei Shibata & Marina M. Tavares, *Gender and Employment in the COVID-19 Recession: Cross-Country Evidence on "She-Cessions*," 81 Lab. Econ. 1 (2023); Anu Madgavkar, Olivia White, Mekala Krishnan, Deepa Mahajan & Xavier Azcue, *COVID-19 and Gender Equality: Countering the Regressive Effects*, McKinsey Glob. Inst. (July 15, 2020), https://www.mckinsey.com/featured-insights/future-of-work/covid-19-and-gender-equality-countering-the-regressive-effects.

[9] Bureau of Lab. Stat., U.S. Dep't of Lab., *Unemployment Rate Rises to Record High 14.7 Percent in April 2020*, Econ. Daily (May 13, 2020), https://www.bls.gov/opub/ted/2020/unemployment-rate-rises-to-record-high-14-point-7-percent-in-april-2020.htm; Marina Tertilt, Matthias Doepke, Jean Olmstead-Rumsey & Titan Alon, *The Shecession (She-Recession) of 2020: Causes and Consequences*, CEPR VoxEU (Nov. 3, 2020), https://cepr.org/voxeu/columns/shecession-she-recession-2020-causes-and-consequences.

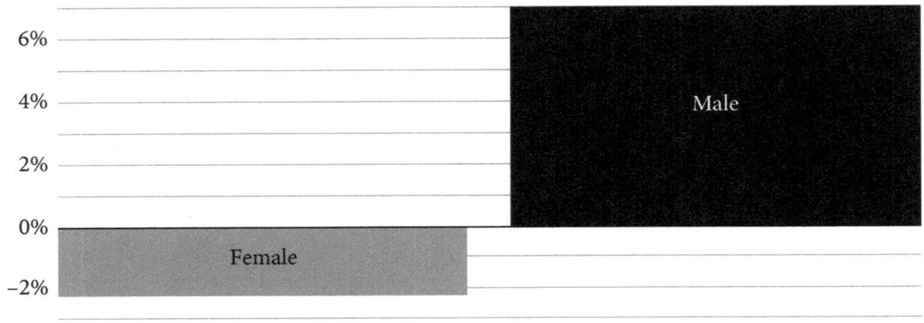

Figure 1.4. Change in copyright registrations for single-authored works by gender of author (February–April 2020)

Women also tended to work in jobs that allow more remote work and those involving more face-to-face activities.[10] It is not immediately obvious how these trends might carry over to creative output for several reasons. First, the gap from making cross-industry and cross-profession comparisons may be less pronounced when the analysis is limited to individuals within similar industries and professions. Second, creative output is not entirely tied to formal employment.

To shed some light on this issue, we build on our previous research[11] by examining the COVID-19 impact on registrations by gender using the copyright registration data.[12] Figure 1.4 shows the changes by gender to copyright registration for single-authored works in the first few months of the pandemic (February–April 2020). Over this period, registrations of male-authored works increased by 7.08 percent, while female-authored works decreased by 2.28 percent. This lowered the share of female-authored works in our sample by 5.41 percent. Note that, as stated in a United States Copyright Office report, total copyright registrations decreased by 3,977 (−1 percent) during this period, largely due to a decline in registrations by organizations (as can be seen below in Figure 1.5).[13] It now becomes clearer

[10] Laura Montenovo, Jiang Xuan, Felipe Lozano-Rojas, Ian Schmutte, Kosali Simon, Bruce A. Weinberg & Coady Wing, *Determinants of Disparities in Early COVID-19 Job Losses*, 59 Demography 827 (2022).

[11] U.S. Copyright Off., The Resilience of Creativity: An Examination of the COVID-19 Impact on Copyright-Reliant Industries and Their Subsequent Recovery (2024).

[12] For this analysis, we first limit our analysis to the 9.4 million registered works with a single individual author (about 87 percent of registrations available in the data, after accounting for empty or missing author data).

[13] Note that there are several key differences in this analysis compared to U.S. Copyright Office, *supra* note 7. These counts are not seasonally adjusted and use the subset of copyright registrations that contain one named author whose gender could be inferred. Registrations of works by authors whose gender could not be robustly inferred declined by 9 percent over this period.

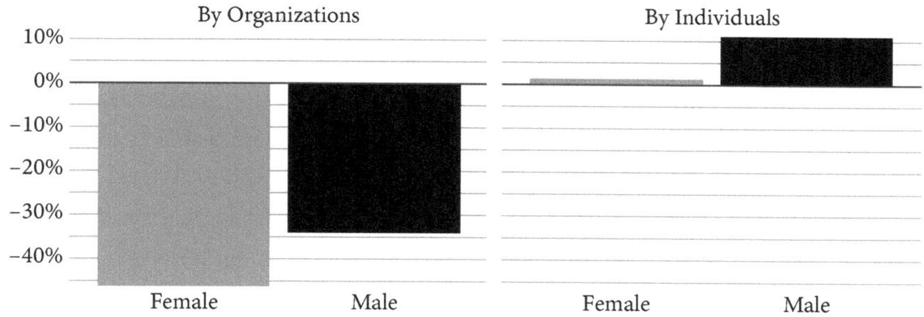

Figure 1.5. Change in copyright registrations by gender of author and type of claimant (February–April 2020)

that a significant share of this decline was borne by female authors relative to male authors.

Figure 1.5 expands Figure 1.4, further splitting the gender-specific effects by the type of claimant—whether the claimants were exclusively individuals or whether at least one of the claimants was an organization. Organizations such as record labels or literary publishers are typically listed as claimants. Independent creators (e.g., those without a record or publishing deal) tend to have only individual claimants listed. Overall, it becomes clearer that most of the decline in registrations originated from organizational claimants, with sharp declines in registrations of works across both male (a 34.6-percent decrease) and female authors (a 46.6-percent decrease). In contrast, there was an 11-percent increase in individual registrations from male authors and a 0.8-percent increase from female authors over the period.

Assuming that works with organizational claimants tend to be tied to an author's primary employment, and registrations from individuals are more likely to be tied to leisure activities or secondary/informal employment or come from early-career creators, these results provide some useful insights. First, the data shows that the COVID-19 employment shock was larger for women even when comparing workers within similar industries and occupations. Second, they suggest substantial differences in how men and women used their time outside of their formal employment (perhaps due to differences in childcare responsibilities). Finally, they imply that early-career female authors may be disadvantaged, compared with their male counterparts, in terms of future career progression—at least to the extent that career opportunities improve as creative output increases.

Although most evidence suggests that women are underrepresented or disadvantaged within creative ecosystems, recent research suggests at least one context in which systemic biases may work in their favor. Luis Aguiar, Joel Waldfogel, and Sofia Waldfogel examine the case of music streaming platforms using data from Spotify.[14] They measure the gender bias using outcome measures to test the difference in performance by male and female artists expected to be of equal promise via Spotify's "New Music Fridays" curated playlists. Across twenty-six countries in 2017, the authors find that Spotify curators appear to give greater weight to music by women—relative to those by men, contrary to popular belief.

While it is clear that gender disparity exists to varying extents within the copyright and creative ecosystems (usually, but not always, to the disadvantage of women), the mere existence of a disparity tells us little about its effects on social welfare. Although it is difficult to measure, and even more so to generalize, the welfare effects of the observed gender disparities, recent work by Joel Waldfogel provides some useful insights within the specific context of book authorship.[15] In particular, he examines the consumer welfare gains associated with the shift toward female authorship that started in the 1960s (relative to a counterfactual world in which the gender gap remained at 1960s-levels).

Waldfogel's model predicts that, in this counterfactual world, more male authors would have entered the market than in the real world, which would have made up for some, but not all, of the welfare decrease associated with the counterfactual world's lost female authors. The quality (as measured by his indicators) of the marginal male authors entering the market would, however, be lower than the quality of the female authors who are excluded from the market in this scenario. This is because, when the split between male and female authorship is skewed as a result of social barriers (and not systematic differences in production capacity), the marginal male author will come from the low end of the quality distribution, and the marginal female author will come from the high end of the quality distribution.

As a stylized and simplified example, suppose the market only had room for 100 authors, and because of social barriers around gender, we start with eighty male and twenty female authors. Aside from the social barriers skewing the gender distribution, authors can enter the market based on

[14] Luis Aguiar, Joel Waldfogel & Sofia Waldfogel, *Playlisting Favorites: Measuring Platform Bias in the Music Industry* (Nat'l Bureau of Econ. Rsch., Working Paper No. 29017, 2021).

[15] Joel Waldfogel, *The Welfare Effects of Gender-Inclusive Intellectual Property Creation: Evidence from Books* (Nat'l Bureau of Econ. Rsch., Working Paper No. 30987, 2023).

their relative quality, such that, in this initial state, the twentieth best female author can enter the market, and the twenty-first best female author does not make the cut. Once gender-oriented barriers are reduced, every ensuing step toward gender parity improves the *average* quality. We would gain the twenty-first best female author at the expense of the eightieth best male author, and twenty-second best female author at the expense of the seventy-ninth best male author, and so on. This intuition is borne out empirically through sales data that reveals, for example, that the twenty-first best female author does in fact produce higher-quality works than the eightieth best male author.

Waldfogel shows that the shift toward female authorship has a net positive effect on overall author revenue, with the increase in female author revenue more than offsetting the decrease in male author revenue. Moreover, the resulting (and substantial) increase in consumer surplus accrues to both readers with preferences for female-authored books and those with preferences for male-authored books (although the former realize the bulk of consumer surplus gains).

Ultimately, the existing evidence tells us the following: (1) the gender gap in copyright and creative ecosystems persists but is shrinking; (2) female authorship tends to be more sensitive to recent economic shocks than male authorship; (3) the roots of the gender gap are likely multifaceted (and a narrowly focused intervention is unlikely to satisfactorily resolve it); and (4) gender disparity is not only a matter of inequity but also a potential source of meaningful economic inefficiency. Existing research, however, does not yet tell us the specific mechanisms that have worked to shrink the gender gap or the factors contributing to the remaining gap.

Socioeconomic Characteristics of Authors

Information on the socioeconomic characteristics of authors can help us better understand how the copyright system is being used, measure how well the system meets its goals, and identify areas for enhancing its utility. However, little research exists on the socioeconomic characteristics of authors, such as income, education, age, and urban/non-urban divides, largely because data on such characteristics is usually unavailable, and those characteristics cannot be inferred from names in the same way gender can. Nonetheless, recently published data has laid the foundation for doing such research.[16] In this section, we provide the first look into several key socioeconomic factors that influence authorship. We first discuss prior research and our methodology.

The only prior empirical work in this area of which we are aware is Brauneis and Oliar, who examine the age of authors.[17] Copyright registrations allow claimants to list authors' birth and death years, the former of which the researchers use to calculate age at the time of registration. They find that the average author is approximately forty years old, with the most productive authors aged 27–36, which accounts for about 30 percent of registrations in their sample. Authors of published works tend to be significantly older (by about 5.5 years) than authors of unpublished works. There is also significant age variation by the type of work: the average age of authors is thirty-six for musical works and sound recordings, forty for software and dramatic works, forty-three for visual art and motion pictures, and forty-six for literary works. They also show that, over time, the age distribution of authors has evened out: in 1980, creativity was highly concentrated, peaking around ages 25–29, whereas in 2012, there is a long plateau of creativity by age group, ranging between ages twenty-five and sixty-four. One methodological limitation of this approach is that "birth year" is not a field claimants are required to fill in, and only about 10 percent opt to do so. Moreover, there may plausibly be systematic age differences between those who elect to report their birth year and those who do not.

With respect to our own socioeconomic analysis of authors, we employ a geographically based system for observing relationships between key characteristics and copyright registration activity. This work builds on the work of one of us (Lutes), Joel Waldfogel, and Jeremy Watson,[18] whose data identifies the physical addresses of claimants, and of the United States Copyright Office,[19] which uses those addresses to measure geographic patterns in copyright registrations. We extend this research by matching geographic patterns of registrations to those of socioeconomic characteristics, which allows us to measure the conditional relationships between those characteristics on the one hand and registration type and volume on the other.

[16] Brent Lutes, Joel Waldfogel & Jeremy Watson, *Extending Intellectual Property Research in Copyright: A New Data Set from the U.S. Copyright Office*. 10 Strategy Sci. 245 (2025).

[17] Brauneis & Oliar, *supra* note 3.

[18] Lutes et al., *supra* note 16.

[19] U.S. Copyright Off., The Geography of Copyright Registrations (2024).

This method, too, has limits. One limit derives from the addresses that are available in the data. In particular, the address that is typically provided is that of the copyright claimant, who may or may not be the author of the work. For example, a claimant may be a publisher, whereas the author is the writer. In that case, the data typically provides the address of the publisher, not the writer. To ensure that we analyze the socioeconomic characteristics of authors, not non-author claimants, we limit the sample of copyright registrations to only those for which the author and the claimant are the same person, meaning that the provided claimant address is also the author's address.[20] This subset of authors, which we informally characterize as "independent creators," should not necessarily be considered a representative sample of broader creative ecosystems, as it systematically excludes important subsets of creators.[21] Moreover, the assignment of an author to this subgroup may not be random across socioeconomic lines. Thus, while our analysis of independent creators provides useful insights into creative ecosystems, the reader should exercise caution in broadly extrapolating the results.

Separately, within a locality, we cannot determine the socioeconomic characteristics of the individuals actually registering copyrights. Thus, we can say that areas with a higher or lower proportion of a particular group tend to have more or fewer registrations than other areas, but we cannot definitively say that the change in registrations comes from that particular group. For example, if young people who live in predominantly older areas systematically differ from young people who live in predominantly younger areas, our methodology would incorrectly characterize the difference as one between young and old, instead of one between two differing subsets of young people. While we control for many systematic differences and are not aware of evidence suggesting that other differences may be driving our results, we cannot definitively rule out the possibility. For the sake of exposition, we assume in what follows that the average propensity to register copyrights, conditional

[20] Our analysis relies on the socioeconomic composition of an area's residents. It may be that authors provide an address other than their residence—for example, a post office box or a business address. However, in analyzing a random sample of these addresses, we find that the vast majority (83 percent) are indeed residential addresses.

[21] For example, when a recording artist has a record deal and produces works as part of that deal, those works are typically registered by the record label, which is the claimant. The address provided in such a case is typically that of the record label headquarters, not that of the recording artist. Thus, the work is excluded from our sample.

on the controls included in our model, is consistent within a socioeconomic subgroup irrespective of geography.

For our analysis, we construct a multidimensional panel dataset consisting of registration counts per year, per ZIP code,[22] per type of work, for the eight most registered types of works over the period 2011–2022.[23] We compare that to data on socioeconomic characteristics of ZIP codes by year using the Poisson panel model:

$$Regs_{i,j,t} = exp(\alpha + \beta Population_{i,t} + \boldsymbol{X}_{i,t} + FE_j + FE_t) \qquad (1)$$

Where $Regs_{i,j,t}$ is the number of registrations originating from ZIP code *i*, for type of work *j*, in year *t*, *Population* is the population of each ZIP code, expressed in 1,000s of people, FE_j are the fixed effects for type of work *j*, and FE_t are the fixed effects for year *t*. Our socioeconomic variables are in the vector $\boldsymbol{X}_{i,t}$, which vary by ZIP code *i* and year *t*. They include the following:[24]

- *Percent Pop College Grad:* the percentage of a ZIP code's adult population with a bachelor's degree or higher;
- *Median Real HH Income*: each ZIP code's median real household income, expressed in thousands of dollars;
- *Percent Land Urban*: the percentage of the tracts within each ZIP code that the Census Bureau classified as "urban" in the 2010 Decennial Census (the classification was based on meeting population and housing density thresholds); and
- *Info & Entertainment*: the share of employed people in a ZIP code that work in either the Information sector (classified under North American Industry Classification System (NAICS 51)) or the Arts and

[22] More precisely, we use the Census Bureau's ZIP Code Tabulation Areas. *ZIP Code Tabulation Areas (ZCTAs)*, U.S. Census Bureau, https://www.census.gov/programs-surveys/geography/guidance/geo-areas/zctas.html (last visited May 6, 2025).

[23] These types of works are artistic works, dramatic works, literary works, machine readable works, motion pictures, musical works, serials, and sound recordings. For more on these types of works, see U.S. Copyright Off., *supra* note 5.

[24] *American Community Survey 5-Year Estimates, 2009–2022*, U.S. Census Bureau (Dec. 7, 2023), https://www.census.gov/data/developers/data-sets/acs-5year.html.

Entertainment sector (NAICS 71) (this data was taken from the Bureau of Labor Statistics).[25]

We report the results of six specifications in Table 1.2. We test the socioeconomic covariates one at a time in columns (1)–(5), and we combine all but one of the factors in column (6). (*Median Real HH Income* is omitted for reasons discussed below.) Each covariate has a positive and significant relationship with registration counts. Note that we report incidence rate ratios (IRR) ($IRR = \tilde{\beta} = e^{\hat{\beta}}$) rather than raw coefficients, the interpretation of which is that a one unit increase in x changes $\hat{y}$ by a factor of $\tilde{\beta}$ (for a change of $(\tilde{\beta} - 1)$ percent in $\hat{y}$). For example, the IRR for *Percent Pop College Grad* is 1.031. This implies that a one percentage point increase in the share of a ZIP code's population with at least a bachelor's degree is associated with 3.1-percent increase in copyright registrations. College education appears to be one of the strongest predictors of copyright registrations (after population size).

Another important predictor is age. People in areas with older populations tend to produce more copyright registrations, increasing at about 1 percent for every one-year increase in median age. About 90 percent of ZIP codes in our data have median ages ranging between thirty and fifty-six, with the median ZIP code falling around forty-two years old. ZIP codes toward the top of that distribution tend to produce more copyright registrations per person, even when accounting for other socioeconomic differences between them.

Similarly, urban ZIP codes tend to produce more registrations than non-urban ones. Again, this holds even after accounting for other systematic differences between urban and non-urban areas. On average, an urban area will produce more registrations than a non-urban area with the same population, median age, median income, and college education rate. While creative industries do tend to agglomerate in urban areas,[26] such agglomeration is unlikely the primary driver of our results—at least not directly so. Recall that our sample of authors are independent authors and thus not associated with organizations within creative industries. Moreover, our model controls for the prevalence of creative industries in an area.

[25] *May 2023 National Industry-Specific Occupational Employment and Wage Estimates*, U.S. Bureau of Lab. Stat. (May 2023), https://www.bls.gov/oes/2023/may/oessrci.htm; *Quarterly Census of Employment and Wages*, U.S. Bureau of Lab. Stat. (2011–2022), https://www.bls.gov/cew (last visited July 29, 2025).

[26] U.S. Copyright Off., *supra* note 19.

Table 1.2. Estimated relationship between socioeconomic factors and copyright registrations

	(1)	(2)	(3)	(4)	(5)	(6)
Population	1.075*** (0.000)	1.082*** (0.000)	1.053*** (0.000)	1.088*** (0.000)	1.083*** (0.000)	1.057*** (0.000)
% Pop College Grad	1.031*** (0.000)					1.026*** (0.000)
Median Real HH Income		1.011*** (0.000)				
% Land Urban			1.020*** (0.000)			1.012*** (0.000)
Median Age				1.011*** (0.001)		1.011*** (0.001)
Info & Entertainment					1.032*** (0.001)	1.036*** (0.001)
Observations	2,800,080	2,746,827	2,788,929	2,803,005	2,798,496	2,735,986
Pseudo R^2	0.488	0.451	0.461	0.423	0.427	0.507

Note: The dependent variable is the number of copyright registrations, by year and ZIP code. Model fit using Poisson regression with year fixed effects and work type fixed effects. Coefficients are reported as IRR ($\exp(\hat{\beta})$) for ease of interpretation. Intercept term is omitted for brevity. Standard errors are clustered at the work type level and transformed using the delta method to match the scale of the exponentiated coefficient estimates. $^{*}P < 0.10$, $^{**}P < 0.05$, $^{***}P < 0.01$.

Median income, at first blush, seems to be an important determinant of copyright registration volume. However, on closer examination, that relationship appears to be spurious and an artifact of the separate relationships between (1) registrations and education; and (2) education and income. Indeed, *Median Real HH Income* is highly correlated with *Percent Pop College Grad*, and inclusion of the latter essentially eliminates the effect of the former. This finding suggests that college education may be the stronger, more direct driver of copyright registrations.[27]

The analysis above uses fixed effects to control for the fact that registration counts differ by the type of work, but it does not indicate whether the relationship between registrations and socioeconomic factors differs along those same lines. To test for these differences, we run another set of tests separately for each type of work. We combine the three types of works covering music and sound recordings into one category of work, which we call "audio works." Table 1.3 reports the results.

[27] This is the reason *Med Real HH Income* is omitted from column (6). The inclusion of both raises multicollinearity concerns.

Table 1.3. Estimated relationship between socioeconomic factors and copyright registrations by the type of work

	(1)	(2)	(3)	(4)	(5)	(6)
	Art works	**Dramatic works**	**Literary works**	**Machine-readable**	**Motion pictures**	**Audio works**
Population	1.052*** (0.001)	1.063*** (0.001)	1.056*** (0.001)	1.058*** (0.002)	1.085*** (0.007)	1.059*** (0.000)
% Pop College Grad	1.030*** (0.001)	1.035*** (0.000)	1.030*** (0.001)	1.030*** (0.001)	1.027*** (0.002)	1.016*** (0.000)
% Land Urban	1.013*** (0.001)	1.017*** (0.000)	1.010*** (0.000)	1.012*** (0.001)	1.017*** (0.001)	1.013*** (0.000)
Median Age	1.011*** (0.001)	1.023*** (0.001)	1.006*** (0.001)	1.018*** (0.003)	1.035*** (0.005)	1.013*** (0.000)
Info & Entertainment	1.046*** (0.002)	1.070*** (0.002)	1.026*** (0.001)	1.021*** (0.004)	1.071*** (0.003)	1.030*** (0.000)
Observations	309,554	309,554	309,554	309,554	309,554	309,554
Pseudo R^2	0.335	0.423	0.488	0.183	0.271	0.464

Note: The dependent variable is the number of copyright registrations, by year and ZIP code. Model fit using Poisson regression with year fixed effects and work type fixed effects. Coefficients are reported as IRR ($exp(\hat{\beta})$) for ease of interpretation. Intercept term is omitted for brevity. Robust standard errors are transformed using the delta method to match the scale of the exponentiated coefficient estimates. $^{*}P < 0.10$, $^{**}P < 0.05$, $^{***}P < 0.01$.

The IRRs for *Percent Pop College Grad* is the highest for dramatic works, indicating that education is most associated with the registration of this type. It is the lowest for audio works. The IRRs for *Percent Land Urban*, *Median Age*, and *Info & Entertainment* are all the highest for dramatic works and/or motion pictures. The IRRs for *Percent Land Urban* and *Median Age* are the lowest for literary works, indicating that the relationships between urbanity and age on the one hand and registrations of written works on the other are weaker than they are for other types of works. Nonetheless, these relationships are still positive and significant. Overall, these results indicate that the influence of socioeconomic factors is quite heterogeneous between types of works.

Race/Ethnicity of Authors

Like research on socioeconomic factors, research on the role of race/ethnicity in the copyright system is limited. Indeed, we are aware of only one prior study along these lines.[28] This is likely an artifact of the practical challenges in identifying the race/ethnicity of authors. Like the case of gender and other socioeconomic characteristics, direct information about the race/ethnicity of participants is rarely available. However, unlike gender, the correlation between given names and race/ethnicity can be rather weak. While many first names are relatively more or less frequent among various racial/ethnic groups, those patterns tend to be unstable over time, making inference based on given names reliable in only narrow circumstances.[29]

As an alternative, Brauneis and Oliar use surnames to assess the race/ethnicity of authors who have registered copyrights.[30] While this can be a more dependable method than relying on given names in many circumstances, it remains somewhat controversial.[31] For example, surname-based racial/ethnic identification may prove challenging when attempting to distinguish Black individuals from White individuals since the surnames of the two groups tend to exhibit similar patterns in the United States. Additionally, because of traditional surname norms in the United States, such an analysis usually only reflects a person's paternal lineage.

For those reasons, we conduct a novel analysis based on the granular geographic location of authors combined with data on the racial/ethnic composition of those areas. This allows us to examine racial/ethnic trends in copyright registrations. Our findings are, in many respects, consistent with those of Brauneis and Oliar.[32] Moreover, our approach allows for new and important insights into the factors driving racial/ethnic patterns in creative ecosystems. In the remainder of this section, we first outline previous findings and then present novel ones.

Table 1.4 reports Brauneis and Oliar's findings in terms of racial/ethnic representation in copyright registrations relative to the racial/ethnic composition of the U.S. populace.[33] These findings imply that White authors

[28] Brauneis & Oliar, *supra* note 3.

[29] Lisa D. Cook, Trevon Logan & John Parman, *Distinctively Black Names in the American Past*, 53 Explorations Econ. Hist. 64 (2014).

[30] Brauneis & Oliar, *supra* note 3.

[31] For a discussion of limits and criticisms, see, for example, Pablo Mateos, Names, Ethnicity and Populations: Tracing Identity in Space (2014).

[32] Brauneis & Oliar, *supra* note 3.

[33] Note that the Census Bureau considers Hispanic as an ethnicity and the other groups reported in Table 1.4 as racial groups. People in those racial groups can be Hispanic or non-Hispanic. However, to avoid double counting, the Bureau includes Hispanic populations of all races within the "Hispanic" group and excludes ethnically Hispanic people from other racial groups. Thus, for example, "White" is more accurately characterized as "Non-Hispanic White," "Black" as "Non-Hispanic Black," and so on. For ease of exposition, we adopt Brauneis and Oliar's convention of omitting the "Non-Hispanic" prefix from the names of Census Bureau racial groups.

Table 1.4. Racial/ethnic shares reported by Brauneis and Oliar

(1)	(2)	(3)	(4)
Race/ethnicity	**Share of 2010 registrations (%)**	**Share of 2010 population (%)**	**Reg. share/Pop. share (%)**
White	74.0	63.7	116.1
Hispanic	7.3	16.3	44.6
Black	15.1	12.6	119.9
Asian or Pacific Islander	4.1	4.9	82.7
American Indian/ Alaskan Natives	0.7	0.9	77.8

Note: The first two columns, "Share of 2010 registrations" and "Share of 2010 population" are as reported by Brauneis and Oliar. The third column is calculated as the ratio of the first two columns.

tend to be significantly overrepresented in copyright registrations as of 2010, producing about 16 percent more registrations than the White share of the U.S. population would otherwise predict. Brauneis and Oliar hypothesize that this overrepresentation may be the result of two factors. First, the U.S. White population is, on average, significantly older than other racial/ethnic groups in the United States, which may lead to more registrations. Indeed, this is consistent with our findings discussed in the previous section: older Americans tend to register copyrights more frequently than younger Americans. Second, the overrepresentation of White authors is the reciprocal of a large and significantly underrepresented Hispanic population in the United States. As a simple matter of mathematics, the underrepresentation of one group must be accompanied by the overrepresentation of some other group(s). The implication of this second point is that the overrepresentation of White authors could feasibly stem from shortcomings in the system with respect to Hispanic authors in particular, rather than (or in addition to) overtly advantaging White authors.

The underrepresentation of Hispanic authors in Brauneis and Oliar's analysis is indeed significant, with Hispanic authors registering about 55 percent fewer works than the Hispanic share of the U.S. population would predict. Brauneis and Oliar identify potential factors driving this disparity as, first, the relatively young average age of the Hispanic population and, second, the inclusion of undocumented Hispanic immigrants in the Census Bureau's measure of population shares. The first is simply the converse of the issue discussed above: younger Americans tend to register copyrights at a lower frequency. The second stems from an implicit hypothesis that undocumented immigrants are less likely to register copyrights due to their reluctance to engage with government institutions.

Brauneis and Oliar also find that Pacific Islander and Native American populations are underrepresented in terms of copyright registrations. In contrast, their results indicate that, of all racial/ethnic groups examined, the Black population tends to register copyrights at the highest rate (relative to the Black share of the population). As noted above, surname-based identification of Black people is methodologically controversial. Nonetheless, Brauneis and Oliar's results on this front are consistent with the results of our own analysis, which are not based on name-based identification, and which we turn to now.

We employ the same method used for socioeconomic characteristics discussed in the previous section (recall that this methodology limits our sample of authors to independent creators, which is a narrower sample than the one used by Brauneis and Oliar). In particular, we compare geographic patterns of race/ethnicity to those of copyright registrations by estimating a modified version of the Poisson model in equation (1):

$$Regs_{i,j,t} = exp(\alpha + \beta_{1-6} GroupPop_{i,t} + \boldsymbol{X}_{i,t} + FE_j + FE_t) \qquad (2)$$

Equation (2) replaces $Population_{i,t}$ with $GroupPop_{i,t}$, which is a vector of six racial/ethnic population variables that vary by ZIP code i and year t. These variables measure the number of residents in each ZIP code that identified themselves to the Census Bureau as belonging to one of six racial/ethnic groups listed in the 2010 Decennial Census: Asian, Black, Hispanic, Native American, White, or Multiracial.[34] $\boldsymbol{X}_{i,t}$ is the same vector of socioeconomic control variables discussed in the previous section.

Table 1.5 presents the results. As in the last section, coefficient estimates are transformed into IRRs for ease of interpretation. Column (1) reports the simple, unconditional relationships between race/ethnicity and registrations without controlling for any of the systematic socioeconomic differences between racial/ethnic groups. These results imply that Black and White populations have roughly the same relationship with registrations,

[34] The Census Bureau also reports the populations of people who identify as Pacific Islanders or members of another racial group, but these populations by ZIP code are very small and often equal to zero, hindering reliable estimation. Thus, we do not include these residents in our analysis.

Table 1.5. Estimated relationship between race/ethnicity and copyright registrations

	(1)	(2)	(3)	(4)	(5)	(6)	(7)
Population (Thousands)							
White	1.085*** (0.001)	1.060*** (0.001)	1.076*** (0.001)	1.056*** (0.001)	1.086*** (0.001)	1.085*** (0.001)	1.049*** (0.001)
Black	1.092*** (0.001)	1.107*** (0.001)	1.107*** (0.001)	1.058*** (0.001)	1.094*** (0.001)	1.089*** (0.001)	1.090*** (0.001)
Hispanic	1.062*** (0.001)	1.091*** (0.001)	1.075*** (0.001)	1.029*** (0.001)	1.065*** (0.001)	1.057*** (0.001)	1.069*** (0.001)
Asian	1.137*** (0.002)	1.038*** (0.002)	1.081*** (0.002)	1.098*** (0.002)	1.137*** (0.002)	1.136*** (0.002)	1.031*** 0.002)
Native American	0.721*** (0.010)	0.976*** (0.008)	0.882*** (0.009)	0.794*** (0.010)	0.733*** (0.010)	0.710*** (0.010)	1.00 (0.008)
Multiracial	1.149*** (0.008)	1.213*** (0.010)	1.158*** (0.009)	1.076*** (0.008)	1.159*** (0.009)	1.115*** (0.008)	1.157*** (0.009)
Socioeconomic Controls							
% Pop College Grad		X					X
Median Real HH Income			X				
% Land Urban				X			X
Median Age					X		X
Info & Entertainment						X	X
Observations	2,803,023	2,800,080	2,746,827	2,788,929	2,803,005	2,798,496	2,785,986
Pseudo R^2	0.429	0.496	0.455	0.466	0.429	0.434	0.513

Note: The dependent variable is the number of copyright registrations, by year and ZIP code. Model fit using Poisson regression with year fixed effects and work type fixed effects. Coefficients are reported as IRR ($exp(\hat{\beta})$) for ease of interpretation. Intercept term and estimates for control variables are omitted for brevity. Standard errors are clustered at the work type level and transformed using the delta method to match the scale of the exponentiated coefficient estimates. $^{*}P < 0.10$, $^{**}P < 0.05$, $^{***}P < 0.01$.

which increase at respective rates of 8.5 and 9.2 percent for every additional 1,000 people in a ZIP code. Asian and Multiracial populations are associated with somewhat larger increases in registrations and Hispanic populations with smaller ones. The IRR for Native Americans is 0.721, indicating that increasing the population by 1,000 more Native Americans is associated with a 27.9-percent *reduction* in copyright registrations.

Importantly, examining these unconditional relationships does not tell the full story. As demonstrated in the previous section, registrations are strongly driven by socioeconomic factors, and it is well known that there are systematic socioeconomic differences between racial/ethnic groups in the United States. While these unconditional relationships may indicate certain disparities in creative ecosystems, examining how other socioeconomic factors influence those relationships provides useful insights into the mechanisms behind the issue.

To that end, columns (2)–(6) test each of the socioeconomic factors individually, and column (7) includes all factors (aside from median income for the reasons discussed in the previous section). Of all the socioeconomic factors for which we control, college education (in column (2)) appears to have the largest impact on the relationship between race/ethnicity and registrations. When comparing racial/ethnic populations with the same college education profile, registrations from Black, Multiracial, and Hispanic authors significantly outpace those from White and Asian authors. Registrations from Native American populations are very close to zero.

When all socioeconomic controls are included (column (7)), the disparity between racial/ethnic groups shrinks substantially. The IRRs for Black, Hispanic, and Multiracial groups are higher than those for the other groups, suggesting that more registrations originate from areas with larger shares of these populations relative to socioeconomically similar areas that are more heavily White, Asian, or Native American. This does not mean that the full measure of racial/ethnic disparity is smaller than what is implied by column (1). Rather, it means that racial/ethnic disparities in creative ecosystems are, to a large extent, driven by broader socioeconomic disparities between racial/ethnic groups. Moreover, some disparity remains unexplained by those inter-group socioeconomic differences.

While these results are informative, they do not account for potentially differing relationships for different types of works. To further explore such differences, we re-estimate equation (2) on work type–specific subsets of the data. Results are reported in Table 1.6. The relationship between registrations and White populations is the highest for motion pictures and the lowest for artworks. For Black populations, the highest IRR is for audio works and the lowest is for machine-readable works. The relationship between registrations and Hispanic populations are the highest for motion pictures and the lowest for literary works. For Asian populations, the effect is the highest for motion pictures and the lowest for audio works.

The IRRs for Native Americans are not uniformly significant across all types of works, ranging from 1.085 for literary works to 0.310 for motion pictures. These figures imply that an increase of 1,000 Native American

Table 1.6. Estimated relationship between race/ethnicity and copyright registrations by the type of work with all socioeconomic controls

	(1)	(2)	(3)	(4)	(5)	(6)
	Art works	Dramatic works	Literary works	Machine-readable	Motion pictures	Audio works
Population (Thousands)						
White	1.039***	1.042***	1.053***	1.056***	1.032***	1.048***
	(0.001)	(0.001)	(0.001)	(0.003)	(0.012)	(0.000)
Black	1.065***	1.090***	1.086***	1.046***	1.048***	1.101***
	(0.002)	(0.001)	(0.002)	(0.006)	(0.011)	(0.000)
Hispanic	1.070***	1.104***	1.058***	1.071***	1.119***	1.071***
	(0.002)	(0.002)	(0.001)	(0.005)	(0.007)	(0.000)
Asian	1.043***	1.038***	1.024***	1.045***	1.135***	1.023***
	(0.004)	(0.003)	(0.005)	(0.008)	(0.024)	(0.000)
Native American	1.041*	0.311***	1.085***	1.015	0.314*	0.999***
	(0.022)	(0.023)	(0.013)	(0.051)	(0.195)	(0.000)
Multiracial	1.231***	1.335***	1.110***	1.144***	0.985	1.002***
	(0.022)	(0.020)	(0.018)	(0.042)	(0.094)	(0.000)
Observations	309,554	309,554	309,554	309,554	309,554	309,554
Pseudo R^2	0.339	0.437	0.494	0.183	0.283	0.482

Note: The dependent variable is the number of copyright registrations, by year and ZIP code. Model fit using Poisson regression with year fixed effects and work type fixed effects. Coefficients are reported as IRR ($exp(\hat{\beta})$) for ease of interpretation. Model control variables are the same as those in column (7) of Table 1.5. Intercept term and estimates for control variables are omitted for brevity. Robust standard errors are transformed using the delta method to match the scale of the exponentiated coefficient estimates. $^{*}P < 0.10$, $^{**}P < 0.05$, $^{***}P < 0.01$.

people in a ZIP code's population would be associated with an 8.5-percent increase in literary work registrations and a 69-percent decrease in motion picture registrations (though this decrease is only weakly statistically significant and may be largely driven by the mostly nonoverlapping geographic clustering of Native American communities and motion picture production). The largest positive relationship we observe is between Multiracial and dramatic works registrations, which implies registration increase by 34 percent when the Multiracial population increases by 1,000 people.

Overall, Table 1.6 shows that different racial/ethnic groups have differing registration patterns across various types of works. This type of specialization is similar to findings in the United States Copyright Office report, which states that different geographic regions tend to specialize in the registrations of different types of works.[35] As a cautionary note, identifying patterns of copyright activity along racial and ethnic lines is necessary, but not sufficient, for determining optimal policy interventions. As a preliminary matter, the mere existence of differences does not necessarily imply inequity or economic inefficiency. Observed differences could plausibly be attributable to cultural factors or systemically differing preferences. Moreover, even when the racial and ethnic variation is the result of inequity, a number of different mechanisms may drive that inequity. The efficacy of an intervention depends on the degree to which it addresses the specific mechanisms at play. Thus, the next necessary steps in this line of research are, first, to determine whether the disparities we uncover are indicative of inequities, and second, to understand the underlying mechanism driving that inequity.

Disclaimer

All statements are the opinions of the authors and do not necessarily reflect the views of the United States Copyright Office.

[35] U.S. Copyright Off., *supra* note 19.

2

Understanding Demographics in Patent Data

Michelle Saksena and Gauri Subramani

Introduction

Patents offer a valuable framework for examining innovation, as they are quantifiable indicators of technological progress. Analyses of patent data have shed light on a wide range of topics, including scientific developments, immigration, and information flows.[1] Additionally, patent data have been utilized to draw insights into the demographics of inventors. For instance, data from the United States Patent and Trademark Office (USPTO) have been employed to explore gender disparities in patenting[2] and post-grant patent outcomes[3] and to investigate the correlation between age and innovation.[4]

[1] Ajay Agrawal, Devesh Kapur, John McHale & Alexander Oettl, *Brain Drain or Brain Bank? The Impact of Skilled Emigration on Poor-Country Innovation*, 69 J. URB. ECON. 43 (2011); Prithwiraj Choudhury, *Return Migration and Geography of Innovation in MNEs: A Natural Experiment of Knowledge Production by Local Workers Reporting to Return Migrants*, 16 J. ECON. GEOGRAPHY 585 (2016); Adam B. Jaffe & Manuel Trajtenberg, *Flows of Knowledge from Universities and Federal Laboratories: Modeling the Flow of Patent Citations over Time and Across Institutional and Geographic Boundaries*, 93 PROC. NAT'L ACAD. SCI. 12671 (1996); Heidi L. Williams, *How Do Patents Affect Research Investments?*, 9 ANN. REV. ECON. 441 (2017).

[2] JESSICA MILLI, EMMA WILLIAMS-BARON, MEIKA BERLAN, JENNY XIA & BARBARA GAULT, EQUITY IN INNOVATION: WOMEN INVENTORS AND PATENTS (2016), https://iwpr.org/equity-in-innovation-women-inventors-and-patents/; U.S. Pat. & Trademark Off., Off. of the Chief Economist, *Progress and Potential: A Profile of Women Inventors on U.S. Patents* (U.S. Patent & Trademark Off., Off. of the Chief Economist, IP Data Highlights No. 2, 2019); Abhay Aneja, Oren Reshef & Gauri Subramani, *Attrition and the Gender Patenting Gap*, 107 REV. ECON. & STAT. (forthcoming 2025); Waverly W. Ding, Fiona Murray & Toby E. Stuart, *Gender Differences in Patenting in the Academic Life Sciences*, 313 SCI. 665 (2006).

[3] Gauri Subramani & Michelle Saksena, *Investigating Gender Disparities in Patent Citations Reveals Untapped Potential: Patents*, 43 NATURE BIOTECH. 1613 (2025).

[4] Mary Kaltenberg, Adam B. Jaffe & Margie E. Lachman, *Invention and the Life Course: Age Differences in Patenting*, 52 RSCH. POL'Y 104629 (2023); Mary Kaltenberg, Adam B. Jaffe & Margie E. Lachman, *The Age of Invention: Matching Inventor Ages to Patents Based on Web-Scraped Sources* (Nat'l Bureau of Econ. Rsch., Working Paper No. 28768, 2021).

Michelle Saksena and Gauri Subramani, *Understanding Demographics in Patent Data* In: *Inclusive Innovation in the Age of AI and Big Data*. Edited by: Daryl Lim and Peter K. Yu, Oxford University Press.
 DOI: 10.1093/9780197799444.003.0003

Patent data are a staple in research, largely due to their timeliness and easy accessibility. PatentsView, an award-winning open data platform, hosts and disseminates USPTO data on granted patents and patent applications. Updated quarterly, PatentsView is a popular public source for data on U.S. patents. Between April 30, 2023, and April 30, 2024, there were 34,880 unique PatentsView users and 39,103 bulk downloads of PatentsView data. Along with direct downloads, PatentsView's application programming interface (API) received nearly one million requests in the first four months of 2024.[5] One of the reasons researchers use PatentsView is to take advantage of its value-added algorithms. Specifically, PatentsView utilizes the latest disambiguation and gender attribution techniques, enabling researchers to identify unique inventors, track their patenting behavior over time, and determine their gender—the only demographic information currently available to researchers. As a result, PatentsView plays a significant role in supporting patent-based research, making it crucial for researchers to use the platform thoughtfully and understand the nuances of the data and how these details affect results. We discuss these nuances, their effects on interpreting results, and their influence on research.

We begin by providing an overview of trends in USPTO inventor demographics. We then describe how two key features of PatentsView's value-added data are generated: name-based inventor disambiguation and gender attribution. We discuss both the accuracy of these data and their limitations. Finally, we provide clarification on how to accurately use and interpret PatentsView data and highlight opportunities for future research.

This chapter examines disparities in patenting participation by gender and assesses how name-based disambiguation and gender attribution influence our understanding of these gaps. By evaluating the accuracy and limitations of PatentsView data, we contribute to the broader literature on diversity in innovation, offering insights into both methodological challenges and empirical trends in patenting. Our findings help clarify how demographic imputation methods shape patent data interpretation and highlight opportunities for future research to refine these approaches and enhance inclusivity in innovation studies.

[5] Nicholas Rada, PatentsView: Building Confidence in Patent Data, Presentation at the 7th Annual IP Data & Research Conference in Canada (Nov. 4, 2024).

Demographic Trends in Patenting

Prior literature has found that the demographics of inventors affect both participation in patenting and the content of inventions. Research linking inventors to tax records shows that individuals' demographic characteristics at birth—socioeconomic class, race, and gender—predict their propensity to patent as adults.[6] These researchers find that children born to more affluent parents—disproportionately White and Asian children—and boys are far more likely to become inventors. They also demonstrate that exposure to invention in childhood is a strong determinant of adult participation in patenting. In addition, existing work has identified that diversity among researchers benefits innovation as measured by patents and publication outputs. For example, immigrant inventors are more productive than nonimmigrant inventors in the United States,[7] and minority researchers have a higher propensity to develop novel insights.[8] Prior research has found that while women inventors make substantial contributions to overall invention, they are also more likely to produce inventions that address women's health concerns.[9]

If, conditional on having an innovative contribution, some populations do not patent at the same rates as others, their inventions may be lost, with negative implications for potential inventors and the progress of innovation. Such loss can have distributional consequences, as innovation comes not only from expertise but also from exposure to contexts that could benefit from innovation and situational awareness.[10] If women are less likely to participate in innovation, the female population may lose out disproportionately. Thus, having a clear understanding of who participates in the invention is important for policymakers and researchers to accurately evaluate the status of the patent system.

[6] Alex Bell, Raj Chetty, Xavier Jaravel, Neviana Petkova & John Van Reenen, *Who Becomes an Inventor in America? The Importance of Exposure to Innovation*, 134 Q.J. Econ. 647 (2019).

[7] Shai Bernstein, Rebecca Diamond, Abhisit Jiranaphawiboon, Timothy McQuade & Beatriz Pousada, *The Contribution of High-Skilled Immigrants to Innovation in the United States* (Nat'l Bureau of Econ. Rsch., Working Paper No. 30797, 2022).

[8] Bas Hofstra, Vivek V. Kulkarni, Sebastian Munoz-Najar Galvez & Daniel A. McFarland, *The Diversity-Innovation Paradox in Science*, 117 Proc. Nat'l Acad. Sci. 9284 (2020); Lars Bo Jeppesen & Karim R. Lakhani, *Marginality and Problem-Solving Effectiveness in Broadcast Search*, 21 Org. Sci. 1016 (2010).

[9] Rembrand Koning, Sampsa Samila & John-Paul Ferguson, *Who Do We Invent for? Patents by Women Focus More on Women's Health, but Few Women Get to Invent*, 372 Sci. 1345 (2021).

[10] Elias Einiö, Josh Feng & Xavier Jaravel, *Social Push and the Direction of Innovation* (Ctr. for Econ. Performance, Discussion Paper No. 1861, 2022).

By many measures, women remain underrepresented in patenting, both in the United States and globally. They are even less likely to receive patents than to pursue entrepreneurship.[11] In 2019, women accounted for 12.8 percent of U.S. inventors who received patents,[12] compared with 16.5 percent of inventors worldwide.[13] Additionally, only 21.9 percent of all patents granted by the USPTO included at least one female inventor, a share lagging behind global trends. Figure 2.1 illustrates that this gender gap has progressively narrowed. By 2023, women represented 14.5 percent of all U.S. inventors and 16 percent of inventors globally.[14] However, despite this progress, the pace of change remains slow. At the current rate, gender parity among inventors is projected to be reached globally by 2118, whereas in the United States, it is expected that such parity will not be achieved until 2171, more than fifty years later.[15] This stark contrast underscores the persistent underrepresentation of U.S. women inventors, even when compared with their counterparts in other countries.

Inventors are not required to disclose their demographic information when applying for a patent. As a result, inventors have no self-identified demographic information. Researchers who have gained access to restricted data from the U.S. Census Bureau have leveraged the Census' detailed employment and address data to match individuals' tax data with patent records.[16] However, even this data-rich approach requires triangulation and matching to identify inventor demographics. Owing to these data limitations, most studies of inventor demographics have focused on gender representation because of the reliability of name-based gender attribution algorithms in predicting gender. We discuss PatentsView's gender attribution in greater detail in the section "Gender Attribution."

Despite significant interest in expanding research to examine racial representation among U.S. inventors, limited data availability has hindered

[11] U.S. Pat. & Trademark Off., *supra* note 2.

[12] U.S. Pat. & Trademark Off., Off. of the Chief Economist, *Progress and Potential: 2020 Update on U.S. Women Inventor-Patentees* (U.S. Patent & Trademark Off., Off. of the Chief Economist, IP Data Highlights No. 4, 2020).

[13] Elodie Carpentier & Julio Raffo, The Global Gender Gap in Innovation and Creativity: An International Comparison of the Gender Gap in Global Patenting over Two Decades (2023).

[14] *Id.*

[15] *Id.*

[16] Bell et al., *supra* note 6; Ufuk Akcigit & Nathan Goldschlag, *Measuring the Characteristics and Employment Dynamics of U.S. Inventors* (Nat'l Bureau of Econ. Rsch., Working Paper No. 31086, 2023).

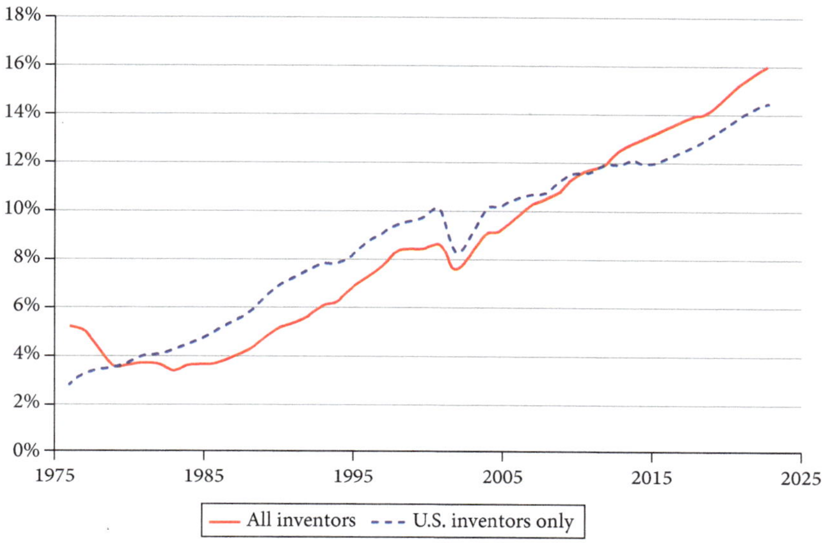

Figure 2.1. Annual woman inventor rate for patents granted in the United States from 1975 to 2025

Note: Women make up between 2 and 16 percent of all named inventors during this time.

progress. Recent work uses restricted, individual-level Census data to impute inventor race and ethnicity.[17] They find that as of 2016, 74.6 percent of U.S. patent recipients self-identify as White, 22 percent as Asian or Pacific Islander (AAPI), 3.7 percent as Hispanic, 1.6 percent as Black or African American, and 0.3 percent as American Indian or Native American (AIAN). For Hispanic, Black or African American, and AIAN populations, these participation rates reflect woefully low representation relative to their population shares.[18]

Another dimension of inventor background that has been studied is immigration status.[19] A recent study imputed immigration status by matching USPTO inventors based on their names and addresses to a dataset that includes addresses and Social Security numbers.[20] They find that 16 percent of U.S. inventors are immigrants and that immigrants are more productive

[17] Akcigit & Goldschlag, *supra* note 16.
[18] *Id.*
[19] Jennifer Hunt & Marjolaine Gauthier-Loiselle, *How Much Does Immigration Boost Innovation?*, 2 Am. Econ. J. 31 (2010).
[20] Bernstein et al., *supra* note 7.

than U.S.-born inventors. The former received more patents, and their patents are more economically valuable and receive a higher number of citations. Immigrant inventors can also facilitate the import of foreign knowledge into the United States, as they rely more on foreign technologies and collaborate more with foreign inventors.[21]

Further work is needed to continue to explore the extent and causes of demographic disparities among individuals who apply for and receive patents. Patenting can increase inventors' incomes,[22] affect who can leverage their inventions,[23] and influence both the types of extant innovation and the population benefiting from innovations.[24] Research identifying potential interventions and policies that can close gender and race gaps in patenting can add enormous value for inventors, the patent system, and society at large.

Individual Disambiguation

We next discuss the process by which PatentsView identifies individual patent applicants and recipients. Researchers have undertaken significant efforts to track individual patent recipients across time.[25] The current approach to inventor disambiguation results from an Inventor Disambiguation Workshop hosted by the USPTO on September 24, 2015. A research team from the University of Massachusetts Amherst, led by Andrew McCallum

[21] Choudhury, *supra* note 1; William R. Kerr, *Ethnic Scientific Communities and International Technology Diffusion*, 90 Rev. Econ. & Stat. 518 (2008).

[22] Philippe Aghion, Ufuk Akcigit, Ari Hyytinen & Otto Toivanen, *On the Returns to Invention Within Firms: Evidence from Finland*, 108 AEA Papers & Proc. 208 (2018).

[23] Joan Farre-Mensa, Deepak Hegde & Alexander Ljungqvist, *What Is a Patent Worth? Evidence from the U.S. Patent "Lottery,"* 75 J. Fin. 639 (2020); Patrick Gaulé, *Patents and the Success of Venture-Capital Backed Startups: Using Examiner Assignment to Estimate Causal Effects*, 66 J. Indus. Econ. 350 (2018).

[24] Einiö et al., *supra* note 10; Koning et al., *supra* note 9.

[25] Lee Fleming & Adam Juda, *A Network of Invention*, Harv. Bus. Rev., Apr. 2004, https://hbr.org/2004/04/a-network-of-invention; Li Guan-Cheng, Ronald Lai, Alexander D'Amour, David M. Doolin, Sun Ye, Vetle I. Torvik, Amy Z. Yu & Lee Fleming, *Disambiguation and Co-Authorship Networks of the U.S. Patent Inventor Database (1975–2010)*, 43 Rsch. Pol'y 941 (2014); Michele Pezzoni, Francesco Lissoni & Gianluca Tarasconi, *How to Kill Inventors: Testing the Massacrator© Algorithm for Inventor Disambiguation*, 101 Scientometrics 477 (2014); Julio Raffo & Stéphane Lhuillery, *How to Play the "Names Game": Patent Retrieval Comparing Different Heuristics*, 38 Rsch. Pol'y 1617 (2009); Jasjit Singh, *Collaborative Networks as Determinants of Knowledge Diffusion Patterns*, 51 Mgmt. Sci. 756 (2005); Manuel Trajtenberg, Gil Shiff & Ran Melamed, *The "Names Game": Harnessing Inventors, Patent Data for Economic Research*, Annals Econ. & Stat., no. 93/94, at 79 (2009); Nicolas Carayol & Lorenzo Cassi, *Who's Who in Patents: A Bayesian Approach* (Groupe de Recherche en Économie Théorique et Appliquée, Cahiers du GREThA, Working Paper No. 2009-07, 2009).

and Nicholas Monath, authored the successful algorithm integrated into the PatentsView data platform in March 2016. The algorithm uses discriminative hierarchical coreference to increase the quality of PatentsView data.[26]

A key challenge to identifying patent applicants over time is the lack of unique identifiers assigned to inventors when they apply for patents. This complicates the task of linking multiple applications or patents to a single individual, especially as inventors are not required to standardize their names and may use various iterations across multiple applications—for example, Will Smith, W. Smith, Will L. Smith, and W.L. Smith. The disambiguation leverages inventor name, address, and assignee affiliation to cluster these name variations, forming a list of unique identifiers for inventors and assignees. Beyond name and address, no individual-specific information is solicited to enable researchers to link a given application to an individual's prior (or subsequent) patent applications, if any exist.

A recent study assesses the disambiguation accuracy of PatentsView and finds precision rates between 79 and 91 percent and recall rates between 91 and 95 percent.[27] Precision measures the fraction of correctly grouped pairs, while recall indicates the fraction of correctly identified name pairs. High precision means the algorithm often correctly groups similar names, while high recall means frequently identifying all names belonging to the same inventor.[28] Additionally, Ufuk Akcigit and Nathan Goldschlag use Census employment data to track individuals in the patent assignment data by a triangulation process[29] and find strong agreement between PatentsView's inventor disambiguation and their disambiguation. Ninety-five percent of disambiguated PatentsView inventors match a single inventor in their triangulated data, while the remaining 5 percent match multiple records.

There are reasons to believe that disambiguation is less likely to perform well for female inventors because the vast majority (84 percent) of American women married to a man change their last name following marriage.[30]

[26] *PatentsView Project Disambiguation Algorithms*, U.S. Pat. & Trademark Off., https://patentsview.org/disambiguation (last visited July 9, 2025).

[27] Olivier Binette, Sokhna A. York, Emma Hickerson, Youngsoo Baek, Sarvo Madhavan & Christina Jones, *Estimating the Performance of Entity Resolution Algorithms: Lessons Learned Through PatentsView.org*, 77 Am. Statistician 370 (2023).

[28] The construction of precision and recall measures is described in greater detail in the section "Gender Attribution."

[29] Akcigit & Goldschlag, *supra* note 16.

[30] Luona Lin, *About 8 in 10 Women in Opposite-Sex Marriages Say They Took Their Husband's Last Name*, Pew Rsch. Ctr. (Sept. 7, 2023), https://www.pewresearch.org/short-reads/2023/09/07/about-eight-in-ten-women-in-opposite-sex-marriages-say-they-took-their-husbands-last-name/.

As individuals are tracked by name in the patent data, if an inventor's last name changes after applying for or receiving a patent, their subsequent applications are unlikely to be connected to their prior patenting activity. This is more likely to affect female inventors than male inventors.[31] As a result, a female inventor who applies for more than one patent is more likely to be incorrectly identified as two separate individuals than a similar male inventor. This can inflate our understanding of the number of unique women participating in patenting.

Gender Attribution

Once inventor names are disambiguated, PatentsView uses a gender attribution algorithm to impute inventor gender. This step is necessary because inventors do not disclose their gender or demographic information when applying for a patent. To fill this data gap, the USPTO implements a name-to-gender attribution approach.

PatentsView uses the gender-it package developed by the World Intellectual Property Organization (WIPO) based on data from their Worldwide Gender-Name Dictionary (WGND) 2.0. This approach provides a customized version of WIPO's attribution method (WIPO 2.0). It uses country-specific lists of approximate probabilities for each gender associated with names within that country. The updated Worldwide Gender-Name Dictionary (WGND 2.0) builds on its previous version, significantly expanding its global coverage of names, including over 26 million records that link given names to 195 countries and territories.[32]

PatentsView uses two country-specific records' datasets from WGND 2.0 to customize their gender-prediction model. The Language Group Agreement Dataset groups countries by language. If countries within a language group report that a majority of individuals with a certain name share the same gender, that gender is associated with that name. If there is no singular gender associated with a name, the language group excludes that name. The Global Agreement Dataset is used when all countries in the WGND

[31] *Id.*; Meredith Whitaker, *Married Scientists and the Name Change Dilemma*, PLOS Blogs: ECR Cmty. (July 7, 2018), https://ecrcommunity.plos.org/2018/07/07/married-scientists-and-the-name-change-dilemma/.

[32] Gema Lax Martínez, Helena Saenz de Juano-i-Ribes, Deyun Yin, Bruno Le Feuvre, Intan Hamdan-Livramento, Kaori Saito & Julio Raffo, *Expanding the World Gender-Name Dictionary: WGND 2.0* (World Intell. Prop. Org., Econ. Rsch. Working Paper No. 64, 2021).

2.0 dataset report that a majority of individuals with a given name share the same gender. In this case, the name is associated with that gender; otherwise, it is excluded.

Using these country-specific gender-attributed names, the gender-it algorithm first assigns gender to inventor names as they appear on individual USPTO-published applications and patents. The algorithm begins by searching for an inventor's given name(s) in the records specific to their country of residence. Matching records provide a "weight" for male and female labels based on the proportion of individuals with that name and gender in the country. If the resulting weight meets or exceeds PatentsView's confidence threshold for that country, the inventor is attributed to the corresponding gender. If the inventor has multiple given names and conflicting attributions, the earliest attributable name is given preference (the first name is preferred over the middle name). If data are available for the inventor's name(s) within their country of residence but no names reach the confidence threshold, the name is considered ambiguous, and the inventor is not assigned a gender.

If data are unavailable for an inventor's given name(s) in their country of residence, the algorithm checks for the name(s) within the language group for that country. If a record is present, meaning that all countries in that language group share the same majority gender for individuals with that name, that gender is assigned to the inventor.

Names not assigned based on data from the inventor's country of residence or language group are then checked against the set of names for which every country in the WGND 2.0 dataset reports the same majority gender. If all countries with records of that name identify the name as belonging to the same gender category, that gender is assigned to the inventor.

Any names that could not be attributed based on the inventor's country, language group, or global agreement are considered ambiguous and not assigned a gender. After individual inventor records are disambiguated, conflicts in gender attribution between any records associated with the same individual are resolved by assigning the disambiguated inventor the gender associated with the majority of records. If an equal number of records associated with the same inventor are attributed as male and female, the disambiguated inventor is not attributed a gender. As of March 31, 2024, the PatentsView dataset included 4,015,791 unique inventors. Of these inventors, 3,669,307 names (91 percent) were assigned a gender (either female or male), while 346,484 remained unattributed.

There are notable limitations to this attribution process. Gender is identified as either male or female, and PatentsView cannot identify inventor gender outside these binary categories. Therefore, any analysis using PatentsView's gender data can only evaluate male–female disparities in patenting and cannot provide insights into the inventive activities of individuals whose gender identities do not fit this binary framework.

Because the USPTO does not collect inventor gender directly, there is no ground truth of inventor data against which the gender disambiguation process is validated. To evaluate the accuracy of gender attribution, the USPTO leveraged internal administrative and demographic data collected on USPTO examiners, which include examiner gender. Using these data, PatentsView's gender attribution approach can be applied to these examiners, and the results of that attribution can be compared with examiners' self-reported gender data. It is important to note that there are relatively fewer examiners with Asian names in our validation set than Asian inventors. As a result, the accuracy of this gender attribution process for Asian names is not as well validated as for names of Western origin.

We compare the performance of eight gender attribution approaches—including WIPO 2.0, which most closely resembles PatentsView's approach. We name and evaluate the following methods:

1. WIPO 1.0: This approach matches the USPTO examiners' first names to names and countries in the WGND 1.0 dataset. When evaluating this algorithm against USPTO examiner names, it assigns all names to the United States as the country of origin.
2. WIPO 1.0GNR: This approach is similar to WIPO 1.0 but departs from the latter by inferring each examiner's country of origin from the IBM-GNR database, thereby relaxing the restriction of the WIPO 1.0 approach in which all examiners are presumed to have the United States as their country of origin.
3. WIPO 2.0: This approach uses the gender-it package and leverages WGND 2.0. WGND 2.0 differs from WGND 1.0 in terms of coverage and the number of data sources.
4. WIPO 2.0GNR: This approach is the same as WIPO 2.0, except that it infers examiners' countries of origin from the IBM-GNR database.
5. WIPO 2.0GNRname: This approach builds on WIPO 2.0GNR by selecting a list of potential countries of origin based on countries most

frequently associated with both first name *and* surname, as per IBM-GNR, and expands the definition of country of origin to all countries sharing the same language.

6. Gender API: Gender-API.com is a commercial product by the eponymous German company that uses data from publicly available governmental sources and social networks to identify gender by first name.
7. Gender API Country: This approach uses the same methodology as the Gender API approach, adding IBM-GNR data to determine a likely country of origin.
8. Inference using U.S. Social Security Administration (SSA) data: This approach takes advantage of a publicly available dataset of first names downloaded from the SSA to generate a gender distribution by first name and chooses a threshold for determining if a name is male or female. We test such distribution using a 90-percent certainty threshold.

To evaluate the efficacy of a gender attribution algorithm, we first calculate an overall prediction score. This score identifies the proportion of names assigned to a gender prediction. To measure the performance and accuracy of these gender attribution algorithms, we calculate the total number of predictions, precision, recall, and F1 score, detailed below.

The F1 score relies on the balance between true positives, false positives, and false negatives. Each measure is calculated separately for inventors identified as male and inventors identified as female. If, for a given observation, the attributed gender is the same as the ground-truth gender, this is a true positive. For example, female true positives are individuals who are female and are attributed as female by the algorithm. Next, we are interested in false positives. Female false positives, for example, are individuals identified by the WIPO algorithm as female but are male based on the administrative data. Thus, this entry is wrongly attributed as being in this female gender cluster. The reverse is true for male false positives; an example is a female examiner incorrectly identified as male by the WIPO algorithm.

Finally, we measure false negatives. Female false negatives are observations that are female based on the administrative data but are identified as male by the algorithm. That is, this observation *should* be clustered with the other female observations and is incorrectly excluded from this cluster. Equivalently, male false negatives are observations that are male based on the administrative data but are wrongly identified as female by the algorithm.

Using these measures, precision, recall, and F1 score are defined as follows:[33]

$$\text{Precision:} \quad \frac{\#\ \text{true positives}}{\#\ \text{true positives} + \#\ \text{false positives}}$$

Precision provides a measure of how precise the gender attribution is by indicating the proportion of correctly identified names.

$$\text{Recall:} \quad \frac{\#\ \text{true positives}}{\#\ \text{true positives} + \#\ \text{false negatives}}$$

Recall measures what fraction of observations that should have been in a gender cluster were correctly predicted to be in that cluster.

$$\text{F1 score:} \quad 2 * \frac{\text{precision} * \text{recall}}{\text{precision} + \text{recall}}$$

F1 score measures the balance between precision and recall. There is an inherent tension between recall and precision. High precision requires that entries are only included in a cluster (that is, identified as male or female) if they actually belong there. High recall, on the other hand, requires that entries are not left out of the cluster in which they belong.

Table 2.1 presents prediction rates, precision, recall, and F1 scores for all the approaches described above. We see that the WIPO 2.0 gender attribution algorithm performs well overall. For female names, precision, recall, and F1 scores are 0.888, 0.929, and 0.908, respectively. For male names, these

[33] Nicholas Monath, Sarvo Madhavan, Christopher DiPietro, Andrew McCallum & Christina Jones, *Disambiguating Patent Inventors, Assignees, and Their Locations in PatentsView*, https://s3.amazonaws.com/data.patentsview.org/documents/PatentsView_Disambiguation.pdf (last visited July 9, 2025).

Table 2.1. Comparing gender-name prediction methods

	WIPO 1.0	WIPO 1.0 GNR	WIPO 2.0	WIPO 2.0 GNR	WIPO 2.0 GNR name	Gender API	Gender API Country	SSA
Total predictions:	6,639	6,612	6,726	6,749	6,781	5,919	5,763	6,031
Out of:	7,287	7,287	7,287	7,287	7,287	7,287	7,287	7,287
Prediction rate	0.911	0.907	0.923	0.926	0.931	0.812	0.791	0.828
Female names:								
Precision	0.889	0.887	0.886	0.888	0.881	0.981	0.976	0.943
Recall	0.934	0.931	0.923	0.929	0.923	0.97	0.963	0.965
F1	0.911	0.908	0.904	0.908	0.902	0.975	0.97	0.954
Male names:								
Precision	0.975	0.973	0.971	0.973	0.971	0.99	0.988	0.987
Recall	0.956	0.955	0.956	0.956	0.953	0.993	0.992	0.978
F1	0.965	0.964	0.963	0.964	0.962	0.992	0.99	0.983
Harmonic mean	0.928	0.926	0.93	0.932	0.931	0.919	0.907	0.916

Note: This table presents the performance of eight different gender-name attribution methods when evaluated against a ground-truth dataset with USPTO examiner names and administratively recorded genders.

scores are 0.973, 0.956, and 0.964, respectively.[34] Since patent examiners and inventors share similar training and backgrounds, this exercise provides a close approximation of what is likely true for inventors. However, because the USPTO is not legally permitted to collect inventor demographic data, there is no way to directly evaluate the accuracy of gender identification for inventors.

We are interested in the balance between F1 scores and the number of names that are predicted. If, for example, one approach performs very well but only predicts a small proportion of names, this limitation is relevant when assessing if this is a good approach or not. Thus, we calculate the harmonic mean of the prediction rate and the F1 score for *both* male and female names. The range of harmonic means for the set of approaches we evaluate is from 0.907 to 0.932, and the value of this measure for WIPO 2.0 is 0.930. Thus, we see that PatentsView's chosen gender attribution approach performs well for both male and female names and also uses a free and publicly available algorithm.

Understanding Representation in Patent Applications Versus Granted Patents

While most research has focused on granted patents, even ungranted patent applications can have effects on future inventions. It is, therefore, useful to link individuals' patent applications to their other inventive behavior—as opposed to just tracking granted patents, which represent a subset of all applications. Doing so has become easier since 2021, when PatentsView began publishing a dataset of disambiguated patent applicants in addition to disambiguated inventors on granted patents.

To apply for a patent, an inventor must believe they have produced an invention of novel value and must have the knowledge, and expend the effort, to file an application. Filing a patent application requires time and financial investment. Application fees vary depending on the applicant, type of patent application, the application's level of complexity, and other features of the application, but the total cost of fees paid to the USPTO are a minimum of

[34] Michelle Saksena, Assessing Approaches for Identifying the Gender of Inventors on Patents, Presentation at the USPTO Symposium on Advancing Research on Inventor Demographics (2022). Note that precision, recall, and F1 statistics for male names are not equivalent to the reciprocal statistics for female names.

roughly $500 (excluding attorney fees).[35] The assistance of a lawyer is resource intensive, as patent attorneys' hourly billing rates range from $300 to over $700, depending on attorney experience and geographic location.[36]

The value of patent applications is also illustrated by the fact that they are frequently referenced as prior art by USPTO patent examiners. Abandoned patent applications that are made publicly available are used by examiners to narrow the scope of subsequent patents and thus have implications for the patent system more broadly.[37] In fact, Christopher Cotropia and David Schwartz find that patent examiners are more likely to cite abandoned applications as prior art when issuing rejections, due to a lack of novelty and obviousness than they are to cite previously granted patents.[38] This finding indicates that even though abandoned patent applications did not translate to direct value in the form of legal rights for their inventors, they play an important role in influencing *future* innovation by affecting what technologies the USPTO grants patent rights to.

Between 2001 and 2019, only 72.97 percent of all patent applications eventually converted to granted patents.[39] Thus, analyses focusing only on the inventors and ideas represented in granted patents omit 27 percent of applications filed. The costs of this omission are particularly striking when we consider the value of understanding the effects of failure in the patent application process on individuals' innovation paths as well as the broader innovation landscape.

Furthermore, granted patents are not representative of patent applications, particularly with respect to inventor characteristics. As Figure 2.2 shows, when we separately evaluate applications from male and female inventors, we see that female inventors are less likely to convert applications to granted patents.[40] Over this time period, 69.44 percent of female inventors' applications convert to granted patents, while the equivalent statistic for male inventors is 73.54 percent. This indicates that only evaluating inventors who

[35] *Table of Patent Fees—Current, Proposed and Unit Cost*, U.S. PAT. & TRADEMARK OFF., https://www.uspto.gov/sites/default/files/documents/Table_of_Patent_Fees-Current_Proposed_and_Unit_Cost.pdf (last visited July 10, 2025).

[36] Gene Quinn, *Patent Cost: Understanding Patent Attorney Fees*, IPWATCHDOG (Apr. 18, 2015), https://ipwatchdog.com/2015/04/18/patent-cost-understanding-patent-attorney-fees/id=56970/.

[37] Christopher A. Cotropia & David L. Schwartz, *The Hidden Value of Abandoned Applications to the Patent System*, 61 B.C. L. REV. 2809 (2020).

[38] *Id.*

[39] Female inventors' patents have lower grant rates throughout this time period.

[40] In this figure, we define female patents as those with 100 percent female inventors and male patents as those with 100 percent male inventors. Single-gender applications account for 82.43 percent of all applications in this time period.

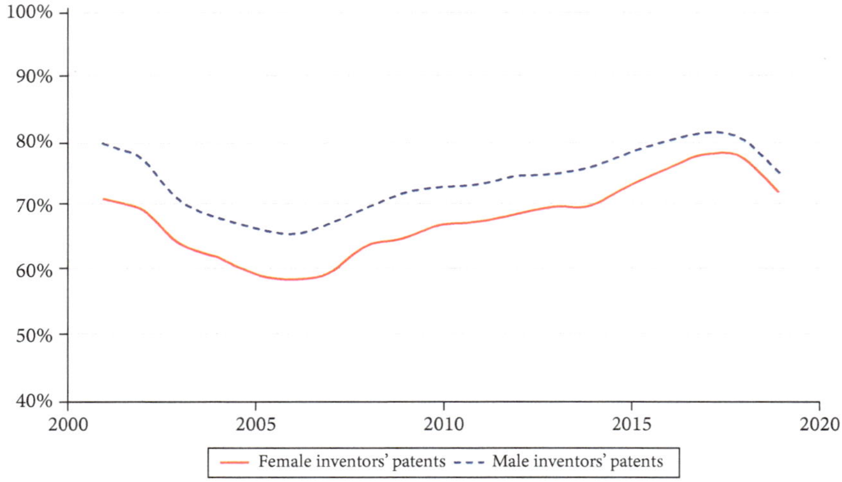

Figure 2.2. Percentage of patent applications granted in the United States from 2002 to 2019

hold patents can lead to sample bias. As previously discussed, women are far less likely than men to apply for patents. Only 23.41 percent of applications contain any female applicants, and this gender disparity only worsens through the patent review process. Conditional on application, women are less likely than men to receive a patent; just 21.31 percent of granted patents include any female inventors, which indicates that women are underrepresented on granted patents and overrepresented on ungranted applications. Prior work finds that this gender gap in application conversion can be partly explained by the increased likelihood of female inventors to abandon patent applications following a rejection in the review process.[41] Thus, just looking at granted patents elides gendered dynamics in representation and success in the patenting process.[42] Studying only granted patents disproportionately ignores the innovative contributions of female inventors, while examining the full set of patent applications gives researchers the opportunity to examine participation in the patent process and the demographic characteristics that affect participation in patenting.

[41] Aneja et al., *supra* note 2.

[42] Kyle Jensen, Balázs Kovács & Olav Sorenson, *Gender Differences in Obtaining and Maintaining Patent Rights*, 36 Nature Biotech. 307 (2018).

Finally, while much research has focused on granted patents, examining patent applications offers a more comprehensive view of inventors' careers. Patent applications provide a valuable comparison to study the effects of patent grants. If granted patents can be seen as successful outcomes or "goals," then applications are like "shots on goal." Unsuccessful patent applications can represent significant learning opportunities for inventors,[43] and linking inventors' successful and unsuccessful applications opens up rich avenues for study.

One potential area for future study is the overlapping relationship between granted patent coinventor networks and application networks. Previous work exploring coinventor networks uses data on granted patents to evaluate relationships between inventors.[44] This may disproportionately exclude female inventors from conceptualizations of inventor networks due to the gendered dynamics discussed above. In line with this, we find instances of wider, more gender-diverse networks on patent applications than the networks constructed by looking only at granted patents. Researchers should consider the value of studying not only granted patents but also ungranted applications when evaluating coinventor networks and relationships.

Discussion

In this chapter, we highlight current demographic trends in participation in patenting as captured by USPTO applications and patents. We discuss how data on individual-level disambiguation and gender are created and identify the limitations of these imputed measures, as well as their implications for our understanding of female representation in the patent system. In addition, we highlight how the historical focus on granted patents, as opposed to patent applications, may disproportionately ignore female inventors' contributions to the patent system due to differential trends in application conversion for male and female inventors.

Through this work, we hope to shed light on nuances in the oft-used but not always well-understood PatentsView data and encourage researchers to continue to evaluate the drivers of gender and other demographic disparities in patent participation and outcomes. Patenting is an important context in

[43] Cotropia & Schwartz, *supra* note 37.

[44] Fleming & Juda, *supra* note 25; Lee Fleming, Santiago Mingo & David Chen, *Collaborative Brokerage, Generative Creativity, and Creative Success*, 52 ADMIN. SCI. Q. 443 (2007).

which researchers not only can study broader economic trends but also can examine the relationship between individual demographics and innovative outcomes. Having an accurate grasp of the opportunities and limitations of the public data available for this research is essential to furthering our understanding of how diversity can strengthen our patent system.

Acknowledgments

Both authors contributed equally. We are grateful to Beth Anne Card (American Institutes for Research), Ernest Miguelez (Institute of Public Goods and Policies, Spanish National Research Council), Nicholas Rada (USPTO), and Andrew Toole (USPTO) for research assistance and feedback.

3

Gender Differences in Intellectual Property Awareness

Evidence from a Global Survey

Carlotta Nani, Martin Correa, and Julio Raffo

Introduction

Innovation is the backbone of economic growth, and technological progress requires a constant influx of ideas.[1] Intellectual property (IP) rights are fundamental assets that promote innovation as they ensure returns for the time and resources employed in the creative and inventive process. They also contribute to the consolidation of intangible assets for entrepreneurs, making innovation an investment rather than a liability.[2] Nevertheless, research and innovation remain male-dominated, with women accounting for less than 20 percent of listed inventors and creators.[3] As ideas become harder to find, overlooking the potential of half the population leads to lost opportunities for innovation, lower quality of ideas, and unexplored market segments.[4]

[1] Alex Bell, Raj Chetty, Xavier Jaravel, Neviana Petkova & John Van Reenen, *Who Becomes an Inventor in America? The Importance of Exposure to Innovation*, 134 Q.J. Econ. 647 (2019); Nicholas Bloom, Charles I. Jones, John Van Reenen & Michael Webb, *Are Ideas Getting Harder to Find?*, 110 Am. Econ. Rev. 1104 (2020); Peter Howitt & Philippe Aghion, *Capital Accumulation and Innovation as Complementary Factors in Long-Run Growth*, 3 J. Econ. Growth 111 (1998); Paul M. Romer, *Endogenous Technological Change*, 98 J. Pol. Econ. S71 (1990).

[2] Otto Toivanen & Lotta Väänänen, *Returns to Inventors*, 94 Rev. Econ. & Stat. 1173 (2012).

[3] Élodie Carpentier & Julio Raffo, The Global Gender Gap in Innovation and Creativity: An International Comparison of the Gender Gap in Global Patenting over Two Decades (2023); *see also* Eur. Union Intell. Prop. Off., Women in Design (2023); U.S. Copyright Off., Women in the Copyright System—An Analysis of Women Authors in Copyright Registrations from 2020 (2022).

[4] Bloom et al., *supra* note 1; Karin Hoisl, Hans Christian Kongsted & Myriam Mariani, *Lost Marie Curies: Parental Impact on the Probability of Becoming an Inventor*, 69 Mgmt. Sci. 1714 (2023); Rembrand Koning, Sampsa Samila & Jason P. Ferguson, *Who Do We Invent for? Patents by Women Focus More on Women's Health, but Few Women Get to Invent*, 372 Sci. 1345 (2021).

Carlotta Nani, Martin Correa, and Julio Raffo, *Gender Differences in Intellectual Property Awareness* In: *Inclusive Innovation in the Age of AI and Big Data*. Edited by: Daryl Lim and Peter K. Yu, Oxford University Press.
 DOI: 10.1093/9780197799444.003.0004

Women's underrepresentation in innovation stems from a combination of individual choices and structural barriers. On the one hand, women may not engage in research and development (R&D) due to a lack of awareness or interest in IP rights. On the other hand, they may face systemic obstacles related to education, employment opportunities, credit access, and recognition for their contributions. In this chapter, we conduct a survey of 25,000 individuals across fifty countries to investigate whether gender differences in IP awareness can explain women's underrepresentation in the field. The survey captures both objective knowledge (measured through factual questions on IP rights) and self-reported awareness, allowing us to study both actual and perceived familiarity with IP. Self-reported measures are crucial, as individuals make decisions based on perceptions about their abilities: someone who believes they know little about IP may self-select out of innovative professions, even if they possess relevant knowledge or skills.[5] Our results indicate that individuals report the highest levels of familiarity with copyrights and trademarks, while designs and geographical indications are the least known forms of IP. Women, compared with men, report lower familiarity with patents and higher familiarity with designs, and these differences remain significant even after controlling for socioeconomic factors. This pattern is mirrored in objective knowledge measures: women are less likely to correctly answer questions about patents and trademarks but more likely to know about designs, copyrights, and geographical indications.

These results align with gendered patterns of specialization: despite having overall more positive perceptions about IP rights and their impact on the economy, women tend to cluster in creative fields like fashion, design, and the arts, while men are overrepresented in entrepreneurship and fields related to mechanics, engineering, and technology. In fact, when we look at areas where individuals report benefitting from innovation, men cite sectors like computing, electrical tools, and sports, whereas women more often mention children's leisure, household appliances, and food products. This specialization affects the types of IP protections individuals seek and highlights the gendered dimensions of innovation ecosystems.[6]

[5] Pedro Bordalo, Katherine Coffman, Nicola Gennaioli & Andrei Shleifer, *Beliefs About Gender*, 109 AM. ECON. REV. 739 (2019); Carlotta Nani, *Perceived Abilities and Gender Stereotypes Within the Household: Experimental Evidence from Bangladesh* (Geneva Graduate Inst., Working Paper No. 19-2024, 2024).

[6] In a forthcoming working paper, we expand this analysis by focusing on students, since universities and other institutes are the hub of research and creativity. We observe that most gender differences in IP awareness disappear in this sample, suggesting that exposure during education can mitigate gaps in knowledge. Carlotta Nani, Martin Alejandro Correa & Julio Raffo, *Common*

When we break down the analysis by the countries' income level, high- and middle-income countries drive the results while gender differences lose significance among low-income countries. This could suggest that the institutional and economic factors specific to high-income environments could also play a role in determining gender differences in awareness. These findings suggest that awareness campaigns and training should be targeted to take into account structural and cultural barriers as well as the level of economic development.

While this study brings evidence of differences in perceptions and awareness about what IP rights are among the general population, future research should focus on awareness about how to effectively use them. Individuals might know what patents and copyrights are, yet they might not know how to use them to protect their ideas, leaving growth opportunities and potential revenues unused. A greater focus on effective use would bring important insights on why certain groups are more present in innovation while others fall behind.

Literature Review

This study contributes to the literature on diversity and inclusion in innovation and IP, with a specific focus on gender. We review the existing literature focusing on three main areas: factors leading to underrepresentation in IP, IP awareness, and consequences of underrepresentation.

Factors Contributing to Women Underrepresentation

Despite the importance of IP rights for innovation and growth, women remain significantly underrepresented in the IP system. The gender gap in STEM (science, technology, engineering, and mathematics) education is progressively reducing, raising important questions about the barriers women face in translating their educational achievements into successful careers in innovation.[7] This finding suggests that underrepresentation

Knowledge? A Cross-Country Analysis of Gender Differences in Awareness About IP rights from the WIPO Pulse Survey (forthcoming).

[7] Hoisl et al., *supra* note 4.

could be due not to a lack of talent or potential but rather to structural and institutional barriers. Compared with men, women face more and stricter constraints related to income, family responsibilities, access to a network and credit, and discrimination, which contribute to their underrepresentation.[8]

One of the key economic factors influencing women's exit from innovation is the differential returns from innovation and IP. Studies have shown that male inventors tend to earn more than female inventors in R&D roles. For instance, Karin Hoisl and Myriam Mariani find a wage gap of approximately 14 percent in favor of male inventors,[9] while Otto Toivanen and Lotta Väänänen estimate a wage gap of 20 percent.[10] A recent report from the European Patent Office shows that, on average, women designers earn 13 percent less than male designers.[11] These wage disparities are particularly pronounced in the long term, suggesting that women face slower career progression and lower returns on their innovations. This gendered wage gap is a critical factor influencing women's decisions to leave careers in science and engineering.[12] These differential returns to innovation appear as the main determinant of women's lower participation, compared with other factors such as family responsibility or lower skill levels.[13]

The legal protection afforded by IP rights does not guarantee equal opportunities for women in the innovation system. Women pursuing careers in research and innovation often face challenges in gaining recognition for their contributions. Kyle Jensen, Balazs Kovács, and Olav Sorenson show that patent applications submitted by women are more likely to be rejected, compared with those submitted by men.[14] Even when women's patents are accepted, they tend to undergo more amendments during prosecution, often reducing their scope and value. Moreover, women's patents are less likely to be cited and maintained in the long term than men's. In some cases, women's

[8] Élodie Carpentier, Jennifer Brant, Utsav Bahl & Aikaterini Kanellia, *Closing Innovation and Intellectual Property Diversity Gaps: A Global Literature Review* (World Intell. Prop. Org., Econ. Rsch. Working Paper No. 86, 2024).

[9] Karin Hoisl & Myriam Mariani, *It's a Man's Job: Income and the Gender Gap in Industrial Research*, 63 Mgmt. Sci. 766 (2017).

[10] Toivanen & Väänänen, *supra* note 2.

[11] Eur. Union Intell. Prop. Off., *supra* note 3.

[12] Hoisl et al., *supra* note 4; Jennifer Hunt, *Why Do Women Leave Science and Engineering?*, 69 ILR Rev. 199 (2016).

[13] Hoisl et al., *supra* note 4; Hunt, *supra* note 12.

[14] Kyle Jensen, Balazs Kovács & Olav Sorenson, *Gender Differences in Obtaining and Maintaining Patent Rights*, 36 Nature Biotech. 307 (2018).

contributions to joint inventions go uncredited, as highlighted by Margaret Rossiter, further exacerbating gender disparities in the IP system.[15]

Awareness about IP Rights and Participation

While these structural barriers are well documented, the role of IP awareness is less explored. The effectiveness of IP systems depends not only on the protection they offer but also on individuals' knowledge of how to leverage them.[16] Studies indicate that a lack of awareness of IP rights is a significant barrier to participation in patenting. The European Patent Office finds that many small and medium-sized enterprises (SMEs) in Europe forego patenting simply due to a lack of IP knowledge.[17] Robert Pitkethly conducts a survey among UK firms and concludes that larger firms own more IP rights and know more about them, compared with smaller firms, and that IP awareness promotion is crucial to preserving innovation of SMEs and micro-enterprises early in their life.[18] According to Janewa Osei-Tutu, women entrepreneurs in Ghana are not aware of the potential market value that IP rights bring and did not know how to leverage trademarks, copyrights, and patents to develop their business.[19] A report by the Institute for Women's Policy Research highlights that women do not see the commercialization of innovation as part of their career paths.[20]

A comprehensive analysis of gender gaps in innovation should, therefore, study whether women are aware of IP rights. If women are not aware of the benefits of IP protection or hold negative perceptions about the IP system, they can be discouraged from seeking IP protection for their inventions and creations, with effects lasting across generations. Exposure to innovation and inventorship, particularly at an early age, plays a significant role in shaping individuals' career trajectories in R&D. Studies show that parental role models can significantly influence a child's likelihood of pursuing a career in innovation, with a notable gender bias in the impact of role models.[21]

[15] Margaret W. Rossiter, *The Matthew Matilda Effect in Science*, 23 Soc. Stud. Sci. 325 (1993).

[16] Francis. F. Balahadia, Rainer R. Fiscal, Jayson N. Olayta, Maricon C. Pablo, Marjean R. Valmote & Joseph Aldrin C. Ganibo, *University Students' Awareness on Intellectual Property Rights*, 3 Int'l J. Academe & Indus. Rsch. 28 (2022); Robert H. Pitkethly, *Intellectual Property Awareness*, 59 Int'l J. Tech. Mgmt. 163 (2012).

[17] Eur. Pat. Off., *Utilization of Patent Protection in Europe*, 17 World Pat. Info. 100 (1995).

[18] Pitkethly, *supra* note 16.

[19] J. Janewa Osei-Tutu, *Using Intellectual Property Law to Promote Human Flourishing for Market Women*, Landslide, Mar.–Apr. 2018, at 38.

[20] Elyse Shaw & Cynthia Hess, Closing the Gender Gap in Patenting, Innovation, and Commercialization: Programs Promoting Equity and Inclusion (2018).

[21] Bell et al., *supra* note 1.

Karin Hoisl, Hans Christian Kongsted, and Myriam Mariani show that parental role models significantly increase the probability of a child becoming an inventor, but the impact is much stronger for boys than for girls.[22] They identify parents' gendered perceptions about returns from inventorship to be the channel of transmission.

Consequences of Underrepresentation

Women's lower rate of participation in research and innovation not only has immediate consequences in terms of unused human capital, mismatched skills, and returns to education, but it also affects the quality and quantity of ideas since inventors innovate based on their personal experiences. The overrepresentation or underrepresentation of certain groups limits the diversity of contributions and skews innovation in certain fields and products, making ideas harder to find, leaving large market opportunities unexploited and preventing a big share of the population to benefit from innovation. Products designed without input from women may not fully address the needs or preferences of a substantial portion of the market. For instance, research indicates that women are underrepresented in medical device design and healthcare innovation, leading to products that do not adequately address women's health issues. According to Rembrand Koning, Sampsa Samila, and Jason Ferguson, the underrepresentation of women has led to thousands of missing women-focused inventions since the 1970s.[23]

If innovation benefits only those who invent, it can lead to a vicious cycle where more women exit innovation because, despite IP rights, they do not see the benefits of it, leading to even less women-focused ideas.

Data and Descriptive Statistics

The data for this chapter comes from the 2023 WIPO Pulse Survey, which examines knowledge and attitudes toward IP rights across fifty countries (the country list is provided in Table A.1 of the Appendix).[24] Designed to be nationally representative, the survey includes approximately 500 interviews per country with individuals aged 18–65. Respondents were selected from

[22] Hoisl et al., *supra* note 4.
[23] Koning et al., *supra* note 4.
[24] World Intell. Prop. Org., WIPO Pulse: Global Intellectual Property Perception Survey 2023 (2023).

panels provided by the surveying company and invited to participate in online interviews conducted between March and April 2023.

The survey collects information on four main areas: (1) IP awareness (actual and self-reported knowledge of each IP right); (2) perceptions about products and services protected by IP rights; (3) the impact of IP rights on the economy of a country; and (4) perceived benefits from innovations in various aspects of life. Furthermore, the survey collects data on the respondents' demographic characteristics (such as gender, age, education, employment status, and perceived income comfort).

Our primary outcomes of interest are perceptions and knowledge of IP rights. We construct two measures of IP knowledge: objective and subjective. Objective knowledge is a binary variable equal to one if the respondent correctly answered questions to identify the most appropriate IP right for protecting a given product.[25] Although only one option per question is correct, respondents could select up to two options. We consider an answer correct if the respondent selected only the correct option. Subjective knowledge is based on the respondents' self-reported knowledge, measured on a Likert scale. We code this as one when respondents indicated they knew either "fairly well" or "very well" about a particular IP right.[26]

We capture perceptions of IP rights using summary indices. One section of the survey asks respondents to indicate their level of agreement with statements about products protected by IP rights, using a Likert scale from one ("strongly disagree") to five ("strongly agree").[27] For each IP right, we create a summary index representing the proportion of statements with which the respondent strongly agreed. For example, if the respondent strongly agreed with four out of six statements about products protected by patents, the index would equal 0.67 (4/6). Additionally, respondents are asked about the perceived impact of IP rights on the economy.[28] In this case, we construct the index using the generalized least-squares weighting

[25] For example, "A brand name can be best protected through? Patent; trademark; registered designs; copyright; geographical indication; or I do not know."

[26] For example, "How would you evaluate your personal understanding of trademarks? I have never heard about it; I have heard about it but the word only; I have heard about it but know very little; or I have heard about it and know fairly or very well about it."

[27] For example, "Please indicate how much you agree or disagree with the following statements about trademarks: Product with a registered trademark are (i) more trustworthy; (ii) better value for money; (iii) better quality; or (iv) my first choice when buying products."

[28] For example, "Please indicate how much you agree or disagree with the following statements: IPRs [IP rights] matter only to big corporations; IPRs lead to economic growth in my country."

procedure by Michael Anderson.[29] Higher values of these indices indicate more positive perceptions and attitudes.

The literature suggests that men and women may perform differently when aware of being tested, and research indicates gender differences in self-confidence, risk aversion, and susceptibility to impostor syndrome.[30] To account for these factors, we create measures of low and high self-confidence based on the discrepancy between objective and subjective knowledge. Low self-confidence is a binary variable equal to one if a respondent reported low knowledge of an IP right but answered the corresponding objective question correctly. High self-confidence is coded as one if a respondent reported knowing about an IP right but answered the objective question incorrectly. In both cases, the comparison category consists of individuals whose subjective and objective awareness matched. (For example, they reported knowing about patents, and they answered correctly the question about patents.) We also construct a measure of "hesitance" or test-related anxiety: whether a respondent decreased the chances of possessing objective knowledge. For each IP right, the variable equals one if, despite knowing the correct answer to the objective knowledge questions, the respondent decided to select two options, compared with individuals who only selected the (one) correct answer. This should allow us to capture in a different way how confident the respondents are about their knowledge and whether they stress under test.

Table 3.1 presents the descriptive statistics for the respondents' demographic characteristics, comparing the sample of men and women using a *t*-test of means differences. Respondents are, on average, thirty-eight years old. Most of the individuals have a higher level of education at the time of the survey (67 percent tertiary and 28 percent secondary), and there are no significant differences between men and women. Almost half of the sample reports currently coping on present income (42 percent) while 30 percent living comfortably. In this case as well, there is no significant difference between men and women. Fifty percent of the sample lives in high-income countries, and 30 percent in upper-middle income countries, according to

[29] Michael L. Anderson, *Multiple Inference and Gender Differences in the Effects of Early Intervention: A Reevaluation of the Abecedarian, Perry Preschool, and Early Training Projects*, 103 J. AM. STAT. ASS'N 1481 (2008).

[30] Shelley J. Correll, *Constraints into Preferences: Gender, Status, and Emerging Career Aspirations*, 69 AM. SOC. REV. 93 (2004); Laura Kamas & Anne Preston, *The Importance of Being Confident: Gender, Career Choice, and Willingness to Compete*, 83 J. ECON. BEHAV. & ORG. 82 (2012); Muriel Niederle & Lise Vesterlund, *Gender and Competition*, 3 ANN. REV. ECON. 601 (2011).

Table 3.1. Baseline characteristics of respondents by gender

	Women	Men	*t*-test difference
	Mean/(SE)	Mean/(SE)	(Women-Men)
Age	38.003 (0.113)	38.674 (0.112)	−0.670***
Education			
No education	0.017 (0.001)	0.017 (0.001)	0.001
Primary	0.036 (0.002)	0.037 (0.002)	−0.001
Secondary	0.276 (0.004)	0.279 (0.004)	−0.003
Tertiary	0.671 (0.004)	0.667 (0.004)	0.003
Employment status			
Full-time	0.534 (0.005)	0.644 (0.004)	−0.110***
Part-time	0.189 (0.004)	0.154 (0.003)	0.035***
Unemployed	0.080 (0.002)	0.064 (0.002)	0.016***

	Women	Men	*t*-test difference
	Mean/(SE)	Mean/(SE)	(Women-Men)
Location			
Urban	0.545 (0.004)	0.534 (0.004)	0.011*
Rural	0.141 (0.003)	0.140 (0.003)	0.001
Semi-urban	0.313 (0.004)	0.326 (0.004)	−0.012**
Global region			
Africa	0.202 (0.004)	0.206 (0.004)	−0.004
Asia-Pacific	0.188 (0.004)	0.212 (0.004)	−0.024***
Eastern Europe	0.204 (0.004)	0.196 (0.003)	0.008
Latin American and Caribbean	0.207 (0.004)	0.189 (0.003)	0.018***
Western European and Other	0.199 (0.004)	0.198 (0.004)	0.002

(continued)

Table 3.1. Continued

	Women	Men	*t*-test difference		Women	Men	*t*-test difference
	Mean/(SE)	Mean/(SE)	(Women-Men)		Mean/(SE)	Mean/(SE)	(Women-Men)
In education	0.053 (0.002)	0.049 (0.002)	0.004	**Country Income**			
Retired	0.144 (0.003)	0.089 (0.003)	0.055***	High income	0.493 (0.004)	0.498 (0.004)	−0.005
Perceived household income				Middle income	0.266 (0.004)	0.260 (0.004)	0.005
Finding it difficult	0.289 (0.004)	0.271 (0.004)	0.018***	Low income	0.241 (0.004)	0.242 (0.004)	−0.000
Coping	0.421 (0.004)	0.425 (0.004)	−0.004				
Living comfortably	0.290 (0.004)	0.304 (0.004)	−0.013**				

Note: The table reports the averages for the sample of women and men, as well as the difference between the sample averages using *t*-tests. Education refers to the level of education at the time of the survey (irrespectively of completion). High income, Middle income, and Low income refer to the World Bank classification.

*** $p < 0.01$

** $p < 0.05$

* $p < 0.1$

the World Bank classification (more details provided in Table A.1). Almost 80 percent of the sample lives in urban or semi-urban areas.

On average, more men than women are employed (79 percent of men against 72 percent women), but significantly more men are employed full-time than women, while more women than men are employed part-time or unemployed.

Empirical Strategy

The goal of this chapter is to explore gender differences in knowledge and perceptions of IP rights. We begin our analysis by conducting a simple comparison of means between men and women using the Student's *t*-test. This initial step provides an unadjusted measure of gender differences, without accounting for factors that might simultaneously influence knowledge and perceptions of IP rights and that might vary systematically by gender.

To account for potential confounding factors, we estimate the coefficients using the following linear regression model:

$$Y_{ic} = \alpha + \beta Woman_i + \gamma X_i + \delta_c + \varepsilon_{ic}$$

where Y_{ic} represents all outcome variables of interest for individual i in country c—namely, objective and subjective knowledge, self-confidence, hesitance, perceptions of IP rights, and perceived benefits of innovation. $Woman_i$ indicates the respondent's gender and corresponds to our primary variable of interest. X_i is a vector of individual's sociodemographic characteristics, such as education, employment status, age, household income, and rural or urban location. δ_c is the country fixed effect that controls for all the country-specific characteristics that might influence outcomes, such as cultural attitudes toward gender, differences in national IP systems, legal frameworks, or enforcement mechanisms. Finally, ε_{ic} is the error term, clustered at the country level to account for the fact that the standard errors might be correlated within countries. This model allows us to isolate the gender effect by holding constant socioeconomic and country-level characteristics (whether observable and not). If the coefficient remains statistically significant after controlling for these factors, it suggests that gender differences in IP knowledge and perceptions persist beyond what can be explained by observable individuals' characteristics and countries fixed effects. In other words, the remaining differences may be attributed to more nuanced gender-specific factors, such as confidence, social norms, and systemic biases (beyond those captured by countries fixed effects).

Furthermore, we explore potential heterogeneity in gender differences and estimate the model separately for high-, middle-, and low-income countries to uncover whether a country group drives the results by IP rights. This approach accounts for how contextual factors, such as the affordability and accessibility of IP rights or the quality of IP-related institutions, might shape gendered patterns in knowledge and perceptions. For instance, lower-cost IP protections might be more widely used in low-income areas, potentially influencing how men and women perceive them. Similarly, more advanced economies may have better dissemination programs and IP user support services affecting men's and women's awareness and perception.

Results

This section presents and discusses the results of these analyses, which are grouped by (1) knowledge about IP rights; and (2) perceptions about IP rights.

Knowledge about IP Rights

The first outcomes we analyze are subjective and objective knowledge (see Table 3.2). Overall, copyrights and trademarks are the IP rights most individuals are familiar with, with 55 and 57 percent of respondents, respectively, stating that they know about these rights. In contrast, designs and geographical indications are the least familiar, with only 36 and 30 percent of respondents reporting knowledge of them, respectively. The comparison of means reveals gendered patterns in self-reported knowledge. Women are significantly less likely than men to report knowledge of patents and geographical indications, though they are slightly more likely to report knowledge of industrial designs. However, these raw comparisons do not account for underlying socioeconomic differences between men and women that could influence knowledge. To address this, we estimate the regression model controlling for education, employment status, income, age, and geographic location.

Table 3.2. Differences in knowledge of IP rights by gender and countries' income level

Subjective knowledge

	Women	Men	t-test difference	Regression coefficients			
	Mean	Mean	(Women-Men)	Full sample	High income	Middle income	Low income
Patents	0.402 (0.004)	0.436 (0.004)	−0.034***	−0.0245** (0.0111)	−0.0271** (0.0111)	0.0072 (0.0232)	−0.0534** (0.0227)
Trademarks	0.572 (0.004)	0.566 (0.004)	0.006	0.0098 (0.0106)	0.0081 (0.0135)	0.0341** (0.0126)	−0.0085 (0.0240)
Designs	0.375 (0.004)	0.358 (0.004)	0.017***	0.0230* (0.0121)	−0.0035 (0.0156)	0.0768*** (0.0199)	0.0173 (0.0220)
Copyrights	0.546 (0.004)	0.549 (0.004)	−0.002	0.0009 (0.0114)	−0.0056 (0.0135)	0.0335** (0.0144)	−0.0164 (0.0238)
Geo. indications	0.294 (0.004)	0.318 (0.004)	−0.025***	−0.0147 (0.0117)	−0.0263** (0.0125)	0.0187 (0.0297)	−0.0253 (0.0187)

Objective knowledge

	Women	Men	t-test difference	Regression coefficients			
	Mean	Mean	(Women-Men)	Full sample	High income	Middle income	Low income
Patents	0.346 (0.004)	0.369 (0.004)	−0.023***	−0.0259*** (0.0080)	−0.0324** (0.0122)	−0.0282* (0.0153)	0.0043 (0.0109)
Trademarks	0.115 (0.003)	0.127 (0.003)	−0.011***	-0.0095* (0.0056)	0.0005 (0.0072)	-0.0256* (0.0137)	−0.0088 (0.0086)
Designs	0.365 (0.004)	0.321 (0.004)	0.044***	0.0424*** (0.0072)	0.0501*** (0.0109)	0.0448*** (0.0090)	0.0331** (0.0121)
Copyrights	0.617 (0.004)	0.589 (0.004)	0.028***	0.0239** (0.0099)	0.0288* (0.0147)	0.0329** (0.0119)	0.0229 (0.0203)
Geo. indications	0.285 (0.004)	0.264 (0.004)	0.020***	0.0144 (0.0089)	0.0025 (0.0129)	0.0337 (0.0203)	0.0296** (0.0114)

Note: The left panel reports the average subjective and objective knowledge for the sample of women and men, as well as the difference between the sample averages using *t*-tests. The right panel reports the OLS regression coefficients. For each regression, the outcome variables are the objective and subjective knowledge of each IP right (patents, trademarks, designs, copyrights, geographical indications, and overall). The coefficients reported are those corresponding to "being a woman." High income, Middle income, and Low income refer to the World Bank classification. Coefficients not reported: education, employment, age, household income, and rural or urban location. Each regression includes country fixed effect. Standard errors (in parenthesis) are clustered at the country level. The number of observations (not reported) ranges from 24,000 for the full sample, to 12,000 for high-income countries, to 6,000 for middle and low-income countries.

*** $p < 0.01$

** $p < 0.05$

* $p < 0.1$

The regression results confirm that, even after controlling for observable characteristics, gender differences persist. Holding everything else constant, women, compared with men, remain two and a half percentage points less likely to report knowledge of patents and two percentage points more likely to report knowledge of industrial designs. The coefficient for geographical indications loses statistical significance once controls are added, suggesting that the initial difference observed in the means comparison may be driven by socioeconomic factors rather than gender-specific dynamics. This means that, if we take a man and a woman with the same level of education, employment status, age, and income, the woman will still be less likely to report that she knows about patents and more likely to report knowing about designs than the man. When disaggregating the analysis by the countries' income level, we uncover important heterogeneities. In low-income countries, the gender gap in patent knowledge widens, and women are five percentage points less likely than men to report knowledge of patents. By contrast, in middle-income countries, the gender gap in industrial designs is more pronounced, with women being eight percentage points more likely than men to report knowledge. Interestingly, in these countries, women are also more likely to report knowledge of copyrights and trademarks, while these coefficients are negative but not statistically significant in low-income countries.

Turning to objective knowledge, copyrights are the most well-known IP rights, with 60 percent of respondents answering the relevant questions correctly. This is followed by industrial designs and patents (35 percent) and geographical indications (27 percent), while trademarks are the least known, with only 12 percent of respondents providing correct answers.[31] Gender disparities in subjective knowledge are, to some extent, mirrored in objective knowledge measures. Women score lower than men on objective knowledge of patents and trademarks (by two and one percentage points, respectively), but they outperform men in industrial designs, copyrights, and geographical indications (by four, three, and two percentage points, respectively).

Importantly, these gender gaps persist even after accounting for socioeconomic factors. Therefore, the observed disparities might not be purely the result of educational or employment differences but may instead reflect

[31] By design, WIPO Pulse had two questions related to trademark objective knowledge. The likelihood of guessing two answers right might artificially reduce the indicator for trademark objective knowledge when compared with that in other IP areas.

gender-specific dynamics such as social norms or systemic biases. When we split the sample by the countries' income level, we find that the gender gap in objective knowledge is driven by high- and middle-income countries, where women are systematically more likely to know about copyrights and designs, while men remain more knowledgeable about patents.

These findings suggest that women tend to be more knowledgeable about IP rights that are more prevalent in creative industries (designs and copyrights), but they are less likely to know about IP rights used more in STEM fields (patents) and businesses (trademarks). In other words, awareness about patents and trademarks appears to be male-dominated, with knowledge gaps persisting even after accounting for individual characteristics and country fixed effects.

To accurately interpret the results, it is crucial to rule out the possibility that the survey structure systematically influenced how men and women responded. Research suggests that men and women may behave differently under test conditions.[32] Women may report lower subjective knowledge or select multiple options even when they know the correct answer, reflecting lower confidence or higher risk aversion. To address this, we investigate gender differences in self-confidence when answering, as shown in Table 3.3. We define self-confidence as the alignment between subjective and objective knowledge. Respondents with low self-confidence understate their knowledge. (They report low subjective knowledge but answer the objective question correctly.) Conversely, high self-confidence is captured by respondents who overstate their knowledge. (They report knowing about an IP right but answer the objective question incorrectly.) On average, around 30 percent of respondents exhibit lower self-confidence across IP rights (except for trademarks where the percentage drops to 13 percent). Compared with men, women correctly assess their level of knowledge for patents, but they are more likely to underestimate themselves in areas where they are actually more knowledgeable (such as designs). While for patents and trademarks we do not observe significant differences in lower self-confidence between men and women, for designs, copyrights, and geographical indications, women are significantly more likely than men to fall into this group, even after accounting for socioeconomic characteristics. The coefficients are the largest for industrial designs in high-income countries, where women are significantly likely to underestimate their knowledge. In contrast, gender

[32] Kamas & Preston, *supra* note 30.

Table 3.3. Differences in self-confidence by gender and countries' income level

Lower self-confidence							
	Women	Men	*t*-test difference	Regression coefficients			
	Mean	Mean	(Women-Men)	Full sample	High income	Middle income	Low income
Patents	0.298 (0.005)	0.292 (0.005)	0.006	−0.0017 (0.0082)	0.0010 (0.0121)	−0.0034 (0.0151)	0.0007 (0.0179)
Trademarks	0.131 (0.004)	0.130 (0.004)	0.001	−0.0029 (0.0077)	0.0061 (0.0123)	−0.0159 (0.0137)	−0.0097 (0.0107)
Designs	0.351 (0.005)	0.307 (0.005)	0.044***	0.0386*** (0.0092)	0.0584*** (0.0133)	0.0237* (0.0121)	0.0122 (0.0150)
Copyrights	0.350 (0.005)	0.320 (0.005)	0.030***	0.0263*** (0.0089)	0.0426*** (0.0146)	0.0160 (0.0145)	0.0118 (0.0114)
Geo. Indications	0.288 (0.005)	0.259 (0.004)	0.029***	0.0228*** (0.0085)	0.0296** (0.0134)	0.0263 (0.0151)	0.0144 (0.0104)
Higher self-confidence							
	Women	Men	*t*-test difference	Regression coefficients			
	Mean	Mean	(Women-Men)	Full sample	High income	Middle income	Low income
Patents	0.324 (0.005)	0.335 (0.005)	−0.011	−0.0049 (0.0111)	0.0007 (0.0118)	0.0317 (0.0202)	−0.0557** (0.0207)
Trademarks	0.542 (0.005)	0.528 (0.005)	0.014**	0.0144 (0.0111)	0.0105 (0.0139)	0.0415** (0.0157)	−0.0048 (0.0258)
Designs	0.338 (0.005)	0.321 (0.005)	0.018***	0.0186 (0.0112)	0.0081 (0.0133)	0.0536** (0.0178)	−0.0012 (0.0229)
Copyrights	0.276 (0.005)	0.274 (0.005)	0.002	0.0005 (0.0115)	0.0087 (0.0143)	0.0176 (0.0191)	−0.0330 (0.0246)
Geo. indications	0.274 (0.005)	0.286 (0.004)	−0.012*	−0.0028 (0.0113)	0.0033 (0.0125)	0.0111 (0.0279)	−0.0286 (0.0194)

Note: The left panel reports the average self-confidence (lower and higher) for the sample of women and men, as well as the difference between the sample averages using *t*-tests. The right panel reports the OLS regression coefficients. For each regression, the outcome variables are the self-confidence (lower and higher) for each IP right (patents, trademarks, designs, copyrights, geographical indications, and overall). The coefficients reported are those corresponding to "being a woman." High income, Middle income, and Low income refer to the World Bank classification. Coefficients not reported: education, employment, age, household income, and rural or urban location. Each regression includes country fixed effect. Standard errors (in parenthesis) are clustered at the country level. The number of observations (not reported) ranges from 24,000 for the full sample, to 12,000 for high-income countries, to 6,000 for middle and low-income countries.

*** $p < 0.01$

** $p < 0.05$

* $p < 0.1$

differences in self-confidence are not significant in low-income countries, suggesting that they may be amplified in environments where the knowledge of IP rights is already more widespread. (As Table A.2 shows, low-income countries report lower levels of subjective and objective IP awareness, compared with middle- and high-income ones.) Conversely, we do not observe significant differences between men's and women's likelihood of being more self-confident. The only exceptions are trademarks and designs in middle-income countries where women are more likely to be overly self-confident than men, and patents in low-income countries where they are less likely to be overly self-confident.

While women are more likely to underestimate their knowledge, there is no strong evidence that they are more hesitant when answering questions. For instance, across income levels women appear less likely than men to hesitate when answering (Table A.3). However, the coefficients are not statistically significant, with the exception of designs and geographical indications, indicating no significant gender differences in the likelihood of selecting two options when only one is correct. This suggests that the observed gender gaps in knowledge, especially for patents and trademarks, do not depend on the stress related to being tested that might impact men and women differently.

Perceptions of IP Rights

In Table 3.4, we present the results for perceptions toward IP rights. Overall, individuals express positive perceptions toward products protected by IP rights, with agreement around 70 percent. Across all categories of IP rights, women tend to hold more positive attitudes than men, and these differences remain statistically significant even after controlling for socioeconomic characteristics.

The gender differences in perceptions diminishes substantially when focusing on low-income countries, where attitudes toward IP rights appear to be more homogeneous across genders. This finding suggests that in high-income countries, where exposure to and awareness of IP rights appear more widespread (Table A.2), gender differences in perceptions may reflect broader societal or cultural factors influencing how men and women value innovation and creativity.

In addition to product-level perceptions, women also have more favorable views on the overall impact of IP rights on the economy. This gender gap is

Table 3.4. Differences in perceptions about IP rights by gender and countries' income level

Perceptions	Women	Men	*t*-test difference	Regression coefficients			
	Mean	Mean	(Women-Men)	Full sample	High income	Middle income	Low income
Patents	0.698 (0.003)	0.691 (0.003)	0.007*	0.0128** (0.0059)	0.0160** (0.0075)	0.0180 (0.0132)	0.0053 (0.0107)
Trademarks	0.720 (0.003)	0.709 (0.003)	0.011**	0.0156** (0.0065)	0.0156 (0.0101)	0.0245** (0.0102)	0.0077 (0.0116)
Designs	0.691 (0.003)	0.677 (0.003)	0.014***	0.0183*** (0.0066)	0.0208** (0.0099)	0.0238* (0.0117)	0.0083 (0.0115)
Copyrights	0.738 (0.003)	0.721 (0.003)	0.016***	0.0199*** (0.0061)	0.0244** (0.0090)	0.0308*** (0.0099)	0.0032 (0.0093)
Geo. indications	0.736 (0.003)	0.713 (0.003)	0.023***	0.0263*** (0.0058)	0.0284*** (0.0089)	0.0271** (0.0121)	0.0238*** (0.0071)
Perceptions about IPRs in the economy	0.017 (0.009)	−0.016 (0.009)	0.033**	0.0445** (0.0172)	0.0942*** (0.0165)	0.0528 (0.0306)	−0.0244 (0.0310)

Note: The left panel reports the average perceptions about IP rights for the sample of women and men, as well as the difference between the sample averages using *t*-tests. The right panel reports the OLS regression coefficients. For each regression, the outcome variables capture perceptions about IP rights. The coefficients reported are those corresponding to "being a woman." High income, Middle income, and Low income refer to the World Bank classification. Coefficients not reported: education, employment, age, household income, and rural or urban location. Each regression includes country fixed effect. Standard errors (in parenthesis) are clustered at the country level. The number of observations (not reported) ranges from 24,000 for the full sample, to 12,000 for high-income countries, to 6,000 for middle and low-income countries.

*** $p < 0.01$

** $p < 0.05$

* $p < 0.1$

most pronounced in high-income countries, where women express higher than average beliefs in the economic benefits of IP protection. In low- and middle-income countries, these gender differences in perception about the impact of IP rights in the economy fade.

These results indicate that socioeconomic factors alone do not fully account for the differences in knowledge about IP rights between men and women. One plausible explanation lies in gender-based specialization in education, career paths, and household roles. Research suggests that women are more likely to pursue studies and careers in fields such as fashion, design, and creative industries, while men are more concentrated in machinery, engineering, and technology-intensive sectors.[33] These patterns of specialization

[33] Carolyn M. Sloane, Erik G. Hurst & Dan A. Black. *College Majors, Occupations, and the Gender Wage Gap*, 35 J. Econ. Persp. 223 (2021).

could naturally translate into increasing knowledge of copyrights and industrial designs among women, and greater familiarity with patents and trademarks among men.

To explore this hypothesis, we examine the aspects of life in which respondents report benefiting the most from innovation (see Table 3.5). The results support this theory: Men are significantly more likely to report

Table 3.5. Differences in perceived benefits from innovation in life aspects by gender and countries' income level

Benefits from innovation	Women	Men	*t*-test difference	Regression coefficients			
	Mean	Mean	(Women-Men)	Full sample	High income	Middle income	Low income
Computer technologies	0.757 (0.004)	0.792 (0.004)	−0.035***	−0.0315*** (0.0074)	−0.0456*** (0.0098)	−0.0098 (0.0125)	−0.0199 (0.0138)
Electrical tools	0.626 (0.004)	0.668 (0.004)	−0.042***	−0.0394*** (0.0108)	−0.0550*** (0.0121)	−0.0379 (0.0266)	−0.0056 (0.0202)
Sport and leisure	0.565 (0.005)	0.606 (0.004)	−0.041***	−0.0380*** (0.0102)	−0.0189 (0.0114)	−0.0368* (0.0201)	−0.0791*** (0.0232)
Medicine	0.704 (0.004)	0.653 (0.004)	0.051***	0.0492*** (0.0082)	0.0530*** (0.0106)	0.0684*** (0.0152)	0.0265 (0.0148)
Household appliances	0.786 (0.004)	0.725 (0.004)	0.060***	0.0617*** (0.0073)	0.0667*** (0.0077)	0.0789*** (0.0143)	0.0320* (0.0150)
Digital communication	0.850 (0.003)	0.822 (0.003)	0.027***	0.0277*** (0.0061)	0.0346*** (0.0070)	0.0355*** (0.0109)	0.0114 (0.0130)
Transport	0.707 (0.004)	0.678 (0.004)	0.029***	0.0316*** (0.0089)	0.0347** (0.0132)	0.0447*** (0.0145)	0.0141 (0.0169)
Children entertainment	0.471 (0.005)	0.400 (0.004)	0.071***	0.0798*** (0.0092)	0.0659*** (0.0121)	0.0895*** (0.0198)	0.0837*** (0.0177)
Renewable energies	0.549 (0.005)	0.527 (0.004)	0.022***	0.0223** (0.0089)	0.0213** (0.0095)	0.0285 (0.0227)	0.0201 (0.0180)
Food	0.799 (0.004)	0.738 (0.004)	0.061***	0.0627*** (0.0074)	0.0804*** (0.0088)	0.0539*** (0.0130)	0.0335* (0.0158)

Note: The left panel reports the average for whether individuals benefit from innovation in different life aspects, for the sample of women and men, as well as the difference between the sample averages using *t*-tests. The right panel reports the OLS regression coefficients. For each regression, the outcome variables equal 1 if the respondent indicates they benefit from innovation, for each life aspect. The coefficients reported are those corresponding to "being a woman." High income, Middle income, and Low income refer to the World Bank classification. Coefficients not reported: education, employment, age, household income, and rural or urban location. Each regression includes country fixed effect. Standard errors (in parenthesis) are clustered at the country level. The number of observations (not reported) ranges from 24,000 for the full sample, to 12,000 for high-income countries, to 6,000 for middle and low-income countries.

*** $p < 0.01$

** $p < 0.05$

* $p < 0.1$

benefiting from innovation in computing technologies, electrical tools, and sports and leisure, while women report higher benefits in areas such as childcare, household appliances, and food products. These patterns align with traditional gender roles and point to differential exposure to IP-protected products through both professional and domestic spheres.

These findings hold even after controlling for socioeconomic characteristics and across different country-income levels. In low-income countries, gender differences are even more pronounced for specific categories. For example, women are substantially more likely to benefit from innovation in children's products and entertainment, while men benefit more from innovations in sports and leisure. In contrast, gender differences in the perceived benefits of innovation in medicine, digital communication, and transport largely disappear in low-income settings, suggesting that, in these domains, innovation may be perceived as more universally beneficial regardless of gender.

Overall, these results suggest that both professional specialization and household roles contribute to shaping knowledge and perceptions of IP rights. The persistence of gender differences even after accounting for observable characteristics reinforces the idea that exposure to innovation is shaped not only by individual attributes but also by broader social and cultural factors that influence how men and women interact with technology and creative outputs in their daily lives.

Discussion and Conclusions

Innovation is a fundamental driver of economic growth, yet persistent gender disparities in IP rights limit the full potential of innovation and creative outputs. Women remain significantly underrepresented among inventors and creators, despite increasing participation in higher education and STEM fields. This underrepresentation is not only a matter of equity but also of economic inefficiency, as it restricts the diversity of ideas and potential market innovations. While structural barriers such as income disparities, limited access to networks, and biases in patenting processes have been well documented, less attention has been given to the role of IP awareness and knowledge in shaping women's engagement with IP and innovation. If individuals make career choices based on their perceptions of their own knowledge and capabilities, gaps in IP awareness could be a contributing factor to the gender imbalance in innovation ecosystems. This chapter examines the extent of gender disparities in IP knowledge, distinguishing between subjective (self-reported) and objective (tested) knowledge, and explores how these disparities vary across the countries' income level.

To investigate these issues, we analyze data from a survey conducted with 25,000 individuals across fifty countries. The survey assessed both subjective and objective knowledge of different types of IP rights—namely, patents, trademarks, copyrights, industrial designs, and geographical indications. The analysis accounted for key socioeconomic factors, such as education, employment status, income, and geographic location, to isolate the effects of gender on IP awareness. Our findings reveal significant gender differences in both subjective and objective knowledge of IP rights. Women consistently report lower familiarity with patents, while they are more likely than men to report familiarity with industrial designs. These patterns persist even after controlling for socioeconomic characteristics, suggesting that gender disparities in IP awareness are not solely driven by differences in observable characteristics of respondents. When examining objective knowledge, a similar trend emerges: Women score lower than men on patents and trademarks but outperform them in industrial designs, copyrights, and geographical indications. The gender gap in IP knowledge is more pronounced in low-income countries, where women are less likely than men to report familiarity with patents. However, in middle-income countries, women show higher awareness of copyrights, trademarks, and industrial designs.

An important aspect of our study is the exploration of self-confidence in IP knowledge. Women exhibit lower self-confidence in areas where they perform well, particularly in high-income countries. This finding aligns with existing literature on gender differences in self-perception and confidence, particularly in competitive and technical fields. The fact that women show more positive perceptions of the benefits from IP rights suggests that gender differences in awareness and self-confidence could reflect differences in occupational specialization and exposure to IP-protected products. Women are more likely to report benefiting from innovation in areas such as childcare, household appliances, and food products, while men are more likely to cite computing, electrical tools, and sports. Broader social norms and occupational segregation could therefore shape exposure to innovation and technology, reinforcing gendered patterns in IP knowledge and participation.

Our results suggest that addressing gender disparities in IP awareness and participation requires a multifaceted policy approach that combines targeted interventions. Gender disparities in IP knowledge and participation are not simply a reflection of individual choices but are shaped by systemic factors, occupational patterns, and societal norms. Specifically, interventions should be developed at three critical stages: (1) educational environments where equitable IP knowledge can be fostered and maintained; (2) workforce entry where institutional barriers and gendered specialization might reduce career opportunities, especially for those related to IP; and (3) career progression where recognition barriers might limit participation in IP. Policies aimed at increasing IP awareness, reducing biases, and supporting women in innovation are critical to unlocking the full potential of diverse talent in R&D. By addressing barriers at different stages, they can create a sustainable pipeline of women innovators, ensuring that IP knowledge translates into active participation in innovation ecosystems.

While this study provides valuable insights into the gender disparities in IP awareness and participation, several limitations should be acknowledged. First, the analysis relies on self-reported survey data, which may be subject to biases such as social desirability bias or differences in self-assessment across genders. (Although we cannot test for the former, our analysis of self-confidence and hesitance allows us to rule out the latter.) Moreover, while this study focuses on knowledge and perceptions, it does not assess how individuals apply IP knowledge in real-world contexts and, specifically, their understanding and actual usage of IP rights. Understanding whether increased awareness translates into higher engagement with the IP system is crucial for designing effective policies. Future research should focus on these aspects.

Acknowledgments

The views expressed herein are those of the authors and do not necessarily reflect the views of the World Intellectual Property Organization or its member states. The analysis presented in this chapter will be further expanded in a forthcoming working paper, Carlotta Nani, Martin Alejandro Correa & Julio Raffo, *Common Knowledge? A Cross-Country Analysis of Gender Differences in Awareness About IP rights from the WIPO Pulse Survey* (forthcoming).

Appendix

Table A.1. List of countries included in the survey, and corresponding sample size

African States		Asia-Pacific States		Eastern European States		Latin American and Caribbean States		Western Europe and Other States	
Algeria	559	Bangladesh	500	Azerbaijan	522	Argentina	500	Australia	500
Angola	501	China	501	Bulgaria	503	Brazil	500	France	501
Egypt, Arab Rep.	500	India	501	Croatia	506	Chile	501	Germany	503
Ghana	500	Indonesia	562	Czechia	500	Colombia	501	Italy	501
Kenya	530	Japan	500	Hungary	501	Jamaica	500	Spain	501
Mozambique	562	Pakistan	500	Kazakhstan	518	Mexico	500	Sweden	502
Nigeria	513	Republic of Korea	502	Lithuania	501	Panama	500	Switzerland	508
Senegal	502	Saudi Arabia	500	Poland	500	Peru	500	United Kingdom	507
South Africa	502	United Arab Emirates	500	Romania	501	Trinidad and Tobago	500	United States	501
Tanzania	504	Vietnam	504			Uruguay	500		
				Slovak Republic	506				
				Türkiye	500				

Note: The table reports the number of interviews completed for each country.

Table A.2. Average values of the outcome variables for the sample of men by countries' income level

	Subjective knowledge			Low self-confidence		
	High income	Middle income	Low income	High income	Middle income	Low income
Patents	0.4252	0.4517	0.4416	0.3399	0.2708	0.2048
Trademarks	0.5218	0.5805	0.6410	0.1474	0.1087	0.1088
Designs	0.3161	0.3680	0.4351	0.3403	0.2804	0.2561
Copyrights	0.5041	0.5539	0.6352	0.3541	0.3107	0.2485
Geo. indications	0.3098	0.3007	0.3552	0.2936	0.2227	0.2232
	Objective knowledge			**High self-confidence**		
	High income	Middle income	Low income	High income	Middle income	Low income
Patents	0.4441	0.3484	0.2384	0.3045	0.3483	0.3761
Trademarks	0.1395	0.1067	0.1224	0.4886	0.5462	0.5882
Designs	0.3565	0.2968	0.2729	0.2815	0.3286	0.3838
Copyrights	0.6286	0.5706	0.5268	0.2288	0.2874	0.3414
Geo. indications	0.3167	0.2139	0.2114	0.2617	0.2857	0.3312
	Hesitance			**Perceptions**		
	High income	Middle income	Low income	High income	Middle income	Low income
Patents	0.3920	0.4922	0.5436	0.6292	0.7388	0.7680
Trademarks	0.3383	0.3983	0.3609	0.6313	0.7687	0.8037
Designs	0.4451	0.5028	0.5514	0.6179	0.7198	0.7527
Copyrights	0.2264	0.3125	0.3585	0.6554	0.7660	0.8096
Geo. indications	0.3991	0.5138	0.5058	0.6717	0.7468	0.7635
Perceptions about IPRs in the economy				−0.1033	0.0571	0.0823

Note: The table reports the average values of the outcome variables for the sample of men.

Table A.3. Differences in hesitance by gender and countries' income level

Hesitance	Women	Men	*t*-test difference	Regression coefficients			
	Mean	Mean	(Women-Men)	Full sample	High income	Middle income	Low income
Patents	0.451 (0.006)	0.448 (0.005)	0.004	0.0066 (0.0094)	0.0107 (0.0122)	−0.0008 (0.0157)	−0.0124 (0.0265)
Trademarks	0.365 (0.010)	0.358 (0.010)	0.007	0.0150 (0.0156)	−0.0171 (0.0179)	0.0524 (0.0392)	0.0353 (0.0306)
Designs	0.447 (0.006)	0.485 (0.006)	−0.038***	−0.0360*** (0.0081)	−0.0583*** (0.0099)	−0.0057 (0.0108)	−0.0294 (0.0178)
Copyrights	0.268 (0.004)	0.281 (0.004)	−0.013**	−0.0106 (0.0083)	−0.0121 (0.0120)	−0.0067 (0.0130)	−0.0248 (0.0191)
Geo. indications	0.412 (0.006)	0.450 (0.006)	−0.038***	−0.0306*** (0.0110)	−0.0182 (0.0175)	−0.0402* (0.0187)	−0.0637*** (0.0127)

Note: The left panel reports the average hesitance when answering questions for the sample of women and men, as well as the difference between the sample averages using *t*-tests. The right panel reports the OLS regression coefficients. For each regression, the outcome variable is hesitance for each IP right (patents, trademarks, designs, copyrights, geographical indications, and overall). The coefficients reported are those corresponding to "being a woman." High income, Middle income, and Low income refer to the World Bank classification. Coefficients not reported: education, employment, age, household income, and rural or urban location. Each regression includes country fixed effect. Standard errors (in parenthesis) are clustered at the country level. The number of observations (not reported) ranges from 24,000 for the full sample, to 12,000 for high-income countries, to 6,000 for middle and low-income countries.

*** $p < 0.01$

** $p < 0.05$

* $p < 0.1$

II.

DISPARITIES IN THE PATENT SYSTEM

4

The Gender Gap in Academic Patenting

W. Michael Schuster, Miriam Marcowitz-Bitton, and Deborah R. Gerhardt

Introduction

Gender disparities in academia have long vexed institutions whose core responsibilities include promoting equality, inclusion, and success for all members of university communities. Integrating women into senior faculty positions is essential to promoting women's advancement in society. The possibility of attaining these positions encourages the pursuit of higher education and recognition of scholarly achievement. The rising percentage of women professors is often touted as proof of academia's success in promoting gender equity.[1]

With this in mind, we sought to learn more about women's academic success by examining the extent to which women transfer their knowledge from universities to industry. Identifying whether a gender gap exists in this domain is necessary to understand whether research universities are doing enough to promote equality in scientific inquiry and technology transfer. The U.S. academic sector provides an excellent case study because the United States is a world leader in scientific research and pioneered technology transfer beginning in the early 1960s.

Patent prosecution is often facilitated through university technology transfer offices that assist in securing patents to promote the commercialization of technology.[2] To measure the extent to which women's scientific discoveries are supported through this process, we examined how frequently women are named as inventors in university patent applications. We used

[1] *See, e.g.*, Bettina J. Casad, Jillian E. Franks, Christina E. Garasky, Melinda M. Kittleman, Alanna C. Roesler, Deidre Y. Hall & Zachary W. Petzel, *Gender Inequality in Academia: Problems and Solutions for Women Faculty in STEM*, 99 J. Neurosci. Rsch. 13, 16 (2020).

[2] David Orozco, *Assessing the Efficacy of the Bayh-Dole Act Through the Lens of University Technology Transfer Offices (TTOS)*, 21 N.C. J.L. & Tech. 115, 146 (2019).

W. Michael Schuster, Miriam Marcowitz-Bitton, and Deborah R. Gerhardt, *The Gender Gap in Academic Patenting*
In: *Inclusive Innovation in the Age of AI and Big Data*. Edited by: Daryl Lim and Peter K. Yu, Oxford University Press.
 DOI: 10.1093/9780197799444.003.0006

the inventor names listed in patent applications filed by universities to identify the likely gender of each inventor. From this information, we counted the number of patent applications that named women inventors alone or as part of a group. We then determined the rates at which those applications succeeded and associated metrics.

We are not, however, the first to address women's ownership of intellectual property rights. Many studies show a sizable gender gap in both patent applications and issued patents.[3] In the most comprehensive research to date, the World Intellectual Property Organization surveyed international patent applications in 182 countries and found that only 29 percent of them listed women as inventors.[4] Although this percentage has increased over time, it is still low relative to the population and differs substantially across countries, technologies, and sectors.

Research addressing the United States presents similar findings. Between 1977 and 2010, only 7.7 percent of U.S. patents named a woman as the lead inventor.[5] In 1977, only 3.4 percent of patents named at least one woman as an inventor,[6] while the rate had grown to 21.9 percent in 2019.[7] Notwithstanding this growth, women are still underrepresented as inventors named in patents.

Some of this disparity may be explained by underrepresentation in STEM (science, technology, engineering, and mathematics) fields generally and in patent-intensive fields specifically.[8] However, this disparity does not appear to account for the entire gender gap in patenting.

[3] Allie Porter, *Where Are the Women? The Gender Gap Within Intellectual Property*, 28 TEX. INTELL. PROP. L.J. 511, 512–16 (2020).

[4] Gema Lax Martinez, Julio Raffo & Kaori Saito, *Identifying the Gender of PCT Inventors* 8 (World Intell. Prop. Org., Econ. Rsch. Working Paper No. 33, 2016).

[5] JESSICA MILLI, EMMA WILLIAMS-BARON, MEIKA BERLAN, JENNY XIA & BARBARA GAULT, EQUITY IN INNOVATION: WOMEN INVENTORS AND PATENTS 8 n.2 (2016), https://iwpr.org/wp-content/uploads/2020/12/C448-Equity-in-Innovation.pdf; Jessica Milli, Barbara Gault, Emma Williams-Baron, Jenny Xia & Meika Berlan, *The Gender Patenting Gap* 2 (Inst. for Women's Pol'y Rsch., Briefing Paper No. C441, 2016), https://iwpr.org/wp-content/uploads/2020/12/C441_Gender-Patenting-Gap_BP-1.pdf.

[6] MILLI ET AL., *supra* note 5, at 7.

[7] U.S. Pat. & Trademark Off., Off. of the Chief Economist, *Progress and Potential: 2020 Update on U.S. Women Inventor-Patentees* (U.S. Patent & Trademark Off., Off. of the Chief Economist, IP Data Highlights No. 4, 2020).

[8] David Beede, Tiffany Julian, David Langdon, George Mckittrick, Beethika Khan & Mark Doms, *Women in STEM: A Gender Gap to Innovation* 2–3 (U.S. Dep't of Com., Econ. & Stat. Admin. Issue Brief No. 04-11, 2011); Lisa D. Cook & Chaleampong Kongcharoen, *The Idea Gap in Pink and Black* 2 (Nat'l Bureau of Econ. Rsch., Working Paper No. 16331, 2010).

Among college graduates, women are less likely to apply for a patent,[9] and they hold a disproportionately low number of positions in patent-intensive areas, such as development and design.[10] The Institute for Women's Policy Research found that, even if the current rate of progress holds, the United States will not reach gender parity in patenting until around 2092.[11]

Beyond trends in aggregate application filing, women also succeed less often when prosecuting their applications before the United States Patent and Trademark Office (USPTO). Research from Kyle Jensen, Balázs Kovács, and Olav Sorenson found that, even after accounting for differences in technological fields, women inventors were 7–21 percent less likely to secure a patent than men.[12] When women did secure a patent, the USPTO allowed fewer of their claims and disproportionately narrowed their claims so that claims in patents prosecuted by women ended up narrower in scope and potentially less valuable. Once granted, patents secured by women are cited less frequently, and their assignees are less likely to pay maintenance fees to maximize the duration of their patents.[13]

In academia, prior research found that women professors are less likely to seek and obtain patents than men, even in fields approaching gender parity.[14] A 2006 study by Waverly Ding, Fiona Murray, and Toby Stuart found that women faculty members in the American academy patent at about 40 percent of the rate of men.[15] Similarly, Rainer Frietsch, Inna Haller, Melanie Funken-Vrohlings, and Hariolf Grupp found that women scholars patent their research less frequently than they publish it.[16]

[9] MILLI ET AL., *supra* note 5, at 5; *see also* Zhang Qiantao, Mary Frank Fox, Shiri M. Breznitz & Talia Capozzoli Kessler, *Analyzing the Impact of Gender on Entrepreneurship and Innovation: Evidence from University Graduates*, 50 J. TECH. TRANSFER 1080 (2025), https://link.springer.com/article/10.1007/s10961-024-10128-z.

[10] Jennifer Hunt, Jean-Phillippe Garant, Hannah Herman & David J. Munroe, *Why Don't Women Patent?* 2 (Nat'l Bureau of Econ. Rsch., Working Paper No. 17888, 2012).

[11] MILLI ET AL., *supra* note 5, at 5.

[12] Kyle Jensen, Balázs Kovács & Olav Sorenson, *Gender Differences in Obtaining and Maintaining Patent Rights*, 36 NATURE BIOTECH. 307, 307 (2018); *see also* W. Michael Schuster, R. Evan Davis, Kourtenay Schley & Julie Ravenscraft, *An Empirical Study of Patent Grant Rates as a Function of Race and Gender*, 57 AM. BUS. L.J. 281, 306 (2020).

[13] Jensen et al., *supra* note 12, at 307.

[14] Annette I. Kahler, *Examining Exclusion in Woman-Inventor Patenting: A Comparison of Educational Trends and Patent Data in the Era of Computer Engineer Barbie*, 19 AM. U. J. GENDER, SOC. POL'Y & L. 773, 787–91 (2011).

[15] Waverly W. Ding, Fiona Murray & Toby E. Stuart, *Gender Differences in Patenting in the Academic Life Sciences*, 313 SCI. 665 (2006).

[16] Rainer Frietsch, Inna Haller, Melanie Funken-Vrohlings & Hariolf Grupp, *Gender-Specific Patterns in Patenting and Publishing*, 38 RSCH. POL'Y 590, 595 (2009).

Data Reflecting Academic Patent Applications

In this section, we explain our methodology and our approach to quantifying women academics' interaction with the patent system. We began by identifying patent applications filed by university researchers,[17] the gender of named inventors, and other relevant information. Next, we coded patent filings for gender, grant status, technology classification, forward citations, and filing years. We also describe the challenges we faced in identifying university applications, limitations of our approach, and why these limitations do not introduce bias into our data. After explaining our methodology in greater detail, we present our findings.

Analysis of Patent Applications

Patent applications reveal a trove of information about new inventions. To meet the specification requirements for issuance, a patent application must instruct a person having ordinary skill in the relevant field how to recreate and use the disclosed technology. This requirement fulfills one of the core missions of patent law—to promote the progress of science by contributing new inventions to human knowledge through public dissemination. Beyond disclosure of the new knowledge, an application includes the names of the inventors and may also identify who acquired their rights by assignment.

This information facilitates quantitative analysis of inventor collaboration, demographic information, and technology transfer.[18] From large datasets containing this information, we devised means for locating patent applications filed by research universities and analyzed this data to identify trends in inventor team composition, fields of innovation, and inventor demographics. However, findings based on patent prosecution data have some limitations.

While patent applications identify inventors and describe inventions, they show us only a narrow snapshot of the broad innovation ecosystem. Some inventors and their assignees choose to maintain their discoveries as trade secrets or forgo filing a patent application for other reasons. A cost-benefit analysis may favor the choice to forego patent prosecution; in such cases,

[17] University researchers include academic staff as well as student researchers.

[18] *See, e.g.*, Richard Gruner, *The Golden West: Influential Innovation from the San Francisco Region Revealed in Patent Records*, 20 Tul. J. Tech. & Intell. Prop. 43, 66 (2017).

data about the innovation will not be reflected in patent datasets.[19] Assigning all patents equal weight presents another limitation because not all patents reflect the same inventive contributions. A patent can protect multiple radical innovations or a single incremental improvement to prior technology. These concerns should not, however, prevent us from effectively studying patenting trends within the university system.

Data Collection

Our primary source of data was the USPTO's Office of the Chief Economist (OCE) Patent Assignment Dataset.[20] The version we analyzed contained data on utility patents from 2001 to 2016 and was updated with grant data through 2019.[21]

To focus our analysis on academics within a digestible number of universities, we limited our dataset to the top 250 universities[22] by research expenditures for the financial year 2019.[23] Consistent with past USPTO research on university patenting, we then matched university names (or their known patent-holding entity names) with assignee names in the database.

Identifying universities within the assignment data was a multistep process. We initially ran a search identifying assignments with terms indicating academic involvement, such as "university," "college," or "academy." Next, we culled the data to include only assignees that shared a relevant term with a university included in the study—for example, assignee names including the word "Oregon" were included because of "Oregon State University" and

[19] Org. for Econ. Coop. & Dev., OECD Patent Statistics Manual 27–28 (2009).

[20] *Patent Assignment Dataset*, U.S. Pat. & Trademark Off., https://www.uspto.gov/ip-policy/economic-research/research-datasets/patent-assignment-dataset (June 13, 2022).

[21] The patent grant data was through August 2019 and came from the USPTO's PatentsView dataset. We omitted plant patents, design patents, and reissued patents from the data. This dataset comprises self-reported patent ownership information, including assignment, security interests, name changes, and firm mergers. Each filing includes ownership information on one or more patents, including the name of the party obtaining the interest in the patent. We initially associated these filings with the patent application(s) relevant to that document. Likewise, filings were identified as being an assignment or a recording of some other property interest—for example, a security interest or patentee name change. Data unrelated to assignments was discarded because it is irrelevant to application ownership.

[22] The 250-university threshold was adopted from prior USPTO research. *U.S. Colleges and Universities—Utility Patent Grants 1969–2012*, U.S. Pat. & Trademark Off., https://www.uspto.gov/web/offices/ac/ido/oeip/taf/univ/doc/doc_info_2012.htm [hereinafter *U.S. Colleges and Universities*].

[23] *Higher Education Research and Development: Fiscal Year 2019*, Nat'l Sci. Found. (Jan. 29, 2021), https://ncses.nsf.gov/pubs/nsf21314#data-tables.

"University of Oregon." We then manually reviewed the list and excluded any non-university assignees. This approach is consistent with the methodology used by other researchers.[24]

One challenge we faced is that universities may report ownership of patents under various names.[25] While such variation poses some difficulty in identifying all university applications, it is not a critical drawback. We were interested in trends over time, not simply reporting the number of applications filed. Therefore, while our data may not include every relevant application, we can still achieve our goal of recognizing trends and patterns.[26]

After identifying the scope of applications assigned to universities, we excluded applications that did not name university researchers as inventors. For example, patents that were assigned to a university by some entity outside the institution are not representative of academic patenting and, thus, are excluded from our data. We used the OCE dataset's "employer assignment" code to identify employee-to-employer assignments.[27] Using this coding, we excluded applications that were not assigned to a university via an employee-to-employer assignment.[28] We included an application in our data if at least one academic inventor signed an employee-to-employer assignment. This strategy made it possible to collect data on inventors who are professors (or other academic researchers, like graduate students) at colleges and universities.

Next, we created two distinct datasets. The first set identified all university applications and the inventors who signed "employer assignments." This data identified university inventors, to the exclusion of non-university inventors (who may have signed later assignments to other entities). We call this the "University Researcher Only Dataset," as it excluded non-university inventors. Using this dataset, we identified trends in the attributes of university inventors and their patenting activities.

[24] *U.S. Colleges and Universities*, *supra* note 22.

[25] Examples include "JOHNS HOPKINS UNIVERSITY, THE, A NOT-FOR-PROFIT CORP. OF MD.," and "JOHNS HOPKINS UNIVERSITY, A CORP. OF MD."

[26] This approach proved robust. As described in our prior research, this approach provided data with a strong correlation to prior USPTO work. Deborah R. Gerhardt, Miriam Marcowitz-Bitton & W. Michael Schuster, *The Gender Gap in Academic Patenting*, 56 U.C. DAVIS L. REV. 759, 789 fig.1 (2022).

[27] Alan C. Marco, Amanda F. Myers, Stuart Graham, Paul D'Agostino & Kirsten Apple, *The USPTO Patent Assignment Dataset: Descriptions and Analysis* 11 (U.S. Pat. & Trademark Off., Econ. Working Paper No. 2015-2, 2015) (describing the available data).

[28] For further information on this choice, see Gerhardt et al., *supra* note 26, at 790–92.

Due to its exclusion of inventors from outside the academy, the University Researcher Only Dataset did not allow us to study inventor team attributes comprising both university and non-university inventors. Because we were interested in learning about the presence of women on inventor teams, we created a second dataset, the All Inventor Dataset, that includes *all* inventors named on applications assigned to a university.

After the two datasets were created, we began the work of estimating the gender of each inventor. The USPTO does not collect gender data from patent applicants, and due to the large size of the dataset, hand-coding was not feasible. Accordingly, we adopted a method common in the literature: identifying gender from each inventor's name.[29]

We used data from the Gender API website,[30] which contains gender data for over six million names from 189 countries. We uploaded the first name and country of residence for each inventor, and Gender API associated over 96 percent of inventors with the likelihood that someone with that name is of a particular gender.

Next, we assigned each inventor name a binary gender code if the likelihood of that gender exceeded 50 percent.[31] We then coded each application for which the gender of all inventors was available and sorted them into categories of only women inventors (Women Only), only male inventors (Men Only), or inventors who are men and women (Mixed Genders).[32]

Descriptive Analysis

Our initial findings reflected a dramatic increase in patent applications filed by university researchers since 2000. Between 2001 and 2015, the number

[29] *See, e.g.*, Jensen et al., *supra* note 12, at 307; Schuster et al., *supra* note 12, at 295–98; William Michael Schuster, Miriam Marcowitz-Bitton & Deborah R. Gerhardt, *An Empirical Study of Gender and Race in Trademark Prosecution*, 94 S. Cal. L. Rev. 1407, 1433–34 (2021).

[30] Gender API, https://gender-api.com/ (last visited Feb. 12, 2022).

[31] There may be miscoding in some instances, but given the size of the dataset and the nonsystemic nature of any miscoding, it is safe to assume that the miscodings will largely cancel out.

[32] As a robustness check for the use of Gender API, we took a sample of 100 patents assigned to research universities and randomly pulled one inventor's name for each patent. We then conducted a Google search to identify the apparent gender of the inventor through an online photo or gendered pronoun. We also ran those 100 first names and the inventor's location through Gender API, which returned a gender for ninety-seven of the names. Of those ninety-seven, the perceived gender of ninety-four was identified via Google search. Of those ninety-four, Gender API coded ninety-one of them correctly (96.8 percent). This robustness check supports the validity of our approach.

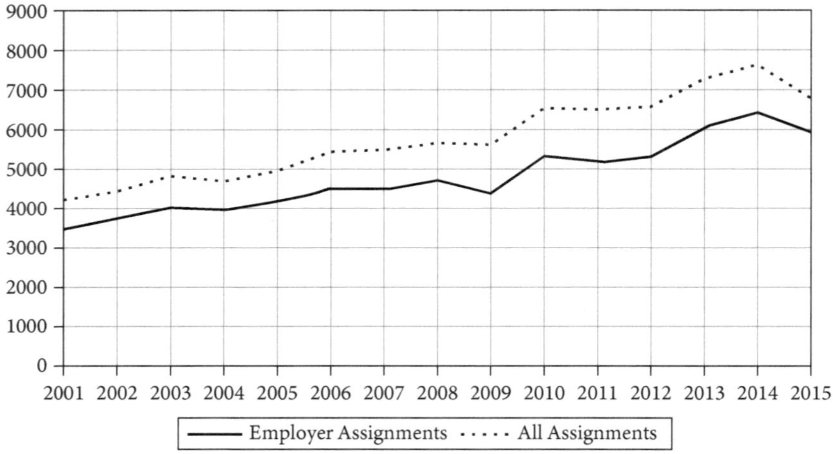

Figure 4.1. University patent applications by year

of employer-assigned university applications increased over 70 percent.[33] Figure 4.1 illustrates the distribution of patent applications filed by the top 250 U.S. research universities (by research-and-development (R&D) expenditures) from 2001 to 2015.[34] For robustness purposes, Figure 4.1 includes applications that were transferred to universities via employee-to-employer assignments and via any assignment (from an employee or otherwise). The correlation between the two groups is high (0.991).

Figure 4.2 depicts the gender profiles of inventor teams by year. This analysis draws from the All Inventor Dataset, as we are interested in the breakdown of the entire inventor group, not just the inventors employed by the university. The graph shows the number of applications filed annually between 2001 and 2014.

As illustrated in Figure 4.2, teams of all men (light gray) constitute the greatest percentage of academic patent applications filed each year. However, teams including women gained ground over time. The number of applications filed by all-women teams (dark gray) and mixed-gender teams (medium gray) doubled over this fifteen-year period. The number of applications filed by men-only teams also increased, but not at the same rate.

[33] Applications filed on or after November 29, 2000, are, with certain limitations, available for inspection eighteen months after filing. 35 U.S.C. § 122(b)(1)(A). Accordingly, we started our analysis in 2001.

[34] The filing year was the actual filing year of each application (not the effective filing year).

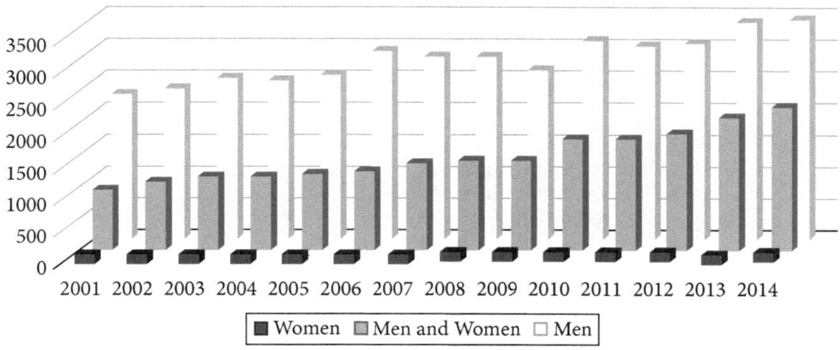

Figure 4.2. Gender profiles of inventor teams, 2001–2014

Table 4.1. Comparison of patent applications to granted patents, 2001–2015 application year

Group	Patent applications	Granted patents	Grant Rate (%)
Women Only	2,105	1,244	59.10
Men Only	41,980	28,622	68.18
Mixed Genders	22,394	14,340	64.04
Total	66,519	44,238	66.50

Recognizing the significant disparities in the aggregate rate of application filings shown in Figure 4.2, we will next evaluate how often applications are granted. Table 4.1 sets forth the total grant rate for patent applications filed by university inventors between 2001 and 2015 and also the totals for teams that are mixed genders, women only, and men only.[35]

The results show that men working with other men (or alone) have the highest grant rate. While 68.18 percent of patent applications filed by teams of only men were granted, the mixed-gender teams had a 64.04 percent rate and teams of only women had a 59.10 percent grant rate. This disparity is an important topic for further research to determine whether this difference may be explained by subject matter, bias, or other variables.

[35] This is by actual year filed, not priority date.

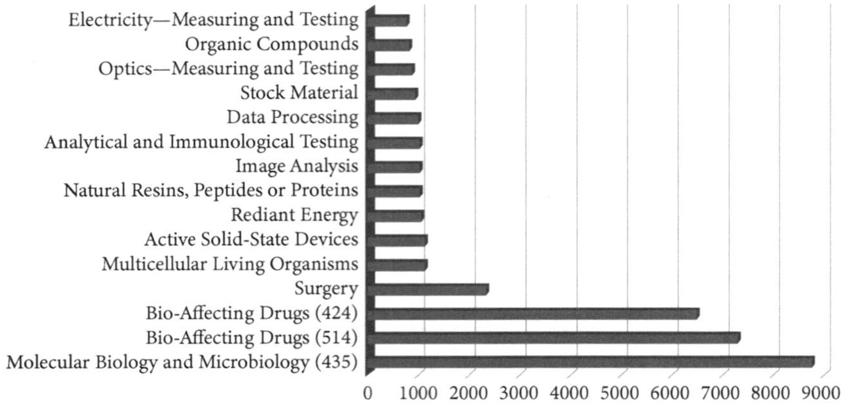

Figure 4.3. Applications filed by USPC class, 2001–2014

Figure 4.3 describes university inventor applications by United States Patent Class (USPC) for the top fifteen most popular technological classes out of 370 represented in the data.[36] The substantial skew toward the bottom of the figure is notable, with the largest three classes (USPC Classes 435, 514, and 424) accounting for 36 percent of all filings. The second and third classes (USPC Classes 514 and 424, both including "drug, bio-affecting and body treating compositions") are largely interchangeable, with 514 being "considered to be an integral part of Class 424" by the USPTO.[37] The skew toward a few classes continues throughout the data with 74.1 percent of all applications falling in 10 percent of the classes represented and 86.7 percent being represented in 20 percent of the classes.

The findings depicted in Figure 4.3 are notable in comparison to patents issued to the general public. The three dominant classes in university applications (435, 514, and 424) were the sixth, fourth, and ninth most common classes among all patents issued from 2001 to 2014.[38]

Figure 4.4 displays the number of patent applications filed by teams of only men, only women, and mixed genders from 2001 to 2014 in the ten most common USPC classes.

[36] USPC data collected from the OCE's application_data_2015 dataset.

[37] *Class 514 Drug, Bio-Affecting and Body Treating Compositions*, U.S. Pat. & Trademark Off., https://www.uspto.gov/web/patents/classification/uspc514/sched514.htm (last visited Feb. 13, 2022).

[38] *Patent Counts by Class by Year January 1977–December 2015*, U.S. Pat. & Trademark Off., https://www.uspto.gov/web/offices/ac/ido/oeip/taf/cbcby.htm (last visited Feb. 13, 2022).

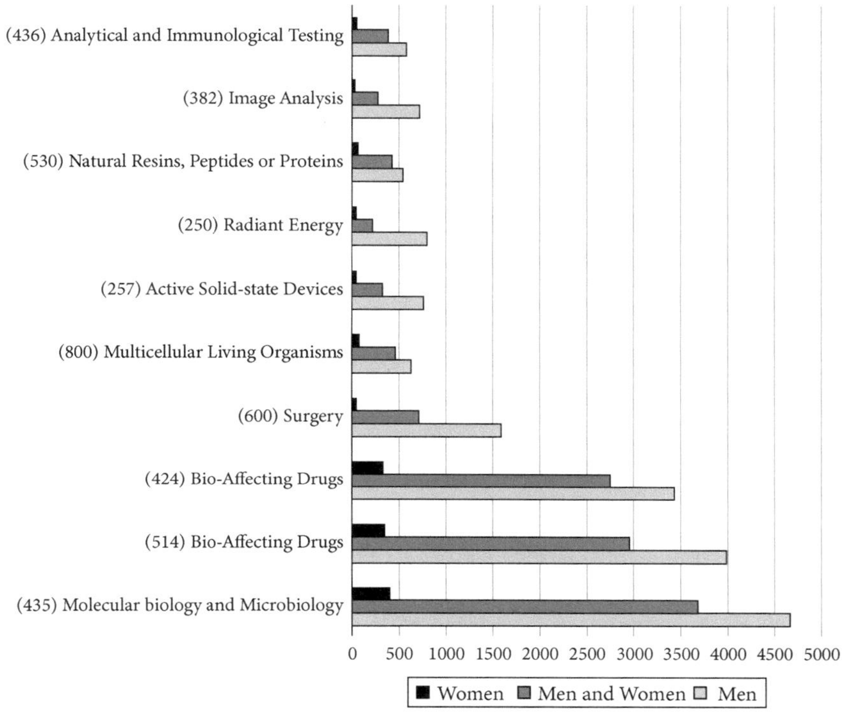

Figure 4.4. Gender composition of inventor teams in top ten patent application fields

Figure 4.4 illustrates that chemistry (molecular biology and microbiology) and drug classes have been the dominant fields of innovation for teams of only men, only women, and mixed genders.

Teams of only women accounted for 4.10 percent of the applications across these top ten USPC classes, compared with 3.15 percent in the aggregate. Classes 800 (multicellular living organisms and unmodified parts thereof and related processes) and 530 (chemistry: natural resins or derivatives; peptides or proteins; lignins or reaction products thereof) had the highest rates of women inventor teams: 5.74 and 5.49 percent, respectively. Classes 600 (surgery), 257 (active solid-state devices—e.g., transistors, solid-state diodes), and 382 (image analysis) reflected the lowest representation of women inventor teams. In these fields, teams of women filed less than 1.80 percent of patent applications.

Figure 4.5 shows the top ten USPC classes for applications from women inventor teams at universities from 2001 to 2014.

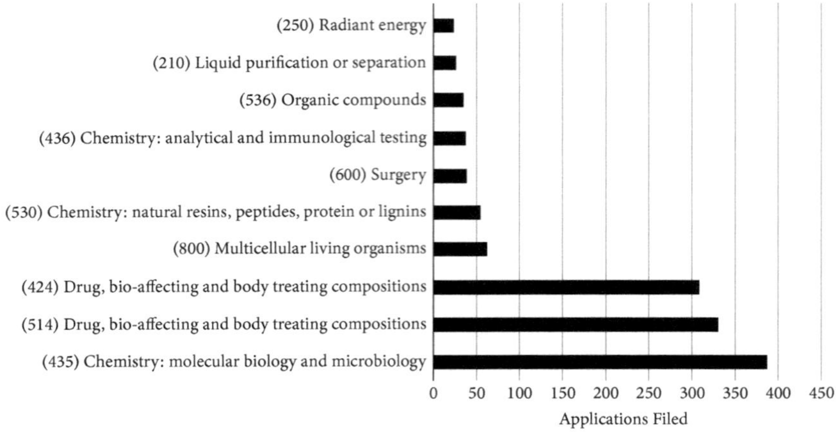

Figure 4.5. Top ten fields naming only women as inventors in patent applications

Consistent with Figure 4.4 (detailing all university applications by USPC class), chemistry (molecular biology and microbiology, USPC Class 435) and pharmaceuticals (bio-affecting and body treating compositions, USPC Classes 514 and 424) dominate applications by women inventor teams.

Table 4.2 breaks down citation patterns for granted patents arising from applications filed from 2001 to 2015 (as of August 2019) for the different inventor gender categories. Forward citations serve as a measure of patent quality in the literature, and therefore, it is important to explore this measure in our dataset.[39]

Table 4.2 shows that 89.32 percent of patents filed by teams of women have been cited ten or fewer times, compared with 86.60 percent for mixed-gender teams and 82.69 percent for teams of men. We see a general trend of patents with male inventors being cited more often than those with female inventors. Within our data, teams of men were cited more often than those of women and mixed genders in every category (except for ten or fewer citations). Likewise, mixed-gender patents were cited more often than those prosecuted by women in all categories except 81–90 citations and ten or fewer citations.

One possible explanation for women's lower citation rates may be that a larger percentage of patents with all-male inventors issued earlier (as

[39] W. Michael Schuster & Kristen Green Valentine, *An Empirical Analysis of Patent Citation Relevance and Applicant Strategy*, 59 Am. Bus. L.J. 231 (2022).

Table 4.2. Percentage of patents by forward citations count by inventor team breakdown

Cites	Men (%)	Women (%)	Mixed (%)
0–10	82.69	89.32	86.60
11–20	7.85	6.10	6.62
21–30	3.43	2.09	2.68
31–40	1.92	0.96	1.35
41–50	1.11	0.64	0.67
51–60	0.66	0.32	0.52
61–70	0.45	0.08	0.36
71–80	0.37	0.08	0.22
81–90	0.32	0.24	0.20
91–100	0.17	0.00	0.13
over 100	1.02	0.16	0.67

male-only grants have been increasing at a slower rate than the others). Therefore, a greater number of male-only patents had a longer period to attract citations.

To check whether longevity may account for this difference, we ran the same data for patents granted in 2010 and 2015, so all relevant patents would have had the same amount of time to garner citations. Our findings were largely consistent. For the 2010 group, ignoring the ten or fewer citation group, the group of women inventors had the largest percentage of patents with 31–40 and 41–50 citations, and the mixed group had the largest percentage of patents with 71–80 and over 100 citations. For the 2015 group, ignoring the ten or fewer citation group, the all-male group was equal to or greater than the other groups in every category except 11–20 citations, where the mixed group was less than 0.02 percent ahead of the male-only group. Therefore, even accounting for the possibility that older patents will have more citations, inventor groups that included men had citation rates exceeding those of women inventor groups.

Additionally, we analyzed the breakdown of inventor groups by gender and team size. For this analysis, we evaluated all university applications in the All Inventor Dataset between 2001 and 2014 for which gender data was available for all inventors. Unsurprisingly, the percentage of patent applications with some missing gender information continues to climb as the number of inventors goes up. Thus, we acted in accordance with past

Table 4.3. Distribution of applications with 2–4 inventors by group

Group	No. of applications	Percentage (%)
Men Only	27,472	62.84
Women Only	705	1.61
Mixed Genders	15,538	35.54
Total	43,715	100

Table 4.4. Inventor team size (men- and women-only)

	Men-only teams		Women-only teams	
Inventors on team	Application count	Percentage (%)	Application Count	Percentage (%)
4	4,352	11.92	23	1.17
3	8,561	23.45	110	5.61
2	14,559	39.87	572	29.17
1	9,041	24.76	1,256	64.05
4 or less	36,513	1	1,961	1

research and only analyzed teams with four or fewer inventors because using larger inventor groups would have required eliminating more than 10 percent of applications due to missing inventor gender data. Our data included 43,715 applications naming 2–4 inventors with the distributions shown in Table 4.3.

Next, we analyzed inventor-team breakdown by size for groups of only men (left side of table) and only women (right side of table)—including single inventor teams, which were not included in Table 4.3. The inventor-team size distribution is shown in Table 4.4.

Surprisingly, this analysis revealed a significant deviation in the prevalence of solo invention by gender for men- and women-only inventor teams.[40] Over 60 percent of patent applications filed by women-only teams name solo inventors, compared with less than 25 percent of patent applications filed by men.

[40] Similar findings have been made regarding non-professor patenting. Bridget Diakun, *Data Reveals Strong Growth in the Number of Female Inventors, but There Is Still a Long Way to Go*, IAM

Looking to mixed-gender teams, we see that group size tends to be well distributed, with two-, three-, and four-member teams accounting for 34.18, 38.18, and 27.64 percent, respectively. Consistent with the general under-representation of women in our data, it was not surprising to see that male-majority teams are significantly more common than female-majority teams. Among mixed-gender teams with three inventors, groups of two men (and one woman) occur more than three times as often (3.77:1 ratio) as groups of two women (and one man). Looking at four-member teams, teams of three men (and one woman) are more than ten times (13.58:1 ratio) as common as teams of three women (and one man).

Our analysis so far has focused on the All Inventor Dataset, which gives us information about all inventors named on applications assigned to research universities. However, we now turn to the University Researcher Only Dataset, which only includes data on individuals that signed an employer assignment to a research university, indicating they are professors or researchers. Figure 4.6 depicts the percentage of named inventors[41] who are women from 2001 to 2016 by application year.

To check this data, we compared our findings with contemporaneous research conducted by Jordana Goodman.[42] She reported the percentage of female inventors on patents granted to schools in four groups. The groups and percentage of women inventors from 2000 to 2015 were as follows: Ivy League colleges (14.4 percent), highly ranked schools outside of the Historically Black Colleges and Universities (HBCU) system with the most tenured Black faculty (17.5 percent), HBCUs (20.1 percent), and research institutions (12.3 percent). Our annual data from 2001 to 2016 was largely consistent, finding that women represented 14–19 percent of named inventors from universities annually.

Analyzing the data further, Figure 4.6 notably shows an increase in the percentage of named inventors who are women over the period studied. However, data shows that the number of university researchers—for

(Oct. 11, 2019), https://www.iam-media.com/patents/data-reveals-strong-growth-number-female-inventors-there-still-long-way-go.

[41] Figure 4.6 depicts the percentage of named inventors whose gender could be identified by their name.

[42] Jordana R. Goodman, *Sy-STEM-ic Bias: An Exploration of Gender and Race Representation on University Patents*, 87 Brook. L. Rev. 853, 882–84 (2022).

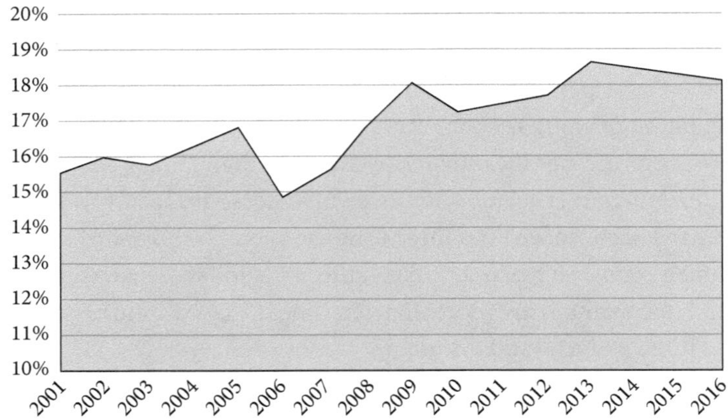

Figure 4.6. Percentage of women inventors named in patent applications, 2001–2016

example, professors—who are women increased over the same period.[43] To compare the relative output of university researchers and professors by gender, data on women's representation within the university as a whole must be ascertained. Ideally, annual data would be available on women's representation in science and engineering faculty at research universities, mimicking our dataset. Unfortunately, this ideal data was not available.

However, one study provided a snapshot of the gender breakdown of science and engineering professors at top research universities for the year 2002.[44] It found that "14.8 percent of the faculty members in top science and engineering research departments are female."[45] That data is similar to our finding that women represented 15.96 percent of named researchers from universities in 2002 (and 15.78 and 16.25 percent in 2003 and 2004, respectively).

[43] *See, e.g.*, Brian L. Yoder, Am. Soc'y for Eng'g Educ., *Engineering by the Numbers* 32, https://aseecmsduq.blob.core.windows.net/aseecmsdev/asee/media/content/papers%20and%20publications/pdfs/16profile-front-section.pdf (last visited Feb. 13, 2022) (showing an increase in the percentage of female engineering professors from 2007 to 2016). The National Science Foundation data is similar. *Survey of Doctorate Recipients Survey Year 2017*, Nat'l Sci. Found. (Feb. 2019), https://ncsesdata.nsf.gov/doctoratework/2017/ (percentage calculated from table 17 data). This was a slight increase from the 2013 finding of 36.4 percent from the same survey. *Survey of Doctorate Recipients Survey Year 2013*, Nat'l Sci. Found. (Sept. 2014), https://ncsesdata.nsf.gov/doctoratework/2013/ (percentage calculated from table 17 data).

[44] Ann M. Beutel & Donna J. Nelson, *The Gender and Race-Ethnicity of Faculty in Top Science and Engineering Research Departments*, 11 J. Women & Minorities Sci. & Eng'g 389 (2005).

[45] *Id.* at 391.

This finding suggests an equal use of the patent system by university researchers regardless of gender. In contrast, recent research by Goodman analyzed a subset of 719 university patents, compared with the percentage of women on the respective schools' faculty, and reported a disparity in patenting rates by gender between 2000 and 2015.[46] Specifically, she found a significant overrepresentation of male professors among named inventors. These disparate preliminary findings indicate that this topic warrants further research.

Primary Findings

Our primary findings are as follows.

First, academic patenting is on the rise. Patent applications originating from universities increased significantly between 2000 and 2015.

Second, inventor teams that included women had patents granted at a lower rate than teams of only men. Teams of all women had the lowest grant rate, mixed teams fared better, and teams of all men had the highest grant rate. The differences between male-only and women-only teams requires further research to understand the reason for their differences and their robustness.

Third, we found that three USPC classes—consisting of drugs and chemistry (molecular biology)—dominate the technological classes of all types of inventor groups.

Fourth, patents from men-only inventors teams tend to be cited more often than those from women-only and mixed-gender teams.

Fifth, we found that there are many more men-only teams than women-only teams, with mixed-gender teams in the middle. This finding is consistent with work showing that researchers tend to work with people of the same gender,[47] as well as literature showing that most university STEM professors are men.[48] Men-only teams were most likely to work in pairs (about 40 percent), but groups of one and three inventors were also common

[46] Goodman, *supra* note 42, at 886–87.

[47] Luke Holman & Claire Morandin, *Researchers Collaborate with Same-Gendered Colleagues More Often than Expected Across the Life Sciences*, 14 PLOS ONE 1, 9 (Apr. 26, 2019), https://www.ncbi.nlm.nih.gov/pmc/articles/PMC6485756/.

[48] Negin Sattari & Rebecca L. Sandefur, *Gender in Academic STEM: A Focus on Men Faculty*, 26 GENDER, WORK & ORG. 158, 158 & n.1 (2019).

(about 24 percent). In contrast, almost two-thirds of women working in all-women teams filed as solo inventors. Mixed-gender teams tended to be two or three people, though groups of four were not uncommon.

Sixth, women academic inventorship has increased over time. However, due to a lack of historical and current data on the representation of female academic researchers in STEM in the U.S. academy, we are unable to determine whether their representation among patentees correlates with their representation in the academy. More research and data in this field is required.

Seventh, the percentage of women participating in academic patenting exceeds women's patenting participation percentage in the United States generally and worldwide. Indeed, our study reveals that women were named as an inventor in 36.5 percent of applications filed by U.S. universities from 2001 to 2014, which is greater than the 29 percent total representation worldwide reported in prior literature.[49] The percentage of American women's academic patenting is also higher than the overall representation of women in patenting worldwide (7.2 percent) and in the United States (8.7 percent).[50]

Proposals

Based on our findings, we recommend the following proposals to better understand the gender gap in patenting and how it may be remediated. More research on global trends should be conducted. While much empirical research focuses on the U.S. market, fewer studies delve into international trends, making it difficult to discern which countries are closing the gender gap and why.

The following initiatives may also help close the gender gap in academic and general patenting:

- *Changes to patent law and policy*. Potential changes include addressing subject matter eligibility criteria, the patent prosecution process (e.g., blind review of patent applications with inventors' names redacted, reduced fees for small businesses, and government guidance through

[49] However, the Martinez, Raffo, and Saito study examined only PCT applications. Martinez et al., *supra* note 4, at 9.

[50] UK Intell. Prop. Off., Gender Profiles in Worldwide Patenting: An Analysis of Female Inventorship 30 (2016).

the process) and introduction of an unregistered patent system to provide more egalitarian protection, which may reduce the patenting gender gap.[51]

- *Introducing data tools to track women's patenting activity.* The lack of available data on the gender of inventors makes research on this subject far more challenging than it would be if the USPTO collected demographic information on inventors. Compounding the absence of inventor data, there is no systematic collection of data on women in STEM in the U.S. academy. To better understand women's patenting activity and make decisions about potential policy solutions, it is crucial to collect data systematically on women in STEM fields in the U.S. academy and to establish methods for studying demographics, such as voluntary surveys and other methods.
- *Developing networks of support services for inventors.* While different resources are available to women in the United States, a comprehensive database of resources could help women and men inventors in all sectors secure assistance in the patenting process.
- *Fostering networks for women entrepreneurs and inventors.* Women often lack mentors and networking opportunities, making it more difficult for them to advance professionally.[52] A 2016 study found that having industry contacts is the most important factor for getting women more involved in patenting.[53] Mentorship and networking programs could be implemented to support research conducted by women. Networks are extremely helpful for inventors and provide industry contacts, access to funding sources, technical assistance with research and development, and opportunities to collaborate on projects. Promoting awareness and familiarity with different networks can promote women's engagement within these groups and lead to increased access to resources and opportunities for collaboration.
- *Supporting efforts to increase women's interest in STEM fields.* Women are still underrepresented among STEM degree holders globally, and women are substantially underrepresented in particular fields in the

[51] Miriam Marcowitz-Bitton, Yotam Kaplan & Emily Michiko Morris, *Unregistered Patents & Gender Equality*, 43 Harv. J.L. & Gender 47, 73 (2020); Miriam Marcowitz-Bitton & Emily Michiko Morris, *The Distributive Effects of IP Registration*, 23 Stan. Tech. L. Rev. 306, 362–63 (2020).

[52] Andie Kramer, *Women Need Mentors Now More than Ever*, Forbes (July 14, 2021), https://www.forbes.com/sites/andiekramer/2021/07/14/women-need-mentors-now-more-than-ever/.

[53] Yu Meng, *Collaboration Patterns and Patenting: Exploring Gender Distinctions*, 45 Rsch. Pol'y 56, 64 (2015).

United States, such as engineering. Therefore, another solution is to encourage girls in middle and high schools to be involved in STEM to prepare them for studying STEM subjects in college. When both boys and girls were asked to draw a scientist, girls were twice as likely to draw a man scientist than a woman.[54] Seventy percent of six-year-old girls drew women scientists, but only 25 percent of sixteen-year-old girls did so.[55] As girls get older, they often lose the courage to enter the STEM world, so it is vital to support girls who want to enter STEM at a young age and keep that support in place during middle and high school. Interpersonal interventions (such as mentorship, outreach, and campaigns against stereotypes) and systematic changes (such as enforcing policies against discrimination and harassment in hiring, promotion, and tenure decisions) should also be employed to address the gap.

- *Supporting family responsibilities.* Research in the United States and elsewhere shows that one of the most significant challenges facing women academic scientists is balancing work and family obligations.[56] STEM faculties in universities often emphasize the importance of keeping up with academic standards and having total devotion to the field. This mentality makes it difficult for women to set aside time to raise children at early stages in their careers. Therefore, institutions need to find ways to support women who would like to work in STEM and have a family. Family-oriented policies, such as pausing the tenure clock for maternity leaves, are important changes that can help recruit and retain more women in science. Women outside of academia face similar issues. In recognizing the importance of family-oriented workplace policies in attracting and retaining talented women and men, employers should consider offering paid maternity and paternity leave.
- *Creating a variety of institutional incentives to apply for patents.* Waverly Ding, Fiona Murray, and Toby Stuart show that gender differences in attitudes toward patenting exist.[57] Women academic scientists report

[54] Carly Berwick, *Keeping Girls in STEM: 3 Barriers, 3 Solutions*, Edutopia (Mar. 12, 2019), https://www.edutopia.org/article/keeping-girls-stem-3-barriers-3-solutions.

[55] Youki Terada, *50 Years of Children Drawing Scientists*, Edutopia (May 22, 2019), https://www.edutopia.org/article/50-years-children-drawing-scientists.

[56] Vicky J. Rosser, *Faculty Members' Intentions to Leave: A National Study on Their Worklife and Satisfaction*, 45 Rsch. Higher Educ. 285, 289–90 (2004).

[57] Ding et al., *supra* note 15, at 665–66.

that patenting activity requires the cost of less time with students, teaching, and university obligations. Men, by contrast, are more likely to state that commercial activity complements their teaching. Fiona Murray and Leigh Graham[58] found that many women scientists were ambivalent about commercial science and expressed reservations about the practice. Institutional policies supporting commercialization and metrics for how such activities factor into the promotion and tenure process could help assuage women's reservations and provide guidance on how the university views patenting activity. For example, in 2006, Texas A&M University approved a measure to include inventions in its promotion and tenure decisions. Since then, many universities have followed suit. The ever-increasing market value for patenting supports making it a measure of success in STEM fields. Additionally, behavioral changes, such as requiring inventors to report whether their inventions are patentable, could encourage more reflection on the possibility of patent prosecution.

- *Funding opportunities for women.* Another explanation for the gender gap in patenting may be related to venture capital funding. Around 76 percent of venture capital investors consider patents when determining which companies to fund.[59] Although around 36.3 percent of all businesses in the United States are owned by women, only 3 percent of venture capital funding went to businesses with a woman CEO between 2011 and 2013.[60] Men who own businesses are significantly more likely than women to receive outsider equity to fund their businesses.[61] Outside funding is extremely important for businesses going through the patenting process because it can be lengthy and expensive. A patent that lasts twelve or more years can have maintenance fees ranging from $3,000 to over $12,000, plus attorney's fees. The lack of funding makes it difficult for women-owned businesses to meet the high costs of patent prosecution.

58 Fiona Murray & Leigh Graham, *Buying Science and Selling Science: Gender Differences in the Market for Commercial Science*, 16 Indus. & Corp. Change 657, 682 (2007).

59 Milli et al., *supra* note 5, at 7.

60 *Id.*

61 Alicia Robb, Small Bus. Admin., Access to Capital Among Young Firms, Minority-Owned Firms, Women-Owners Firms, and High-Tech Firms 17 table 4 (2013), https://www.sba.gov/sites/default/files/files/rs403tot(2).pdf.

- *Implementing initiatives to enhance gender equality generally.* Women in STEM often report feeling ignored, discriminated against, and sexually harassed in the workplace.[62] Institutions with this dynamic should take concrete steps to change their behavior to create a welcoming and inclusive environment for women. Educational and social initiatives to support gender equality generally, and women inventors specifically, would also help narrow the patenting gender gap.

Finally, in October 2021, President Joe Biden nominated Kathi Vidal to be the next USPTO Director. On April 5, 2022, the Senate confirmed this nomination, making Vidal the second female director of the Office in U.S. history. In addition to serving as an inspirational role model, she initiated multiple programs to encourage more women to see themselves as potential leaders in intellectual property–intensive fields.

Conclusion

This study explores a dimension of the gender gap in academia that is often overlooked. Although past studies have examined the disparity in men's and women's representation among faculty in various contexts, our study empirically examines differences in men's and women's participation in technology transfer from academia to industry. Specifically, we examine the gender of inventors named in U.S. patent applications and find that a substantial gender gap exists both in the number of patent applications and how often women's inventions are cited by others.

These findings call for further research to examine the reasons these gaps exist and formulate solutions for optimizing academic women's inventive work. Faculty inventors often earn royalties from commercializing their patents. Accordingly, women's low rate of participation in patenting activity has tangible financial consequences: As a group, women faculty members benefit less than their male colleagues from these financial rewards. Therefore, women's lower representation in patenting may be contributing to the gender pay gap in the general workforce. Moreover, the low integration of women into knowledge transfer activities and patent commercialization

[62] Emmeline de Pillis & Lisette de Pillis, *Are Engineering Schools Masculine and Authoritarian? The Mission Statements Say Yes*, 1 J. Diversity Higher Educ. 33, 34 (2008).

may reduce their exposure to the private market, which can, in turn, diminish their professional opportunities.

Our findings can serve as a springboard for further in-depth research on the different aspects of women's integration in academia. The results of our study clarify that equality in academia is not merely a question of how many women are present. It is also a question of whether women faculty can and do fully participate in the innovation ecosystem as inventors. Because women are not equally represented in patent prosecution, additional research and policy initiatives should target this gender gap to close it.

Acknowledgments

These findings were originally presented in W. Michael Schuster, Miriam Marcowitz-Bitton & Deborah R. Gerhardt, *The Gender Gap in Academic Patenting*, 56 U.C. Davis L. Rev. 759 (2022).

5

Patent Attorneys and the Increasing Use of Artificial Intelligence

A "Thought Experiment" on Our Human and Technological Gatekeepers

Jessica C. Lai

Introduction

Successful innovation is often imagined around an inventor and their invention. It is the inventor who brings this invention to market, and success is determined solely by an objective market demand. Of course, it is understood that innovation is more complex than this imagining. For example, the success of an innovation hinges on the protection of the invention via intellectual property rights and successful enforcement of these rights, the ability of the inventor to "sell" the invention to those who hold the purse strings, and a market that is socially "ready" for the invention and is willing to incur transaction costs to take up the invention.[1] A critical examination of innovation also highlights that the multiple stages of the innovation process are gendered and racialized. To illustrate, society might neither see women or people of color as inventors nor their inventions as inventions. In turn, marginalized people may struggle to finance their inventions because these perceptions mean they are not viewed as entrepreneurs in whom one should invest.[2] Even if they bring a product to market, their social construction

[1] Kara W. Swanson, Banking on the Body 218–19 (2014); Jessica C. Lai, *Patents, Gendered Bodies and Innovation: A Case Study on Contraceptives*, 20 J. Intell. Prop. L. & Prac. 46 (2025).

[2] *See, e.g.*, Jessica C. Lai, *The Role of Patents as a Gendered Chameleon*, 30 Soc. & Legal Stud. 203 (2021); Malin Malmström, Jeaneth Johansson & Joakim Wincent, *Gender Stereotypes and Venture Support Decisions: How Governmental Venture Capitalists Socially Construct Entrepreneurs' Potential*, 41 Entrepreneurship Theory & Prac. 833 (2017); Lisa A. Marovich, *"Let Her Have Brains Too": Commercial Networks, Public Relations, and the Business of Invention*, 27 Bus. & Econ. Hist. 140 (1998).

Jessica C. Lai, *Patent Attorneys and the Increasing Use of Artificial Intelligence* In: *Inclusive Innovation in the Age of AI and Big Data*. Edited by: Daryl Lim and Peter K. Yu, Oxford University Press. © Oxford University Press 2026.
DOI: 10.1093/9780197799444.003.0007

can affect market demand and their ability to enforce their intellectual property.[3]

While the socially and culturally contingent nature of successful innovation has been explored from multiple perspectives, such exploration has typically focused on the social constructions of the inventor,[4] the invention,[5] and the entrepreneur,[6] as well as the consequential behavior of patent examiners,[7] venture capitalists, and consumers.[8] Significant literature is developing around how patenting is gendered and racialized—that is, inventors named on patents are chiefly men and disproportionately Caucasian.[9] Moreover, existing scholarship has identified that the gendered and racialized nature of patenting can result in innovations being gendered and racialized—that is, innovations for women and those of color may not make it to market.[10] Little

[3] Kathy Bowrey, *The Threat Posed by a Woman Inventor: Law, Labour and the Subjugation of Louisa Lawson*, 21 Hist. Austl. 376 (2024); Kara W. Swanson, *Mind the Gaps: Race, Gender, and Intellectual Property*, *in* A Research Agenda for Intellectual Property and Gender (Jessica C. Lai & Kathy Bowrey eds., 2024) [hereinafter Research Agenda].

[4] Christine Battersby, Gender and Genius: Towards a Feminist Aesthetics (1989); Christine MacLeod, Heroes of Invention: Technology, Liberalism and British Identity 1750–1914 (2007).

[5] Dan L. Burk, *Do Patents Have Gender?*, 19 Am. U. J. Gender Soc. Pol'y & L. 881 (2011); Shlomit Yanisky-Ravid, *Eligible Patent Matter—Gender Analysis of Patent Law: International and Comparative Perspectives*, 19 Am. U. J. Gender Soc. Pol'y & L. 85 (2011).

[6] Fiona Murray & Leigh Graham, *Buying Science and Selling Science: Gender Differences in the Market for Commercial Science*, 16 Indus. & Corp. Change 657 (2007); Francisco J. Santos, Muhammad Azam Roomi & Francisco Liñán, *About Gender Differences and the Social Environment in the Development of Entrepreneurial Intentions*, 54 J. Small Bus. Mgmt. 49 (2016).

[7] Jessica Milli, Emma Williams-Baron, Meika Berlan, Jenny Xia & Barbara Gault, Equity in Innovation: Women Inventors and Patents 12 (2016); Vicki T. Huang, Sue Finch & Cameron Patrick, *Patents and Gender: A Big Data Analysis of 15 Years of Australian Patent Applications*, 45 UNSW L.J. 953 (2022); Kyle Jensen, Balázs Kovács & Olav Sorenson, *Gender Differences in Obtaining and Maintaining Patent Rights*, 36 Nature Biotech. 307 (2018); Chahreddine Abbes, Amélie Lafrance-Cooke & Danny Leung, *Patenting Activity of Women-Owned Business in Canada* 8–9 (Statistics Canada, Catalogue No. 36-28-0001, 2023). On how patent offices shape patent law and practice, see Peter Drahos, The Global Governance of Knowledge: Patent Offices and Their Clients (2010).

[8] Kara W. Swanson, *Centering Black Women Inventors: Passing and the Patent Archive*, 25 Stan. Tech. L. Rev. 305, 339–43 (2022).

[9] Eur. Patent Off., Women's Participation in Inventive Activity: Evidence from EPO Data (2022); UK Intell. Prop. Off., Gender Profiles in Worldwide Patenting: An Analysis of Female Inventorship (2019); U.S. Pat. & Trademark Off., Off. of the Chief Economist, *Progress and Potential: 2020 Update on U.S. Women Inventor-Patentees* (U.S. Patent & Trademark Off., Off. of the Chief Economist, IP Data Highlights No. 4, 2020); Susan Corbett, *The Female Inventor: What Price Intellectual Capital?*, 2002 N.Z. Intell. Prop. J. 91; Huang et al., *supra* note 7; Lisa D. Cook & Chaleampong Kongcharoen, *The Idea Gap in Pink and Black* 14–17 (Nat'l Bureau of Econ. Rsch., Working Paper No. 16331, 2010); Gema Lax Martinez, Julio Raffo & Kaori Saito, *Identifying the Gender of PCT Inventors* (World Intell. Prop. Org., Econ. Rsch. Working Paper No. 33, 2016).

[10] Rembrand Koning, Sampsa Samila & John-Paul Ferguson, *Who Do We Invent for? Patents by Women Focus More on Women's Health, but Few Women Get to Invent*, 372 Sci. 1345 (2021).

attention has been paid to patent attorneys and how they might shape who gets patents and what is patented.

This chapter undertakes a "thought experiment" on how patent attorneys might play a role in influencing invention and innovation. It is broadly situated in the United States, the United Kingdom, New Zealand, and Australia, which have some shared history in developing patent law and the patent attorney profession. The section "Some Potential Biases of Patent Attorneys" looks briefly at socialized gendered understandings of the inventor and the invention. It argues that patent attorneys, as nonneutral actors, are likely to embody these understandings in a way that affects their practice and patenting outcomes. Such embodiment is detrimental to women inventors, the protection of their inventions, and women consumers. The chapter contends that the realization of such biases within the patent attorney profession could assist in countering them. However, as explored in the section "Some Potential Effects of Generative AI," the increasing use of generative artificial intelligence (AI) in patent attorney work could retard gains that have been made in increasing the awareness of gender biases in the patent space amongst the patent attorney profession. The chapter concludes with a call for the profession to recognize the negative biases against women (and other marginalized groups) as AI-based technologies are increasingly used in the practice of their trade.

Some Potential Biases of Patent Attorneys

As noted above, strangely little attention has been paid to patent attorneys and the role they play in identifying, shaping, and defining the patented invention. It is well understood that access to a quality lawyer can affect legal outcomes.[11] However, little has been said about patent attorneys being gatekeepers affecting who and what is given exclusive rights. Like how patent law is often framed as neutral, patent attorneys are viewed as mere vessels who only translate their clients' inventions into "patentese" (patent language) and apply their legal skills in patenting.[12] They are not seen as

[11] Simon Chesterman, *Do Better Lawyers Win More Often? Measures of Advocate Quality and Their Impact in Singapore's Supreme Court*, 15 Asian J. Compar. L. 250 (2020); Banks Miller, Linda Camp Keith & Jennifer S. Holmes, *Leveling the Odds: The Effect of Quality Legal Representation in Cases of Asymmetrical Capability*, 19 L. & Soc'y Rev. 209 (2015).

[12] This view is reflected in a study showing that having a patent attorney, compared to filing *pro se*, affects how far along one gets through the examination process, although the authors attribute this solely to knowledge about rules related to patent practice, such as deadlines. Kate S. Gaudry, *The*

active participants in the creation of the invention as represented in a patent document.

However, as Jessica Silbey has highlighted, patent attorneys "harvest" intellectual property, advising their clients at what point there is patentable subject matter (the "right" kind of creation) and a patentable invention (that is novel, has an inventive step or is nonobvious, and is useful or has industrial application) and when to pursue a patent.[13] The flip side of the coin is that patent attorneys also advise clients when they believe there is no patentable subject matter or patentable invention, or no strong patent due to low novelty or low inventiveness. These attorneys likely make these assessments based on their socialized gendered understandings of the inventor and the invention. That the inventor and the invention are gendered is well-explored in the literature and briefly explained in the following section.

Gendered Concepts

The "inventor" has been socially constructed as a man. This construction stems from centuries of only men inventors being raised to the public consciousness. It is partly due to patent law's construction of the "inventor."[14] In the mid-nineteenth century, the intellectual notions of the individual inventor, and inventive activity as an abstract property, took hold in the United Kingdom.[15] The inventor was marked as an exceptional, individualized actor, with different qualities from those who contributed anonymous, collective labor in the workshop.[16] This treatment has gendered outcomes

Lone Inventor: Low Success Rates and Common Errors Associated with Pro-se Patent Applications, 7 PLOS ONE e49504 (2012).

[13] JESSICA SILBEY, THE EUREKA MYTH: CREATORS, INNOVATORS, AND EVERYDAY INTELLECTUAL PROPERTY 184–220 (2015). On the importance of contextualizing inventors, law, lawyers, and the legal system, see Kara W. Swanson, *"Great Men," Law, and the Social Construction of Technology*, 43 L. & SOC. INQUIRY 1093 (2018).

[14] Jessica C. Lai, *An Inventor, a Cyborg and an AI Walk into a Bar: Changing Gendered Narratives in Patent Law?*, *in* RESEARCH AGENDA, *supra* note 3, at 97.

[15] MACLEOD, *supra* note 4. The notions of the inventor and the invention were concretely recognized earlier in the United States through the Constitution, adopted on September 17, 1787. Article I, section 8, clause 8 of the Constitution grants Congress the power to "promote the Progress of Science and useful Arts, by securing for limited Times to Authors and Inventors the exclusive Right to their respective Writings and Discoveries."

[16] Christine MacLeod & Alessandro Nuvolari, *The Pitfalls of Prosopography: Inventors in the Dictionary of National Biography*, 47 TECH. & CULTURE 757 (2006).

as men are ascribed with individuality, intellect, and the "rational" disembodied "mind" to pursue and create the abstract and objective.[17] In contrast, women are constructed as communal, emotional, closely tied to nature, and the "body" inherently grounded in the subjective.[18]

Furthermore, men have been valorized for inventive genius,[19] which is not assisted by the multiple reasons why women are missing from the patent record. This might be because of the material realities women faced, and continue to face, such as not having access to formal education or the (human and financial) resources to seek a patent. It might also be because, until the late nineteenth century, married women could not own property in many English-speaking countries—including the United States, the United Kingdom, Australia, and New Zealand—and, therefore, could not own patents.[20] If a married woman filed for a patent, the laws of coverture meant that her husband would own it. Kara Swanson has noted that, as a result of these laws, married women did not bother to file for patents, and their husbands or brothers, for example, patented their inventions in their own (the husbands' or brothers') names.[21]

There is also evidence that women inventors have been discriminated against, for example, by patent offices,[22] in the selection of named inventors.[23] Discrimination against women inventors and their inventions is not merely a thing of the past. Women continue not to be attributed inventorship when they should be, and they are left of the patent record as a result. By way of example, in 2023, both *Science* and *Nature* reported on how Svetlana Mojsov was left off patent applications and multiple prizes for the work despite being

[17] Joan Acker, *Hierarchies, Jobs, Bodies: A Theory of Gendered Organizations*, 4 GENDER & SOC'Y 139 (1990); Margaret Thornton, *Authority and Corporeality: The Conundrum for Women in Law*, 6 FEMINIST LEGAL STUD. 147, 153 (1998).

[18] EVELYN FOX KELLER, REFLECTIONS ON GENDER AND SCIENCE (1985).

[19] MACLEOD, *supra* note 4; Christine MacLeod, *The Invention of Heroes*, 460 NATURE 572 (2009).

[20] *See, e.g.*, Married Women's Property Act 1882, 45 & 46 Vict. c. 7 (UK); Married Women's Property Act 1884 (N.Z.); *Married Women's Property Act 1890* (Cth) (Austl.). *See also* B. Zorina Khan, *Married Women's Property Laws and Female Commercial Activity: Evidence from United States Patent Records, 1790–1895*, 56 J. ECON. HIST. 356 (1996).

[21] Swanson, *supra* note 3.

[22] Jensen et al., *supra* note 7.

[23] Deborah Merritt, *Hypatia in the Patent Office: Women Inventors and the Law, 1865–1900*, 35 AM. J. LEGAL HIST. 235, 289–90, 300–05 (1991); Kara W. Swanson, *Rubbing Elbows and Blowing Smoke: Gender, Class, and Science in the Nineteenth Century Patent Office*, 108 ISIS 40 (2017); *see also* Laura Foster, *Situating Feminism, Patent Law, and the Public Domain*, 20 COLUM. J. GENDER & L. 261, 316 (2011); Annette I. Kahler, *Examining Exclusion in Woman-Inventor Patenting: A Comparison of Educational Trends and Patent Data in the Era of Computer Engineer Barbie*, 19 AM. U. J. GENDER SOC. POL'Y & L. 773, 782 (2011).

a pioneer in the discovery of the hormone GLP-1 (work underpinning diabetes and obesity drugs).[24] She had to fight for the recognition she deserved that the men around her did not have to.

The perception that men are inventors is buttressed by patent case law, which is replete with language and imagery of men inventors.[25] Dan Burk has examined this in depth, including the use of gendered conceptualizations and visualizations in case law concerning the conception of the person having the ordinary skill in the art (PHOSITA).[26] Patent law's "reasonable person" is, thus, a man. The issue is not only that most inventors are men and PHOSITA is framed as a man, but also that expert witnesses are almost always men—it is hard to think of a single patent law case where a woman expert witness was used.[27] Put another way, the physical representations of PHOSITA—those who present at court as the experts of their field—are almost exclusively men, and such representations perpetuate the belief that men, not women, are inventors.

In addition, knowledge typically connected to women (and the non-Western) is often unpatentable. It is framed as part of the public domain, too close to nature to be patentable, not belonging to the technical arts, or not industrial (and belonging in the private sphere).[28] To illustrate, inventions from the areas of the care sector dominated by women, such as medical treatment methods created by nurses or mental health care workers, and inventions for teaching methods from the education sector would not be considered patentable in many jurisdictions. Such inventions are explicitly excluded in statute or case law due to a desire to keep them out of the commercial sphere or because they are considered nontechnical.

[24] Jennifer Couzin-Frankel, *Her Work Paved the Way for Blockbuster Obesity Drugs. Now, She's Fighting for Recognition*, 381 Sci. 1274 (2023); Elie Dolgin, *Weight-Loss-Drug Pioneer: This Biochemist Finally Gained Recognition for Her Work*, 624 Nature 506 (2023).

[25] *See, e.g.*, *In re* Winslow, 365 F.2d 1017, 1020 (C.C.P.A. 1966).

[26] Dan L. Burk, *Diversity Levers*, 23 Duke J. Gender L. & Pol'y 25 (2015); Chris Dent, *The "Reasonable Man", His Nineteenth-Century "Siblings", and Their Legacy*, 44 J.L. & Soc'y 406, 426–27 (2017).

[27] Jessica C. Lai, Ronelle Geldenhuys & Maryam Khajeh Tabari, *Invisible Women in Invisible Professions: Voices from Australian and New Zealand Women in Intellectual Property* (Sept. 1, 2023), https://ssrn.com/abstract=4556301; *see also* Dent, *supra* note 26.

[28] Jessica C. Lai, Patent Law and Women: Tackling Gender Bias in Knowledge Governance ch. 2 (2022); Jessica C. Lai, *A Feminist Perspective on Food-Related Patents: On Messiness, Nature and the Social*, 56 Int'l Rev. Intell. Prop. & Competition L. 35 (2025).

The Patent Attorney

Traditionally, patent attorneys draft patent applications (including a "specification"[29] that "discloses"[30] the invention in relation to the "prior art"[31] and "claims" that delineate the claimed invention).[32] Patent attorneys also prosecute patent applications through patent offices, filing them and obtaining them through examination to grant. Patent attorneys are increasingly involved in commercialization as intellectual property strategists and within in-house roles.[33] In a profession historically and continually dominated by men, it is hard to imagine that patent attorneys are free from the abovementioned presumptions about the inventor and the invention. Even in the twenty-first century, most patent attorneys are men, and often Caucasian men.[34] For example, in 2023, almost 70 percent of patent attorneys in Australia and New Zealand were men.[35]

The gender bias that patent attorneys might display when advising clients is underexplored. Reporting on a qualitative study of Canadian women inventors and entrepreneurs in the clean technology sector conducted by Myra Tawfik and Heather Pratt,[36] Tawfik and Marcia Valiante stated that the "most disheartening aspect" was "that many of the women reported feeling dismissed, diminished, underestimated, and undermined in their interactions with third parties, like lawyers, patent examiners, and

[29] The patent specification is the main patent document.

[30] The invention must be disclosed sufficiently to allow PHOSITA to make (or work) the invention.

[31] The prior art is everything preexisting in the field of the invention.

[32] It is the claims that circumscribe the property embodied by a patent. The specification is used to interpret the claims (to varying degrees, depending on the jurisdiction).

[33] Li Changli, Tony Lan, and Liu Shang-Jyh have argued that this is a positive extension of the role of patent attorneys vis-à-vis technology transfer in developing countries. Li Changli, Tony Lan & Liu Shang-Jyh, *Patent Attorney as Technology Intermediary: A Patent Attorney-Facilitated Model of Technology Transfer in Developing Countries*, 43 World Pat. Info. 62 (2015).

[34] This is true in the United States. Elaine Spector & LaTia Brand, *Diversity in Patent Law: A Data Analysis of Diversity in the Patent Practice by Technology Background and Region*, Landslide, Sept.–Oct. 2020, at 32. For the United Kingdom, see Hayleigh Bosher, *Females and Felines in Intellectual Property Law*, IPKat (Dec. 3, 2017), http://ipkitten.blogspot.com/2017/12/females-and-felines-in-intellectual.html. For New Zealand and Australia, see Jessica C. Lai, Ronelle Geldenhuys, Maryam Khajeh Tabari & Mark Summerfield, *Female Patent Attorneys and Movements Around the Profession: Achieving Non-gendered Decision Making*, 19 J. Intell. Prop. L. & Prac. 596 (2024).

[35] This is unsurprising, as having a STEM background is often a prerequisite to becoming a patent attorney or examiner, and fewer women than men are educated in STEM. J. Shontavia Johnson, Tonya M. Evans & Yolanda M. King, *Diversifying Intellectual Property Law: Why Women of Color Remain "Invisible" and How to Provide More Seats at the Table*, Landslide, Mar.–Apr. 2018, at 30.

[36] Myra Tawfik & Heather Pratt, Study of the Underrepresentation of Women and Women-Identifying IP-Rights Holders, Company Founders and Senior Leadership: Final Report to Innovation Asset Collective 10–11 (2021), https://www.ipcollective.ca/wp-content/uploads/2022/03/Study-on-Women-in-IP-ENG.pdf.

investors."[37] Reflecting gender biases, patent attorneys might not see women as inventors, or their inventions as inventions. Such perception can affect the advice they give and the way they draft and prosecute a patent application. For example, they might advise a woman client not to file a patent because they do not see any patentable subject matter or they do not consider the invention novel or inventive. They might have taken such a view because the invention is for women and, as such, is in an unfamiliar field or solves a problem that the patent attorney cannot appreciate. Alternatively, thinking little of the inventive contribution, the patent attorney perhaps would draft narrow claims, resulting in weak property rights. The patent attorney might do this because the claims of a patent must be fairly based or supported by the disclosure. That is, there must be a connection between what gets property (the claims) and the inventor's contribution (as disclosed). However, if the patent attorney believes there is little contribution, they will draft narrow claims to prevent the claims from being rejected for a lack of fair basis or support.

Finally, a patent attorney's gender bias could result in the attorney not advocating as strongly for a woman client in the patent office, as they would for a man client. Note that there is some evidence that the inventor's gender affects examination outcomes, with women more likely to have claims rejected or reduced in scope.[38] This has been attributed to bias from patent offices. However, it could also be attributed to the extent to which the patent attorney negotiates with the examiner. The attorney might not have represented women clients as zealously as they would have represented men clients. Arguably, bias from a patent attorney against a woman inventor (or from a patent examiner against a woman patent attorney) is more likely to affect examination outcomes negatively than bias from a patent examiner against a woman inventor, as patent examiners do not typically interact directly with inventors.

That gender biases of patent attorneys could affect how a patent attorney provides advice and practices is supported by quantitative evidence that patent attorneys are not mere filters of inventions from inventors. Instead, their experiences are reflected in their advice and their practice. More

[37] Myra Tawfik & Marcia Valiante, *SDG 9: Innovation, Intellectual Property and Gender Equity*, *in* The Elgar Companion to Intellectual Property and the Sustainable Development Goals 281, 295–96 (Bita Amani, Caroline B. Ncube & Matthew Rimmer eds., 2024). They bring together a sample of quotes from the participants regarding their experiences with lawyers, examiners, and investors. *Id.* at 296.

[38] Jensen et al., *supra* note 7.

specifically, existing studies indicate that patent attorneys, where they work and have worked, and their prior experiences affect the success and quality of patent applications.[39] Arguably, other social and cultural experiences must also affect how patent attorneys practice, including their socialized framings of inventors and inventions.

Furthermore, a patent attorney might have gendered perceptions of inventors and inventions, which influences the patent examination outcome not only because of how they draft an application but also because of how they influence patent examiners. As noted above, patent attorneys negotiate with patent examiners in the prosecution of a patent application. To illustrate the effect they can have on patent examiners, Gaétan de Rassenfosse and his coauthors looked at the United States, the European Patent Office, Japan, South Korea, and China and found evidence that patent attorney firms had strong effects on patenting outcomes—for example, a high-quality firm could push through a patent application for a low-quality invention.[40] In addition, undertaking interviews with patent examiners in Spain, Benedicto Acosta noted that the examiners acknowledged that patent examination is "very subjective" and not free from external influences, including interactions with patent attorneys.[41] Put another way, how patent attorneys advocate for their clients before patent examiners can impact examination outcomes. Thus, how a patent attorney views a woman client and her invention matters. If the attorney thinks little or less of the client as an inventor, or of the invention and its contribution, the attorney might provide weaker advocacy.

The influence that a patent attorney can exert on a patent examiner affects not only the examination outcome but also the content of the examination report. In a quantitative study showing the influence of patent attorneys

[39] Dimitris Andriosopoulos, Pawel Czarnowski & Andrew Marshall, *Do Corporate Lawyers Matter? Evidence from Patents*, 83 J. Corp. Fin. 102473 (2023); Rainer Frietsch & Peter Neuhäusler, *The Role of the Patent Attorney in the Filing Process*, *in* Springer Handbook of Science and Technology Indicators 875 (Wolfgang Glänzel, Henk F. Moed, Ulrich Schmoch & Mike Thelwall eds., 2019); Krzysztof Klincewics & Szymon Szumiał, *Successful Patenting—Not Only How, but with Whom: The Importance of Patent Attorneys*, 127 Scientometrics 5111 (2022).

[40] Gaétan de Rassenfosse, Paul H. Jensen, T'Mir Julius, Alfons Palangkaraya & Elizabeth Webster, *Is the Patent System a Level Playing Field? The Effect of Patent Attorney Firms*, 71 J. Indus. Econ. 124 (2023); *see also* Andriosopoulos et al., *supra* note 39.

[41] Benedicto Acosta, *Impartiality at the Patent Office*, 2023 Pub. Integrity 1, 5. In addition, interviewees noted feeling more pressure when they examined applications from "important" or "large" companies, and spending more time on them, because such applicants were more likely to push back if they found anything amiss. Given that men generally have more social power than women, and arguably more so in the inventorship and entrepreneurship space, one could postulate that patent examiners might attribute little power to women to challenge the examination process and might spend less time on their applications, which could negatively affect their quality or result in rejection due to less care being taken.

on patent examiners, Patrick Doran and Elizabeth Webster identified that, in the United States, when examining an application from a patent attorney, examiners cite patents from that attorney at a disproportionate rate, indicating that patent attorneys have a strong influence on the drafting of examiners' reports.[42] Any bias a patent attorney might have could be translated into the examiner's report. For example, if patent attorneys tend to think more highly of their men clients and the work of men inventors and attribute less value to their women clients and the work of women inventors, the former might be cited disproportionately more in the examiners' reports. Similarly, men's patents would be disproportionately more likely to be cited in patent applications.[43] Citations matter because citation rates of patents are often used as a proxy for their value and the value of the embodied inventions.[44] If the patents and inventions of men are cited disproportionately more than those of women, they will be attributed more value by proxy. Moreover, the patents and inventions of men would get disproportionately more visibility, which also affects their perceived value.

Note that the extent of the influence of a patent attorney on the examination outcome and report depends on a local patent office's processes and the norms around attorney-examiner interactions. For example, at some offices, it is normal for an attorney to call and verbally negotiate with an examiner, but this would be rare at other offices. As a further illustration, in some jurisdictions, the local culture and norms mean that an attorney is unlikely to challenge an examiner's report and more likely to try to appease the examiner to get the application to grant.

Overall, gender biases in the social constructions of the inventor and the invention can result in patent attorneys not perceiving women as inventors, not taking their inventions seriously, drafting narrow claims, and not advocating zealously on their behalf in patent offices. These biases arguably

[42] Patrick Doran & Elizabeth Webster, *Who Influences USPTO Patent Examiners?*, 56 World Pat. Info. 39 (2019). In the United States, there is also some evidence that the political ideology of a patent examiner can affect outcomes where there is more discretion—for example, in relation to software patents. Joseph Faffiee, Florenta Teodoridis & Daniel Fehder, *Partisan Patent Examiners? Exploring the Link Between the Political Ideology of Patent Examiners and Patent Office Outcomes*, 52 Rsch. Pol'y 104853 (2023).

[43] Women's patents are indeed cited less than men's. Cassidy R. Sugimoto, Ni Chaoqun, Jevin D. West & Vincent Larivière, *The Academic Advantage: Gender Disparities in Patenting*, 10 PLoS ONE e0128000 (2015); Gauri Subramani & Michelle Saksena, *Untapped Potential: Investigating Gender Disparities in Patent Citations* (U.S. Pat. & Trademark Off., Econ. Working Paper No. 2024-3, 2024).

[44] Bronwyn H. Hall, Adam Jaffe & Manuel Trajtenberg, *Market Value and Patent Citations*, 36 RAND J. Econ. 16 (2005).

contribute to women being omitted from the patent record. Yet when women do get patents, the grants might be comparatively narrower in scope and, thus, of a lower commercial value. Furthermore, patent attorneys reflecting gender biases in their practice could result in fewer inventions for women being patented and subsequently commercialized. Even if patented and commercialized, such biases could affect the intellectual property strategies patent attorneys develop for women inventors, or for inventions targeting women consumers.

In light of these findings, one could consider whether it might benefit women inventors to have women patent attorneys because they will see them as inventors, understand their inventions, and better advocate for them in patent offices. Put another way, the solution, which will be further discussed below, might be the presence of more women patent attorneys.

The Body but Not the Mind

The argument that a woman patent attorney is required for a woman inventor is particularly salient if the invention is aimed at women. As the argument goes, women patent attorneys are more likely to understand the invention, perceive it as patentable subject matter and a patentable invention,[45] and draft the application and negotiate with the patent examiner accordingly. Furthermore, women inventors seeing women patent attorneys might encourage them to use the patent system, as they might feel a greater sense of belonging in the space.[46] It is also possible that having more women patent attorneys could change the nature of the "inventor" and "invention" as they might use their networks (which differ from those of men patent attorneys) to access a more diverse range of inventors and (potential) inventions.[47] For example, they might extend inventions beyond those from science, technology,

[45] *How Spanx Got Started*, Inc. (Jan. 20, 2012), https://www.inc.com/sara-blakely/how-sara-blakley-started-spanx.html; Madeleine Kelly, *Will More Women Patent Attorneys Lead to More Women Inventors?*, Forbes (Nov. 21, 2022), https://www.forbes.com/sites/madeleinekey/2022/11/21/will-more-women-patent-attorneys--lead-to-more-women-inventors/. Note that Jordana Goodman has made analogous arguments that there needs to be diversity in patent examiners, otherwise marginalized peoples might struggle to have their inventions perceived as inventions, as they might be categorized incorrectly or compared to irrelevant prior art, using an incorrectly constructed PHOSITA. Jordana R. Goodman, *Patently Inequitable*, 105 B.U. L. Rev. 987 (2025).

[46] Mary T. Hannon, *The Patent Bar Gender Gap: Expanding the Eligibility Requirements to Foster Inclusion and Innovation in the U.S. Patent System*, 10 IP Theory 1, 19 (2020).

[47] *Id.* at 20.

engineering, and mathematics (STEM), resulting in patenting inventions from women-dominated industries, and inventions aimed at women.

It is important not to overstate the potential effect of having more women patent attorneys, as they can also be socialized to have gendered perspectives on the inventor and the invention. People are often expected to bring change with their bodies when all minds are socialized. For example, Indigenous peoples are often expected to represent the Indigenous perspective by their mere presence, or women are expected to represent a specific vision of femininity. Such expectations fail to acknowledge that women and people of color hired into roles like patent attorneys fit certain measures of merit that typically require them to go through an education that shapes the lens through which they see the world. Patent attorneys are trained to understand what a patentable invention is. They are trained through legal definition and case law, which are almost all about inventions from men-dominated industries, use masculine terminology, and have only men as expert witnesses. Patent attorneys are also trained through the examples lecturers use when teaching patent drafting, which are stereotypically mechanical. Such training presumes that all trainees will understand basic mechanics, whereas only some will understand, for example, basic chemistry or biotechnology. However, it is incidentally gendered because mechanics is socially constructed as a realm for men. Furthermore, that patent attorneys largely encounter men inventors trains them to presume that inventors are men rather than women. Thus, simply because a patent attorney is a woman does not necessarily mean that she would not have the same prejudices (or unconscious biases) against women inventors and the inventions of, or for, women.

While this chapter is not about the biases of examiners, it is worth noting that, even with more diverse thinking, patent attorneys will not bring about proportionate change if patent examiners exhibit gender bias against these attorneys.[48] One might think that the solution is for patent offices to require more women examiners. Yet the foregoing discussion regarding attorneys applies similarly to examiners; increasing the number of women examiners will not bring about commensurate change because of how examiners are trained and socialized.

[48] On the biases that women patent attorneys face, see Jessica C. Lai, Ronelle Geldenhuys & Maryam Khajeh Tabari, *Women in Intellectual Property: Not Taken Seriously?*, 46 EUR. INTELL. PROP. REV. 602 (2024).

The problem is not solely the absence of women but the absence of the feminine (or what is socially associated with women). Simply having women who have been trained to see and protect the masculine around will not proportionately change the inventor or the invention. This is not to say that the presence of women (and other marginalized groups) would not bring change. It would. People bring their lived experiences, which shape their perspective. However, because becoming a patent attorney (or a patent examiner) also shapes that perspective, more is required than mere presence to proportionately increase diversity and change perceptions of the inventor and the invention. This could include, among other things, altering how patent law and practice is taught, and thus the way the inventor and the patentable invention is perceived. Yet might any efforts in this vein be thwarted by the advent of generative AI, trained on existing law and practice, and its growing presence in patent practice? The next section will examine this question.

Some Potential Effects of Generative AI

One often sees in the news media that AI will take over legal work,[49] especially patent work due to its technical nature. Patent law is often presumed to be more objective (with patent attorneys having little discretion), when compared with other areas of law. Patent law and practice is, thus, perceived as being riper for AI takeover. Whether this is true or not is, of course, highly debatable. In 2024, with the rise of generative AI, a patent attorney and friend, who teaches patent drafting to trainee patent attorneys, decided to see how ChatGPT fared when asked to draft patent claims. She was astounded by how good it was. She noted that the claims were not great, but they were sufficient and could serve as a good starting point.[50] She concluded that generative AI is a tool for patent attorneys.

The fact that algorithmic bias might exist in applying generative AI to patent work has not been explored.[51] Generative AI learns from what

[49] *Generative AI Could Radically Alter the Practice of Law*, Economist (June 6, 2023), https://www.economist.com/business/2023/06/06/generative-ai-could-radically-alter-the-practice-of-law; Steve Lohr, *A.I. Is Coming for Lawyers, Again*, N.Y. Times (Apr. 10, 2023), https://www.nytimes.com/2023/04/10/technology/ai-is-coming-for-lawyers-again.html.

[50] See also Mark Sellick, *Can AI Replace Patent Attorneys?*, HGF (Dec. 2022), https://www.hgf.com/news/can-ai-replace-patent-attorneys/.

[51] Indeed, the literature on the potential biased effects of using AI in legal practice is sparse outside of criminal law.

exists and is available, which embodies dominant and hegemonic views. It is now well documented that AI can learn and perpetuate existing biases.[52] Such biases can include sexist stereotypes and gender tropes,[53] such as men being economists and CEOs and boys interested in science and technology, whereas girls are artistic, empathetic, and nurturing.[54] It is not difficult to imagine that generative AI would associate inventors with men, and inventions with a narrow class of technologies. Thus, it is concerning that AI-based technology is being used to search for prior art, draft disclosure statements and claims, sketch patent drawings, and develop commercialization strategies.

With powerful search and language processing abilities, AI can quickly identify relevant prior art from big datasets. This information can then be used to draft a patent disclosure that avoids prior art and ensures an inventive step.[55] Generative AI can do this by modeling its output on existing patent disclosures. But what if most existing patent disclosures are based on technologies from men-dominated industries or inventions for men? What if there are insufficient examples of technologies from women-dominated industries or inventions for women? Or what if the AI, like the humans it imitates, cannot identify the novelty or the inventive step in an invention (from a description provided by the inventor) because the language patterns it encounters are unfamiliar? This could result in poor drafting.

A paucity of existing patent disclosures could also result in the invention being misconstrued altogether. To begin with, it might not identify an "invention" at all. Statutes and centuries of case law typically define what constitutes patentable subject matter. Presuming to have access to all of this,

[52] Ruha Benjamin, Race After Technology: Abolitionist Tools for the New Jim Code (2019); Safiya Umoja Noble, Algorithms of Oppression: How Search Engines Reinforce Racism (2018); Nima Kordzadeh & Maryam Ghasemaghaei, *Algorithmic Bias: Review, Synthesis, and Future Research Directions*, 31 Eur. J. Info. Sys. 388 (2022); Eirini Ntoutsi et al., *Bias in Data-Driven Artificial Intelligence Systems—An Introductory Survey*, 10 WIREs Data Mining & Knowledge Discovery e1356 (2020).

[53] Juliana Castaneda, Assumpta Jover, Laura Calvet, Sergi Yanes, Angel A. Juan & Milagros Sainz, *Dealing with Gender Bias Issues in Data-Algorithmic Processes: A Social-Statistical Perspective*, 15 Algorithms 303 (2022); Emily Dinan, Angela Fan, Adina Williams, Jack Urbanek, Douwe Kiela & Jason Weston, *Queens Are Powerful Too: Mitigating Gender Bias in Dialogue Generation*, Proc. Conf. on Empirical Methods in Natural Language Processing 2020, at 8173 (2020); Noor ul Ain, *Gender Biases in Generative AI: Unveiling Prejudices and Prospects in the Age of ChatGPT*, 2 Magna Carta 85 (2023); Galit Wellner, *When AI Is Gender-Biased: The Effects of Biased AI on the Everyday Experiences of Women*, 13 HUMANA.MENTE J. Phil. Stud. 127 (2020).

[54] Nicole Gross, *What ChatGPT Tells Us About Gender: A Cautionary Tale About Performativity and Gender Biases in AI*, 12 Soc. Sci. 435 (2023).

[55] Alex Tran, *5+ Advantages of AI Powered Patent Drafting*, Power Patent Blog (May 28, 2023), https://powerpatent.com/blog/ai-patent-drafting-benefits.

the AI being used must correctly "apply" its "understanding" through its language model to the invention at hand. The AI might deem an invention with no predecessors to be "different" and, thus, unpatentable. For example, an invention derived from Indigenous knowledge might be deemed a mere discovery or natural product because most existing literature points in this direction. Furthermore, generative AI cannot address the complicating fact that patentable subject matter has typically expanded over several centuries. That is, the subject matter is not static, and there is some legal capacity to broaden the scope of patentable subject matter. After all, patents are about the new and the inventive, not just what has come before.

In addition, patents are classified by technology type.[56] One could imagine that AI could be used to classify inventions. However, as Jordana Goodman has exemplified, these classifications are neither neutral nor all-encompassing.[57] More specifically, she used the example of hair sponges for styling Black hair being classified as "cleaning sponges" to show how the existing classes reflect the hegemony. She argued that such classification can have negative consequences for patent prosecution because of the incorrect prior art being located—in this case, soap sponges, kitchen cleaners, and a deodorant applicator. It is not difficult to extrapolate from her analysis that AI could also incorrectly classify an invention and locate the incorrect body of prior art. As a result, AI could then poorly construe the invention and describe it incorrectly, potentially missing, or only narrowly capturing, how the invention is patentable subject matter, novel, and inventive.

Similarly, if the invention has few predecessors, AI might struggle to draft robust claims, resulting in a patent that could be challenged, offering weaker intellectual property rights, or both. The AI in use might have insufficient training to draft wide claims that are unlikely to be challenged (based on a lack of patentable subject matter, novelty, or nonobviousness), or the technology might identify the wrong dataset. For example, the AI might adopt the language used to claim soap sponges to draft claims regarding hair sponges to style hair. Similarly, if the invention is a technology that has never been patented before, and of which the AI cannot find existing examples, the AI would not be able to adequately create patent drawings for the invention that correctly depict the invention.

[56] World Intell. Prop. Org., International Patent Classification (IPC) (2022).
[57] Goodman, *supra* note 45.

One would hope that the patent attorney using AI would notice flaws like those described in the foregoing and that the attorney, frustrated with the ineffectiveness of using AI to address the invention at hand, would prepare much of the patent specification manually. However, let us not forget that AI mirrors society. Discussing the hair sponge case above, Goodman stated that the attorney who was prosecuting the case bore significant responsibility for its outcome, as he

> failed to put his clients' inventive language in the patent application, and instead chose to substitute his own description of the invention. The attorney failed to amend the claims to include structural limitations, differentiation the product at hand from the cited prior art. The attorney did not argue that the cited art was irrelevant.[58]

Thus, a patent attorney might be just as prone to misconstruing the invention as AI. As noted above, the patent attorney profession remains relatively homogeneous, and this homogeneity is reinforced through its professional training and practice, which decreases the likelihood that the patent attorney might see that AI has reflected gendered (and racialized) biases.

Finally, it has been suggested that AI could assist with developing intellectual property commercialization strategies.[59] However, if the world is largely filled with examples of inventions and patents in men-dominated industries and their strategies for commercializing and protecting their inventions, AI might struggle to come up with such strategies for people who might have different motivations for commercialization and who might be trying to commercialize something from which there are few examples to draw. If a patent attorney were to ask AI to detect patterns in potential markets or potential threats of litigation, it might not have sufficient high-quality data to make such assessments. It might not even identify the right market to make such an assessment. For example, it might analyze the threat of kitchen cleaners to the market of hair sponges to style hair.

Another way to view this is that AI, like the patent attorney, perpetuates gender (and other) biases, which it inevitably learns from the preexisting. In doing so, AI also shapes those gender biases. When patent attorneys use

[58] *Id.*

[59] Aaron Lepoidevin, *Generative AI and Its Impact on the IP System*, GRIFFITH HACK (July 13, 2023), https://www.griffithhack.com/insights/publications/generative-ai-and-its-impact-on-the-ip-system/.

words and images created by AI based on preexisting scripts to identify an invention, suitably classify the invention, draft claims, create patent drawings, and develop a commercialization strategy, those words and images are performative; they determine and dictate what an invention is and how it is represented.[60] Like a traditional patent attorney, AI is not a mere neutral filter. It can affect the notions of the inventor and the invention.

One could argue that, in using AI to replace some of the work done by patent attorneys, marginalized inventors and inventions are not worse off than when this work is wholly done by these attorneys. After all, AI is merely replicating existing biases. Such an argument is flawed for two reasons, however. First, it supports the status quo rather than looks forward to developing a system that minimizes negative biases. Second, AI perpetuating biases could be viewed as more dangerous than humans doing so, as there is a general perception that AI is objective. This perception partly arises because AI uses large datasets, and because AI is presumed to be free of the biases and vagaries of the human condition. Of course, those large datasets embody those biases and vagaries. Nevertheless, generative AI can appear authoritative and persuasive in a way that results in users not questioning the veracity of their outputs.[61]

Learning from Our Mistakes

As the World Intellectual Property Organization, national patent offices, and academics pay greater attention to gender inequality in patenting, they should not overlook a hitherto-ignored gatekeeper to patents: patent attorneys, who undoubtedly reflect gendered constructions of the inventor and the invention in their interactions with clients and their practice. Moreover, as gatekeepers increasingly rely on AI tools for patent practice, consideration must be made of how such tools might perpetuate negative biases, which could result in the perpetuation of inequities for women (and other marginalized groups), who are not seen as inventors and whose inventions are unpatentable subject matter, receive derision, or are granted narrow property rights.

[60] On patents and performativity, see Dan Burk, *Patent Performativity*, 29 J. INTELL. PROP. L. 280 (2022).
[61] Gross, *supra* note 54.

Humans, as individuals and collectives, are capable of learning from their mistakes. They can be taught to see biases in the law, change the law, and adapt. In contrast, it is difficult to imagine that AI can take a critical lens and identify the opaque ways in which an aspect of the law might appear neutral but is in fact sexist, racist, or otherwise biased against a marginalized group.[62] As the academy increasingly works toward highlighting how patent law reflects hidden biases, including within the constructions of the inventor and the invention, and patent attorneys learn of this work and reflect it in their practice, the employment of AI might inadvertently push against this movement because it relies on and reflects the hegemonic status quo. Put another way, research into the nonneutral role of patent attorneys is only nascent, and it behooves the profession to pause on developing automated tools for patent attorneys that might reflect negative biases before those biases have been fully uncovered and understood. Once the negative biases are understood, they should be front and center in the mind of those developing AI-based tools for patent practice and of patent attorneys using these tools. To illustrate, given the supposedly new and inventive nature of an invention, perhaps it should never be up to a computer program, AI-powered or not, to assess whether there is a patentable subject matter and how to classify the invention in relation to what is in existence. The assessment should remain the domain of humans.

To conclude, society should not give up the gains that it has won in making hidden biases visible because of the convenience offered by AI. After all, what is the purpose of creating a technology, particularly one that is supposed to imitate human intelligence, if that technology pushes human societies backwards? The patent attorney profession should do more than reflect on how AI can be a tool. The profession should also acknowledge that AI can reverse progress made in uncovering and trying to address biases that negatively affect the marginalized, including those reflected in their practice. The profession should consciously and actively resist this.

[62] Galit Wellner & Tiran Rothman, *Feminist AI: Can We Expect Our AI Systems to Become Feminist*, 33 PHIL. & TECH. 191, 200–02 (2020).

6

Inventing Fairness

Exploring AI's Role in Patent Reform

Jordana Goodman, Yan Li, Regan Murphy, and Khamal Patterson

Introduction

Patenting is inequitable. Black and Hispanic patentees "are woefully underrepresented in America," as are female patentees.[1] Although many, including the United States Patent and Trademark Office (USPTO), are trying to increase equitable representation of patentees, there is still a significant race and gender imbalance for credited inventors in the United States.[2]

Scholars offer a myriad of reasons for this imbalance—financial reasons, education gaps, and everything in between. Disparities in representation and cultural capital exist among patent examiners and patent practitioners, who serve as gatekeepers to the patent system. We argue that these disparities limit access to patent protection for underrepresented inventors. We then use AI-assisted experiments to investigate how currently available generative AI interprets and potentially remedies these disparities in culturally nuanced inventions, specialized terminology, and legal standards.

To some extent, every invention stems from a person's collective set of experiences. To create something new, inventors can leverage their cultural capital—knowledge, skills, and education gained from life experiences.[3]

[1] *See, e.g.*, Jordana R. Goodman, *Patently Inequitable*, 105 B.U. L. Rev. 987 (2025); Jordana R. Goodman, *Sy-STEM-ic Bias: An Exploration of Gender and Race Representation on University Patents*, 87 Brook. L. Rev. 853, 855 (2022) [hereinafter Goodman, *Sy-STEM-ic Bias*]; Shontavia Jackson Johnson, *The Colorblind Patent System and Black Inventors*, GPSolo, Mar.–Apr. 2021, at 30.

[2] *Diversity in Innovation: Best Practices*, U.S. Pat. & Trademark Off., https://www.uspto.gov/about-us/events/diversity-innovation-best-practices (last visited May 16, 2025); Eric S. Hintz, *Tearing Down the Barriers for Black Inventors Begins with Honoring Their Historic Breakthroughs*, Smithsonian Mag. (Mar. 1, 2022), https://www.smithsonianmag.com/smithsonian-institution/tearing-down-barriers-black-inventors-honoring-historic-breakthroughs-180979652.

[3] Pierre Bourdieu, The State Nobility: Elite Schools in the Field of Power 264–66 (Lauretta C. Clough trans., Stanford Univ. Press 1996); Pierre Bourdieu, *Cultural Reproduction and Social Reproduction*, *in* Knowledge, Education and Cultural Change 71, 71–112 (Richard

Jordana Goodman, Yan Li, Regan Murphy, and Khamal Patterson, *Inventing Fairness* In: *Inclusive Innovation in the Age of AI and Big Data*. Edited by: Daryl Lim and Peter K. Yu, Oxford University Press.
 DOI: 10.1093/9780197799444.003.0008

These novel ideas "have become the principal wellsprings of economic growth and competitive business advantage."[4]

Having a good idea is not the same as patenting an invention. Once an inventor develops an idea such that a "person having ordinary skill in the art" (PHOSITA) would judge it to be novel and nonobvious, the inventor must file a patent application that is written in a way that enables any person skilled in the art to make and use the invention.[5]

The USPTO evaluates patent applications using standards and practices meant to be objective.[6] We posit that all procedures implemented by humans in the patent process are subject to bias. These procedures range from an inventor seeking out a patent practitioner, to an attorney assisting the inventor in writing and arguing a patent application, to an examiner evaluating the patent application and researching relevant prior art. Although this chapter discusses only utility patent applications, the inequality themes likely also extend to design patents, copyrights, and trademarks.

Participants in the patent process come from significantly different social, cultural, and economic communities. Inventors seeking to patent innovations unique to their communities may face disadvantages when the cultural context necessary to understand their inventions is not widely known among patent practitioners and examiners. This cultural disconnect undermines both the patent practitioner's ability to effectively write and argue the patent application and the examiner's ability to evaluate the application.

These knowledge gaps pose additional obstacles to those already disadvantaged in inventive spaces.[7] Not only does an inventor need knowledge and money to access the patent system, but they also must explain their invention to the patent practitioner and examiner, who may be unfamiliar with

Brown ed., 1973); Pierre Bourdieu, *The Forms of Capital*, *in* HANDBOOK OF THEORY AND RESEARCH FOR THE SOCIOLOGY OF EDUCATION 241, 241–58 (John G. Richardson ed., 1986).

[4] Nilanjana Bhaduri, Nee Chakraborty & Mary Mathew, *Patent Intelligence and Its Implications for Patent Productivity*, *in* PEOPLE, KNOWLEDGE AND TECHNOLOGY: WHAT HAVE WE LEARNT SO FAR? 305, 305 (Bruno Trezzini, Patrick Lambe & Suliman Hawamdeh eds., 2004).

[5] U.S. CONST. art. I, § 8, cl. 8; 35 U.S.C. §§ 102, 103, 112; U.S. PAT. & TRADEMARK OFF., MANUAL OF PATENT EXAMINING PROCEDURE § 2141.03 (9th ed. rev. 2020) [hereinafter MPEP].

[6] Steven P. Smith & Kurt R. Van Thomme, *Bridge over Troubled Water: The Supreme Court's New Patent Obviousness Standard in* KSR *Should Be Readily Apparent and Benefit the Public*, 17 ALB. L.J. SCI. & TECH. 127, 162–63 (2007).

[7] Jordana Goodman, *Addressing Patent Gender Disparities*, 376 SCI. 706, 707 (2022); *see also* ELYSE SHAW & HALIE MARIANO, TACKLING THE GENDER AND RACIAL PATENTING GAP TO DRIVE INNOVATION: LESSONS FROM WOMEN'S EXPERIENCES 2 (2021), https://iwpr.org/wp-content/uploads/2021/07/Tackling-the-Gender-and-Racial-Patenting-Gap_FINAL38.pdf.

the inventor's nonmajority culture forming the basis of their invention.[8] This chapter explores extra barriers disparately affecting underrepresented inventors and uses the term "bias" accordingly, although biases can manifest in both minority- and majority-group settings.[9]

The default majority culture among practitioners and examiners likely affects inventors of many minority groups. In sociology, the term "minority group" refers to a category of people who do not belong to a dominant (often majority) social group based on observable characteristics or practices, such as ethnicity, race, religion, sexual orientation, or disability.[10] When pursuing a patent, an inventor must effectively communicate their invention to at least one attorney or examiner—likely in the majority group—regardless of whether (1) the inventor belongs to the majority group; (2) the invention would be used by the majority group; or (3) the majority group would recognize valuable distinctions of the invention over current technology.[11]

We note that group identification does not always overlap with cultural literacy. Cultural identity is complex.[12] As one of us explains in a recent article:

> [I]ndividuals can have in-depth cultural knowledge of a culture that they do not identify with, and others can identify with a particular culture but lack in-depth cultural knowledge. Some who have a majority culture identity may have in-depth minority cultural knowledge, and others who have a minority culture identity may lack in-depth cultural knowledge about their self-identified minority culture.[13]

Correlations between cultural identity and literacy do not obviate their distinct nature.[14] However, we must also emphasize that distinct gaps in cultural literacy and knowledge in the patent system are likely derived, at least in part, from access to that knowledge.[15] Such access, and differences in access,

[8] Edmund W. Kitch, *The Nature and Function of the Patent System*, 20 J.L. & Econ. 265, 266–67 (1977).

[9] Ashley W. Doane Jr., *Dominant Group Ethnic Identity in the United States: The Role of "Hidden" Ethnicity in Intergroup Relations*, 38 Socio. Q. 375, 376 (1997).

[10] George Ritzer, Essentials of Sociology 216–18 (4th ed. 2021).

[11] J. Shontavia Johnson, Tonya M. Evans & Yolanda M. King, *Diversifying Intellectual Property Law: Why Women of Color Remain "Invisible" and How to Provide More Seats at the Table*, Landslide, Mar.–Apr. 2018, at 30.

[12] Ching Wan & Pony Yuen-Ga Chew, *Cultural Knowledge, Category Label, and Social Connections: Components of Cultural Identity in the Global, Multicultural Context*, 16 Asian J. Soc. Psych. 247 (2013).

[13] Goodman, *Patently Inequitable*, *supra* note 1, at 1004.

[14] Wan & Chew, *supra* note 12, at 251.

[15] *Id.* at 248.

can overlap significantly with cultural identity and the identity of those in a person's community.

Certain differences in majority- and minority-group culture, including communication practices and cultural capital held by individuals in each group, are not acknowledged openly in a consistent manner during the intake, writing, or argument phases of patent prosecution. Patent practitioners will often acknowledge when they are asked to write a patent application outside of their trained subject matter—for instance, a patent practitioner trained as a chemist being asked to write a software patent. However, this discussion is likely absent or lacking when the majority-group/minority-group divide is based on cultural education, such as differences in haircare needs, rather than standardized academic education.

This chapter examines the disparities already entrenched in the patent system through the lens of the Black haircare space. The cultural capital necessary for Black haircare inventions—including knowledge of Black hair texture and style, the perceived monetary value of the Black haircare industry, and existing product expertise—rarely overlaps with the practitioner writing the patent application or the examiner reviewing the application. This lack of overlap and subsequent failed communication results in hermeneutical injustice, where the knower (inventor) attempts to share their knowledge, but their communication does not get the inventor to a place of justice (due to prejudicial flaws in a system).[16] Here, that place of justice is patent protection equal to those pursuing patents for inventions developed for and by members of the cultural majority. Although we do not argue that only African American and Black attorneys have sufficient cultural capital to pursue Black haircare patents, the interview of Brigitte Gopou and Bruce Boyd, the inventors of the NuDred Hair Sponge, suggests that their invention would have been better prosecuted by someone who had developed cultural competency related to Black haircare externally to the client.

Conversations surrounding artificial intelligence (AI) and machine learning tools to reduce these disparities have recently emerged. These tools can streamline patent searches, enhance clarity in documentation, facilitate communication between inventors and examiners, and reduce the cost of patent prosecution, potentially leveling the playing field. Conversely, AI's inherent biases and limitations could further entrench existing disparities by

[16] Miranda Fricker, Epistemic Injustice: Power and the Ethics of Knowing 147, 152 (2007).

misinterpreting cultural nuances or failing to recognize the value of diverse innovations. In a prior article, two of us engaged in an analysis about some injustices in the patent system for Black inventors.[17] Here, we expand upon this analysis by implementing machine learning–assisted experiments (colloquially referred to as AI) to test if these tools can remedy known biases. We found that AI can potentially bridge the gap between inventors' cultural knowledge and prosecutors' technical assessments, mitigating biases in the prosecution process. AI tools can create definitions for words that cross the cultural majority-minority line and identify when a patent drafter uses a term that may be considered inappropriate in the inventors' cultural context.[18] We also explore the limitations of relying on AI in patent analysis, particularly in the examination and final communication contexts.

We urge the USPTO, patent attorneys, and academics to consider the implications of these tools in patent practice, legal education, and ethics, advocating for reforms that foster a more inclusive and equitable patent landscape. Through this exploration, we aim to illuminate the critical intersection of culture, technology, and intellectual property rights, highlighting the urgent need for systemic change in the patent examination process.

Case Study

This chapter focuses on the case study of Brigitte Gopou and Bruce Boyd's journey to obtain a patent for their haircare invention, commonly known as a hair sponge. Addressed in greater detail in a prior article, "Access to Justice for Black Inventors," this case study shows how a mismatch of nonacademic cultural knowledge between practitioners, examiners, and inventors creates inequities for those inventing in underrepresented spaces. Later, we will address how machine-learning tools can exacerbate and minimize these issues.

Gopou and Boyd invented NuDred, a hair-sculpting tool designed to twist 4A–4C hair, and formed Nu-You Technologies, LLC to manufacture and sell their hair-sculpting device.[19] The hair-sculpting device is colloquially

[17] Jordana R. Goodman & Khamal Patterson, *Access to Justice for Black Inventors*, 77 Vand. L. Rev. 109 (2024).

[18] Sondos Mahmoud Bsharat, Aidar Myrzakhan & Zhiqiang Shen, *Principled Instructions Are All You Need for Questioning LLaMA-1/2, GPT-3.5/4* (Dec. 26, 2023) (unpublished manuscript), https://arxiv.org/abs/2312.16171.

[19] McDole Williams, *Nu-You Technologies Files Patent Infringement Lawsuits Against Industry Competitors*, PR Newswire (Oct. 27, 2015), https://www.prnewswire.com/news-releases/nu-you-technologies-files-patent-infringement-lawsuits-against-industry-competitors-300167060.html;

referred to as a hair sponge and has a handle portion attached to a pliable portion (sponge) with bores spaced and sized to shape and style hair.[20] Their sponge created a twisted hairstyle within minutes when the hand-twisting method took hours. It could be used for children and adults who did not have the time, money, or patience for a hand-twisted style, and it was versatile enough to work for those with short and long hair. Gopou (who worked in the Black hair industry as a stylist) and Boyd (who had worn his hair in an Afro and dreadlocks) knew they could leverage their cultural capital—their knowledge derived from these experiences—to experiment with different materials, including those popular in Africa, to arrive at their final prototype. Gopou emphasized that, as a stylist, she used to hate doing the twist style before inventing the hair sponge because "it was so nasty [with] the comb, [and] the gel."[21] When Gopou and Boyd successfully used their invention on their toddler to quickly create a twisted hairstyle, they knew they "had a tiger by the tail."[22]

Gopou and Boyd enlisted an attorney to patent the device. As Gopou recalls, "[They (as inventors)] didn't know the questions [they] could ask [the attorney], because [they] didn't know the process."[23] During the intake process, Boyd gave the patent attorney a full disclosure of the invention before the attorney filed the application.

The application discussed how the device is used, describing how the sponge is pulled across the hair tangentially and the bores "caus[e] clumps of said hair to be formed at substantially regular intervals that are a function of the distance between ones of said spaced-apart bores."[24] Although the patent attorney used the word "clump" in the patent application, neither Boyd nor Gopou used the term "clump" to describe their invention or hairstyle. They specifically used the word "twist" to describe both the style and the method of use.[25] The different word choice may indicate a language gap between the

Interview with Brigitte Gopou and Bruce Boyd, Inventors of the NuDred Hair Sponge, Nu-You Techs., LLC (Aug. 31, 2022) [hereinafter Gopou–Boyd Interview].

20 *NuDreds: Categories*, NuDred, https://nudred.com/collections/sponges (last visited Dec. 19, 2023).

21 Gopou–Boyd Interview, *supra* note 19.

22 *Id.* (meaning they had discovered something powerful but potentially difficult to control).

23 *Id.*

24 U.S. Patent Application Serial No. 10/925,126 (filed Aug. 24, 2004).

25 *Id.* Note that the patent application does not use the term "sponge," but both Gopou and Boyd use that term when describing their invention. Gopou–Boyd Interview, *supra* note 19.

inventors and their attorney that persisted throughout the initial patent intake and prosecution process.

The USPTO sorted the application into two Cooperative Patent Classification (CPC) areas: A45D (hairdressing or shaving equipment) and A47K (sanitary equipment).[26] Although there is no record of how the application for a haircare product was classified as a piece of sanitary equipment, we suspect that the sponge-like appearance of the device played a primary role in this misclassification.

Injustices in the patent prosecution process only began to snowball after the classification process was complete. In the inventors' first rejection, mailed from the USPTO on February 3, 2006, the examiner rejected the device claims and allowed the method claims.[27] The examiner claimed that the hair device was not novel or obvious in light of two *bath* sponges, neither of which discusses how they could be used to shape hair.[28]

In the obviousness rejection, the examiner concluded that an ordinarily skilled person would read two bath sponge patent applications and, drawing from their teachings and common sense, find that the claimed invention is merely "the predictable use of prior art elements."[29] Here, the examiner essentially alleged that a PHOSITA would find bath sponges analogous to a hair sponge and that any innovation for using a bath sponge on a person's hair would be an obvious leap. In reality, it is unlikely that a person could use a bath sponge to shape hair like Gopou and Boyd's hair sponge, given that bath sponges are made of rubber and the hair sponge is made of polyurethane (a plastic material).[30] These materials are decidedly different and have distinct purposes in the haircare space. Rubber, like a rubber band, can pull and break hair but can be excellent at cleaning the body and gripping slippery items like soap. Plastic, which is used in many hair combs today, does no such thing and is much more suited for a hair application. It is not simply a matter of "select[ing] a known material on the basis of its suitability for the intended use as a matter of obvious design choice"; the differences highlight how this prior art is not "from the same field of endeavor as the claimed

[26] *Cooperative Patent Classification* 9, 11, U.S. Pat. & Trademark Off., https://www.uspto.gov/web/patents/classification/cpc/pdf/cpc-scheme-A.pdf (last visited July 31, 2025).

[27] Non-final Rejection, U.S. Patent Application Serial No. 10/925,126 (Feb. 3, 2006).

[28] *Id.*

[29] MPEP, *supra* note 5, § 2141.03 (quoting KSR Int'l Co. v. Teleflex Inc., 550 U.S. 398, 417 (2007)).

[30] U.S. Patent Application Serial No. 10/925,126 (filed Aug. 24, 2004); U.S. Patent No. 2,588,773 (filed Mar. 22, 1948); U.S. Patent No. 1,943,365 (filed Jan. 13, 1933).

invention," nor are they "reasonably pertinent to the problem faced by the endeavor."[31]

The examiner continued to reject the claims over U.S. Patent No. 6,325,565 (Girardot), which is a patent for an antiperspirant applicator.[32] The examiner argued that placing the antiperspirant applicator on hair would cause clumps to be formed at the bores. The attorney rightfully pointed out in the response that the examiner provided "no supporting rationale for such alleged inherency."[33]

By rejecting the hair-sponge claims over body sponges and antiperspirant applicators, the examiner alleged that a PHOSITA would view these items as analogous art for a hairstyling device. We believe that attempts to compare bath sponges and antiperspirant applicators to hairstyling tools are, at best, based on cultural misunderstandings. Eventually, Gopou and Boyd received a method patent for their invention. They have been very successful in litigation. This patent has been asserted at least seven times in court—with five permanent injunctions, one sanction, and one undisclosed settlement.[34] However, there is no way to determine how much money the patent owner could have earned if the application had been classified, written, and argued differently. The final outcomes of these cases might have been different if the examination process had been less biased and if the attorney had gained more cultural capital in Black haircare during or before the patent prosecution process.

Human Biases in the Patent Process

Every interaction with another human can be tainted by bias, and the patent process is no exception.[35] These biases manifest in unequal treatment of

[31] Non-final Rejection, U.S. Patent Application Serial No. 10/925,126 (Feb. 3, 2006); *In re* Bigio, 381 F.3d 1320, 1325 (Fed. Cir. 2004).

[32] Anti-perspirant/Deodorant Applicator, U.S. Patent No. 6,325,565 (filed Nov. 4, 1998) (issued Dec. 4, 2001).

[33] Applicant Arguments/Remarks Made in an Amendment, U.S. Patent Application Serial No. 10/925,126, at 10 (Aug. 14, 2006).

[34] Nu-You Techs., LLC v. Beauty Town Int'l Inc., No. 3:15-cv-03433, 2017 WL 4297229 (N.D. Tex. Aug. 24, 2017) (undisclosed settlement as to Nu-You's indirect infringement claims); Nu-You Techs. LLC v. Dream World Inc., No. 3:15-cv-03438 (N.D. Tex. Nov. 22, 2016) (permanent injunction); Nu-You Techs., LLC v. Eltoweissy, No. 3:15-cv-03434 (N.D. Tex. Sept. 27, 2016) (awarding Nu-You $4,481 in attorney's fees); Nu-You Techs. LLC v. Chee-Ping, No. 3:15-cv-03437 (N.D. Tex. Sept. 22, 2016) (permanent injunction); Nu-You Techs. LLC v. Jehan Corp., No. 3:15-cv-03436 (N.D. Tex. Sept. 2, 2016) (permanent injunction); Nu-You Techs. LLC v. DSK Corp., No. 3:15-cv-03435 (N.D. Tex. Aug. 15, 2016) (permanent injunction); Nu-You Techs. LLC v. Bee Sales Co., No. 3:15-cv-03432 (N.D. Tex. May 23, 2016) (settling with permanent injunction).

[35] Karen Steinhauser, *Everyone Is a Little Bit Biased*, Am. Bar Ass'n (Mar. 16, 2020), https://www.americanbar.org/groups/business_law/resources/business-law-today/2020-april/everyone-is-a-little-bit-biased/.

inventors, which likely contributes to the systemic underrepresentation of people most likely to be negatively affected by bias: those "other" to people in power.[36]

Among the three key players in the patent prosecution process—the inventor, the practitioner, and the examiner—the practitioner and examiner often have more power than the inventor. We, therefore, categorize them as the gatekeepers to patentability. The practitioner writes the patent application, sets the price of patent prosecution, and takes primary responsibility for the vast majority of the patent application's content. The practitioner chooses questions to ask the inventor, advises on how to write claims in the application, and, in the case of a patent attorney, provides legal counsel relating to future licenses and potential infringement suits. Once the practitioner sends the application to the USPTO, the examiner determines whether the claims, as written, are allowable. If the examiner rejects the application, the practitioner reviews the rejection and can make judgments about the reasonableness of the rejection and how to amend the claims in response. These judgments form the basis for their recommendation to the inventor, who can choose to accept or reject the practitioner's advice.

Every judgment call within the patent process is subject to bias. These biases manifest both as interpersonal bias (occurring between individuals) and as systemic bias (existing across society and between its institutions).[37]

Hypothetically, after describing the invention to the practitioner, the client asks the practitioner, "Can you write the application?" Whether the practitioner is qualified to write the application necessarily calls into question whether the practitioner understands the invention. Such understanding is influenced by the practitioner's cultural capital, the inventor's cultural capital, and the cultural capital necessary for a skilled person to make and use the invention.

When the practitioner is a member of a majority group, the inventor is a member of a minority group, and the inventor's invention relies on cultural capital of that minority group, the cultural-capital gap between the practitioner and the inventor may affect the patent prosecution process, especially if the practitioner cannot acquire the cultural capital necessary to prosecute the patent application.

Similar disparate cultural-capital concerns arise at the USPTO and in litigation. The cultural capital of examiners, judges, litigators, and juries

[36] Allie Bunch, *Epistemic Violence in the Process of Othering: Real-World Applications and Moving Forward*, 1 Scholarly Undergraduate Rsch. J. Clark 11, 11 (2015).
[37] *Levels of Racism: Systemic vs Individual*, Fitchburg St. Univ., https://fitchburgstate.libguides.com/c.php?g=1046516&p=7602969 (Mar. 15, 2023).

will affect how they view the patent application. Examiners reviewing applications will make connections to prior art that they are innately familiar with, and this exposure influences their judgment of novelty and obviousness. If the examiner determines that the application fails the enablement requirement, the examiner "must establish on the record a reasonable basis for questioning the adequacy of the disclosure to enable a [PHOSITA] to make and use the claimed invention without resorting to undue experimentation."[38] To reject the application for a lack of written description, the examiner must establish that the specification failed to convey "with reasonable clarity to those skilled in the art that, as of the filing date sought, [the] applicant was in possession of the invention as now claimed."[39] All of these questions are affected by personal biases, which affect the application writing, the application cost, and the arguments and strategy employed when amending claims based on rejections from the USPTO.

Before delving further, it is of the utmost importance to understand that the PHOSITA standard for judging a patent application is inherently biased.[40] As described by various scholars, the supposed neutral standard of the PHOSITA is a fallacy;[41] the standard is constructed and interpreted by biased humans and excludes criteria accounting for the cultural biases intertwined in every decision made by these biased humans. We recognize and endorse wholeheartedly that the biased PHOSITA standard infiltrates and negatively affects almost every standard of patentability, from obviousness to enablement to written description.

Biases in Writing the Patent Application

When deciding to take on a client, the practitioner must first determine if they have the skills and cultural capital necessary to capture the inventor's idea in a patent application. If not, can they acquire such skills and cultural capital during the writing process?

Almost always, if a practitioner has passed the patent bar, patent law deems the practitioner to have relevant expertise to handle this type of case. Any

[38] MPEP, *supra* note 5, § 2161.
[39] *Id.* § 2163.
[40] Goodman, *Sy-STEM-ic Bias*, *supra* note 1.
[41] Dan L. Burk, *Do Patents Have Gender?*, 19 AM. U. J. GENDER SOC. POL'Y & L. 881, 903 (2011).

practitioner who has passed the patent bar can legally write and prosecute patent applications about any subject.

There will always be times when the inventor's knowledge or skill level does not overlap with the practitioner's; the divergence is likely part of the invention's novelty. It is the practitioner's job to recognize and effectively bridge this gap to write a good patent application. Patent practitioners are trained to identify when overlap gaps derive from differences in academic education and understanding. For example, a patent attorney with a Bachelor of Science in chemistry can assess the sufficiency of description in a chemistry-related invention, but they may have difficulty identifying these areas in a computer science–related invention. However, patent practitioners are insufficiently trained to recognize gaps stemming from nonacademic education cultural capital. This insufficient training creates disparate results for underrepresented inventors and the inventions derived from their nonacademic, nonmajority-based cultural capital.

Although interpersonal and systemic biases exist in all areas of patent prosecution, the writing process is primarily intertwined with interpersonal biases. According to sociolinguistic and linguistic anthropology theory, if the inventor and practitioner belong to different speech communities (stemming from different cultures and creating different cultural capital for members of each speech community group), they may have a more difficult time communicating effectively than if they both belonged to the same speech community.[42] The practitioner's communication skill, especially with respect to bridging speech communities, is vital to the success of the patent application writing endeavor.

"A speech community is a group of people who share rules for conducting and interpreting at least one variety of a language or dialect."[43] A speech community does not necessarily encompass all people speaking the same language. For example, "speakers of South Asian English in India and Pakistan share a language with citizens of the United States, but the respective varieties of English and the rules for speaking them are sufficiently distinct to assign the two populations to different speech communities."[44] Speech communities may have different vocabularies, grammar, and pronunciations in the same language. To have mutual intelligibility between two speakers,

[42] Zdenek Salzmann, Language, Culture, and Society: An Introduction to Linguistic Anthropology 244–46 (4th ed. 2007).

[43] Annela Teemant & Stefinee E. Pinnegar, *What Is a Speech Community?*, *in* Principles of Language Acquisition § 1.1 (Bohdana Allman ed., 2019).

[44] Salzmann, *supra* note 42, at 244–46.

their vocabularies must overlap. Inventors of less-represented speech communities in patent law will likely have a more difficult time finding a practitioner who overlaps with their speech community. They must, therefore, find a practitioner with enough cultural capital to bridge the speech community gap.

Miscommunications, especially between speakers from different speech communities, often happen when speakers use slang. For example, the term "knock up" may mean to wake someone up in British English, but it is generally taken to mean "to make pregnant" in American English. If neither the American nor British speaker understands that there is a polysemy—the coexistence of many possible meanings of a term—there will likely be some confusion when this term is used in a sentence.

Furthermore, speakers with different knowledge bases may sometimes belong to slightly different speech communities because their vocabulary differs. In the famous Abbott and Costello "Who's on First?" comedy routine, Bud Abbott is identifying baseball players for Lou Costello, but neither character understands that there is a polysemy problem: Who, What, Why, I Don't Know, and the like all have two meanings.[45] There is a layman's meaning (question words and answers to question words), and there is an expert meaning (the names of the baseball players). Abbott, a person with in-depth knowledge of each baseball player's name, believes he is being incredibly clear by answering Costello's questions with their proper names (Who, What, Why, I Don't Know, etc.). Abbott's subject matter expertise informs his answers, but he assumes that Costello has enough subject matter expertise to perceive these answers as *answers*, not as confusing responses. Costello simultaneously has very different subject matter expertise, such that Abbott's responses only evoke the layman's definition. Their simultaneous, growing frustration stems from each character's unintentional lexical ambiguity—the presence of multiple meanings in a single word.

If a practitioner does not understand the client's invention because of lexical ambiguity, this mismatch in language can manifest in a breakdown in interpersonal communication and result in a poorly written patent application and a fraught intake process.

[45] Universal Pictures, *The Naughty Nineties: Who's on First?—Abbott and Costello*, YouTube (June 28, 2022), https://www.youtube.com/watch?v=sYOUFGfK4bU.

For example, an inventor may ask a practitioner to write a patent application for braces. The practitioner may immediately start asking about teeth, brackets, and metal wiring because, in their speech community, braces are orthodontic appliances. However, the client may come from a speech community where the term "braces" means "suspenders" and may be confused by the practitioner's initial question set. The longer both parties fail to recognize the secondary meaning of "braces," the longer their communication may fail.

Unfamiliarity with a term is commonplace in patent law. If the practitioner is unfamiliar with the client's term or underlying invention, the practitioner will likely ask broad questions to lead the client to describe their invention. The practitioner may offer suggestions or prompts to fully capture the invention's breadth. If the practitioner is familiar with the subject matter, their suggestions might be more helpful to the client. Conversely, if the practitioner is unfamiliar, their suggestions might be less helpful. If the practitioner and client use two very different definitions and have not yet found an overlapping vocabulary, the practitioner may provide erroneous suggestions.

For example, if the client lists that their toothbrush invention could be made of plastic or nylon, the practitioner can prompt the client to see if the brush could be made of other suitable materials, like metal or bamboo. Both may be appropriate materials for brushes, but one may be ideal. An unfamiliar attorney may list that toothbrushes might be made of metal but may neglect to identify that iron would likely be unsuitable because it rusts in water. Other unfamiliar practitioners may import their own biases into the application and may suggest that the brush can be used to clear off a car or clean a sink.

Even if there is an overlap between the practitioner's and client's cultural capital such that the practitioner recognizes both definitions of "braces," or that the practitioner understands why iron would be unsuitable for a toothbrush, the practitioner must recognize the potential disparities between the practitioner and client's collective cultural capital and the examiner's cultural capital before an examiner evaluates the application, or is even assigned to the application. The examiner serves as a gatekeeper, in that, if the examiner fails to have the cultural capital necessary to recognize both definitions of "braces"—or imposes their viewpoint to assert that a PHOSITA would not have the cultural capital to make the same decisions—the inventor may not receive a patent for their work. If the practitioner fails to anticipate future disparate outlooks on the invention described in the application, the application may be doomed.

Inventors can work on their inventions for years before coming to a patent practitioner. As someone with a high level of expertise in this invention and a resulting high level of cultural capital derived from their experience, an inventor may not be forthcoming about details necessary to make or use their invention. This is not because they want to keep their invention a trade secret. Rather, someone with a high subject matter expertise in their invention may have difficulty communicating the importance of every seemingly obvious detail. For an inventor who has styled their hair their entire life, terms like "sealing ends," putting hair in a "protective style," and a "bonnet" need no further explanation. However, if a patent practitioner does not understand these terms, they may use them incorrectly in the application. Furthermore, if an examiner determines that these words lack clarity and are indefinite, the patent practitioner cannot add these details to the patent application after submitting it to the USPTO.

It is more likely that a practitioner will omit these details—like the utility of a design choice—if the practitioner cannot use or relate to the client's invention. With little overlap in relevant cultural spaces between practitioner and inventor, the practitioner must acquire the cultural capital necessary to prosecute the patent application through external sources—from the client, research, or other lived experiences. If a practitioner has never used a toothbrush and cannot use one, they must learn about the toothbrush before writing a patent application because they must be able to communicate this use to a PHOSITA. They will need to learn everything from the client—how the brush scrubs teeth, picks up toothpaste, is cleaned, and is stored—through language rather than experience. This communication requirement places a greater burden on clients whose attorneys are unfamiliar with the cultural capital–derived subject matter of their invention. It also puts an especially large burden on clients whose practitioners cannot experience their invention firsthand.

When a practitioner has no cultural capital relevant to the invention, this communication barrier becomes a larger hurdle to overcome. Even if the practitioner recognizes that the necessary cultural capital derives from a nonacademic source, they may fear making their client uncomfortable if they venture to ask important questions. Practitioners who write patents for feminine hygiene products, for example, may feel uncomfortable asking about what they perceive to be intimate details about a woman's menstrual cycle, especially if the practitioner does not have a menstrual cycle and the inventor does. A practitioner writing a patent for a Black haircare product may be uncomfortable asking about different hair textures, wash day, or specific hairstyles for fear of being perceived as racist (especially if the practitioner does not have 4A–4C hair and the client does).

Practitioners who are uncomfortable bridging gaps between speech communities may choose to import language from their speech communities rather than use their client's language. For example, if a practitioner refers to their toothbrush as an "electric toothbrush," rather than an "electric brush," they may choose to use this language in the application, instead of their client's original "brush" term. Although this may seem harmless, the practitioner must confirm that their use of a different term does not import other definitions, evoke other associations, or otherwise override their client's intent. Improper term use, especially one deviating from the client's intent, may result in the rejection of the inventor's patent application, patent invalidation during litigation, or a finding of noninfringement when a patent owner seeks to enforce their rights.

In some situations, especially when the practitioner does not have sufficient communication and social awareness skills, clients may be required to create a prototype of their invention to communicate to their practitioner how to make and use their invention. Technically, this is unnecessary under patent law. However, for the practitioner to write the patent application effectively, they also need to understand how to make and use the invention. Clients face larger communication barriers and access issues when their practitioners are not equipped to understand the nature of their invention.

It is especially important for practitioners with different lived experiences and speech communities than their clients to have good cultural communication skills to overcome the obstacles commonly found in patent application drafting.

Biases in the Examination Process

Once a patent application is submitted to the USPTO, the patent application will be sorted by a classification system into subject-matter categories, and then an examiner with expertise in these categories will review the application to determine if the claims are allowable. This process, along with the interactions between the practitioner and examiner, introduces another source of bias in the patent examination process.

The USPTO sorts applications by subject matter—ideally by something known as proximate function (or what the invention does)[46]—and then examiners specializing in that subject matter search for prior art relevant to the invention. Both this subject-matter decision and the language within the specification can lead to biased interpretations of the invention scope.

As discussed above, individuals belonging to different speech communities may have a more difficult time communicating effectively than if they belonged to the same speech community. A person's lived experiences inform their speech community, and in the case of an examiner, their art unit classification likely informs their speech community. The examiner's speech community—as well as their perception of the PHOSITA's speech community—informs, for example, choices examiners may make while searching relevant art and interpreting claims in the patent application.

First, the examiner's individual speech choices and the classification system collectively inform their initial search for relevant prior art. "Classification provides a method to search for relevant items independent from the ability of the searcher to think up relevant keywords to include in the search statement."[47] The examiner, or the searcher, determines relevant words to search when evaluating the patent application. Prior art results will vary depending on the classification of the patent application, regardless of whether this was classification by hand or machine.

For example, an examiner in a plumbing unit may reject tracheostomy tube inventions over hoses, but an examiner in a medical device unit may reject tracheostomy tube inventions over other medical devices with tubes because that examiner is more familiar with the prior art. Biases in art unit classification, especially those stemming from a lack of understanding of the invention or the community of people of ordinary skill in the art, will affect the search results.

In the search and the resulting first office action, the examiner compares the claims to the prior art, including previous patents and publications, to determine if the invention in the present patent application is novel and nonobvious according to the examiner's constructed PHOSITA. The

[46] Heather J.E. Simmons, *Categorizing the Useful Arts: Past, Present, and Future Development of Patent Classification in the United States*, 106 L. Libr. J. 563, 568 (2014).
[47] *Id.* at 569.

examiner also evaluates the application on enablement and written description grounds.

Every human is capable of importing their biases into supposedly neutral evaluations. The patent examiner may import their biases both when constructing the PHOSITA and when evaluating the invention's patentability. These biases may be based on their conception of the fictitious skilled person, the language developed in the patent search, and their perception of the language within the specification. This is similar to a biased game of telephone, where the translation from the inventor to the practitioner to the patent office affects later stages of examination: the application's classification and the examiner's perception of relevant art. This is especially true if the claimed invention relies on cultural capital not shared by the examiner or practitioner and not accounted for in the classification system.

If the examiner determines that the application is not allowable, they will issue a rejection, or an office action, on specified grounds for the practitioner to refute. If this rejection is erroneous—made over non-analogous art—the inventor must still pay for the practitioner's time and effort to respond accordingly. The more biased and off-base the examiner's understanding of the invention is, the more difficult the process will likely be to eventually receive an allowance.

Regardless of whether the office action is biased, the practitioner receiving the rejection must evaluate the substance and prepare a response strategy. To succeed, they must communicate this strategy to the inventor so that the inventor understands the strategy and reason for the response. Additionally, the argument must be understandable and persuasive to the examiner such that the response allows the patent prosecution to progress. This requires an overlap in speech communities or an effort on the part of the practitioner to bridge the gap. Thus, a response strategy is more likely to be successful when the practitioner, examiner, inventor, and origin of the invention all derive from the same source of cultural capital. With inventions derived from minority-group cultural capital not shared by the examiner and practitioner, especially if the inventor uses speech derived from the same minority-group cultural capital, this communication response process will be more difficult.

Furthermore, once the lack of speech overlap is discovered in the office action, it may be too late to correct the speech gap between the description of an invention in the specification and the language the examiner needs to understand the invention and properly classify and analyze its patentability. When responding to a rejection—over either analogous or non-analogous art—the practitioner must (1) recognize the analogous nature of the art; and (2) use the disclosure in the original patent application to form the basis of their response. If the practitioner fails to include a detail in the specification (such as the size of the tracheostomy tube), they will likely be unable to use that detail later to overcome a rejection (like a rejection over a garden hose). Furthermore, even if the necessary detail is in the specification, if the practitioner fails to recognize that size differentiates the tracheostomy tube from the garden hose, they will not recommend this amendment option to the client. The inventor may be disadvantaged if their practitioner fails to anticipate the linguistic differences based on the art unit classification and the potential biases of the patent examiner. We suspect this disadvantage happens most frequently when an examiner does not share the cultural capital of the minority-group inventor and fails to bridge the communication gap. The examiner may be unable or unwilling to bridge the cultural gap without explicit language in the application.

The patent system has provided a mechanism for inventors to overcome perceived gaps in the specification: they can file a declaration to traverse the rejection. Specifically, the declaration system allows an inventor to submit evidence outside of the originally filed application to overcome the rejection, but this process is also subject to bias.

The examiner must evaluate a submitted declaration to see whether its contents are sufficient in light of the specification to overcome their rejection, or if the examiner still believes the rejection should stand. The examiner will review all collected evidence, previously submitted materials, and rebuttal evidence provided in the declaration. Based on this review, the examiner will determine whether the "totality of the rebuttal evidence . . . fails to outweigh the evidence"[48] identified during examination. The decision still lies with the examiner.

AI Experiment

We experimented with currently available AI models to determine if they could address human biases discussed herein or if AI would exacerbate these issues. AI uses neural networks comprising interconnected "neural nodes."

[48] MPEP, *supra* note 5, § 716.

These nodes are computational units designed to mimic the function of neurons in the human brain. Unlike structured databases—for example, spreadsheets—AI organizes data within these interconnected neural nodes, retrieving information probabilistically based on user input. Rather than programming a new AI model, we utilized prompt engineering to guide the system in a patent prosecution experiment.

We used ChatGPT-4o (ChatGPT) to address concerns in the Gopou–Boyd patent case, though we predict other currently available machine learning platforms in October 2024 would have performed similarly.

We instructed ChatGPT to "answer a question from the perspective of a specific culture within a given context." We explicitly told ChatGPT to "provide an authentic response that reflects the values, beliefs, and worldview of the specified culture." We then gave ChatGPT context to frame its answer, plus additional guidance to "immerse [itself] in the mindset of a person from the specified culture." We required the AI to be immersed in the mindset of a person from the specified culture, encouraging it to consider cultural history, traditions, and values in formulating its response.

When we prompted ChatGPT to immerse itself in African American/Black culture and to distinguish between "twists" and "clumps"—terms between which the attorney in the case study did not distinguish—ChatGPT generated the following answer:

> Alright, let me break it down for you about these natural hairstyles we rock in our community.
>
> A "twist" is a popular style where we take two sections of hair and wrap them around each other from root to tip. It's like a two-strand braid, but instead of braiding, you're twisting. Twists can be big or small, depending on how much hair you use for each section. They can hang down or be styled up in different ways. Twists are versatile and can protect our hair while looking fresh.
>
> Now, when it comes to "clumps," that's not really a hairstyle we typically talk about in our community. I think you might be referring to "locs" or "dreadlocks." Locs are formed when our naturally coily or kinky hair is allowed to mat and form rope-like strands. They're not just clumped together; it's a deliberate process that takes time and care.
>
> The main difference is that twists are a temporary style that can be undone, while locs are a more permanent commitment. Twists can be a protective style for a few weeks, or even a way to start locs. But true locs are a

> long-term journey that represents a connection to our African roots and natural hair texture.
>
> Both styles celebrate our hair's natural texture and are ways for us to express our identity and culture. Whether you're rocking twists or locs, it's all about embracing and showcasing the beauty of our Black hair.

At first read, the opening is quite jarring. After presenting this response to a group of diverse law students, many found that the opening sentence and the use of the term "fresh" and other linguistic choices carried potentially racist undertones, or at least a misappropriation of community-specific language. Others appreciated the inclusion of speech not typically found in white-dominant spaces, questioning whether expecting a certain language dialect output may lead to the erasure of minority community speech. There is value in preserving and respecting different forms of language expression, particularly those emerging from distinct cultural contexts. While we support generative AI models' freedom to use diverse linguistic expressions, including jargon commonly found in minority communities, the issue of appropriate usage remains complex. AI models have not mastered technical jargon or slang, regardless of their minority or majority cultural context.[49] ChatGPT's use of community-specific language without proper context or cultural understanding can be problematic and potentially disrespectful. We note that the tension between linguistic freedom and cultural sensitivity presents a crucial consideration in the future role of machine learning. We further note that, as of November 2025, ChatGPT, Google Gemini, and Claude all produced results that did not include any noticeable specific racial, cultural linguistic choices. We encourage continued development to improve AI models' holistic vocabulary and culturally appropriate and properly contextualized vernacular.[50]

Going beyond the initial opening, ChatGPT provided a greater depth of information than the Gopou–Boyd patent specification. It correctly identified the term "twist," explained the inappropriate use of the term "clump," and offered an alternative word—locs or dreadlocks—as a substitute for clump. This clarification of culturally nuanced terms corrects the miscommunication between Gopou, Boyd, and their attorney. Additionally,

[49] Michael Sharp, *Teaching Computers to Read "Industry Lingo"—Technical vs. Natural Language Processing*, Nat'l Inst. Standards & Tech. (Oct. 26, 2022), https://www.nist.gov/blogs/taking-measure/teaching-computers-read-industry-lingo-technical-vs-natural-language-processing.

[50] *Id.*

ChatGPT uses the term "protective style" when describing how members of the Black community often wear twists, which shows an understanding of cultural traditions. None of these words were used in the Gopou–Boyd patent specification. In many ways, careful consideration of this model answer when constructing a patent specification may remedy lexical gaps between the inventor's disclosure and the practitioner's summation. Further development of tools to reduce linguistic bias may help overall patent composition, prior art search, and the office action-response processes.

Conclusion

Profound inequities are embedded in the patent system. Underrepresentation of Black inventors reflects systemic biases pervading the patent process. The cultural capital necessary to navigate this complex landscape effectively and equitably can be absent or misaligned between inventors and the patent gatekeepers—practitioners and examiners.

AI-assisted tools can bridge cultural gaps and enhance communication while simultaneously perpetuating existing biases. AI is not a replacement for human actors in the patent process. Instead, AI is another tool to assist humans in their efforts to create more equitable pathways for underrepresented inventors.

By enhancing the clarity of cultural nuances in patent applications, these tools may aid the broader effort to reform inequities in the patent system. We can work toward a patent landscape that truly reflects the richness of human innovation by embracing diversity, enhancing cultural competency, and employing AI responsibly. Ultimately, the path to equity in the patent system is a collective responsibility, necessitating ongoing dialogue and reform to ensure that all inventors, regardless of their background, have equal opportunities to protect their innovations and contribute to our shared economic future.

Acknowledgments

Portions of this chapter were originally published as "Access to Justice for Black Inventors" in the *Vanderbilt Law Review*.

III.

INITIATIVES TO PROMOTE INCLUSIVE INNOVATION

7

Inclusive Innovation in an Age of AI

Insights from the Innovator Diversity Pilots Initiative

Margo A. Bagley and Colleen V. Chien

Introduction

When we launched the Innovator Diversity Pilots Initiative (IDPI) in the winter of 2022, the world was recovering from a global pandemic that highlighted both the critical importance of having all hands on deck, like those of Nobel Prize winner Katalin Karikó and Kizzmekia Corbett-Helaire, the co-inventors of the Moderna COVID-19 vaccine, and the profound challenges of inequality in our innovation infrastructure.[1] Since then, the evidence base for including a broad range and diversity of people in ideating, developing, and commercializing innovations has only grown stronger, especially as artificial intelligence (AI) transforms how we work, create, and innovate. As a recent policy brief on the policy and science of AI puts it, "scientific creativity is undermined by the relative homogeneity of the scientific workforce, which narrows the diversity of ideas."[2] And yet, the composition of the computer scientist workforce powering AI advances remains skewed.[3]

At the time of the creation of the IDPI, we had two key goals: (1) support collaborations between academics and others to develop rigorous evidence to advance inclusive innovation; and (2) highlight and uplift the efforts of others—including firms, policymakers, and practitioners—doing

[1] Particularly in the realm of digital inequality, which impacted the ability of individuals to work from home, stay connected, and safely access health services. Elisabeth Beaunoyer, Sophie Dupéré & Matthieu J. Guitton, *COVID-19 and Digital Inequalities: Reciprocal Impacts and Mitigation Strategies*, 111 Computs. Hum. Behav. 106424 (2020).

[2] *A New Golden Age of Discovery*, AI Pol'y Persp. (Nov. 26, 2024), https://www.aipolicyperspectives.com/p/a-new-golden-age-of-discovery.

[3] Stanford Univ., Inst. for Human-Centered A.I., Artificial Intelligence Index Report 2024, at 411–34 (2024).

Margo A. Bagley and Colleen V. Chien, *Inclusive Innovation in an Age of AI* In: *Inclusive Innovation in the Age of AI and Big Data*. Edited by: Daryl Lim and Peter K. Yu, Oxford University Press. © Oxford University Press 2026.
DOI: 10.1093/9780197799444.003.0010

the same, to create a space in which we could learn from and share with each other. This chapter revisits some of the insights developed in pursuit of both goals through conferences, blog posts, and related research publications.[4] It also focuses on learnings from the 2024 IDPI Conference held at Emory University School of Law at the intersection of human relationships, inclusive innovation, and AI.

We begin by stating the case for inclusive innovation and why it is so crucial to innovation quality, the expansion and efficient allocation of talent, and global competitiveness. We then share insights that have emerged about its challenges, in both corporate and legal settings, and three ways they might be overcome: (1) through education, awareness-raising, networking, and mentorship, all of which build the "invention capital" essential for fostering innovation in technical and legal professions in an age of AI;[5] (2) through institutional support and process design, whether through the building of the pipeline or resources for helping people successfully navigate various stages of it; and (3) through private- and public-sector policy leadership. We conclude by describing several promising applications of AI that could serve as the basis for future "AI diversity pilots" that would apply the power of AI to the mechanisms identified as effective for fostering inclusive innovation.

Why Inclusive Innovation Matters

We begin by synthesizing research about why inclusive innovation is important: It broadens the direction and impact of research and improves its quality, it strengthens the economy, and it boosts international competitiveness. It does so through several mechanisms, including the application of novel insights, experiences, and motivations to existing and new problems, the challenging of assumptions leading to new solutions, and the deepening of the talent pool and improvements of the allocation of talent.[6]

[4] Available at Innovator Diversity Pilots Initiative, https://diversitypilots.org (last visited May 7, 2025), with blog entries cross-posted at PatentlyO and Written Description blogs.

[5] Colleen V. Chien, *The Inequalities of Innovation*, 72 Emory L.J. 1, 33–34 (2022).

[6] *Id.* at 12.

Direction, Impact, and Quality of Innovation

A striking line of recent research confirms that an innovator's identity can influence what and how research is conducted and who benefits from it. When diverse innovators bring their personal experiences, knowledge, and motivations to advancing the frontiers of science and technology, the focus and reach of innovation expand.

Several recent studies show how innovators are more likely to work on problems that impact them or others like them. For example, Rembrand Koning, Sampsa Samila, and John-Paul Ferguson's analysis of U.S. biomedical patents from 1976 to 2010 revealed that all-female research teams were more likely to focus on women's health conditions and study how treatments differently affect women than were all-male teams.[7] Forthcoming research, presented at the IDPI Conference by Gaia Dossi, traces how researcher race has also shaped scientific priorities.[8] Her analysis of scientific articles and patents found that Black researchers were more likely to study diseases that disproportionately impact Black Americans, like HIV (where the match is driven by demographics) and sickle-cell anemia (where the match is driven by genetics). Similar patterns were found across Hispanic, Asian-American, and White scientists (who, for example, were more likely to focus on melanoma).[9] Analyzing publication patterns, Diego Kozlowski and his coauthors have also found researcher characteristics to be strongly correlated with research topics—for instance, Black and African American authors were more likely to study racial disparities, while Latinx researchers frequently focused on topics related to Hispanic language and cultural identity.[10]

This pattern extends to student inventors as well. In their analysis of 2,000 collegiate inventors competing in a national prize competition, April Burrage and her coauthors documented clear differences in invention focus based on innovator demographics. Their study revealed distinct patterns in how different groups approached innovation.[11]

[7] Rembrand Koning, Sampsa Samila & John-Paul Ferguson, *Inventor Gender and the Direction of Invention*, 110 AEA Papers & Proc. 250 (2020).

[8] Gaia Dossi, Race and Science, Address at the Second Innovator Diversity Pilots Conference at Emory University School of Law (Sept. 20, 2024) (unpublished manuscript) (on file with authors).

[9] *Id.*

[10] Diego Kozlowski, Vincent Larivière, Cassidy R. Sugimoto & Thema Monroe-White, *Intersectional Inequalities in Science*, 119 Proc. Nat'l Acad. Scis. e2113067119, at 4 (2022).

[11] For example, men of color showed particular interest in developing consumer-oriented inventions. April Burrage, Janell Ciemiecki, Stephanie Couch & Ina Ganguli, *Inclusive Pathways to Invention: Racial and Ethnic Diversity Among Collegiate Student Inventors in a National Prize Competition*, 22 Tech. & Innovation 341, 342 (2022).

Research by Elias Einiö, Josh Feng, and Xavier Jaravel has established a similar link between innovator and innovation in the realm of mobile and desktop applications.[12] Their study found that engineers tended to create products serving people similar to themselves and that even indirect experience shaped innovation focus: Developers who had significant exposure to lower-income peers were more likely to create "necessity products."[13]

To be clear, this is not to say that inventor research foci are solely determined by demographic or group factors; they are not. Women develop solutions to problems that predominantly affect men,[14] and minority inventors solve problems affecting majority group members. Rather, collectively, these studies demonstrate that increasing the inclusion of diverse groups in the innovation ecosystem is not only about who innovates but also what problems get solved and which communities stand to benefit from research.

Team diversity also yields benefits. Yang Yang, Tanya Tian, and Teresa Woodruff have found that diverse teams in science produce papers that are more novel and highly cited than papers produced by all-women or all-men teams.[15] Davidson Heath, Nathan Seegert, and Jeffrey Yang's recent analysis of open source software teams found that increased team diversity generated more diverse ideas and improved project outcomes across various metrics including survival, development, and popularity.[16] Notably, teams with low starting levels of diversity benefited the most from increasing it. Studies have also found teams that are diverse on a range of dimensions to have produced insights and innovations with greater originality, impact, and radical innovation than less diverse teams.[17]

[12] Elias Einiö, Josh Feng & Xavier Jaravel, *Social Push and the Direction of Innovation* (Ctr. for Econ. Performance, Discussion Paper No. 1861, 2022), https://cep.lse.ac.uk/pubs/download/dp1861.pdf.

[13] The study documented a geographic dimension as well, with apps gaining particular traction in their creators' home states. *Id.* at 9.

[14] For example, a librarian helping one of us gather research on this topic described a female inventor she knew who patented a prosthetic testicle for men who need to have one removed for testicular cancer or other reasons. Women are just more likely than men to invent solutions to problems that affect women uniquely. Margo A. Bagley, *Deploying Our Secret Weapon*, Marq. Law., Summer 2024, at 28.

[15] Yang Yang, Tanya Y. Tian & Teresa K. Woodruff, *Gender-Diverse Teams Produce More Novel and Higher-Impact Scientific Ideas*, 119 Proc. Nat'l Acad. Scis. e2200841119 (2022).

[16] Davidson Heath, Nathan Seegert & Jeffrey Yang, *Team Production and the Homophily Trap: Evidence from Open Source Software* (Apr. 16, 2025), https://ssrn.com/abstract=4655458.

[17] Colleen Chien, *Redefining Progress: The Case for Diversity in Innovation and Inventing*, 71 UCLA L. Rev. 540, 564 (2024).

Growing the Economy through Expansion of the Talent Pool and the Efficient Allocation of Talent

Beyond shaping research priorities, inclusive innovation can yield economic benefits through the expansion and improved allocation of talent. Federal Reserve Governor Lisa Cook has estimated that including more women and African Americans in innovation could grow the U.S. economy by 0.6–4.4 percent, roughly equivalent to $1 trillion in potential annual growth to the U.S. economy.[18]

Historical evidence reinforces the economic impact of diversifying the innovator pool. Petra Moser, Alessandra Voena, and Fabian Waldinger document how Jewish émigrés from Nazi Germany to the United States drove a 31-percent increase in U.S. chemical innovations.[19] More broadly, immigrant innovators contributed an estimated 23 percent of all U.S. inventions from 1990 to 2012 while comprising only about 16 percent of inventors.[20]

The potential dividends from inclusive innovation are substantial. Research by Alex Bell and his coauthors found that, if women, minorities, and individuals from low-income families were to invent at the same rate as white men from affluent families, there would be four times as many inventors.[21] This finding points to the possibility of a significant number of "lost geniuses"—individuals who could have made substantial contributions if given proper exposure and opportunity. The economic impact of missing innovators is particularly acute given the outsized influence of "star inventors" on their peers and on technological progress. Jennifer Hunt and her coauthors calculated that closing just the gender gap in engineering jobs and patents would increase U.S. GDP per capita by 2.7 percent.[22]

[18] *U.S.-China: Winning the Economic Competition: Hearing Before the S. Subcomm. on Econ. Pol'y of the S. Comm. on Banking, Hous., & Urb. Affs.*, 116th Cong. 2 (2020) (testimony of Lisa D. Cook, Professor of Economics and International Relations, Michigan State University) (referencing Lisa D. Cook & Yang Yanyan, *Missing Women and Minorities: Implications for Innovation and Growth*, http://www.yanyanyang.com/uploads/5/6/5/2/56523543/aeapinkblack_cookyang.pdf).

[19] Petra Moser, Alessandra Voena & Fabian Waldinger, *German Jewish Émigrés and US Invention*, 104 Am. Econ. Rev. 3222, 3224 (2014).

[20] Shai Bernstein, Rebecca Diamond, Abhisit Jiranaphawiboon, Timothy McQuade & Beatriz Pousada, *The Contribution of High-Skilled Immigrants to Innovation in the United States* 3 (Nat'l Bureau of Econ. Rsch., Working Paper No. 30797, 2022).

[21] Alex Bell, Raj Chetty, Xavier Jaravel, Neviana Petkova & John Van Reenen, *Who Becomes an Inventor in America? The Importance of Exposure to Innovation*, 134 Q.J. Econ. 647, 710 (2019).

[22] Jennifer Hunt, Jean-Philippe Garant, Hannah Herman & David J. Munroe, *Why Are Women Underrepresented Amongst Patentees?*, 42 Rsch. Pol'y 831 (2013); Dev Stahlkopf & Liz Centoni, *Building a Bridge: Closing the Gender Gap for Women Inventors*, CISCO (Mar. 8, 2023), https://newsroom.cisco.com/c/r/newsroom/en/us/a/y2023/m03/building-a-bridge-closing-the-gender-gap-for-women-inventors.html.

These gaps persist, in part, due to unequal access to key resources like STEM (science, technology, engineering, and mathematics) education, role models, and professional networks (or "invention capital"[23]) as well as underrepresentation in patent-intensive fields.[24] However, as history demonstrates, the "misallocation of talent" can be corrected with systemic action. Just as the percentage of white male doctors and lawyers in the United States declined from 94 percent in 1960 to 62 percent in 2010, following civil rights advances and reduced discrimination,[25] the current composition of innovators can shift over time as barriers to participation are dismantled.[26]

These studies underscore the importance of an inclusive innovation ecosystem for expanding the scope and impact of innovation across society and the presence of what has been called "a triple dividend"[27] of reduced inequality (as frictions to participating in the scientific labor market diminish), increased innovation (as the pool of innovators grows), and more inclusive innovation (as the direction of innovation is shaped by those who create it).

Inclusive Innovation as a Global Competitiveness Lever

Inclusive innovation also matters to international competitiveness. In today's global landscape, innovation has emerged as a critical driver of national security and geopolitical strength.[28] Technology leadership is now seen as a cornerstone of competitiveness, and countries actively strive to foster innovation within their borders. The Trump and Biden administrations have explicitly stated that technology is central to geopolitical competition and national security, particularly concerning China. As one of Trump's top advisors on science and technology policy recently put it, "China has emerged as both our preeminent geopolitical rival and our most formidable technological and scientific competitor."[29] His statement echoes the Biden

[23] Chien, *supra* note 5.
[24] As documented in Hunt et al., *supra* note 22.
[25] Hsieh Chang-Tai, Erik Hurst, Charles I. Jones & Peter J. Klenow, *The Allocation of Talent and U.S. Economic Growth*, 87 ECONOMETRICA 1439, 1440 (2019).
[26] Dossi, *supra* note 8, estimates that removing race-specific frictions could increase the share of inventors and scientists by up to 10 percent.
[27] *Id.*
[28] See Suzanne Harrison and Bowman Heiden's chapter in this volume.
[29] *Nominations Hearing Before the S. Comm. on Com., Sci. & Transp.*, 119th Cong. 1 (2025) (testimony of Michael J.K. Kratsios, nominee for the Director of the Office of Science and Technology Policy).

administration's 2022 National Security Strategy, according to which China is the only U.S. competitor "with both the intent to reshape the international order and, increasingly, the economic, diplomatic, military, and technological power to [do so]."[30]

In terms of technological advancement and protection, China has long been an American concern, due to rampant copying and counterfeiting activity, lax intellectual property laws, and low damages awards for infringement.[31] According to a 2011 report from the International Trade Commission, China's intellectual property rights infringement cost the U.S. economy approximately $48 billion in 2009. The report stated that, if China complied with its then-current international obligations to protect and enforce intellectual property rights, 2.1 million jobs could be created in the United States, with "[t]he most direct jobs impact in high-tech, innovative industries."[32]

But of course, China's goal is not to create jobs in the United States; China wants to create jobs in China. Pressure from the United States and others has contributed to China's revised view of intellectual property as a tool for economic growth and geopolitical dominance. In fact, the goal of its "Made in China 2025" plan is apparently to have "China dominate technology markets by 2049."[33]

To accomplish this objective, the Chinese government began a massive, concerted effort to drive inclusive innovation and to get "all hands on deck" in terms of citizens developing inventions and, importantly, patenting them. As a result, Chinese nationals began filing patent applications at an unheard-of rate. After a few years, not only did many countries see a vast influx of applications from China, but China's patent office also overtook the United States Patent and Trademark Office (USPTO) as the patent office

[30] White House, National Security Strategy 8 (2022), https://bidenwhitehouse.archives.gov/wp-content/uploads/2022/10/Biden-Harris-Administrations-National-Security-Strategy-10.2022.pdf.

[31] Comm'n on the Theft of Am. Intell. Prop., The IP Commission Report 11, 16, 19 (2013).

[32] China: Effects of Intellectual Property Infringement and Indigenous Innovation Policies on the U.S. Economy, Inv. No. 332-519, USITC Pub. 4226 (May 2011); *see also* Chuck Grassley, *Colleagues Call for China to End Intellectual Property Rights Infringement*, N. Iowa Today (May 18, 2011), https://northiowatoday.com/2011/05/19/grassley-colleagues-call-for-china-to-end-intellectual-property-rights-infringement/.

[33] Kal Raustiala, *Innovation in the Information Age: The United States, China, and the Struggle over Intellectual Property in the 21st Century*, 58 Colum. J. Transnat'l L. 531, 550–51 (2020); *see also "Made in China 2025" Plan Issued*, The State Council of the People's Republic of China (May 19, 2015), https://english.www.gov.cn/policies/latest_releases/2015/05/19/content_281475110703534.htm.

receiving the most patent applications worldwide, a title it shows no sign of relinquishing any time soon.[34]

In this era of intensifying global competition, the United States faces a critical imperative to activate all available talent. It too needs an "all hands on deck" approach to mobilizing a diversity of inventors in technological innovation. This is no easy feat: women, racial minorities, and other underrepresented groups face historical and continuing barriers to full participation in the innovation ecosystem as inventors and as those who protect inventions, such as patent attorneys.[35] But, as explained above, this mobilization is critically important.

This is why goal number 1 of the USPTO's Strategic Plan 2022–2026 is to "drive inclusive U.S. innovation and global competitiveness" by "ensur[ing] all Americans can participate fully in the innovation and entrepreneurial ecosystems that drive economic growth. . . . We, along with every sector of the innovation community, must incentivize more Americans to enter, innovate in, and bring more innovation to impact in these fields."[36]

Collectively, the research makes a compelling case that inclusive innovation can deliver not only a broader societal impact through diversified research priorities but also substantial economic gains through expanded talent pools and improved competitiveness because our diversity is our strength. Addressing persistent gaps in participation could redirect innovation toward previously neglected problems while simultaneously driving economic growth and international advantage through more optimal talent allocation.

Insights about Challenges to Inclusive Innovation and Invention and How to Overcome Them

Against this backdrop, one objective of the IDPI has been to support and elevate research on the blockers and enablers of broad-based participation in innovation and invention, as well as to raise awareness of various inclusive

[34] Ana Maria Santacreu & Heting Zhu, *Has China Overtaken the U.S. in Terms of Innovation?*, Fed. Rsrv. Bank of St. Louis (Feb. 20, 2018), https://www.stlouisfed.org/on-the-economy/2018/february/china-overtaken-us-terms-innovation.

[35] See *supra* note 14; Kara W. Swanson, *Race and Selective Legal Memory: Reflections on Invention of a Slave*, 120 Colum. L. Rev. 1077, 1085 (2022). *See also* Brian L. Frye, *Invention of a Slave*, 68 Syracuse L. Rev. 181, 186 (2018).

[36] U.S. Pat. & Trademark Off. [USPTO], 2022–2026 Strategic Plan 9 (2023).

innovation initiatives and "what works." Within the settings of innovation, we have focused, in particular, on the "innovator-inventor" gap—the differential rate of participation in invention by innovators[37] that has contributed to a women's inventor rate (the share of women inventors, which is not expected to reach parity until 2092)[38]—and efforts to narrow it. Because lawyers and other professionals play a critical role in turning ideas into inventions and supporting their commercialization, we also discuss efforts to increase inclusivity for women and underrepresented minorities in the patent procurement and enforcement professions by law firms, corporations, and the USPTO.[39]

Frictions in the Innovation Process

While the gender gap in patenting and entrepreneurship has been widely documented, recent research, including research supported by the IDPI, has pinpointed a number of frictions that have contributed to it. Far from being limited to one particular phase of innovation, these frictions span the initial development of ideas within organizations through the commercialization of patented inventions.

Prefiling Barriers

Through partnerships with several high-tech and chemical companies, IDPI researchers have surveyed over 4,000 innovators to gain a more robust understanding of the factors that work for and against participation in innovation and invention within companies.[40] Understanding these barriers is critical since 90 percent of patenting happens within firms.[41] However, because public tracking only begins when patent applications are filed and made public, there has been, to date, limited understanding of the prefiling dynamics that shape who participates.

[37] See *supra* note 17.
[38] Gauri Subramani & Michelle Saksena, *Untapped Potential: Investigating Gender Disparities in Patent Citations* 2 (USPTO, Econ. Working Paper No. 2024-3, 2024).
[39] While the Supreme Court overturned decades of precedent supporting race-based affirmative action in admissions decisions in *Students for Fair Admissions, Inc. v. President and Fellows of Harvard College*, 600 U.S. 181 (2023), that decision is distinguishable from the inclusivity programs described in this chapter on multiple grounds.
[40] Colleen Chien & Jillian Grennan, *Unpacking the Innovator-Inventor Gap: Evidence from Engineers* (Apr. 3, 2024), https://ssrn.com/abstract=4721522.
[41] Chien, *supra* note 5, 33 fig.3.

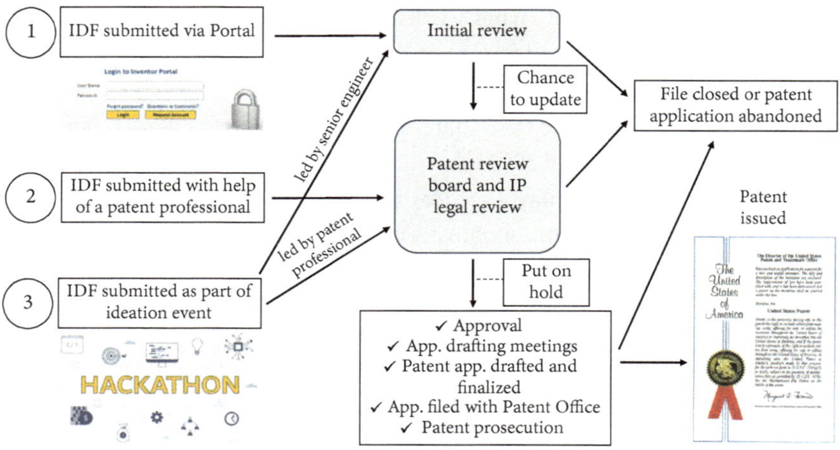

Figure 7.1. The path from idea to invention in a large company setting
Source: Adopted from Chien & Grennan, *supra* note 40, fig.1.

By analyzing new administrative data and survey responses from thousands of engineers, one of us (Chien) and Jillian Grennan attempt to unpack, for the first time, the conversion of innovators to inventors and how firm dynamics, culture, and demographic differences shape it.[42] The study documents that the patent system within firms is competitive and opt-in, with only one-third of engineers submitting ideas for patenting, only a subset of these ideas advancing to patent applications, and an even smaller subset advancing to eventual grants.

Their research shows how heavily the process of inventing relies on social dynamics (Figure 7.1). For example, for an idea to be submitted as an official invention disclosure, some firms have patent professionals reach out to inventors to see what they are working on and gather any ideas worthy of intellectual property protection. Women are much more likely to submit through an anonymous inventor portal than through more social means, such as with the help of a patent professional or at brainstorming sessions, suggesting a potential for social isolation or friction in the idea-collection process.[43] In addition, the "black box" nature of internal rejection decisions particularly impacts first-time inventors, who often do not know what they are being judged on and may not receive an explanation as to why their idea was rejected.[44]

[42] Chien & Grennan, *supra* note 40, at 1.
[43] *Id.* at 17.
[44] *Id.* at 10.

Moreover, women were less likely to report that managers explained important details to them or that they were able to find collaborators or experienced fair decisions from management.[45] These frictions have consequences. Using administrative data from collaborating firms, Chien and Grennan estimate that being female correlates with a nine percentage point reduction in the probability of an idea being initially submitted and another five percentage point reduction in a submitted idea being converted into a patent application.[46] Interestingly however, in high-friction environments, the ideas that survive tend to be of high quality. Conditional upon making it through the patenting process in such settings, female patent holders receive significantly more forward citations than their male counterparts,[47] suggesting the quality of the marginal idea lost to frictions in the process is higher. This finding is broadly consistent with Moritz Lubczyk and Petra Moser's finding that women must be much more talented to enter science than men.[48]

Similar performance losses have been documented in homogeneous teams in the software industry. Heath, Seegert, and Yang's analysis of over 40,000 open source software teams demonstrates how homophily—the tendency to associate with similar people—creates meaningful barriers.[49] Despite having access to a pool of over a million coders from 170 countries, the median team has members from only five countries and three ethnicities, with monoculture being the most common team composition.[50] Their research shows that the tendency to associate and work with people of similar backgrounds and locations, consistent with homophily, is strong and directly affects team composition.

The costs of this tendency can be significant; teams that escape the "homophily trap" experience increased productivity across various metrics, including survival, development, and popularity. Paradoxically, policies aimed at broadening participation can backfire due to strong sorting effects. For example, initiatives to teach women or underrepresented minorities to code can have the unintended effect of inadvertently encouraging them to join homogenous teams.[51]

[45] *Id.* at 3.
[46] *Id.* at 4.
[47] *Id.*
[48] Moritz Lubczyk & Petra Moser, *The Ms. Allocation of Talent* 2 (Dec. 10, 2024), https://www.aeaweb.org/conference/2025/program/paper/5YQT5GRr ("[W]omen face much higher talent thresholds to enter research fields with patenting than men.").
[49] Heath et al., *supra* note 16, at 1.
[50] *Id.*
[51] *Id.* at 3.

The patent attribution process presents additional barriers shaped by both social dynamics and institutional rules. Women are 58 percent less likely to be named on patents versus on papers for similar contributions.[52] While part of this could be due to bias, the legal definition of inventorship likely plays a role as well. Colleen Chien and Lisa Ouellette's analysis shows women make up only 38 percent of individuals credited with "conceptualization" but comprise 45 percent of people given "investigation" credit. Since patent law requires one to contribute to "conception" to be an inventor, the standard may operate to systematically exclude women from the ranks of patent inventors.

Patent Prosecution Barriers

Even after filing, gender disparities persist through the patent examination process. Using quasi-random assignment of applications to examiners, Abhay Aneja, Oren Reshef, and Gauri Subramani document that women are 3.6–6.9 percentage points less likely to continue pursuing applications after receiving an initial rejection.[53] This differential attrition explains approximately half of the overall gender gap in granted patents. It is not explained by alternative evidence like discrimination or differences in application quality.

This finding complements that of other scholars who have found that female inventors with feminine names are less likely to have patents granted than female inventors with androgynous names.[54] Their research suggests this bias is introduced during prosecution, independent of application quality, and points to the possibility of implicit bias even in the supposedly objective and neutral evaluation of patent applications.

Post-Grant Commercialization Barriers

The challenges continue and, in some ways, intensify after the patent grant. Gauri Subramani and Michelle Saksena's work documents that female inventors' patents are 4–22 percent less likely to be cited than similar male inventors' patents.[55] Their study further reveals how homophily operates even in citation practices: "patents by majority male teams are more likely

[52] Colleen V. Chien & Lisa Larrimore Ouellette, *Improving Equity in Patent Inventorship*, 382 Sci. 1128, 1128 (2023).
[53] Abhay Aneja, Oren Reshef & Gauri Subramani, *Attrition and the Gender Patenting Gap*, 2024 Rev. Econ. Stat. 1 (2024).
[54] Kyle Jensen, Balázs Kovács & Olav Sorenson, *Gender Differences in Obtaining and Maintaining Patent Rights*, 36 Nature Biotech. 307, 309 (2018).
[55] Subramani & Saksena, *supra* note 38, at 1.

to cite other patents granted to majority male teams," which they trace to applicant- rather than examiner-added citations and the higher rate of reuse of technologies developed by men.[56] The implication is that, once patented, female inventions are not noticed or built upon to the extent male patents are.

In their aptly titled *Cassatts in the Attic* study, Marlène Koffi and Matt Marx find that even high-quality, highly cited patents by women face systematically greater commercialization barriers.[57] Examining 70 million scientific articles and controlling for invention quality, they document a double-digit gender gap in the commercialization of scientific discoveries. Troublingly, this gap is the largest among discoveries that are more highly cited and have higher commercial potential. The researchers find articles with "boastful language" both more likely to be written by men and more likely to be commercialized. They also observe gender homophily between scientific authors and commercializing inventors, the majority of whom are male.[58] As the researchers document, these findings, especially given that they implicate high-quality discoveries, have welfare implications.

The work of Roger Masclans-Armengol, Sharique Hasan, and Wesley Cohen[59] highlights how bias not only causes individuals to be overlooked but also institutions, particularly those which may have lower amounts of prestige, as is true of some minority serving institutions. This form of institutional prestige bias also can cause worthy inventions to be underappreciated. Their analysis reveals that research from less prominent institutions is systematically overlooked despite its commercial potential. An article in the top quartile of commercial potential authored by a researcher from a prominent institution has a markedly higher chance of commercialization than an equivalent publication from a bottom-ranked institution.[60] Even when other variables are held constant, the difference between the relative likelihood of articles from highly ranked institutions being cited and that of those from less prominent institutions is close to 20 percent.[61] These findings, the researchers conclude, imply that "valuable research from less prominent sources is more likely to be overlooked."[62]

[56] *Id.*
[57] Marlène Koffi & Matt Marx, *Cassatts in the Attic* 3 (Nat'l Bureau of Econ. Rsch., Working Paper No. 31316, 2023).
[58] *Id.*
[59] Roger Masclans-Armengol, Sharique Hasan & Wesley M. Cohen, *Measuring the Commercial Potential of Science* (Nat'l Bureau of Econ. Rsch., Working Paper No. 32262, 2024).
[60] *Id.* at 24.
[61] When comparing "maintain" patents. *Id.*
[62] *Id.* at 25.

Enablers of Inclusivity in Innovation and Invention

Fortunately, research has uncovered not only barriers to inclusive innovation but also ways that many of them may be addressed, and AI is included in the mix. The most effective solutions work by addressing both individual and institutional factors—providing direct support while also reshaping the broader dynamics that can exclude underrepresented innovators. These interventions are particularly powerful when they help disrupt patterns of unhelpful homophily, provide support, and create opportunities for broader participation.

Education and Mentorship

Several studies conducted as part of the IDPI suggest how education, structured mentorship programs, and arrangements that foster social connection can facilitate the development of the know-how and information needed to be successful in innovation and invention.

For example, when Chien and Grennan asked engineers about the factors that would facilitate greater participation in intellectual property development, respondents cited more training, followed by mentorship by senior engineers and scientists.[63] Mentorship was significantly more likely to be valued by women; women and underrepresented groups also were much more likely to cite brainstorming sessions to get early ideas[64] as a way to encourage involvement in intellectual property. These responses suggest ways of overcoming the challenge of determining whether an idea is worth submitting.[65]

What happens when inventor mentorship programs are rolled out? As part of an IDPI partnership, Colleen Chien, Jillian Grennan, and Jason Sandvik evaluated a program at a major technology firm that paired experienced inventors with small mentee groups.[66] Using data on over 66,000 invention disclosures and analyzing the program's staggered rollout over seven cohorts, they found that mentored innovators produced 1–1.5 additional disclosures annually versus baseline rates of 0.5 per year.[67] The impacts persisted well beyond the program period and created positive spillovers to nonparticipants through expanded collaboration networks.

[63] *Id.* tbl.C.4.
[64] *Id.*
[65] *Id.*
[66] Colleen Chien, Jillian Grennan, & Jason Sandvik, *Small-Scale Mentoring, Large-Scale Innovation: Evidence from a Superstar Firm* (unpublished manuscript) (on file with authors).
[67] *Id.*

The program worked by addressing multiple barriers simultaneously: direct knowledge transfer demystified the "black box" of patent processes, expanded networks countered social isolation, and increased confidence helped overcome hesitancy to put forward ideas. Crucially, mentored innovators went on to form more diverse teams, suggesting mentorship can help break persistent cycles of homophily.

Institutional Support and Process Design

Institutional backing and resources have emerged as critical enablers across pilots and studies. During 2014–2015, the USPTO carried out a randomized control trial involving a "pro se" unit that specifically provided extra one-on-one support to a cohort of self-represented inventors. A subsequent analysis found that women applicants were eleven percentage points more likely to benefit from the assistance.[68] Further, the benefits were largest "for new U.S. inventors, and in technology areas where women had the worst relative outcomes."[69] This work is particularly important given that most first-time female inventors are independent or affiliated with a small entity.[70] Shifting from the examiner to the applicant side, Aneja, Reshef, and Subramani demonstrate that organizational support substantially reduces gender gaps in patent prosecution. When applicants have firm backing or legal representation, the gender attrition gap after rejection decreases significantly.[71]

Managerial support and institutional structures and features at the idea submission stage also make a difference. Through analysis of submission data and engineer surveys, Chien and Grennan find that management practices and corporate culture play an outsized role in influencing participation in invention.[72] Specific practices that tend to increase participation include offering training, boosting extrinsic rewards and recognition, and greater encouragement from management.[73] Anonymous submission options can help overcome social barriers, while clear communication of evaluation criteria particularly aids first-time inventors.

[68] Nicholas A. Pairolero, Andrew A. Toole, Peter-Anthony Pappas, Charles deGrazia & Mike Teodorescu, *Closing the Gender Gap in Patenting: Evidence from a Randomized Control Trial at the USPTO* 7–10 (USPTO, Econ. Working Paper No. 2022-1, 2022).

[69] *Id.* at 1.

[70] *Id.* at 4–5.

[71] Aneja et al., *supra* note 53, at 15 (finding the gender gap to be substantially decreased, though not totally eliminated, when the application is supported by an employer or firm).

[72] Chien & Grennan, *supra* note 40, at 22.

[73] *Id.* tbl.C.5.

Even in the post-grant phase, institutional support matters. Masclans-Armengol, Hasan, and Cohen not only show the presence of a "realization gap" between patent grant and commercialization at more versus less prominent organizations, but they also introduce a promising new metric for assessing the ex ante commercialization potential of a publication that firms could rely on and thereby diminish the potentially distortionary role of reputation.[74] They suggest that their measure of the commercial potential of science could serve as a proxy for the otherwise unobserved "technological opportunity."[75] When deployed properly, this measure would help identify promising commercialization candidates, even from less prominent institutions, boosting the realization of potential across research realms.[76]

AI Facilitation of Inclusive Innovation

AI can be part of the solution as well. A key finding of the IDPI highlights the critical role of collaboration across groups and disciplines—for example, through teamwork, mentorship, and information sharing—in overcoming friction in the inventive process. As Nia Nixon, Lin Yiwen, and Lauren Snow discuss, AI-driven tools can significantly enhance these human-centric efforts.[77] Their research illustrates how generative AI can promote inclusivity in teams, act as a bridging participant in diverse groups, and create simulations that challenge stereotypes and promote diverse role models, thereby fostering an inclusive environment. An AI-enhanced approach can promote the IDPI's goal of supporting collaboration and ensuring that diverse talent receives personalized support to foster professional growth and innovation contributions.

The potential for AI to mitigate bias while "meeting people where they are" represents another promising convergence between technological capabilities and institutional needs. As the field experiments of Mallory Avery, Andreas Leibbrandt, and Joseph Vecci demonstrate, AI-based evaluation can increase women's participation in male-dominated fields while helping combat evaluator bias. These findings complement IDPI research

[74] Masclans-Armengol et al., *supra* note 59.
[75] *Id.* at 30.
[76] *Id.* at 35.
[77] Nia Nixon, Lin Yiwen & Lauren Snow, *Catalyzing Equity in STEM Teams: Harnessing Generative AI for Inclusion and Diversity*, 11 Pol'y Insights Behav. Brain Sci. 85, 85 (2024).

showing how institutional practices and evaluation criteria can dismantle barriers for underrepresented innovators.[78] By leveraging AI's ability to provide more objective assessments while maintaining human oversight, organizations can work to ensure their processes promote rather than inhibit diversity, whether in idea evaluation, patent prosecution, or commercialization contexts.

Cultural competency is another area where human and technological approaches can collaborate to boost inclusive innovation. The work of Lin Ying-Tung, Hung Tzu-Wei, and Linus Ta-Lun Huang on "engineering equity" through AI emphasizes how technology can help create personalized, context-sensitive strategies for bias mitigation.[79] This technological capability could help address the cultural competency challenges in patent practices. As both the legal and technical fields wrestle with making their practices more inclusive, AI tools that enhance cultural awareness while facilitating meaningful cross-cultural engagement may prove valuable.

Policy Solutions for Systemic Change

Beyond organizational interventions, policy changes can help reshape systemic barriers. For example, Chien and Ouellette estimate that expanding recognition beyond conception to the performance of experiments could boost female patent recognition by as much as 75 percent.[80]

Enhanced attention to applicants has also proven effective. Using randomized controlled trials, the USPTO has demonstrated that providing additional support to patent applicants without legal representation increases persistence through the patent process and eliminates gender gaps in some technology areas.[81] Looking at evaluation metrics of an invention's value beyond the traditional measure of citation counts, as proposed by Subramani and Saksena,[82] could also prevent biases in status quo citation patterns from turning into the systematic devaluation of women's inventions.[83]

[78] Mallory Avery, Andreas Leibbrandt & Joseph Vecci, *Does Artificial Intelligence Help or Hurt Gender Diversity? Evidence from Two Field Experiments on Recruitment in Tech* (Monash Bus. Sch., Discussion Paper No. 2023-09, 2023).

[79] Lin Ying-Tung, Hung Tzu-Wei & Linus Ta-Lun Huang, *Engineering Equity: How AI Can Help Reduce the Harm of Implicit Bias*, 34 PHIL. TECH. 65 (2020).

[80] Chien & Ouellette, *supra* note 52, at 1129.

[81] Pairolero et al., *supra* note 68, at 29.

[82] Subramani & Saksena, *supra* note 38, at 27–29.

[83] *Id.* at 29.

IDPI Spotlight: From Research into Practice and Pilots

Several research findings in this chapter have led to practice and pilot action at the USPTO and elsewhere. For example, in 2023, the USPTO launched a "Welcome Letter" for patent and trademark applicants designed to enable applicants to more quickly and easily navigate the patent and trademark application process and connect them with relevant resources. In doing so, USPTO director Kathi Vidal cited the findings of Aneja, Reshef, and Subramani[84] that applications from females are more likely to be abandoned after an initial rejection. She stated that the letters' goal was to "educate filers about our processes, reaching them where they are and connecting them with valuable resources to help them protect their intellectual property, start new businesses, and drive our economy forward." In the private sector, companies are piloting practices based on research insights developed as part of the IDPI. In a first preregistered pilot, one firm is implementing a randomized control trial that tests the extent to which differential framing (opt-in/opt-out) and rewards (extrinsic/intrinsic) can shape participation and overcome frictions in the invention process.[85] In a second preregistered pilot, a firm is using a rubric, meant to identify who might have contributed to an invention, as a precursor to understanding the impact of broadening attribution.[86] Such interventions should yield actionable insights about ways to boost inclusion in innovation through adjustments to the innovation process.

Together, these findings suggest that the most promising approaches combine multiple reinforcing elements: expanding networks and mentorship to counter isolation, providing clear institutional support and processes, and reforming policies to check bias and recognize diverse contributions.

[84] *New USPTO "Welcome Letter" Seeks to Demystify Patent and Trademark Process Early on by Providing Applicants Helpful Information on Free Trainings, Resource*, U.S. PAT. & TRADEMARK OFF. (Aug. 10, 2023), https://www.uspto.gov/about-us/news-updates/new-uspto-welcome-letter-seeks-demystify-patent-and-trademark-process-early.

[85] Jillian Grennan & Colleen Chien, *Closing the Innovator-Inventor Gap: Evidence from Proactive (Opt-Out) Outreach*, AEA RCT REGISTRY (May 13, 2024), https://www.aeaweb.org/doi/10.1257/rct.12897-1.0.

[86] Frances Gutierrez Winkler, Address at the Second Innovator Diversity Pilots Conference at Emory University School of Law (Sept. 20, 2024), https://law.emory.edu/impact/conferences/innovator-diversity-pilots-conference.html (describing PURE's introduction of an "innovator" badge to recognize employee ingenuity outside of the normal patenting process).

By simultaneously addressing individual and systemic barriers, such interventions can help create a more inclusive innovation ecosystem.

Blockers and Enablers to Inclusive Innovation in the Legal Profession

While issues relating to innovators are of primary concern, there are other players in the innovation ecosystem who affect innovation participation and who occupy roles in which increasing inclusivity is also important. As such, we consider here blockers and enablers relating to those who assist in protecting inventions.

Barriers to Becoming a Patent Professional

Inventors often need assistance with protecting their inventions through the patent system, assistance that is normally provided by patent attorneys or agents. However, representing inventors before the USPTO in patent matters requires one to have the requisite science or technical background both to be a patent examiner and to sit for the Office's registration examination to become a patent agent or attorney.[87] As such, the underrepresentation of women and minorities in STEM fields cascades into further representation deficits in the patent legal profession.

Focusing on attorneys, law schools have made strides to increase the matriculation of diverse students, with 33 percent of law students identifying as people of color and 56 percent as women in 2022 (up from 9 and 20 percent, respectively, in 1977).[88] Unfortunately, these gains are not translating into comparable demographic advances in law firms. According to Wayne Stacey, this is largely due to structural features of large law firms that result in women and attorneys of color leaving these firms at significantly higher rates than men.[89] While associate attrition is built into the financial metrics

[87] USPTO, Off. of Enrollment & Discipline, General Requirements Bulletin for Admission to the Examination for Registration to Practice in Patent Cases Before the United States Patent and Trademark Office 2 (2024), https://www.uspto.gov/sites/default/files/documents/OED_GRB.pdf.

[88] Wayne Stacey, *Law Firms Have Abandoned Their Underrepresented Junior Attorneys*, Am. Law. (July 12, 2024), https://www.law.com/americanlawyer/2024/07/12/law-firms-have-abandoned-their-underrepresented-junior-attorneys/.

[89] *Id.* In addition, in a survey of 200 women who left large law firms, the respondents cited "gender biases, microaggressions, billable hour target pressure, preservation of mental health, lack of mentorship, unequal pay, isolation, long hours and unpredictable schedules, lackluster career trajectory

of such firms, the attrition is unequal. It appears to be related to "haphazard training" and the toleration of "disparate, discriminatory development practices" for junior attorneys.[90] Moreover, the imbalance in attrition rates has worsened over the past twenty years.

There is no reason to think patent attorney attrition is any different, especially considering the smaller numbers of women and underrepresented individuals even eligible to be patent attorneys and the likelihood that they might experience increased isolation in a field dominated by white men. For example, it is estimated that only 17–21 percent of patent attorneys are women.[91] For racial and ethnic minorities, the numbers are considerably worse: 14 percent of practicing attorneys are people of color, and only 5 percent of registered patent attorneys are racially diverse.

Turning the Tide and Enabling Inclusivity

Fortunately, several law firms and corporations are making intentional efforts to advance equity and inclusivity to enhance diversity in the patent profession, some of which were highlighted at our 2024 IDPI Conference. Many of these efforts can be found at ADAPT.Legal,[92] a hub and clearinghouse for a variety of diversity piloting initiatives within the patent profession. ADAPT.Legal members include some of the biggest tech companies and law firm intellectual property groups, all willing to share information on their inclusivity efforts. The idea is that a company, law firm, or government agency wanting to begin a pilot but not knowing where to start can go to ADAPT.Legal and gather a wealth of ideas based on what others have tried.[93] Details of initiatives vary, but they largely can be grouped into three kinds of interventions (with some areas of overlap): education and awareness-raising, pipeline building, and networking and mentoring.

Education and Awareness-Raising

Recognizing the importance of raising awareness about the patent system and the career opportunities available in patent procurement and enforcement,

prospects and insufficient work-life balance" among the drivers of their decision to leave. Laura Leopard, *Why Are Women Leaving Big Law and What Can Law Firms Do About It?*, JD Supra (July 25, 2022).

[90] *Id.*

[91] *Patent Attorney Demographics and Statistics in the US*, Zippia, https://www.zippia.com/patent-attorney-jobs/demographics/ (last visited July 26, 2025); *see also* Paul R. Gugliuzza & Rachel Rebouché, *Gender Inequality in Patent Litigation*, 100 N.C. L. Rev. 1683, 1692 (2022) (reporting 17 percent).

[92] Advancing Diversity Across Pat. Teams, https://www.adapt.legal/ (last visited May 7, 2025).

[93] Jeremiah Chan, Patent Pipeline, Address at the Innovator Diversity Pilots Conference at the U.S. Patent & Trademark Office (Nov. 18, 2022), https://law.scu.edu/wp-content/uploads/20.-Chan.pdf.

several firms have focused on providing relevant information in a broadly accessible format. For example, Finnegan, Henderson, Farabow, Garrett & Dunner (Finnegan), an Adapt.Legal member, showcases on that hub its *IP University*, a free online program that provides information on patent career options for STEM college and graduate students.[94] The program focuses particularly on technical specialists and explains the patent prosecution process before the USPTO.

The creation of the *SLW Academy* by Schwegman Lundberg & Woessner (SLW) was motivated in part by the 2020 murder of George Floyd in Minneapolis, the firm's headquarters.[95] The Academy is designed to facilitate increases in underrepresented group members pursuing careers in patent law through educational content geared toward high school, college, and law students.[96] The firm created a holistic series of free videos and quizzes on patents and other career success information to educate and equip not only minority candidates but all who choose to use the materials. A certificate of completion is also available, and the firm is working on facilitating career connections and other ways to scale the benefits of the Academy's content.[97]

Harrity and Harrity (Harrity) is another Adapt.Legal member with a range of inclusivity initiatives, including the *Harrity Academy*.[98] The Academy offers a flexible learning platform for both experienced and aspiring patent professionals. It provides access to tools, resources, and expert-led training to enhance skills in drafting and prosecuting patent applications. The goal is to equip individuals, particularly from underrepresented groups, to find greater success in the patent profession.

Wilson Sonsini Goodrich & Rosati, ranked number 2 among large firms by Law360 for the highest representation of minorities in its partnership, has launched several education and pipeline-focused inclusivity initiatives.[99] In addition to sponsoring events to assist college students with navigating the law school application process and resumé improvement workshops for law students, the firm has a mentoring program targeting women and

[94] *Finnegan IP University*, ADVANCING DIVERSITY ACROSS PAT. TEAMS, https://www.adapt.legal/dei-programs/finnegan-ip-university (last visited May 7, 2025).
[95] *Commitment to Diversity and Inclusion*, SCHWEGMAN LUNDBERG & WOESSNER, https://www.slwip.com/about/about-the-firm/commitment-diversity-inclusion/ (last visited Dec. 1, 2024).
[96] *SLW Academy Opens the Door to Careers in IP*, SCHWEGMAN LUNDBERG & WOESSNER, https://www.slwip.com/slw-academy-opens-the-door-to-careers-in-ip/ (last visited Dec. 1, 2024).
[97] SLW ACADEMY, https://slwacademy.com/ (last visited Dec. 1, 2024).
[98] *What Is the Harrity Academy?*, HARRITY ACADEMY, https://harrityllp.com/commitment-to-progress/the-harrity-academy/ (last visited May 7, 2025).
[99] Derek Rowe, Address at the Innovator Diversity Pilots Conference at Emory University School of Law (Sept. 20, 2024), https://law.emory.edu/impact/conferences/innovator-diversity-pilots-conference.html.

underrepresented minorities. It also has a special focus on startups, and sponsors incubator events for underrepresented minority and women founders to aid their understanding of the startup process and assist with pitch development. The firm also hosts competitions for financial support for founders, including lab space in incubators and access to other resources, tools, and networks.

Pipeline Building

Raising awareness and providing knowledge about the patent system is a great start, but more is needed to increase the numbers of women and underrepresented group members participating at all levels of the innovation protection ecosystem. Creating a pipeline of students equipped to join the workforce as patent examiners, patent agents, patent attorneys, and scientific advisors, as well as to proceed through levels of promotion to corporate, agency, and firm management positions is crucial. The following programs target these goals.

The *Patent Pipeline Program* (PPP) is an initiative of the National Council on Patent Practicum and focuses on debiasing the patent profession and helping minorities and women holding STEM degrees become patent agents through exposure and training.[100] The program partners with law firms and corporate legal departments to recruit candidates, facilitate the development and training of novice patent practitioners, and increase the diversity of the profession. In one recent cycle, it received 230 applications. PPP then provides patent training, mentoring, and internships in conjunction with partner law firms.

A particularly promising Harrity initiative is the *Patent Pathways* program, which, like the PPP, is designed to create a pipeline of diverse patent professionals.[101] It is geared toward expanding opportunities in patent law and provides mentoring, patent career education, free preparation support for the USPTO "patent bar" exam, and job opportunities to a new cohort of STEM-qualified individuals each year. Also, Harrity's *Minority Firm Incubator* provides free tools and training for women and minority-owned patent law firms, including strategy classes with in-house intellectual property attorneys.[102] This incubator is a creative way of contributing

[100] Pat. Pipeline Program, https://thencpp.org/patent-pipeline-program/ (last visited Dec. 19, 2024).
[101] Pat. Pathways, https://www.patentpathways.org/ (last visited Dec. 19, 2024).
[102] *Minority Firm Incubator Overview*, Harrity & Harrity, https://harrityllp.com/incubator/ (last visited Dec. 19, 2024).

to pipeline expansion through all ranks and stages of the innovation protection ecosystem. However, at the time of writing, the application window is closed.

SLW is one of more than 365 U.S., Canadian, and UK law firms to have achieved Mansfield certification, a distinction that recognizes tangible commitments to increasing and sustaining diversity in law firm leadership through a process that promotes accountability, transparency, and knowledge-sharing.[103] The firm also uses the data generated for the certification process to help understand how it provides opportunities such as client pitches and promotion consideration and to help ensure accountability in increasing diversity and effectiveness in firm leadership.

Finnegan's signature inclusivity program is the *IP Summit*, a multiday in-person conference in Washington, D.C., which targets underrepresented communities of all backgrounds and experiences to pursue careers in intellectual property. The initiative provides networking and mentoring opportunities and highlights different career paths in patent law.[104] It has also proven to be a recruiting tool for Finnegan to bring more women and underrepresented minorities into the firm. Finnegan is also Mansfield-certified, evidencing a commitment to multiple levels of pipeline building.

Double Attribution: From IDPI Conference to Practice

Because pipeline issues do not end with entry-level hiring, one initiative of Western Digital holds particular promise for assisting women and underrepresented minorities as they advance their careers. The intervention is based on a presentation by Professor Jordana Goodman at the 2022 IDPI Conference, who shared her work on "misattribution": the fact that, on many documents filed with the USPTO during patent prosecution, the name of the person doing most of the actual work, often a junior associate, does not appear on the document.[105] Instead, a partner, who is more likely to be a white male, signs the filing.

[103] *Mansfield Certification*, DIVERSITY LAB, https://www.diversitylab.com/what-we-do/mansfield-certification/ (last visited Dec. 19, 2024).

[104] *Finnegan IP Summit*, FINNEGAN (Aug. 2024), https://www.finnegan.com/en/finnegan-ip-summit.html.

[105] Jordana R. Goodman, *Ms. Attribution: How Authorship Credit Contributes to the Gender Gap*, 25 YALE J.L. & TECH. 309, 316 (2023).

This lack of recognition of the work done by an associate can have multiple negative impacts throughout their career, making it difficult to show the kind and quality of work they have performed. Sabra Truesdale, Associate General Counsel for Intellectual Property at Western Digital, learned about Goodman's work at the IDPI Conference and implemented a new rule for outside counsel preparing the company's patent filings: the individual who spends the most time drafting a patent application or office action response must sign the document if they have a registration number. While a partner can still be listed as an additional signer, the junior practitioner's contributions must be acknowledged.[106] It is hoped that other companies will adopt this approach as well.

Networking and Mentoring

Many law firms, companies, and even government agencies have become more aware of the necessity of assisting in the creation of support networks and potential mentors for women and underrepresented group members who may otherwise experience isolation in majority-dominant settings. These initiatives can be crucial to not only entry into the innovation protection ecosystem but also retention in patent-related careers.

Affinity group formation is one way to facilitate connection. In addition to its other efforts, Finnegan has created affinity groups, such as a women's group and a LGBTQ+ group, to enhance career satisfaction and build networks.[107] The USPTO has also supported the creation of affinity groups, such as the National Society of Black Engineers chapter within the agency.[108]

Harrity's *Harrity for Parity* program is an annual four-day workshop that provides female science and engineering students, law school students, recent graduates, and practitioners with exposure to, and intensive patent training from, some of the top female patent prosecutors in the country. As such, it contributes to the creation of supportive networks and identification of potential mentors for participants.

[106] Sabra-Anne Truesdale, Address at the Innovator Diversity Pilots Conference at Emory University School of Law (Sept. 20, 2024), https://law.emory.edu/impact/conferences/innovator-diversity-pilots-conference.html.

[107] Kara Specht, Address at Emory University School of Law Conference: Innovator Diversity Pilots Conference at Emory University School of Law (Sept. 20, 2024), https://law.emory.edu/impact/conferences/innovator-diversity-pilots-conference.html.

[108] Valencia Martin-Wallace, Address at the Innovator Diversity Pilots Conference at Emory University School of Law (Sept. 20, 2024), https://law.emory.edu/impact/conferences/innovator-diversity-pilots-conference.html.

Why Patent Practitioner Diversity Matters

It may not be immediately apparent why increasing inclusivity and diversity in the ranks of patent practitioners should be relevant to inclusive innovation, but recent research showcased at the IDPI and a variety of sources suggests it does matter. For example, a study commissioned by Invent Together, an alliance of companies, universities, and other stakeholders, found that potential inventors who had people in their networks they could trust to help them develop ideas were significantly more likely to feel confident about understanding the requirements for obtaining a patent—where to start and who to talk to—and the ability to finance patent protection.[109]

Conversely, those who had minimal or no knowledge of patents and services available were less likely to trust patent examiners, the USPTO, or even their tech transfer office.[110] To the extent the numbers of women and underrepresented minorities in the patent profession are increased, the trust and patent participation of potential inventors in their networks should also increase as they would then be able to interact with a patent professional.

In addition, as noted earlier, Subramani and Saksena found that female-inventor patents are less likely to be cited than male-inventor patents, which has implications for, among other things, the growth rate of technology areas with more female inventors and the ability of female inventors to extract benefits from their inventions.[111] Because the applicant adds the majority of citations in patents, the authors posit that the onus is on not only inventors but also patent attorneys and agents preparing applications to think proactively about the ways in which they find and include citations. Having a more diverse and inclusive patent attorney/agent corp could also facilitate increased citations of female-inventor patents and perhaps those of other underrepresented groups as well.

Moreover, in a recent article, Jordana Goodman and Khamal Patterson explain how a lack of cultural competency in both practitioners and patent examiners can negatively impact inventors from underrepresented groups.[112] They highlight challenges some Black inventors face in the U.S. patent system

[109] Jessica Milli & Breann Branch, The Role of Trust in Advancing Equity in Innovation 13 (2024); *see also* Holly Fechner, Address at the Innovator Diversity Pilots Conference at Emory University School of Law (Sept. 20, 2024), https://law.emory.edu/impact/conferences/innovator-diversity-pilots-conference.html.

[110] Milli & Branch, *supra* note 109; Fechner, *supra* note 109.

[111] Subramani & Saksena, *supra* note 38, at 25.

[112] Jordana Goodman & Khamal Patterson, *Access to Justice for Black Inventors*, 77 Vand. L. Rev. 109, 113 (2024).

due to cultural and systemic biases, and how the lack of shared cultural capital between inventors, patent practitioners, and examiners can lead to communication barriers that can result in inadequate patent protection for the inventors.[113]

In reviewing the article, which described difficulties experienced by inventors of Black haircare inventions, Sarah Fackrell provocatively asks:

> So what if, in addition to trying to make sure people who currently qualify to be registered patent practitioners . . . get more cultural education, we allowed more people with the relevant cultural education and experiences to become registered patent practitioners? Perhaps inventors like the ones featured in this article would be better served if the patent bar were opened up to allow people with this type of cultural knowledge to prosecute . . . patent applications.[114]

Having a more inclusive and diverse base of examiners and patent practitioners can ameliorate these cultural competency concerns both directly (with inventors being able to seek assistance from practitioners having a shared cultural paradigm) and indirectly (by increasing the opportunities for majority patent practitioners to interact with and learn from minority practitioners in ways that ultimately benefit underrepresented inventors).

Public-Sector Policy Leadership

The SUCCESS Act (Study of Underrepresented Classes Chasing Engineering and Science Success Act of 2018) required the USPTO, in conjunction with the Small Business Administration, to prepare a study on the number of patents applied for by women, veterans, and minorities. The study was prepared using publicly available data, as the USPTO does not collect demographic information from applicants.[115] The resulting study reported that innovation in the United States is highly concentrated, with vast swaths of the population not fully participating.[116]

[113] *Id.* at 131.

[114] Sarah Fackrell, *The (White) Person of Skill in the Art?*, JOTWELL (Mar. 12, 2024), https://ip.jotwell.com/the-white-person-of-skill-in-the-art/ (reviewing Goodman & Patterson, *supra* note 112).

[115] Study of Underrepresented Classes Chasing Engineering and Science Success Act of 2018, Pub. L. No.115-273, 132 Stat. 4158.

[116] USPTO, Study of Underrepresented Classes Chasing Engineering and Science Success (SUCCESS) Act of 2018 (2019), https://www.uspto.gov/ip-policy/legislative-resources/successact.

The disconcerting findings catalyzed action within the USPTO to take a leading role in (1) leveling the playing field and increasing the participation of underrepresented groups in innovation processes, and (2) working to obtain the data necessary to ascertain who is and is not participating in the innovation ecosystem. Over the past few years, the USPTO has launched a plethora of initiatives, primarily through the Council for Inclusive Innovation (CI^2), whose creation was proposed in the study required by the statute and whose remit is to expand American innovation "by tapping into the strength of our nation's diversity and increasing the opportunities for all Americans to participate in innovation."[117]

These initiatives include a paid innovation internship program for university and community college students to provide hands-on training in the innovation-supporting work of the USPTO, a first-time-filer expedited examination pilot to increase patent system accessibility for those new to patenting, and expansion of free legal services through a network of twenty-one pro bono attorney organizations and more than sixty certified law school clinics that, due to income and other limiting criteria, tend to serve predominantly women and underrepresented minority inventors. This is important because USPTO data shows that, "while the number of women inventors named on patents remains around 12–13%, the percentage of pro bono participants benefitting from [these free] services is 41% women, 30% African American or black, 14% Hispanic American, 5.6% Asian American or Native Pacific Islander, and 1.5% Native American."[118]

The USPTO has also lowered fee barriers to entry for small businesses and universities, and for inventors new to the patent system. Pursuant to the Unleashing American Innovators Act of 2022, the Office increased discounts from 50 to 60 percent for small entity applicants, and from 75 to 80 percent for micro-entities.[119]

The free legal services programs also include an educational component, which supplements other CI^2 initiatives that leverage the USPTO's expansive network of teleworking patent examiners nationwide in community

[117] *Council for Inclusive Innovation (CI2) Initiatives*, U.S. PAT. & TRADEMARK OFF., https://www.uspto.gov/initiatives/equity/ci2/initiatives (last visited Dec. 2, 2024); *see also IP Champions: Connecting USPTO Employees with Their Communities*, U.S. PAT. & TRADEMARK OFF., https://www.uspto.gov/initiatives/ci2/ip-champions (last visited May 7, 2025) [hereinafter *IP Champions*].

[118] Kathy Vidal, *The Unleashing American Innovators Act: Promoting Inclusive Innovation Under the New Law*, U.S. PAT. & TRADEMARK OFF. (Jan. 10, 2023), https://www.uspto.gov/blog/the-unleashing-american-innovators-act.

[119] *Id.*

outreach and education activities, including ones targeting K-12 education, through the *IP Champions* program.[120] On the data front, the CI^2 launched the *Diversity Information Platform*, which is designed to provide access to the latest available demographic data geographically and by industry with a template that allows organizations to compare their demographic profiles with other entities.[121]

The USPTO has also lowered barriers to entry for would-be patent practitioners. As noted above, it sets specific scientific and technical criteria for those seeking to represent inventors in the patent procurement process. Recognizing that some of the criteria might be creating barriers with no concomitant benefit in terms of competency, the Office loosened the accreditation requirement for computer science degrees such that any degree from an accredited program would qualify. It also committed to reviewing categories every three years to ensure the criteria are still appropriate.[122]

In an even bigger nod to the need to increase inclusivity in applicant representation, the USPTO created a new design patent bar, enabling individuals with degrees in industrial design, product design, architecture, applied arts, graphic design, fine/studio arts, and art teacher education to sit for the regular patent registration exam and represent clients seeking design patent protection.[123] One can expect that many more women will be able to qualify as practitioners via this route.

These initiatives have ramifications beyond the direct representation of inventors and designers before the USPTO. Although being a registered patent attorney is not a requirement to be a patent litigator, research by Jordana Goodman, Paul Gugliuzza, and Rachel Rebouché shows that many firms require entry-level patent litigators to have passed the patent bar.[124] Yet their data indicates that, in the vast majority of cases, having passed the patent bar does not result in higher win rates for attorneys, suggesting that it may be an unnecessary and artificial barrier, erected by firms, that disadvantages women and underrepresented group members.

[120] *IP Champions*, *supra* note 117.

[121] *Welcome to the Diversity Information Platform*, U.S. PAT. & TRADEMARK OFF., https://developer.uspto.gov/diversity-data/home (last visited May 7, 2025).

[122] *USPTO Opens Opportunities to Practice Before the Agency by Evolving Admissions Criteria for Patent Bar*, U.S. PAT. & TRADEMARK OFF. (Mar. 16, 2023), https://www.uspto.gov/subscription-center/2023/uspto-opens-opportunities-practice-agency-evolving-admissions-criteria.

[123] *Apply to Become a Design Patent Practitioner*, U.S. PAT. & TRADEMARK OFF. (Jan. 5, 2024), https://www.uspto.gov/subscription-center/2024/apply-become-design-patent-practitioner.

[124] Jordana Goodman, Paul R. Gugliuzza & Rachel Rebouché, *Inequality on Appeal: The Intersection of Race and Gender in Patent Litigation*, 58 U.C. DAVIS L. REV. 829, 832 (2024).

CI^2's 2024 *Strategy for Inclusive Innovation*[125] describes a wealth of barrier-reducing initiatives, most of which take the form of public-private partnerships. For example, most of the law school clinic and pro bono programs described above are public-private partnerships. Others include the Intellectual Property Owners Educational Foundation's IP Patch program (including a Girl Scouts IP patch),[126] the Boy Scouts of America Inventing Badge,[127] innovation-related internships for high school students through the Urban Alliance,[128] The Congressional App Challenge (in which members of Congress encourage students in their districts to learn to code and consider careers in computer science),[129] The Diversity Pledge through the US Intellectual Property Alliance, and partnering with us and other members of the IDPI to facilitate connections between firms piloting diversity initiatives with researchers willing to support rigorous evaluation of such initiatives.[130]

These USPTO initiatives are long overdue. As noted earlier, for several years, China has engaged in a concerted campaign to increase inclusive innovation and dominate patenting metrics. In 2019, Chinese entities were the fourth-largest group using the U.S. patent system,[131] dramatically increasing their filings by 93 percent over the prior ten years.[132] This increase has largely been attributed to China's patent subsidy program and the national and provincial-level financial support provided to putative inventors.[133] For several years, Chinese patent applicants could receive a wide variety of incentives for developing inventions and filing for patent protection. Incentives could be monetary (such as payment of filing fees and direct payments to inventors) and non-monetary (including reduced prison sentences for convicted criminals). As expected, these policy interventions

[125] USPTO & U.S. Dep't of Com., National Strategy for Inclusive Innovation 37 (2024), https://www.uspto.gov/sites/default/files/documents/NationalStrategy.pdf.

[126] *Teach Intellectual Property in Your Community*, Intell. Prop. Owners Educ. Found., https://www.ipoef.org/ip-patch/ (last visited May 7, 2025).

[127] *Inventing Merit Badge*, Scouting, https://www.scouting.org/merit-badges/inventing/ (last visited May 7, 2025).

[128] Urban Alliance, https://www.urbanalliance.org/ (last visited May 7, 2025).

[129] Cong. App Challenge, https://www.congressionalappchallenge.us/ (last visited May 7, 2025).

[130] Innovator Diversity Pilots Initiative, *supra* note 4.

[131] *WIPO IP Statistics Data Center*, World Intell. Prop. Org., https://www3.wipo.int/ipstats/index.htm?tab=patent (set the Indicator to "1"; then the Report Type to "Count by filing office and applicant's origin"; then add "United States of America" in the Office menu; then select "add all" in the Origin menu; then create a pie chart in the upper right-hand corner; then set the year range to 2019).

[132] Santacreu & Zhu, *supra* note 34.

[133] Erik Baark, *China's Indigenous Innovation Policies*, 11 E. Asian Pol'y 5, 11 (2019).

opened a floodgate of patent application filings by Chinese residents both in China and abroad.

Unsurprisingly, not all of these applications covered true inventions; many were effectively junk. So, to increase the proportion of truly meritorious inventions, the patent subsidy system has been modified.[134] However, it still exists and currently consists of the following: tax breaks, patent application filing and examination subsidies, monetary awards for granted patents, housing benefits, and reduced prison sentences. In addition, funding incentives are available for commercialization, particularly for university-generated inventions and those from small and medium-sized enterprises, including subsidies, loans, and assistance in evaluating commercial potential.[135] All of these policies and initiatives have as their goal increasing and incentivizing innovative output from all sectors of society; in other words, they are designed to facilitate inclusive innovation.

Conclusion

This chapter has explored why inclusive innovation—participation in innovation by people of all backgrounds—matters and how it can be hindered or advanced through various mechanisms operating across both corporate and legal settings. Through research supported by the IDPI and insights shared

[134] A key government planning document states: "We will optimize the patent subsidy and incentive policies and evaluation mechanisms to better protect and encourage high-value patents and develop patent-intensive industries. By reforming the ownership and distribution mechanism of state-owned intellectual property rights, we will give research institutions and institutions of higher learning a greater say in the disposition of intellectual properties." NAT'L DEV. & REFORM COMM'N, THE OUTLINE OF THE 14TH FIVE-YEAR PLAN FOR ECONOMIC AND SOCIAL DEVELOPMENT AND LONG-RANGE OBJECTIVES THROUGH THE YEAR 2035 OF THE PEOPLE'S REPUBLIC OF CHINA (2021) (China), https://en.ndrc.gov.cn/policies/202203/P020220315511326748336.pdf (translated by Shizhen Tong, 2025 J.D. Graduate, Emory University School of Law).

[135] Notice on the Implementation of the Special Plan for Patent Transformation to Assist in the Innovative Development of Small and Medium-Sized Enterprises, Notice of the Ministry of Finance No. 23 [2021] (issued by the Gen. Off. Ministry of Fin. & Gen. Office Nat'l Intell. Prop. Admin., Mar. 19, 2021), https://www.cnipa.gov.cn/art/2021/3/22/art_75_157912.html. Part II, section 2 of the Notice states: "The National Intellectual Property Administration and the Ministry of Finance will provide the following policy support for relevant provinces in carrying out special plans for patent transformation: . . . (3) Financial awards and subsidies shall be granted. The National Intellectual Property Administration and the Ministry of Finance will, based on the results of performance evaluation, give an award of 100 million yuan to provinces with perfect plans, proper measures, strong work promotion, and remarkable achievements in the transformation and application of patented technologies. . . . They may encourage measures including but not limited to awarding in place of subsidizing, service purchase, equity investment, and interest subsidy for loans to support related parties in their efforts to sort out, check and issue the patented technology that can be transformed. Moreover, they may provide the supply and demand matching of patented technologies to help small and medium-sized enterprises to obtain patented technologies." *Id.* (translated by Shizhen Tong).

at its 2024 Conference, common themes have emerged about the barriers faced by underrepresented groups and promising approaches to overcome them, centered around three key factors: (1) social dynamics and networks; (2) institutional support and process design; and (3) policy leadership.

While non-human AI is becoming a more prominent part of the landscape, the social dimension of innovation remains critical whether across companies creating new technology or law firms helping them protect their intellectual property. In corporate settings, research has shown how isolation and homophily—the tendency to associate with similar others—reinforces the status quo. Similarly, in legal settings, the lack of diverse mentors and professional networks can impede the development and advancement of patent practitioners from underrepresented backgrounds. In both domains, structured mentorship programs and intentional network-building have proven effective counters to these dynamics. At the institutional level, clear processes, resources, and leadership commitment emerge as essential enablers—whether supporting engineers, submitting invention disclosures, or helping diverse attorneys navigate career advancement. Policy leadership—whether through corporate diversity initiatives or USPTO programs to expand participation—plays a vital role in creating systemic change.

Looking ahead, the success of inclusive innovation efforts will likely depend on responses to the prevailing political environment as well as thoughtfully integrating AI technological capabilities with human-centered approaches. While AI offers powerful new tools for expanding participation, the IDPI's findings underscore that technology alone cannot substitute for the human relationships, networks, and institutional commitment needed to create truly inclusive environments. Rather, AI is best positioned as an enabler and enhancer of human connection—helping match mentors and mentees, facilitating cross-cultural understanding, and providing objective evaluation frameworks while preserving the irreplaceable value of human judgment and oversight. By combining technological innovation with a sustained focus on human factors, the innovation ecosystem can work toward realizing the full creative potential of our increasingly diverse society.

Acknowledgments

The authors thank Audry Im, Andrew Lo, Huaqing Cai, Shizhen Tong, and Usayd Siddiqi for terrific research assistance.

8

Improving Diversity and Inclusivity Measurements in Inventorship

A Competitiveness Perspective

Suzanne Harrison and Bowman Heiden

Introduction

Innovation is the new global currency. Much like the realization of the importance of oil in the 1970s, countries are working diligently to become more innovative as a means to better bolster their national security and competitiveness, which are increasingly built on technology leadership. Only recently have countries recognized that economic security *is* national security.[1] The Biden Administration's National Security Strategy states:

> Technology is central to today's geopolitical competition and to the future of our national security, economy, and democracy. U.S. and allied leadership in technology and innovation has long underpinned our economic prosperity and military strength. In the next decade, critical and emerging technologies are poised to retool economies, transform militaries, and reshape the world.[2]

This linkage between technology, innovation, and national competitiveness has focused on increasing technology and innovation within one's economy. It has heightened interest in understanding the relationship between STEM (science, technology, engineering, and mathematics) graduates, invention

[1] U.S. Dep't of Com., *Strengthen U.S. Economic and National Security*, https://2017-2021.commerce.gov/about/strategic-plan/strengthen-us-economic-and-national-security.html (last visited May 1, 2025).

[2] *Biden-Harris Administration's National Security Strategy* (Oct. 2022), https://www.whitehouse.gov/wp-content/uploads/2022/10/Biden-Harris-Administrations-National-Security-Strategy-10.2022.pdf.

Suzanne Harrison and Bowman Heiden, *Improving Diversity and Inclusivity Measurements in Inventorship*
In: *Inclusive Innovation in the Age of AI and Big Data*. Edited by: Daryl Lim and Peter K. Yu, Oxford University Press.
 DOI: 10.1093/9780197799444.003.0011

rates, and GDP growth. In the United States, 20 percent of graduates currently come from STEM fields, which is far behind China (40 percent), Russia (37 percent), Germany (36 percent), Iran (33 percent), and India (30 percent).[3] The United States Patent and Trademark Office (USPTO) has successfully highlighted the linkage between invention and GDP in the last several years. According to Professor Lisa Cook, a former Edison Fellow at the USPTO and current member of The Board of Governors for the Federal Reserve, "If we quadruple the number of inventors, we could increase the overall U.S. GDP by up to 4.4 percent. For some reference, 4.4 percent of the $23 Trillion U.S. GDP in 2021 represents about $1 trillion in potential annual growth to the U.S. economy."[4] The only way we can quadruple the number of inventors in the innovation ecosystem is to bring in inventors who are currently not participating or who are participating at a low rate in the innovation and inventorship ecosystem. Research at Harvard shows that innovation in the United States could quadruple if women, minorities, and children from low-income families became inventors at the same rate as men from high-income families.[5]

Looking specifically at the potential of women's inventorship, the USPTO calculated that, in 2019, women made up only 12.8 percent of all inventor-patentees in the United States. One could compare this figure to the 35 percent of STEM graduates in the United States who are women.[6] The persistent underrepresentation of women has created an unnecessary drag on American innovation and prosperity. Some economists suggest that, if women were to patent at the same rate as men, commercialized patents could increase by 24 percent, and per capita GDP could increase by 2.7 percent.[7]

If invention and innovation are the engines of growth and economic and technological competitiveness, the United States must pay more attention to the health of the innovation and invention ecosystems. For nations and firms to improve the scale and productivity of STEM workers and inventors, we

[3] *The Global Distribution of STEM Graduates: Which Countries Lead the Way?*, CTR. FOR SEC. & EMERGING TECH. (June 8, 2020), https://cset.georgetown.edu/article/the-global-distribution-of-stem-graduates-which-countries-lead-the-way/.

[4] U.S. PAT. & TRADEMARK OFF., PAT. PUB. ADVISORY COMM., 2022 ANNUAL REPORT 7 (2022).

[5] Alex Bell, Raj Chetty, Xavier Jaravel, Neviana Petkova & John Van Reenen, *Who Becomes an Inventor in America? The Importance of Exposure to Innovation*, 134 Q.J. ECON. 647 (2019).

[6] NAT'L SCI. FOUND., NAT'L CTR. FOR SCI. & ENG'G STAT., DIVERSITY AND STEM: WOMEN, MINORITIES, AND PERSONS WITH DISABILITIES 2023 (2023).

[7] Michelle Saksena, Nicholas Rada & Lisa D. Cook, *Where Are U.S. Women Patentees? Assessing Three Decades of Growth* (U.S. Patent & Trademark Off., Off. of the Chief Economist, IP Data Highlights No. 6, 2022).

must find better ways to attract and utilize talented people. One first step is to create better ways to measure and report these critical activities.

This chapter critiques current diversity metrics and explore the potential for inclusivity metrics that better capture an organization's inventive capacity and productivity as a key input of its technology competitiveness and leadership. The discussion includes (1) the limitations of patents as a means to measure inventive and innovative activities in the economy, (2) the challenge of benchmarking diversity in inventorship, (3) the differences between measuring diversity and measuring inclusivity, and (4) a call for an "inclusivity first" approach to inventorship based on the results of the Diversity Pledge Program.

Patents as a Sensor for Invention and Innovation Activities

Invention vs. Innovation

Innovation is the engine of growth for many companies worldwide. To better understand how innovation fuels growth and provides value for organizations, one must understand the difference between invention and innovation.

Invention is a new or unique solution to a technical problem such as a device, composition, method, or process. Inventions that meet eligibility criteria and are novel and nonobvious may receive patent protection. Legally protectable inventions are typically viewed through the lens of patentability criteria.

Innovation is the implementation of an invention or several inventions, or an existing idea, product, or process in a way that ultimately creates value for customers or society. It involves adapting inventions and other creative solutions for practical use, finding new applications, and bringing them to market so that people can use them.

For practical purposes, an invention on its own is not an innovation. An innovation that is brought to market may include an invention or many inventions. For example, today's smartphones are estimated to include more than 250,000 patented inventions.[8] Inventions underpin technology

[8] Steve Brachman, *Smartphone Innovation Has Soared Because of Patents*, IPWATCHDOG (Mar. 17, 2015), https://ipwatchdog.com/2015/03/17/smartphone-innovation-soared-because-of-patents/id=55667/.

development, which is often protected by patents in many industries, but not all innovative industries that are important to the economy.

The distinction between inventions and innovation has created two main measurement challenges. First, inventions provide an input measurement, while innovation is an output measurement. If not all inventions lead to innovation and not all innovation is based on invention, invention metrics can both overestimate and underestimate the measurement of innovation and economic growth. A focus on technological competitiveness reduces the error of the latter but not the former. Second, the use of patent information as a proxy for inventive activity is an imperfect measure, which will be discussed further below.

Patents Are Imperfect Sensors of Inventive Activity

Patent data provides a useful glimpse into technological development around the world. Patents are legally protectable inventions that are granted jurisdiction-based protection. U.S.-granted patents do not confer any legal basis outside the United States. However, patents are prosecuted, examined, and ultimately granted worldwide using similar processes, and the data is collected and shared worldwide in a publicly accessible manner. Because patent applications often precede product development, patent information can be a good early indicator of research-and-development (R&D) activity, technology trends, and corporate strategy, all of which are key determinants of competitiveness.

From an inventive capacity perspective, the USPTO, the World Intellectual Property Organization (WIPO), and the European Patent Office (EPO) have utilized patent data to measure gender diversity in inventorship in several studies.[9] These studies provide an aggregate look into the participation of women in the inventive workforce around the world as a means to better understand the latent potential of women inventors in society.

However, patents are an imperfect measure of inventive activity as patents only capture legally protectable inventive activity regarded as valuable or

[9] Élodie Carpentier & Julio Raffo, The Global Gender Gap in Innovation and Creativity: An International Comparison of the Gender Gap in Global Patenting over Two Decades (2023); Eur. Pat. Off., Women's Participation in Inventive Activity: Evidence from EPO Data (2022); U.S. Pat. & Trademark Off., Off. of the Chief Economist, *Progress and Potential: A Profile of Women Inventors on U.S. Patents* (U.S. Patent & Trademark Off., Off. of the Chief Economist, IP Data Highlights No. 2, 2019).

worthwhile by firms. Thus, patent information provides a useful approximation of gender inventorship but has several limitations:

1. Not all inventive activity is patented.
   The more a firm relies on other nonpatent methods of securing its return on R&D—for example, through trade secrets, first-mover advantage, and open source—the less informative patents are as an R&D measure of inventive activity. Furthermore, not all patentable inventions are captured through invention disclosures, and not all invention disclosures lead to patent applications. Thus, one key assumption underpinning the current measurements of the women inventor rate (WIR) in different industries and countries is that inventive activity captured by patents is a reasonable proxy for the actual diversity of inventorship. This assumption may not be true in all companies and industries, especially those that do not rely heavily on patents.
2. Gendering inventors has challenges.
   Most studies employ a gender algorithm based on inventor names. A significant number of patents cannot be accurately identified or misidentified. In particular, anglicized Asian names make it quite difficult to predict gender accurately.
3. Patent metrics may include gender bias in the patent process, not inventive activities.
   When the USPTO released the first "Progress and Potential" report in 2019,[10] it responded to a specific request from Congress to determine the gender makeup of inventors using patent data. The WIR was created and used for that purpose. For companies, the WIR is an interesting benchmark. However, it is not very useful for managing the inventorship process inside the company. To manage inventive activities, companies must first get a baseline of gender inventorship activities, spanning the inventorship decision lifecycle—including invention disclosure form (IDF), patent application, patent grant, maintenance, and renewals. From there, one can evaluate the decision processes at each stage and ensure no biases or other issues would create a gender imbalance.

[10] U.S. Pat. & Trademark Off., *supra* note 9.

4. Patents do not capture the potential pool of inventors—that is, inclusivity.

   Companies have been using patent data for many years to both help visualize various activities and improve executives' decision-making around corporate strategy, R&D investment, technology trajectories, litigation risk, competitive assessment, and R&D productivity. Such data has recently been used to visualize who is and is not participating in the innovation and inventorship processes. However, measurements of who participated in the inventorship process, such as the WIR, do not adequately address the totality of potential inventors within a company or society.

   The total inventor pool and associated genders must be known to understand inventive capacity and productivity to address any imbalances in the inventorship process. Consider the following hypothetical. A company has 200 IDFs with a 50 percent gender split between men and women. Of that pool, only 100 make it to the patent application stage, with a gender split of 20 women and 80 men, creating a WIR of 20 percent, which is well above the USPTO national figure of 13 percent. All looks good. However, looking at the total pool of inventors, which consists of 500 inventors with only 20 percent of women in total, we can see the emergence of a different pattern. Of the 200 IDFs, 100 were submitted by women, in parity with the number of women in the inventor pool. A great outcome! For the men, however, 100 IDFs out of 400 men means 300 men are not currently participating in the inventorship process, which is not good news for the company. As this example highlights, it is imperative to know the total inventor pool for companies wanting to measure and manage these activities for growth. This topic will be further discussed in the section "Differences Between Measuring Diversity and Measuring Inclusivity."

5. Patents do not capture the experience of the inventor.

   New inventors do not invent at the same rate as more established inventors. Thus, there is a learning curve to get new technical staff to invent consistently. The process can take several years in some technical areas. Thus, gender comparisons using inventorship rates need to be adjusted for inventor experience as a key productivity factor.

Building on the above limitations, the next section will describe the challenges associated with comparing patent metrics across technology fields and industries that have very different gender profiles.

The Challenges of Benchmarking Diversity in Inventorship

One major challenge of measuring and benchmarking diversity in gender inventorship is that industries are very heterogeneous in terms of the level of participation by men and women. Statistically, this means that the average WIR for a country or region does not properly illustrate the broad range of WIR across different technology fields and industries. Using data from the study conducted by the European Patent Office (EPO), Table 8.1 shows how the WIR varies from 5.2 to 22.4 percent from mechanical engineering to chemistry (a multiple of 4.3).[11] Even within the chemistry sector, a broad range was identified: from 9.2 to 30.7 percent and from environmental technology to biotechnology.[12]

The WIRs for the different technology sectors are useful for understanding the gender diversity in inventorship across industries. The significant variance allows for a more nuanced and strategic understanding of which technology fields and industries struggle the most to attract and/or empower women inventors. A further analysis could then be made on critical and emerging technologies as an indicator of the fields that have the most latent potential for engagement of women to improve capacity and competitiveness in most highly prioritized areas. Equally important, however, these

Table 8.1. WIR for technology sectors (2010–2019)

Technology sectors	WIR (%)
Chemistry	22.4
Instruments	10.1
Electrical engineering	7.3
Mechanical engineering	5.2
Other fields	7.0

Source: EUR. PAT. OFF., *supra* note 9, at 25.

[11] EUR. PAT. OFF., *supra* note 9, at 25.
[12] *Id.* at 26.

Table 8.2. Nominal vs. Real WIR adjusted by the technology sector

Company	Nominal WIR (%)	Technology WIR (%)	Real WIR
Bristol Myers Squibb	26	30.2	0.86
Caterpillar	7	5.2	1.35

Source: U.S. Pat. & Trademark Off., Off. of the Chief Economist, *supra* note 13.

technology-specific WIRs allow for the development of an index to calculate the real WIR by sector, which is crucial for benchmarking and cross-sector comparison. Without this index, it is impossible to accurately understand whether a firm or country is overperforming or underperforming. Let us explain with an example.

The USPTO's 2020 "Progress and Potential" report ranks 29 top patent assignees by average WIR.[13] The second highest-ranked company is Bristol Myers Squibb (BMS) with a WIR of approximately 26 percent, and the second to last is Caterpillar with a WIR of approximately 7 percent. This information is accurate but only provides the nominal WIR, as it is not adjusted for the high variance in gender participation and inventorship across different technology sectors. For firms to accurately benchmark their WIR, a real WIR value must be calculated considering the mean technology WIR, as shown in Equation 1 below. Using the EPO technology sector data and applying the mean technology WIR for pharmaceuticals (30.2 percent) and mechanical engineering (5.2 percent), the real WIR for each company looks much different, as shown in Table 8.2. BMS has a much higher nominal WIR but a lower real WIR than Caterpillar. Furthermore, the real WIR for BMS is now below the mean technology WIR for its industry (0.86), while Caterpillar is above the mean (1.35). The implications of these differences are quite important for firms working to improve diversity and inclusivity as they provide a starkly different benchmark and assessment of the challenge.

$$Real\ WIR = Nominal\ WIR \,/\, Technology\ WIR \qquad (1)$$

[13] U.S. Pat. & Trademark Off., Off. of the Chief Economist, *Progress and Potential: 2020 Update on U.S. Women Inventor-Patentees* (U.S. Patent & Trademark Off., Off. of the Chief Economist, IP Data Highlights No. 4, 2020).

It should be noted that these calculations are done by mixing USPTO inventor data and EPO technology index data. However, the need for an index is clear. For a completely accurate index of the technology WIR for companies to use as an internal and external benchmark, use Equations 2 and 3 below.

$$\text{Company} - \text{specific techWIR} = \frac{\sum_{n}^{i=1} WIR_{ipc}(i)}{n} \tag{2}$$

$$\text{Company} - \text{specific realWIR} = \frac{nomWIR}{techWIR} = \frac{nomWIR \cdot n}{\sum_{n}^{i=1} WIR_{ipc}(i)} \tag{3}$$

nomWIR = nominal women inventor rate
techWIR = technology women inventor rate
realWIR = real women inventor rate (indexed)
WIRipc = the mean WIR for every International Patent Classification (IPC)[14]
n = number of patents in the company's portfolio

A company's real WIR is calculated by adding the mean WIR for each IPC represented by a patent in its portfolio and dividing it by the total number of patents in the portfolio. This technique will create an accurate index based on a company's unique composite of technology fields, instead of general technology sector categories.[15]

Below are additional areas where further indexing may be needed to compare different firms and industries more accurately:

- the distribution of experience among inventors;
- the inventorship propensity among different positions in R&D; and
- the patenting propensity of different industries.

[14] The WIR for each IPC will also need to be calculated separately by applying the inventor name algorithm to all patents by the IPC on a defined aggregate level.
[15] An alternative method to estimate the company WIR index is to create an industry WIR index by identifying and averaging the WIR of several similar firms.

Differences Between Measuring Diversity and Measuring Inclusivity

There are many potential definitions of diversity and inclusivity, which are explained below as two related but different concepts. The discussion focuses on the gender perspective.

Diversity refers to who is represented in a population (e.g., the workplace) and is intrinsically measured by another group. For example, gender diversity is measured as a distribution of men, women, and nonbinary persons in a specific context. The WIR is a good illustration; it defines the percentage of women inventors compared to men inventors, where the men inventor rate (MIR) is equal to 1-WIR.[16] Diversity metrics are typically evaluated against a chosen norm representing an ideal state. For the WIR, a goal of 50 percent is typically implicit in the evaluation based on the assumption that the aptitude and desire to invent are evenly distributed across men and women.[17] A weakness of diversity measures is that they only provide a comparative distribution, which is useful when evaluating potential gaps in cross-group equality but does not produce an understanding of the magnitude, overall growth, and in-group dynamics. Because of its comparative nature, diversity measures can be interpreted as a competitive, zero-sum game, where one group must lose for another to win. To better contrast with the concept of inclusivity, we will slightly alter the definition of WIR to women inventor diversity rate (WIDR), as shown in Equation 4 to create space for the complementary inclusivity metric discussed below.

$$\text{WIDR} = \text{Women Inventors/Total Inventors} \tag{4}$$

Inclusivity refers to how employees experience the workplace and the degree to which organizations enable them to make meaningful contributions. Inclusivity measures actual participation in relation to potential participation and is particularly useful for measuring in-group participation levels. For example, the women inventor inclusivity rate (WIIR) equals the total number of women inventors divided by the total number of potential

[16] This simplistically overlooks nonbinary persons.

[17] For research questioning this assumption, see Gijsbert Stoet & David C. Geary, *The Gender-Equality Paradox in Science, Technology, Engineering, and Mathematics Education*, 29 Psych. Sci. 581 (2018).

women inventors, as shown in Equation 5 below. Inclusivity is fundamentally a productivity measure of latent participation within a population. It is evaluated under the implicit assumption that capability is evenly distributed, but opportunity is not, with 100 percent inclusion by desire and merit as the goal.

$$\text{WIIR} = \text{Women Inventors/Potential Women Inventors} \tag{5}$$

The hypothetical case below illustrates the differences between measuring diversity and measuring inclusivity in the context of inventorship.

Let's assume that a firm has 150 people working in R&D, of which 50 are women and 100 are men. Of the 150 persons in R&D, only 100 are determined to work in a job with the potential to produce inventions, as determined from a patentability perspective. Of these 100 potential inventors, twenty are women and eighty are men. Furthermore, of the 100 potential inventors, ten women and forty men are inventors on patent applications. Figure 8.1

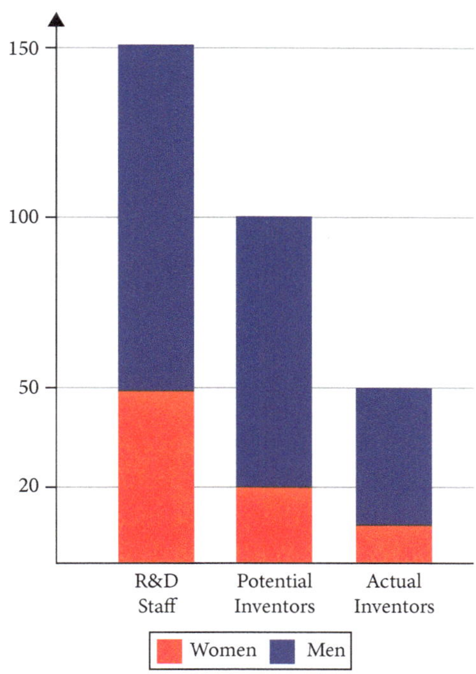

Figure 8.1. Hypothetical R&D firm by gender

provides a graphical illustration of this hypothetical situation, which leads to the following diversity and inclusivity metrics:

- Diversity metrics
  - Total R&D rate = 33 percent women (50) and 67 percent men (100)
  - Total inventors = 50 (ten women / forty men)
  - WIDR = 20 percent (ten women inventors / fifty total)
  - Men inventor diversity rate (MIDR) = 80 percent (forty men inventors / fifty total)
- Inclusivity metrics
  - Total potential inventors = 100 (twenty women + eighty men)
  - Women potential inventor rate (WPIR) = 20 percent (twenty women inventors / 100 total inventors)
  - Men potential inventor rate (MPIR) = 80 percent (eighty men inventors / 100 total inventors)
  - WIIR = 50 percent (ten women inventors / twenty potential women inventors)
  - Men inventor inclusivity rate (MIIR) = 50 percent (forty men inventors / eighty potential men inventors)
  - Gender inclusivity gap (WIIR-MIIR) = 0 percent (50 percent to 50 percent)

The use of both indicators gives a richer understanding of how to increase the inventive capacity of the firm. Some of the key insights are as follows:

1. Inclusivity rates complement diversity by providing the scope of potential inventorship growth available within the firm. This is important because increasing diversity through acquiring new employees is a zero-sum game on the national level in the short term—that is, one firm's gain is another firm's loss.
2. The WIR and WPIR have different denominators. The difference between the two is, therefore, not useful in calculating the inclusivity gap. The WIIR is the proper measurement of that gap. In the example above, WIR-WPIR equals 0 percent, but the WIIR is 50 percent.
3. The WIR can be much lower than the MIR, while at the same time, both the WIIR and MIIR can be similarly distributed with the potential for much improvement for both women and men. In the example

above, the gender inclusivity gap is 0 percent, as men and women have the same inventor inclusivity rate of 50 percent.

4. Increasing inclusivity will alter diversity metrics, depending on the rate of improvement among women and men. In the example above, assume that the number of actual women and men inventors increase by 50 percent—that is, from ten to fifteen women and from forty to sixty men. This will create a jump in WIIR/MIIR from 50 to 75 percent, but the WIR/MIR will stay the same at 20 and 80 percent, respectively. While adding 50 percent more inventors is a great improvement for the firm for both men and women, it will not be seen in the WIR metrics.

Inclusivity First—Insights from the Diversity Pledge

The Diversity Pledge started in 2020 as a collaboration between the US Intellectual Property Alliance and the University of California, Berkeley. Pledgee firms have agreed to collect baseline data of their existing women inventors, investigate root causes, implement potential improvements, and measure and report on the results confidentially or publicly. In 2023, we released our first Pledgee data analysis with telling results. Pledgee firms that shared at least two years of data, on aggregate, were able to increase WIR by 23 percent in one year. In addition, the key insights gained leading to the "inclusivity first" approach are discussed below.

The framing of diversity and inclusion (D&I) needs to be reversed to inclusion and diversity (I&D)—or better yet, to inclusivity first, then diversity.[18] At any given moment, the population of potential women inventors is fixed, requiring a long-term solution to increase the size of the inventor pool. An "inclusivity first" approach helps to solve the inventorship gap in three important ways:

1. Companies can leverage inclusivity to produce short-term impact. Inclusivity focuses on increasing inventorship from existing human resources that are already employed but are not participating or effectively contributing. This focus on the latent inventorship pool within the firm is something over which the company has complete control, in

[18] See Allen Lo's keynote remarks at CIP FORUM 2021 (https://youtu.be/V5SCzrD69iw) for a discussion on the importance of establishing inclusivity and belonging first.

contrast to educational and governmental measures required nationally to boost STEM graduates and inventors.

2. Inclusivity paves the way for organic growth in diversity.
   Creating inclusivity or belonging lays the groundwork by generating a positive environment and process for the future employment growth of all inventors in the organization. Such groundwork is more important to lower the diversity rate of inventorship in the firm as developing diversity-friendly environments needs a critical mass to become sustainable. For example, the management of Pledgee firms believes that including more inventors in the innovation and inventorship processes provides value to the company in numerous ways. The most common value is a decrease in technical staff turnover, making inventors feel more included in these processes and interested in staying with the company longer.
3. Inclusivity facilitates positive-sum growth in inventorship.
   Inclusivity is nondiscriminatory by definition. It uses a bottom-up approach that focuses on the participation of all underutilized inventors in an organization. Its focus is to remove barriers to maximize contributions from all persons with the desire and talent to invent. While it is clear that a diversity of inventors will require a diversity of solutions, a truly inclusive effort must be grounded to support everyone in need. For example, Pledgee firms have found that different groups of technical staff have different mentoring needs. Intellectual property and R&D groups need to tailor their education and outreach programs to meet the needs of different employee demographics by thinking through the different needs by employee tenure, geographic location, gender, technical area, level of technical experience, and more. Additionally, as women inventorship increased in the Pledgee firms, male inventorship did as well, proving that the amount of inventorship does not need to be a zero-sum game.[19]

[19] Note that increasing the MIR will impact the WIR, likely reducing the statistical impact of increases in women inventorship.

9

Bridging the Gender Gap in Innovation

A Behavioral Approach to Inclusivity

Paola Cecchi-Dimeglio

Introduction

Innovators have a unique capacity to generate transformative ideas that drive both organizational success and societal progress. Their creative potential is crucial, but the pathways to innovation are not always equally accessible, particularly when considering gender diversity and inclusivity.[1] While much attention has been paid to fostering innovation within organizations, significant disparities remain, particularly in fields such as patenting, where male innovators are still vastly overrepresented.[2] Recent studies show that despite gradual improvements, women constitute a small percentage of patent holders.[3] The gender gap in innovation remains pronounced, with women not only less likely to hold patents but also less likely to benefit financially from intellectual property rights.[4] This gender disparity represents a societal

[1] World Intell. Prop. Org., WIPO IP Facts and Figures 2022 (2022); Holly Fechner & Matthew S. Shapanka, *Closing Diversity Gaps in Innovation: Gender, Race, and Income Disparities in Patenting and Commercialization of Inventions*, 19 Tech. & Innovation 727 (2018); Sara Reardon, *Gender Gap in U.S. Patents Leads to Few Inventions That Help Women*, 597 Nature 139 (2021); U.S. Pat. & Trademark Off., *USPTO Pilot Program Reduced Gender Disparities in Patenting* (USPTO, Off. of the Chief Economist, Issue No. 102, 2022).

[2] Margo A. Bagley, *"Just" Sharing: The Virtues of Digital Sequence Information Benefit-Sharing for the Common Good*, 63 Harv. Int'l L.J. 1 (2022); Colleen V. Chien & Lisa Larrimore Ouellette, *Improving Equity in Patent Inventorship*, 382 Sci. 1128 (2023).

[3] Florence P. Haseltine & Mark Chodos, *"Why" vs. "What," or "The Bad Penny Opera": Gender and Bias in Science*, 18 Tech. & Innovation 275 (2017); Jennifer Hunt, Jean-Philippe Garant, Hannah Herman & David J. Munroe, *Why Are Women Underrepresented Amongst Patentees?*, 42 Rsch. Pol'y 831 (2013); Gema Lax-Martinez, Julio D. Raffo & Kaori Saito, *Identifying the Gender of PCT Inventors* (World Intell. Prop. Org., Econ. Rsch. Working 33, 2016).

[4] Élodie Carpentier & Julio Raffo, The Global Gender Gap in Innovation and Creativity: An International Comparison of the Gender Gap in Global Patenting over Two Decades (2023); Patrick Kline, Neviana Petkova, Heidi Williams & Owen Zidar, *Who Profits from Patents? Rent-Sharing at Innovative Firms*, 134 Q.J. Econ. 1343 (2019).

Paola Cecchi- Dimeglio, *Bridging the Gender Gap in Innovation* In: *Inclusive Innovation in the Age of AI and Big Data*. Edited by: Daryl Lim and Peter K. Yu, Oxford University Press. © Oxford University Press 2026.
DOI: 10.1093/9780197799444.003.0012

loss, as innovations from a diverse and underrepresented talent pool are left unrealized.[5]

Gender diversity plays a pivotal role in the evolution of knowledge, helping organizations avoid paradigmatic stagnation and fostering fresh perspectives that fuel innovation. Research consistently shows that countries and organizations grappling with skill shortages could significantly benefit from leveraging the innovative potential of women.[6] Despite this research, the economic and social significance of addressing female underrepresentation in innovation remains underexplored. Current studies often fail to distinguish between innovators with varying productivity levels, especially "star inventors," those whose innovations have an exceptional impact.[7] The concept of "lost Marie Curies," *women who could have become high-impact inventors but faced barriers stifling their potential*, speaks to the profound loss of innovation that results from gender bias.[8] These missed opportunities call for a deeper understanding of how to create more inclusive innovation ecosystems.

This chapter seeks to address these gaps by examining how informed organizational interventions can promote innovation participation, improve the diversity of idea submissions, and enhance employee satisfaction. Through a series of five carefully designed experiments, the chapter delves into the effects of interventions, such as leadership involvement, simplified patent submission processes, dedicated online platforms, storytelling videos, and the adoption of inclusive language. Each intervention addresses critical behavioral and structural factors within organizations that encourage or inhibit innovation participation. By focusing on these interventions, this study offers a comprehensive exploration of how organizations can break down barriers to innovation, especially for groups that have historically not fully participated in these processes.

The findings of this research are significant in that they offer actionable strategies for reducing gender bias and fostering inclusivity in innovation processes. Leadership involvement, for instance, plays a critical role in

[5] Alexander M. Bell, Raj Chetty, Xavier Jaravel, Neviana Petkova & John Van Reenen, *Who Becomes an Inventor in America? The Importance of Exposure to Innovation*, 134 Q.J. ECON. 647 (2019).

[6] Alessandra Colombelli, Elena Grinza, Valentina Meliciani & Mariacristina Rossi, *Pulling Effects in Immigrant Entrepreneurship: Does Gender Matter?*, 97 ECON. GEOGRAPHY 1 (2021); Karin Hoisl & Myriam Mariani, *It's a Man's Job: Income and the Gender Gap in Industrial Research*, 63 MGMT. SCI. 766 (2017).

[7] Boris Groysberg & Linda-Eling Lee, *Hiring Stars and Their Colleagues: Exploration and Exploitation in Professional Service Firms*, 20 ORG. SCI. 740 (2009); Lynne G. Zucker & Michael R. Darby, *Individual Action and the Demand for Institutions: Star Scientists and Institutional Transformation*, 40 AM. BEHAV. SCI. 502 (1997).

[8] Bell et al., *supra* note 5.

encouraging employee engagement and promoting a culture where diverse ideas are welcomed and valued. Simplifying procedural complexities, such as patent submission processes, removes barriers that disproportionately hinder women's participation, while dedicated online platforms and storytelling videos help to democratize the innovation process. Finally, adopting inclusive language is a powerful tool in reshaping organizational culture to make innovation processes more welcoming for all employees.

Through the lens of these five experiments, this chapter provides practical insights into how organizations can create more inclusive environments that increase innovation participation and enrich the diversity of contributions. By addressing both the behavioral and structural barriers that prevent groups with historically limited participation in innovation, these findings extend the current understanding of how inclusivity can drive innovation and ultimately lead to more competitive and impactful outcomes for organizations.

The structure of this chapter is designed to explore those critical factors influencing innovation within organizations, particularly those related to gender inclusivity, process accessibility, and the mechanisms that foster diverse participation. Through this exploration, this chapter contributes to the growing body of research on gender disparities in innovation while offering practical recommendations for organizations seeking to harness the full potential of their diverse talent pools. The goal is to provide evidence that fostering inclusivity enhances innovation outcomes and offers a strategic and competitive advantage in a knowledge-based global economy.

Literature Review

Behavior and Gender in Innovation

Over the past several decades, a growing body of research has sought to understand the specific behaviors and personality traits that distinguish innovators from their peers. Studies consistently show that innovative individuals possess distinct characteristics and cognitive habits, such as connecting seemingly unrelated ideas, asking probing questions, and experimenting through prototyping.[9] Innovators also tend to use observation techniques similar to

[9] JEFF DYER, HAL GREGERSEN & CLAYTON M. CHRISTENSEN, THE INNOVATOR'S DNA: MASTERING THE FIVE SKILLS OF DISRUPTIVE INNOVATORS (2011); Guillaume Fürst & François Grin, *A Comprehensive Method for the Measurement of Everyday Creativity*, 28 THINKING SKILLS &

those used by anthropologists and network with a broad range of experts to gain new perspectives. Additionally, they display a higher tolerance for ambiguity, self-confidence, and a strong drive to take risks.[10]

However, while these traits are often viewed as central to fostering innovation, much of the existing research overlooks the structural and environmental factors enabling or inhibiting these behaviors, particularly for women and other underrepresented groups.[11] For instance, social network theories highlight the importance of occupying central positions in advice networks, where interactions with diverse individuals can enhance knowledge access and expedite the identification of new opportunities.[12] Yet, women and minority groups are often marginalized in these networks, limiting their opportunities for engagement in innovation processes.[13]

Moreover, although the "Eureka!" moment is often romanticized as a spontaneous realization of a groundbreaking idea, innovation rarely occurs in isolation. It is a process driven by continuous communication with key stakeholders.[14] Organizational social network research emphasizes that innovation is deeply rooted in personal and professional interactions, which help refine and develop ideas.[15] Despite the critical role played by these interactions, there is a noticeable gap in the literature regarding the impact of social behaviors and language on innovation outcomes, particularly in informal settings such as internal communication platforms or corporate online forums. This gap is especially relevant when considering the gendered

CREATIVITY 84 (2018); James C. Kaufman, *Counting the Muses: Development of the Kaufman Domains of Creativity Scale (K-DOCS)*, 6 PSYCH. AESTHETICS, CREATIVITY & ARTS 298 (2012).

[10] SALVATORE R. MADDI, PERSONALITY THEORIES: A COMPARATIVE ANALYSIS (6th ed. 1996); Blaine Landis, *Personality and Social Networks in Organizations: A Review and Future Directions*, 37 J. ORGAL. BEHAV. S107 (2016).

[11] Frank T. Rothaermel & Andrew M. Hess, *Building Dynamic Capabilities: Innovation Driven by Individual-, Firm-, and Network-Level Effects*, 18 ORG. SCI. 898 (2007).

[12] PAOLA CECCHI-DIMEGLIO, DIVERSITY DIVIDEND: THE TRANSFORMATIONAL POWER OF SMALL CHANGES TO DEBIAS YOUR COMPANY, ATTRACT DIVERSE TALENT, MANAGE EVERYONE BETTER—AND MAKE MORE MONEY (2023); Niharika Garud & Ganesh N. Prabhu, *Linking R&D Inventors' Social Skills and Bricolage to R&D Performance in Resource Constrained Environments in Emerging Markets*, 68 IEEE TRANS. ENG'G MGMT. 713 (2021); Peter A. Gloor, Andrea Fronzetti Colladon & Francesca Grippa, *The Digital Footprint of Innovators: Using Email to Detect the Most Creative People in Your Organization*, 114 J. BUS. RSCH. 254 (2020).

[13] Herminia Ibarra, *Personal Networks of Women and Minorities in Management: A Conceptual Framework*, 18 ACAD. MGMT. REV. 56 (1993).

[14] Paola Cecchi-Dimeglio, Taha Masood & Andy Ouderkirk, *What Makes Innovation Partnerships Succeed*, HARV. BUS. REV. (July 14, 2022), https://hbr.org/2022/07/what-makes-innovation-partnerships-succeed.

[15] PAOLA CECCHI DIMEGLIO, BUILDING A THRIVING FUTURE, METAVERSE AND MULTIVERSE (2025).

dynamics of communication, where women may face barriers that inhibit their participation in key discussions, especially in male-dominated fields like patenting.

Language, Bias, and Innovation

Language is a powerful tool that shapes individual and group cognition, perception, and behavior.[16] How we communicate innovation can influence who feels encouraged to participate and who is excluded from the conversation. Studies have shown that the language used within organizations can either foster inclusivity or perpetuate existing biases.[17] For instance, narratives are an effective strategy for communicating innovation. Innovators often adjust their communication to align with the group dynamics within their organizations.[18] However, when the language used in innovation contexts emphasizes traditionally masculine traits, such as assertiveness or risk-taking, it can marginalize those who do not conform to these stereotypes, particularly women.[19]

Experimentation with inclusive language is crucial, as recent research underscores the profound effects of subtle language changes on fostering innovation participation. For instance, "harvesting ideas" may seem neutral but can invoke competition and extractive connotations that discourage more collaborative or nurturing forms of innovation.[20] Inclusive language can create an environment where a wider array of perspectives is valued, making it easier for women and other underrepresented groups to contribute to innovation.

[16] Samantha Hookway, Mia Fay Johansson, Anton Svensson & Bowman Heiden, *The Problem with Problems: Reframing and Cognitive Bias in Healthcare Innovation*, 22 Design J. 553 (2019); William Ocasio, Tomi Laamanen & Eero Vaara, *Communication and Attention Dynamics: An Attention-Based View of Strategic Change*, 39 Strategic Mgmt. J. 155 (2018).

[17] Natalya N. Bazarova, Jessie G. Taft & Dan Cosley, *Managing Impressions and Relationships on Facebook: Self-Presentational and Relational Concerns Revealed Through the Analysis of Language Style*, 32 J. Language & Soc. Psych. 121 (2013); Teresa Gil-Lopez, Shen Cuihua, Grace A. Benefield, Nicholas A. Palomares, Michal Kosinski & David Stillwell, *One Size Fits All: Context Collapse, Self-Presentation Strategies and Language Styles on Facebook*, 23 J. Comput.-Mediated Commc'n 127 (2018).

[18] Patrick Weber & Yannick Grauer, *The Effectiveness of Social Media Storytelling in Strategic Innovation Communication: Narrative Form Matters*, 13 Int'l J. Strategic Commc'n 152 (2019).

[19] Londa L. Schiebinger, Gendered Innovations in Science and Engineering (2008).

[20] Catherine Ashcraft, Brad McLain & Elizabeth Eger, Women in Tech: The Facts (2016).

Additionally, innovators tend to communicate more frequently and demonstrate a deep curiosity about learning from others, which enhances their creative potential.[21] Yet research on how language influences innovation, especially in relation to gender bias, remains limited. While innovators are often praised for their ability to connect ideas and network effectively, this narrative does not always extend to women and minority groups that face communication barriers due to biased organizational cultures. Addressing these issues requires a conscious effort to cultivate inclusive communication that invites participation from all demographics, rather than favoring the dominant group's speaking and interaction.

Gender and Innovation Bias

Gender bias in innovation, particularly in patenting, has been widely documented. Female underrepresentation in patent submissions is a persistent issue, with women facing both structural and cultural barriers to fully participating in the innovation ecosystem.[22] Despite some improvements, most patent holders remain male, and women continue to face challenges in accessing the financial and professional benefits of intellectual property ownership.[23] This disparity reflects societal bias and is a source of lost economic opportunity, as it leaves a significant portion of the talent pool untapped.[24]

Research has shown that gender diversity within top management teams or corporate boards can positively impact innovation.[25] Firms with greater gender diversity on their boards are more likely to generate a wider range of ideas and enhance their performance, particularly when innovation is a key part of their strategy. However, this does not fully address the barriers women face at the individual level in engaging in patenting and other innovation processes.

[21] Dyer et al., *supra* note 9; Gloor et al., *supra* note 12.
[22] Haseltine & Chodos, *supra* note 3; Hunt et al., *supra* note 3.
[23] Kline et al., *supra* note 4.
[24] Bell et al., *supra* note 5.
[25] Cristian L. Dezsö & David Gaddis Ross, *Does Female Representation in Top Management Improve Firm Performance? A Panel Data Investigation*, 33 Strategic Mgmt. J. 1072 (2012); Toyah Miller & María Del Carmen Triana, *Demographic Diversity in the Boardroom: Mediators of the Board Diversity—Firm Performance Relationship*, 46 J. Mgmt. Stud. 755 (2009).

Much of the research on gender and innovation has focused on diversity at the leadership level, but there is a need to investigate further the experiences of women at different levels within organizations. Women are often discouraged from participating in patenting due to both visible and invisible barriers, ranging from procedural complexities to cultural biases. Studies have called for a closer examination of how the structure of the patenting process, from idea generation to approval, can either encourage or stifle female participation.

Promoting Gender Inclusion in the Patenting Process

The use of inclusive language in fostering innovation, particularly within the patenting process, has garnered increasing attention in recent years. Research shows that the language used in both organizational and legal contexts can significantly influence who is encouraged to participate in innovation activities. Traditional communication styles within the patenting process, which often rely on technical jargon and legalistic terminology, can be intimidating and exclusionary, especially to women already underrepresented in this field.[26]

When language surrounding innovation is not gender neutral, it can reinforce biases that deter women from engaging in patenting activities.[27] Moreover, the complexity and length of the patenting process—comprising multiple stages of evaluation and approval—can further exacerbate this exclusion. Each stage presents an opportunity for attrition, especially for those less familiar with the process, leading to an overall reduction in participation from diverse groups.[28]

To counter these barriers, scholars argue that adopting inclusive language and creating supportive environments are crucial strategies for increasing female participation in patenting, thus enhancing the diversity of innovation outputs.[29] When organizations implement specific incentives and

[26] Tej Krishan Bhatia & William C. Ritchie, The Handbook of Bilingualism and Multilingualism (2d ed. 2013).

[27] Schiebinger, *supra* note 19; Londa Schiebinger, *Gendered Innovations: Integrating Sex, Gender, and Intersectional Analysis into Science, Health & Medicine, Engineering, and Environment*, 4 Tapuya 1867420 (2021).

[28] Emilio J. Castilla, *Gender, Race, and Meritocracy in Organizational Careers*, 113 Am. J. Soc. 1479 (2008); Chien & Ouellette, *supra* note 2; Dianna G. El Hioum & Gregory Logan, *USPTO Has Ways to Improve Patent Diversity and Inclusion*, Bloomberg L. (Oct. 13, 2021), https://news.bloomberglaw.com/ip-law/uspto-has-ways-to-improve-patent-diversity-and-inclusion.

[29] Ashcraft et al., *supra* note 20.

communication strategies to reduce these barriers, women's participation in patenting has improved significantly, contributing to a richer and more diverse pool of innovations.[30]

In parallel with how biased data can lead to unfair AI systems, biased language and procedures in patenting can exclude underrepresented groups from the innovation pipeline.[31] Addressing these biases requires changes in how patent applications are written and examined and how inventors are supported throughout the patenting process. By promoting more inclusive communication and making structural changes to the patenting process, organizations can help ensure that all potential inventors, particularly women, are encouraged to participate fully.

Data, Methodology, and Results

Five experiments were conducted to evaluate the effectiveness of various interventions on increasing employee participation in innovation, improving the diversity of submissions, and enhancing overall satisfaction within large organizations. Each experiment tests specific hypotheses tied to organizational processes and behaviors. The interventions included leadership involvement, simplifying patent submission processes, implementing a dedicated online platform, utilizing storytelling videos, and modifying language to avoid offensive terms. Below is a detailed methodology and overview of the results of each experiment.

Experiment 1: Leadership Involvement in Inclusive Innovation

This experiment aimed to assess the impact of leadership involvement in fostering inclusive innovation within a company of 122,189 employees, 39 percent of whom were women (47,732 women and 74,457 men) from various departments, including those in nontechnical and administrative roles. For technical and higher-paying roles, women represented 21.2 percent of

[30] Iris Bohnet, What Works: Gender Equality by Design (2016); Frank Dobbin, Alexandra Kalev & Erin Kelly, *Diversity Management in Corporate America*, 6 Contexts 21 (2007).

[31] Daryl Lim, *AI & IP: Innovation & Creativity in an Age of Accelerated Change*, 52 Akron L. Rev. 813 (2018); Peter K. Yu, *Artificial Intelligence, the Law–Machine Interface, and Fair Use Automation*, 72 Ala. L. Rev. 187 (2020).

the workforce. In this case, a sample of 28,478 employees (~23 percent) was selected based on their geography, explicitly focusing on the North American workforce within the company. The premise of this experiment was based on the hypothesis that leadership involvement in promoting inclusive innovation would significantly increase employee participation, enhance the diversity of idea submissions (particularly from women), and result in a higher number of implemented ideas, compared with scenarios without leadership engagement.

Conducted over three months, the experiment compared two groups: a control group (where employees were encouraged to innovate independently without formal leadership involvement) and an experimental group (in which leadership actively participated in the innovation process). In the experimental group, leaders endorsed innovation initiatives (offices and regional hackathons), shared personal stories, and recognized employee contributions. The main variables measured included employee engagement, diversity of ideas (from women), the number of ideas implemented, and participation in storytelling activities (Figure 9.1).

The results demonstrated that leadership involvement significantly enhanced engagement, with 78 percent of the experimental group participating in innovation activities, compared with 57 percent in the control group. The proportion of ideas submitted by women increased from 32 percent in the control group to 43 percent in the experimental group, and the number of implemented ideas rose from 12 to 19 percent. Additionally, participation in storytelling activities was notably higher in the experimental group (26 percent), compared with the control group (8 percent).

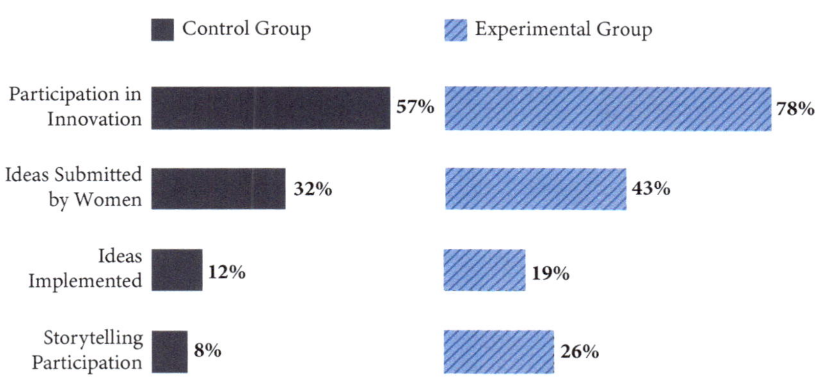

Figure 9.1. Leadership involved in fostering inclusive innovation

These results suggest that leaders who actively engage in innovation processes create a more inclusive environment that encourages a broader range of employees to contribute. From a behavioral perspective, such creation aligns with social network theories that emphasize the importance of influential figures in fostering knowledge sharing and participation. By endorsing innovation initiatives and recognizing contributions, leaders can dismantle traditional hierarchies and create opportunities for more diverse voices to be heard. This is especially critical in large organizations, in which hierarchical structures often suppress bottom-up innovation.

The implication for organizations is clear: leadership should be active in innovation efforts. Leaders should actively participate, share stories, and provide visible recognition to promote inclusivity and diversity. This approach will increase overall participation and ensure a more diverse group involved in innovation.

Experiment 2: Simplifying the Patent Submission Process

This experiment, conducted over sixty days, examined the impact of simplifying the patent submission process and providing regular email nudges to increase participation. The study involved a company of 132,890 employees, of whom 61,129 (46 percent) were women, and 71,761 (54 percent) were men, from various departments, including those in nontechnical and administrative roles. Women made up 24.2 percent of the technical and higher-paying roles. A representative sample of 46,512 U.S. employees was selected for the control and experimental groups. The premise of this experiment was that simplifying the patent submission process, along with regular email nudges, would increase the number of patent submissions, improve the diversity of submissions (particularly by women), and enhance overall employee satisfaction, compared with the existing, more complex process.

In the control group, employees followed the existing, more complex submission process. In contrast, the experimental group was introduced to a simplified process featuring visual aids and biweekly email nudges encouraging idea submissions and outreach by previous inventors. Key variables assessed in this experiment included the number of patent submissions (submission of ideas to the legal department that could be evaluated for patenting), diversity of submissions by gender and department, approval rates, and employee satisfaction.

The results show a significant increase in participation, with the experimental group submitting 1,540 patent ideas, an 87-percent increase compared with 820 submissions in the control group. The proportion of submissions from women rose from 34 to 47 percent, and the approval rate for ideas improved from 15 to 22 percent. Employee satisfaction with the simplified process was significantly higher in the experimental group, with 81 percent expressing satisfaction compared with 59 percent in the control group (Figure 9.2).

These findings demonstrate that simplifying the patent submission process and providing regular, supportive reminders for a certain period can significantly increase participation and diversity while enhancing overall satisfaction with the process. In fact, these results show that complex and opaque processes disproportionately deter underrepresented groups. Simplifying these processes using visual aids, clear guidelines, and regular reminders helps lower the barriers to participation, making innovation more accessible to all employees, regardless of gender or department.

This finding aligns with research suggesting that procedural complexity can act as a gatekeeper, restricting access to innovation opportunities. For organizations, simplifying submission processes and providing clear communication can directly impact diversity in innovation outcomes. Reducing administrative burdens and making submission pathways transparent allows more employees to contribute, thereby increasing the diversity and quality of ideas.

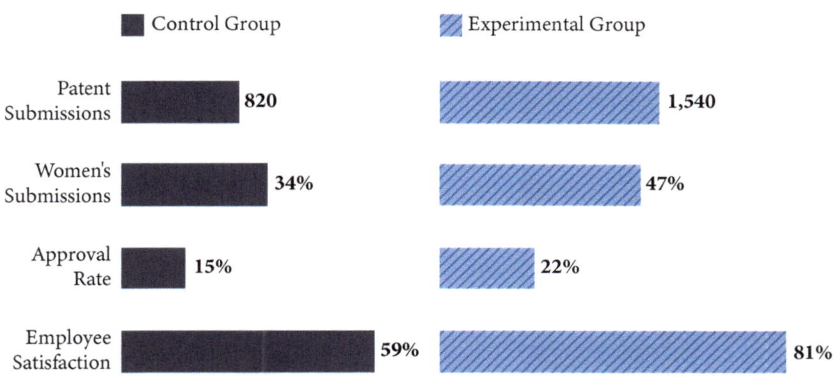

Figure 9.2. Simplifying the patent submission process

Experiment 3: Dedicated Online Submission Platform

This experiment assessed the impact of introducing a dedicated online submission platform on innovation participation. The study involved 234,203 employees worldwide, with 30 percent based in North America (70,261 employees) and a 45–55 gender split. A pre-intervention and post-intervention design was implemented to compare the outcomes of the North American employee population. The hypothesis was that introducing a dedicated, integrated online submission platform would increase employee participation in innovation activities, improve the diversity of submissions, and raise the approval rate for submitted ideas, compared to the submission methods used pre-intervention.

Before the intervention, employees relied on fragmented, ad hoc methods to submit ideas. Following the intervention, employees were provided with a dedicated online platform fully integrated into the company's existing infrastructure. This platform featured real-time tracking, collaboration tools, and feedback mechanisms to streamline the submission process and encourage greater participation.

Key variables measured in this experiment included the number of submissions, the diversity of submissions by gender and department, employee satisfaction, and the number of ideas approved for advancing to the patenting process (Figure 9.3).

The results show a 178-percent increase in submissions post-intervention within the first sixty days, with 5,980 submissions compared with 2,150 pre-intervention. Submissions from women increased from

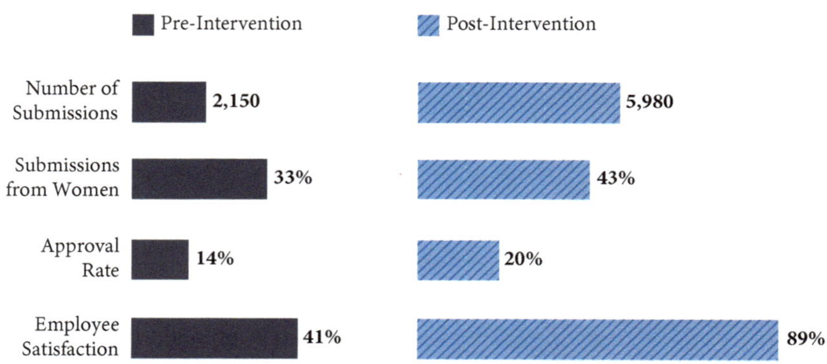

Figure 9.3. Dedicated online submission platform

33 to 43 percent, and the approval rate for submissions rose to 20 percent post-intervention, compared with 14 percent pre-intervention. Employee satisfaction with the submission process was notably higher post-intervention, with 89 percent reporting satisfaction compared with 41 percent pre-intervention.

These results suggest that a dedicated, integrated submission platform can significantly increase participation, improve submission diversity, and enhance overall satisfaction and approval rates for innovation submissions. The findings demonstrate that fragmented, ad hoc systems for submitting ideas inhibit participation and limit diverse contributions. Introducing an integrated platform provided employees with real-time tracking, collaboration tools, and feedback mechanisms, simplifying the process and encouraging engagement from nontechnical departments. This platform highlights the potential of digital tools to level the playing field and create more inclusive innovation ecosystems. For organizations, investing in user-friendly digital platforms that streamline idea submission and provide feedback mechanisms is essential for fostering innovation. These platforms should be designed to be accessible to all employees, regardless of their technical expertise or departmental affiliation.

Experiment 4: Storytelling Videos to Redefine Innovator Perceptions

This three-month experiment investigated the use of storytelling videos to broaden perceptions of who can be an innovator and increase participation in innovation activities. The study involved 92,203 employees, 46 percent of whom were women. A representative sample of 25 percent (23,051 employees, including 10,604 women) was selected. The underlying assumption was that storytelling videos featuring diverse employees sharing their patent experiences would broaden perceptions of who can innovate, increase the number of submissions from nontechnical departments, and improve employee engagement in innovation activities.

In the control group, employees received standard patent submission communications. In contrast, the experimental group was exposed to a video campaign that featured diverse employees from nontechnical and underrepresented departments sharing their patent submission experiences. Key metrics assessed in the study included the number of submissions, diversity of

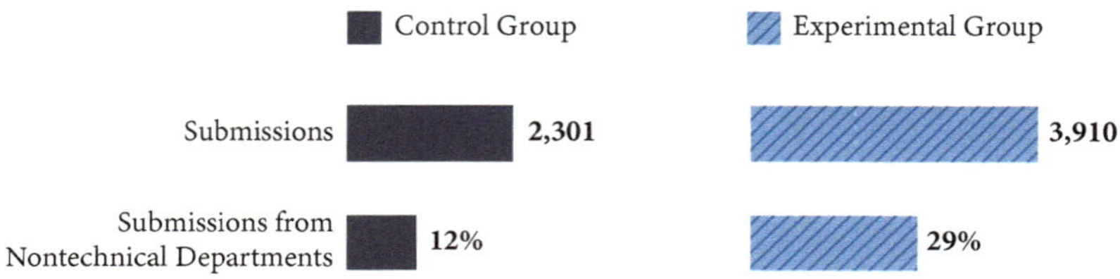

Figure 9.4. Storytelling videos impact on innovation participation

submissions (particularly from nontechnical departments) (Figure 9.4), employee perceptions of innovation, and video engagement.

The results show a 70-percent increase in submissions from the experimental group, with 3,910 submissions, compared with 2,301 in the control group. Submissions from nontechnical departments increased significantly from 12 to 29 percent. Additionally, 83 percent of employees in the experimental group experienced a shift in perception, now believing that anyone, regardless of role, could contribute to innovation. Video engagement was also notably high, with 84 percent of employees watching at least one video and 91 percent providing positive feedback.

These results demonstrate the effectiveness of storytelling in changing perceptions of innovation and encouraging greater participation from diverse groups, particularly those in nontechnical roles. These findings further support the argument that innovation is not limited to technical experts but can come from any part of the organization. The storytelling approach challenged existing stereotypes about innovation by demonstrating that anyone, regardless of their role or background, could contribute. Narratives play a critical role in shaping organizational culture and inclusivity, as they can help broaden the understanding of who can contribute to innovation.

Organizations can leverage storytelling to shift cultural perceptions and encourage diverse participation in innovation activities. Highlighting the stories of innovators from nontechnical roles and/or underrepresented groups can inspire others to contribute, thereby expanding the pool of ideas and fostering a more inclusive innovation environment.

Experiment 5: Removing Biased Terms with Inclusive Language in Innovation Conversations

This experiment examined the impact of removing the term "harvesting ideas," which was considered offensive by some employees, particularly women and other underrepresented groups. A representative sample, comprising 22 percent of the international company's 134,203 employees, was selected for the study. This sample had a gender split of 31 percent women (9,153) and 69 percent men (20,372). The experiment was based on the assumption that replacing biased and potentially offensive language, such as "harvesting ideas" and "brainstorming under-represented inventors," with more inclusive and neutral terminology like "gathering ideas" or "nurturing innovation" would increase participation in innovation activities, improve the diversity of submissions (especially from women and other underrepresented groups), and foster a more inclusive perception of the innovation process.

In the control group, communications continued to use the term "harvesting ideas." In contrast, the experimental group replaced this language with more inclusive terms like "gathering ideas" and "nurturing innovation." Key metrics measured in this study included participation rates, diversity of submissions, and employee perceptions of inclusivity within the innovation process (Figure 9.5).

The results were significant. Over three months, the experimental group saw a 52-percent increase in participation, with 3,832 submissions compared with 2,451 in the control group. Submissions from women increased from 36 to 49 percent, while submissions from underrepresented groups rose from 10 to 23 percent. Additionally, 84 percent of employees in the experimental group reported that the updated language fostered a more inclusive environment, compared with 59 percent in the control group.

These findings underscore the importance of using inclusive language in fostering a more welcoming and diverse environment for innovation, particularly for women and other underrepresented groups. Subtle changes in communication can lead to meaningful increases in participation

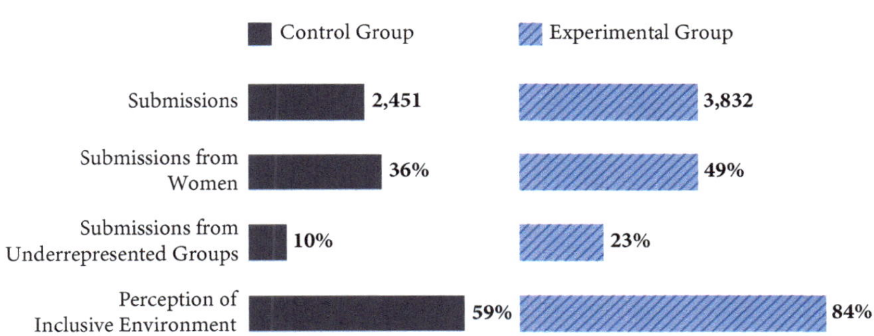

Figure 9.5. Inclusive language impact on innovation participation

and engagement, helping organizations build more inclusive innovation ecosystems. The results also reinforce the idea that biased language can create barriers to participation, particularly for women and minority groups.

The implication for organizations is that the language used in innovation processes should be carefully examined to ensure that it is inclusive and welcoming. Even subtle changes in terminology can profoundly impact who feels comfortable contributing ideas. This impact highlights the need for organizations to adopt inclusive communication strategies that encourage diverse voices to engage in innovation activities.

Discussion

The results from the five experiments provide essential insights into how structural and cultural organizational interventions can foster innovation, increase diversity in idea submissions, and improve employee engagement (see Table 9.1). These findings highlight the dual importance of addressing structural and behavioral barriers to create a more inclusive innovation ecosystem. For organizations looking to increase innovation outcomes, the interplay between leadership, language, process design, and cultural perceptions is key in driving diverse participation.

First, leadership is a catalyst for inclusive innovation, as seen in Experiment 1. The significant increase in participation, particularly among women, when leaders actively engaged in the innovation process (78 percent participation in the experimental group versus 57 percent in the control group) demonstrates the power of leadership as an incentive. This finding aligns with social network theories, which suggest that central figures in organizations, such as leaders, can break down traditional hierarchical barriers and encourage broader participation across the workforce. In the experimental group, women's contributions increased from 32 to 43 percent, emphasizing how visible leadership support creates an environment where underrepresented groups feel empowered to participate.

This outcome is particularly significant because hierarchical structures in large organizations often inhibit bottom-up innovation. Leadership endorsement of innovation initiatives creates a sense of psychological safety, which is crucial for fostering inclusivity.[32] Employees from traditionally

[32] Amy Edmondson, *Psychological Safety and Learning Behavior in Work Teams*, 44 Admin. Sci. Q. 350 (1999).

Table 9.1. Experiments (overview)

Experiment	Objective	Intervention	Total population	Sample size (control & experimental group)	Control group or pre-intervention*	Experimental group or post-intervention*	Key variables	Results (experimental group)	*P*-value
Experiment 1: Leadership involvement	Increase participation in innovation, especially by women	Active leadership involvement (e.g., storytelling, recognition)	122,189 employees 39% women (47,732) 61% men (74,457)	28,478 employees 39% women (11,110) 61% men (17,367)	57% participation in innovation 32% ideas by women	78% participation in innovation 43% ideas by women	Participation in innovation Ideas submitted by women Ideas implemented	78% participation 43% ideas by women 19% ideas implemented 26% participation in storytelling	<0.001
Experiment 2: Simplifying patent submission	Increase patent submissions, particularly from women	Simplified patent submission process with email nudges	132,890 employees 46% women (61,129) 54% men (71,761)	46,512 employees 46% women (21,395) 54% men (25,117)	820 patent submissions 34% submissions by women	1,540 patent submissions 47% submissions by women	Patent submissions Submissions by women Approval rate Employee satisfaction	1,540 submissions 47% submissions by women 22% approval rate 81% satisfaction	<0.001
Experiment 3: Online submission platform*	Improve innovation participation and idea submissions	Dedicated online platform for idea submissions	234,203 employees 45% women (105,391) 55% men (128,812)	70,261 employees 45% women (31,617) 55% men (38,644)	2,150 submissions 33% submissions by women	5,980 submissions 43% submissions by women	Number of submissions Submissions by women Approval rate Employee satisfaction	5,980 submissions 43% submissions by women 20% approval rate 89% satisfaction	<0.001

(continued)

Table 9.1. Continued

Experiment	Objective	Intervention	Total population	Sample size (control & experimental group)	Control group or pre-intervention*	Experimental group or post-intervention*	Key variables	Results (experimental group)	*P*-value
Experiment 4: Storytelling videos	Broaden perceptions of who can innovate and increase submissions	Storytelling videos featuring diverse employee experiences	92,203 employees 46% women (42,413) 54% men (49,790)	23,051 employees 46% women (10,604) 54% men (12,447)	2,301 submissions 12% nontechnical submissions	3,910 submissions 29% nontechnical submissions	Number of submissions Nontechnical submissions Perception of innovation	3,910 submissions 29% nontechnical submissions 83% perception change ("anyone can innovate") 84% video engagement	<0.001
Experiment 5: Removing offensive language	Foster inclusivity in innovation processes	Replacing offensive language (e.g., "harvesting ideas" with "gathering ideas")	134,203 employees 31% women (41,603) 69% men (92,600)	29,525 employees 31% women (9,153) 69% men (20,372)	2,451 submissions 36% submissions by women 10% underrepresented groups	3,832 submissions 49% submissions by women 23% underrepresented groups	Number of submissions Submissions by women Submissions from underrepresented groups Perception of inclusivity	3,832 submissions 49% submissions by women 23% submissions from underrepresented groups 84% perception of inclusive environment	<0.001

underrepresented groups, including women, are often less likely to contribute due to fear of failure or judgment.[33] By sharing personal stories and visibly recognizing contributions, leaders humanize the innovation process, creating an open environment where employees feel supported in contributing new ideas. This experiment highlights that leadership engagement should not be limited to verbal support or distant encouragement but should involve active, hands-on participation in innovation activities.[34] Leaders must act as champions for visible participation in innovation processes and setting an example for others.

Second, the results from Experiment 5 highlight the powerful role language plays in shaping organizational behavior and inclusivity. Replacing the term "harvesting ideas" with more inclusive language, such as "gathering ideas" or "nurturing innovation," led to a 52-percent increase in participation and a substantial improvement in contributions from women (rising from 36 to 49 percent) and underrepresented groups (from 10 to 23 percent). These findings align with research on the role of language in perpetuating or mitigating bias. Subtle language changes can significantly affect whether employees feel welcomed and valued in the innovation process.[35]

Language, as a social tool, influences how people perceive themselves and their contributions within an organization. The traditional terminology around innovation often reflects a competitive, hierarchical mindset that can marginalize individuals who do not see themselves fitting into that culture. For example, terms like "harvesting" evoke images of extracting value, which may feel impersonal or even exploitative to some groups, particularly women. By adopting more inclusive, collaborative language, organizations can shift the focus from extraction to contribution, creating a culture that values diverse perspectives and a growth mindset.

The impact of this change extends beyond participation rates; it also affects how employees view their role in the organization. When language is inclusive, it communicates that everyone's contributions matter, which can significantly boost morale and engagement. This experiment underscores the importance of inclusive communication strategies in fostering a more

[33] Amy C. Edmondson, Right Kind of Wrong: The Science of Failing Well (2023).

[34] Wilmar B. Schaufeli, *Engaging Leadership in the Job Demands-Resources Model*, 20 Career Dev. Int'l 446 (2015).

[35] Michela Menegatti & Monica Rubini, *Gender Bias and Sexism in Language*, Oxford Encyclopedia of Commc'n (Sept. 26, 2017), https://oxfordre.com/communication/view/10.1093/acrefore/9780190228613.001.0001/acrefore-9780190228613-e-470.

diverse and innovative organizational culture. Companies should carefully examine the language used in their innovation processes, ensuring that it invites contributions from all employees, regardless of their gender, race, background, or role.

Third, simplified processes as a pathway to inclusive innovation are critical to increase participation, as Experiment 2 reveals. The 87-percent increase in patent submissions in the experimental group, coupled with a rise in contributions from women (from 34 to 47 percent), suggests that procedural barriers disproportionately deter underrepresented groups. Complex submission processes, often characterized by unclear guidelines and unnecessary bureaucracy, create a psychological barrier for many employees, particularly those already marginalized within the organization.

This finding is critical for organizations seeking to promote diversity in innovation. Procedural complexity often acts as a gatekeeper, restricting access to innovation opportunities for those unfamiliar with, or comfortable navigating, such processes. Women and other underrepresented groups may be susceptible to these barriers, which can exacerbate existing disparities in participation.[36] As demonstrated in this experiment, simplifying these processes facilitates involvement and makes innovation more accessible to a broader range of employees.[37] Introducing visual aids, clear guidelines, and regular reminders further helps to demystify the process, encouraging employees who might otherwise hesitate to submit ideas.[38]

The 22-percent approval rate for ideas in the experimental group (compared with 15 percent in the control group) also highlights that simplifying processes increases participation and improves the quality of submissions. Organizations can focus on nurturing high-quality ideas by reducing administrative burdens, rather than managing cumbersome bureaucratic hurdles. These findings suggest that simplifying innovation processes is a practical and effective strategy for promoting inclusivity and improving innovation outcomes.

Fourth, the results from Experiment 3 illustrate the transformative power of technology in driving inclusive innovation. Introducing a dedicated online submission platform led to a 178-percent increase in submissions,

[36] Herminia Ibarra, *Race, Opportunity, and Diversity of Social Circles in Managerial Networks*, 38 ACAD. MGMT. J. 673 (1995).

[37] Paola Cecchi Dimeglio, *Nudges to Increase Diversity*, 3 THE PRACTICE 1 (2017).

[38] DAVID HALPERN, INSIDE THE NUDGE UNIT: HOW SMALL CHANGES CAN MAKE A BIG DIFFERENCE (2015); RICHARD H. THALER & CASS R. SUNSTEIN, NUDGE: IMPROVING DECISIONS ABOUT HEALTH, WEALTH, AND HAPPINESS (2009).

with women's contributions rising from 33 to 43 percent. This outcome demonstrates that fragmented, ad hoc systems for submitting ideas create barriers to participation. By contrast, the integrated platform in the post-treatment provided real-time tracking, collaboration tools, and feedback mechanisms, making it easier for employees across departments to engage in the innovation process with the legal team.

This experiment supports the growing body of research that suggests digital platforms can democratize access to innovation opportunities.[39] By providing a structured, user-friendly system for submitting ideas, organizations can remove logistical barriers that might otherwise prevent participation from a diverse range of employees. The ability to track submissions, collaborate with peers, and receive real-time feedback empowers employees to take ownership of their contributions and remain engaged throughout the innovation process.

For organizations, this finding underscores the importance of investing in digital tools that facilitate participation from all employees, regardless of their technical expertise or departmental affiliation. In an increasingly digital world, platforms that simplify idea submission and provide transparent feedback loops are essential for fostering a more inclusive innovation ecosystem.

Finally, Experiment 4 reveals the power of storytelling in reshaping perceptions of who can innovate. By showcasing diverse employees from nontechnical and underrepresented departments sharing their patent submission experiences, the experimental group saw a 70-percent increase in submissions, with nontechnical departments contributing 29 percent of the ideas (compared with 12 percent in the control group). Furthermore, 83 percent of employees in the experimental group experienced a shift in perception, now believing that anyone, regardless of their role, could contribute to innovation.

These findings underscore the role of storytelling in driving cultural change within organizations. Narratives are crucial in shaping how individuals perceive their abilities and contributions.[40] When organizations

[39] Philippe Davidson, Democratizing Innovation in Organizations: How to Unleash the Power of Collaboration (2022); Eric von Hippel, Democratizing Innovation (2006); Jim Euchner, *Democratizing Innovation*, 66 Rsch. Tech. Mgmt. 9 (2023).

[40] David M. Marx & Jasmin S. Roman, *Female Role Models: Protecting Women's Math Test Performance*, 28 Pers. & Soc. Psych. Bull. 1183 (2002); Christina Wolbrecht & David E. Campbell, *Leading by Example: Female Members of Parliament as Political Role Models*, 51 Am. J. Pol. Sci. 921 (2007).

elevate the stories of innovators from diverse backgrounds, they challenge the stereotype that innovation is the domain of a select few, typically those in technical roles. By broadening the narrative to include a broader range of voices, organizations can inspire more employees to see themselves as potential innovators.

The high level of engagement with the storytelling videos (84 percent watched at least one video, and 91 percent provided positive feedback) further highlights the effectiveness of this approach. For organizations looking to promote diversity in innovation, storytelling offers a powerful tool for shifting cultural perceptions and encouraging participation from a broader demographic.

Conclusion

The results from these experiments demonstrate that fostering inclusive innovation requires both structural and behavioral changes.[41] Leadership engagement, inclusive language, simplified processes, dedicated digital platforms, and storytelling emerged as effective tools for increasing participation and diversity in idea submissions. Each intervention significantly broke down the barriers that often prevent women and other underrepresented groups from fully engaging in the innovation process.

The findings from this study provide a roadmap for organizations seeking to create a more inclusive and dynamic innovation ecosystem. By addressing the systemic and cultural factors that influence participation, companies can broaden their pool of contributors, resulting in more diverse and innovative outcomes. Moreover, this research highlights the importance of adopting a holistic approach to fostering inclusivity that integrates leadership, process design, communication strategies, and cultural narratives.

As organizations continue to navigate an increasingly competitive global marketplace, harnessing the full potential of their workforce will be critical. The insights gained from these experiments offer practical strategies for achieving this goal, demonstrating that inclusivity is a moral imperative and a strategic advantage that can drive innovation and long-term success.

Future research should explore the long-term effects of these interventions and how they can be scaled across different organizational contexts. By

[41] Cecchi Dimeglio, *supra* note 15.

continuing to investigate the factors that promote inclusivity in innovation, organizations can ensure that they are not only creating a more equitable workplace but also positioning themselves to lead in the innovation-driven economy of the future.

Acknowledgments

Acknowledgment and appreciation are extended to many members of Harvard Law School, Harvard Kennedy School, Harvard Business School, and colleagues at other universities, especially for their faculty scholarship and feedback. The author is particularly thankful to Daryl Lim and Peter Yu, the editors of this book, and offers a special thank you to Amy Edmondson, Robert Eccles, Margo Bagley, Colleen Chien, Suzanne Harrison, Bowman Heiden, Jyotti Uppoli, Christine Foo, Michael Binns, Jeremiah Chan, Allen Lo, Ime Archibong, and the company's executive teams, especially their Chief Technology Officer, Chief Legal Officer, and intellectual property teams, for their trust in running these experiments, as well as the International Telecommunication Union for helping make essential connections to facilitate some of the experiments. Gratitude is also extended to all the participants at the conference organized in August 2023 at Penn State University and to Peter Kamminga for their helpful comments, guidance, assistance, and support. The author also wishes to thank all participants who provided feedback at the Behavioral Insights Institute (summer 2023 and 2024) and the Law and Society Association Annual Meeting (2024).

Table 9.1 summarizes the objective, intervention, total population, sample size, control group, experimental group, key variables, results, and statistical significance (*p*-value) for each of the five experiments.

IV.

AI TECHNOLOGY AND EQUITABLE DEVELOPMENT

10

Identifying Potential Inlets of the Biocentric Man in the Artificial Intelligence Development Process

Deja Workman and Christopher L. Dancy

Introduction

Sylvia Wynter's concept of the biocentric Man genre of human describes the flattening of human existence into the entity of a single, pseudo-imaginary person, which we will also refer to as "Man" for simplicity.[1] The biocentric Man is a concept ill representative of the whole human population because the conditions that created this concept exclude those who, by its definition, are other (than Man). These interlocking systems and conditions of white supremacy, heteropatriarchy, and capitalism enforce boundaries and discriminate based on race, gender, sexuality, and class to dehumanize other people who do not neatly fit into what has been defined as the ideal human.[2] Still, the biocentric Man is a concept around which the world's everyday activities operate. The sociotechnical world is no exception.

Modern service to Man is often unintentional or undetected and can come in many forms, but all forms are exclusionary. The prevalence of Man is especially concerning because, first, human-centered design has not been consistently prioritized, and greater value is often placed on the impact technology has on factors such as productivity or accuracy than on people—be that technology users or those whom the technology tangentially affects. Second, because of the dependence on Man to stand in as a substitute for

[1] Katherine McKittrick, Sylvia Wynter on Being Human as Praxis (2015).

[2] Simone Browne, Dark Matters: On the Surveillance of Blackness (2015); Emily Anne Parker, Elemental Difference and the Climate of the Body (2021).

Deja Workman and Christopher L. Dancy, *Identifying Potential Inlets of the Biocentric Man in the Artificial Intelligence Development Process* In: *Inclusive Innovation in the Age of AI and Big Data*. Edited by: Daryl Lim and Peter K. Yu, Oxford University Press. © Oxford University Press 2026. DOI: 10.1093/9780197799444.003.0014

humanity, the biocentric Man is often used when additional steps are taken to recenter humans.

Although user- or human-centered approaches to developing artificial intelligence (AI) systems[3] provide an opportunity to develop systems that more directly involve people, these approaches fail to explicitly address the prevalence of using a standard, racialized biocentric Man to stand in for human(s) interacting with these systems. Thus, even when people are more directly involved in the AI development process—for example, through forms of co-design—those interactions are (often implicitly) guided by this human genre through expected behaviors, modes of interaction, and power distributions. If end-users and those directly affected by AI systems are not directly involved in the development process—which is often the case—the ubiquitous biocentric Man mediates the model of a person used to guide this process. With the deprioritization of human in the AI development process, the potential for AI systems to be harmful continues to grow with their enlarged presence in society. We have seen examples of these harms more frequently with the increasing ubiquity of these systems. One example is the use of an AI-powered diagnostic tool that has been proven to underdiagnose underserved patients—that is, this technology was more likely to report that Black people, women, and people from lower socioeconomic statuses were healthy when they were in fact ill.[4] People in these categories were more likely not to receive any treatment for their condition because this diagnostic tool was inadequately prepared to diagnose people who were not White men.

Another example concerns the use of surveillance technologies by government entities, especially police. Facial recognition technology has produced a global concern, but this concern has multiple aspects just among the Black community in America. Facial recognition technology is more likely to misidentify people with darker skin tones; it produces a likeness score between faces to match potential subjects. However, it is up to a human employee to make a final call on whether a likeness score is high enough to consider the person a match. This arrangement introduces all of the biases of humans and all the power technology has in creating an extremely dangerous environment for people left in the hands of law enforcement.[5] The creation and

[3] BEN SHNEIDERMAN, HUMAN-CENTERED AI (2022).

[4] Laleh Seyyed-Kalantari, Haoran Zhang, Matthew B. McDermott, Irene Y. Chen & Marzyeh Ghassemi, *Underdiagnosis Bias of Artificial Intelligence Algorithms Applied to Chest Radiographs in Under-Served Patient Populations*, 27 NATURE MED. 2176 (2021).

[5] Adolfo Rafael Mora, *Shades in Gender: Visualizing Gender Diversity Through Color Palettes*, 35 COMMC'N TEACHER 43 (2020); Alex Najibi, *Racial Discrimination in Face Recognition Technology*,

development of facial recognition technology is also blind to the history of Black communities being policed, surveilled, and all too often killed at the hands of the very same people whom we have now equipped with AI systems.[6] Outside the United States, we have seen the same types of technology serving as spyware used to shut down protests, arrest social activists, and quiet civil unrest so that unjust governments can continue calmly oppressing their citizens.[7] The existence of these AI systems, especially in the hands of institutions that work to maintain the biocentric Man, poses a threat to the safety and privacy of Black people.

The many problematic consequences are more than the result of periodic mistakes that happen more frequently due to the rapid expansion of AI. Rather, they arise from the fact that the engineering processes we use today were made to serve the biocentric Man. It is incredibly complex to design technology, particularly AI, in a way that invites, appeals, and attends to people's experiences regardless of their social profile. The way forward is to recenter these technologies on humans as a whole and encourage a foundational shift that insists upon the careful consideration of diverse perspectives in the context of overlapping systems of oppression that result in the biocentric Man. In this chapter, we define and dissect an interpretation of a formalized, generic AI development process, aiming to identify common practices that remain more susceptible to producing malignant outcomes, particularly antiblackness.

Understanding the Biocentric Man

Grasping the idea of the biocentric Man genre of human is an important part of understanding the issue of antiblackness in the AI development process because those being othered by the definition of this human genre are the same people being disproportionately harmed by AI systems that eventually

HARV. GRIFFIN GSAS SCI. POL'Y GRP. (Oct. 24, 2020), https://sciencepolicy.hsites.harvard.edu/blog/racial-discrimination-face-recognition-technology; *Project Green Light Map*, CITY DETROIT, https://detroitmi.gov/webapp/project-green-light-map (last visited May 31, 2023).

[6] Lynne Peeples, *What the Data Say About Police Brutality and Racial Bias—and Which Reforms Might Work*, 583 NATURE 22 (2020).

[7] Elizabeth Dwoskin, *Israel Escalates Surveillance of Palestinians with Facial Recognition Program in West Bank*, WASH. POST (Nov. 5, 2021), https://www.washingtonpost.com/world/middle_east/israel-palestinians-surveillance-facial-recognition/2021/11/05/3787bf42-26b2-11ec-8739-5cb6aba30a30_story.html.

end up having unintended consequences. Broadly, the biocentric Man is characterized by the western White, middle-class, cisgender man. It is no one in particular but rather the notion of one—as indicated by the term genre—a momentary frame, form, culture, or kind of human. The concept was created out of a history of wealth, colonialism, and position of power tied to the western White man—the same power allotted them the ability to define humanness, which was used to deselect variations from the norm. The biocentric Man originates from the idea of a person protected from social injustices due to their lack of any identity that has been historically discriminated against or otherwise disadvantaged. Man is for whom the world has been built. Accordingly, society, sociotechnical systems, and particularly AI systems functionally accommodate this human genre. With Black people and many more removed from the definition of the biocentric Man, society (and thus sociotechnical systems and technologies) is not built with them in mind. Wynter has suggested that our way forward is to reconceptualize our representation of humans, and we argue that one can begin to achieve such reconceptualization by reinviting previously excluded human genres back into the structures that are being built.[8]

The AI Development Process

In this chapter, we aim to create a generic development process that helps understand the organizational support of the biocentric Man. This project differs from those seeking to understand the type of appeals to Man that occur on an individual or team-level scale, such as what is sometimes called bias. While individual-level matters are important to address, those matters differ from the problems we hope to tackle here—in that personal biases happen in singular moments, and organizational inlets present routinely in a manner.

Having a single model of the AI development process such as the one created in this chapter will benefit from an organized deconstruction. In this deconstruction, we will highlight how the different steps in this process play to the biocentric Man. We will also focus on organizational and individual-level perspectives on Man in the different steps carried out in the dataset development and data processing subprocess. We have developed this

[8] McKittrick, *supra* note 1.

representation of the AI development process by reviewing available engineering processes from Microsoft, the CRISP-DM Model, the field of SE4AI, several DevOps and MLOps guides or textbooks, and other sources.[9] While more literature could be referenced, the literature review conducted is appropriate to the scope and aims of this chapter. These references represent commonly found development methods. Although not all institutions, or all departments within an institution, use the same development process, we managed to identify some common themes and shared steps across several institutions. To limit the scope of the chapter, we will delve into the different stages and substages in only the dataset development and data processing subprocess. We pay particular attention to discussing the biocentric Man in these stages and substages at both the organizational and individual levels. To help understand how Man may mediate AI design and development, we have broken the AI development process down into six subprocesses, as shown in Figure 10.1.

Identifying Problems and AI-Based Solutions

Identifying a problem one hopes to resolve can be thought of as the "why," while managing resources can be thought of as the "how." The label of "problem" is misleading in a way, as there does not necessarily need to be a problem for an institution to begin developing AI. This has always been true, but in some ways, it has become more obvious as our technological capabilities advance. This issue both precedes and exceeds AI.

Some would argue that there has been a scientific shift from creating technology for the benefit of the people to creating technology for the benefit of companies and other organizations, showing that there are times in which profits are taken more seriously than the technology's disproportionate impacts. This argument has been revisited especially as OpenAI made headlines in 2022. It has long since been discovered that OpenAI subjected

[9] Mark Treveil, Nicolas Omont, Kenji Lefevre, Clement Stenac & Leo Dreyfus-Schmidt, Introducing MLOps: How to Scale Machine Learning in the Enterprise (2020); Saleema Amershi, Andrew Begel, Christian Bird, Robert DeLine, Harald Gall & Ece Kamar, *Software Engineering for Machine Learning: A Case Study*, *in* 2019 IEEE/ACM 41st International Conference on Software Engineering: Software Engineering in Practice 291 (2019), https://ieeexplore.ieee.org/document/8804457; Daswin De Silva & Damminda Alahakoon, *An Artificial Intelligence Life Cycle: From Conception to Production*, 3 Patterns 100489 (2022); Colin Shearer, *The CRISP-DM Model: The New Blueprint for Data Mining*, 5 J. Data Warehousing 13 (2000).

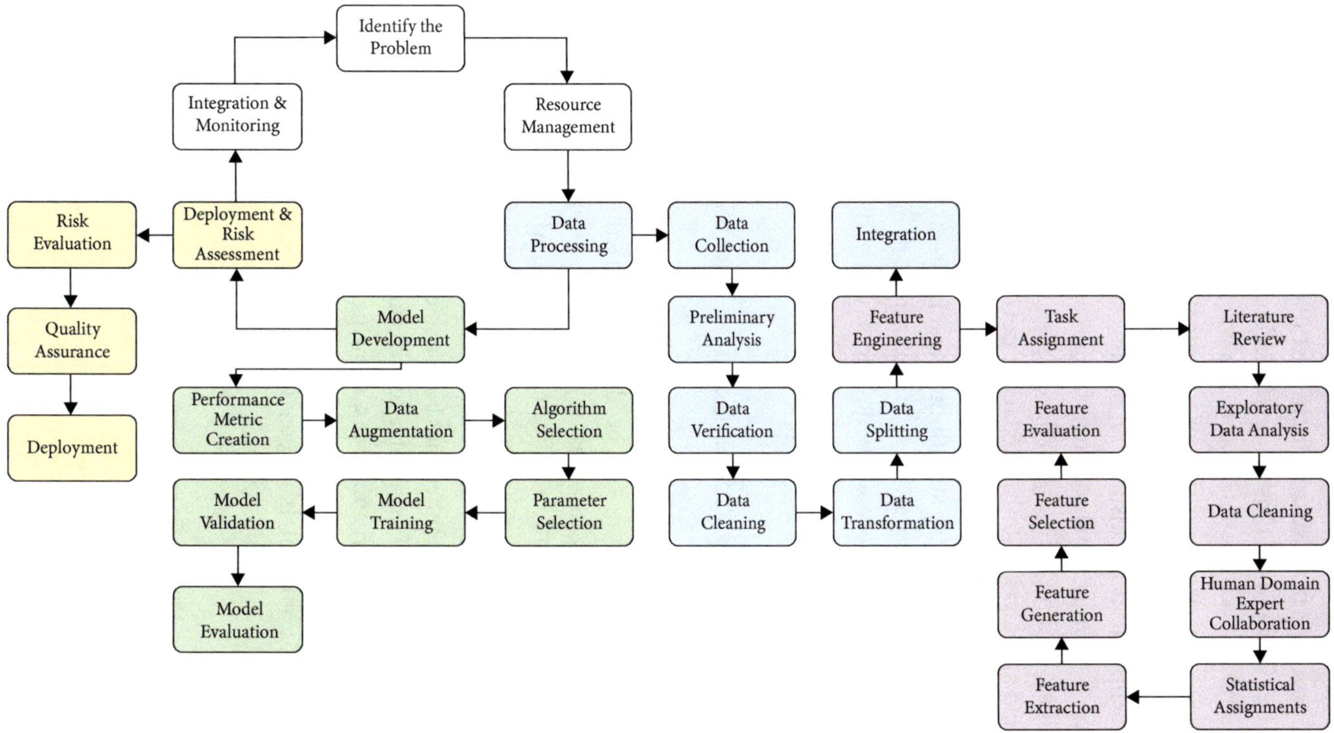

Figure 10.1. Our model of the AI development process

poorly paid workers, who were very often people of color, to traumatizing content to create the GPT-4 dataset, which stores all of the data used by ChatGPT.[10] For around $2 an hour, employees sifted through copious amounts of text, which often included explicit content about gore, violence, and sexual abuse. Thus, some employees have come out stating that they now suffer from workplace-induced post-traumatic stress disorder. This was a common enough narrative that counselors were additionally hired for the employees, but that simply was not enough.

The dissemination of this knowledge has not appeared to curb the popularity of ChatGPT, and the unethicality of how it came to exist is rarely mentioned. The fact that OpenAI has not faced any real form of repercussion for its actions is a direct example of how we have generally disregarded the harm to poor, racialized people caused by AI technology. We can see this lack of accountability in the repeated failure to mention the labor behind AI technology as time passes and in the continued pursuit of profit by OpenAI. This is the main point of what we want to highlight in this subprocess: we routinely find that marginalized people are disproportionately impacted in the decision-making process that leads to the generation of new technologies because we do not consistently consider the motivations, contexts, or broader impacts of their work.

Selecting Development Processes and Managing Resources

Resource management is an unconfined subprocess because it can affect the order and iteration of the remainder of the AI development process. For the sake of having a simple process to deconstruct, our model is configured like that of a waterfall development process. Typically, however, we now see less sequential subprocesses more often. This difference will change how, when, and how often each stage of the AI project is completed, but each stage will remain present in one way or another. The different configuration is especially important because more iteration and evolutionary approaches may be able to produce results that differ from those of sequential development models.[11] The term "resource management" refers to any and all approaches or tools

[10] Billy Perrigo, *OpenAI Used Kenyan Workers on Less Than $2 Per Hour: Exclusive*, Time (Jan. 2023), https://time.com/6247678/openai-chatgpt-kenya-workers/.

[11] Richard W. Pew & Anne S. Mavor, Human-System Integration in the System Development Process: A New Look (2007).

used to complete the AI development process—ranging from philosophies to frameworks—despite the fact these approaches or tools may not belong in the same category individually outside of the present analysis.

Dataset Development and Data Processing

The dataset development and data processing subprocess can vary according to project needs and data availability, but it is an extremely important step with many factors. Thus, we have broken this subprocess down into eight stages: data collection, preliminary analysis, data verification, data cleaning, data transformation, data splitting, feature engineering, and integration.

The first stage of this subprocess is data collection. In this stage, a data scientist, or someone in an adjacent role, will locate a source of data that fits the project's needs. AI development projects will often utilize preexisting datasets to some extent. It is worth examining this fact further for several reasons, beginning with the risks that come with data reuse. All data is generated from somewhere, and data has roots and can never truly be separated from its origins. When data is not used for its intended purposes, there can be adverse effects. As Timnit Gebru and her coauthors assert, when an attempt is made to reuse data in a way that is unaligned with its original purposes, that attempt can negatively impact the functioning of the resulting model in future stages.[12] A common theme of this chapter is that these adverse effects are not experienced equally.

A similar phenomenon occurs when the sourced data differs too drastically from the deployment context of the AI, which Gebru and her coauthors refer to as a "mismatch."[13] A mismatch occurs regularly when the sourced data does not truly represent the input received by the AI system or the environment it exists within. Data collection also tends to instill data biases and advocate for the biocentric Man due to poor sourcing techniques. When dataset developers are not educated on how the data source might impact the characteristics of the data, there is a risk of reifying both the data and its characteristics in the data collection process and substantially reproducing them in model development down the line.

[12] Timnit Gebru, Jamie Morgenstern, Briana Vecchione, Jennifer Wortman Vaughan, Hanna Wallach, Hal Daumé III & Kate Crawford, *Datasheets for Datasets*, 64 COMMC'N ACM 86 (2021).
[13] *Id.*

Another way the data collection stage risks upholding the biocentric Man is through the possibility of data collection being an extractive process. The extraction and generation of data with no consideration of how to contribute back to the places from which data has been taken is harmful, especially since the data represent, in a way, capital that the communities from which the data have been sourced will never see unless an active attempt has been made for recompensation.[14] To collect is to take. When discussing datasets containing the information of people, one must consider how one can move away from taking to trading, and from extracting to transacting (or, better, transforming). One must ask the question of how one can use the data taken to assist and support the communities from which the data has been taken.

Preliminary analysis is a stage in which the goal is to explore data, often using statistical approaches and visualization techniques. The purpose of this stage is to identify trends and patterns within the dataset and begin exploring what kinds of statistical analysis can be done within the boundaries of the dataset. This preliminary analysis might include univariate, multivariate, and correlative analyses. This analysis could also play a role in determining the fitness of a dataset for inclusion as a data source in the project. Exploring the data may include examining how it has been used in the past—perhaps by comparing the objectives and stages of the current AI project with those done previously to identify overlap and, thus, commonly useful datasets. We find occurrences in which the same dataset has been used for multiple pieces of technology or combined with other datasets to create a new, larger dataset. For example, GPT-4 incorporates data from several sources and informs ChatGPT. We argued above that the tendencies to uphold the biocentric Man could arrive from using datasets that are "mismatched" with the environment within which the technology exists. Perhaps preliminary analysis would reveal when this is the case if one were to normalize those specific considerations in this stage.

The data verification stage is often more implicit, but we want to draw explicit attention to this occurrence because it is still an active decision. This stage represents the decision to include or use a dataset for the AI project. It continues to tie into the theme of "mismatching" and brings us to question what one should consider when choosing to include certain data in an analysis or model training. Dataset developers should at least ask whether

[14] Jathan Sadowski, *When Data Is Capital: Datafication, Accumulation, and Extraction*, 6 Big Data & Soc'y 1 (2019).

the data they choose to include is truly representative of who will be affected by the AI system they are constructing. They should also begin asking what patterns or trends they have noticed in the data that might be potentially harmful or overly representative of the biocentric Man and its identities.

Data cleaning is the fourth stage of dataset development and data processing. It can easily become exclusive and discriminatory toward those not representative of the biocentric Man. When dealing with data that is supposed to represent humanity to a degree—such as human data or data points that have incorporated the data of one person or a group of persons—data cleaning becomes a form of erasure because the removal of human data can be akin to the removal of a person or a group of persons. It is a decision of whether someone, or a human genre, gets to be represented in a technology that may come back to affect them. It is yet again the power of deciding who will be allowed here as themselves and who will be othered.[15] Those identities aligned with the biocentric Man are considered to be central, while those not typically humanized can become outliers—at risk for removal or being treated as deviant. Complicating matters at this stage is the fact that inclusion here can amount to a form of *predatory inclusion* in the AI development process.[16] Thus, the overall goals (and their interactions with Man) must be considered during data cleaning.

Data transformation is a stage in which dataset developers manipulate the form in which certain aspects of the data exist. This stage comes down to data representation, such as the choice to represent something as binary, numerical, or textual. How data appears can affect statistical approaches in using the dataset down the line.

Data splitting is the process of breaking up a whole dataset into multiple smaller datasets or subsets with different purposes. Usually, we can expect to see a training dataset, a testing dataset, and sometimes a validation dataset. All three datasets, each corresponding to a subset, are used during model development—for training, validation, and evaluation, respectively.

The seventh stage of dataset development and data processing is feature engineering. We have outlined ten substages that we believe make up this stage, which we accomplished using many of the same reference sources mentioned above. We are aware that the AI development process, including

[15] Katie Rawson & Trevor Muñoz, *Against Cleaning*, *in* Debates in the Digital Humanities 2019, at 279 (Matthew K. Gold & Lauren F. Klein eds., 2019).

[16] Christopher L. Dancy & P. Khalil Saucier, *AI and Blackness: Towards Moving Beyond Bias and Representation*, 3 IEEE Transactions on Tech. & Soc'y 31 (2022).

feature engineering, is loosely defined and does not always consist of every single step shown in Figure 10.1, and this section has not yet listed some additional potential steps. We see this approach as acceptable because our goal was not mainly to set out and define the feature engineering stage but to create an analyzable artifact that is adequate to critique the real world from which it comes. We will individually analyze these ten substages and identify some ways in which they serve the biocentric Man.

The first substage is task assignment. In this substage, the feature engineer receives information necessary to complete their task, including previous decisions. Centering this small part in the rest of the AI development process, the feature engineer may be given a dataset that has already been chosen and that has a predefined objective. Even more intertwined, they could inherit some pieces of the assignment from themselves if they occupied the same role that completed the previous nearby tasks. The important thing to note about task assignment—and why we call it out specifically, despite it being rarely discussed in literature on feature engineering—is that we need to acknowledge that a lot of decisions have already been made by this point. Feature engineers are sometimes called on to continue to uphold those decisions, and this can be an easy entry point for the biocentric Man. According to our definition of the AI development process, the technology's objectives have already been defined, and it is dangerous for the goals of a technology to be defined before we know what the data is capable of. Molding the data to a task presents unwarranted expectations that the data may not have been meant for. All data has origins. While our intentions with data may change, those origins do not and always pose a chance of negatively influencing technological outcomes, which are always unequal.

The second substage is literature review. In this substage, the feature engineer may explore external reports or other contents given to them to become informed about the domain in which they are working. This exploration assumes that the feature engineer is not yet familiar with the domain and also is not using automatic feature engineering techniques like deep neural networks, which can virtually eliminate the need for domain knowledge. This search for information may also be unnecessary if the feature engineer has access to a human domain expert. In addition, the literature being reviewed may exist as attachments to the dataset or as related reports in the same or similar domain. This literature review and human domain expert collaboration substages overlap considerably in relation to their vulnerabilities for serving the biocentric Man. We can further review this overlap during the human domain expert collaboration substage. In both substages, lacking domain knowledge can lead to uninformed decisions which will, in turn, make the technology more susceptible to unforeseen outcomes.

The third substage is exploratory data analysis. In this substage, the feature engineer conducts a preliminary analysis to understand better the available data and how it fits the task. This substage is not unlike the preliminary analysis stage in the overall dataset development and data processing subprocess, but what sets this substage apart is its purpose. The purpose of exploratory data analysis at this level is not only to explore data but also to begin identifying what attributes of the present data may translate into useful features in later substages. Service to the biocentric Man in the exploratory data analysis substage finds its way into how we interpret the data and the personal biases we inflict upon it, or the general lack of consideration for how those interpretations may affect different groups of persons. The question for a feature engineer in this substage is, who benefits and is represented by these different data types and attributes?

The fourth substage is data cleaning. In this substage, the feature engineer will transform the dataset in various ways so that the data can serve its purpose better. This transformation can include but is not limited to removing corrupted data, eliminating outliers, storing data in a different format, separating or combining attributes, winsorizing the data, and filling in missing data. Data cleaning is another substage that appears twice in the overall schema, and this substage does not need to be considered explicitly a part of the feature engineering stage, even though it is relevant enough that we feel the need to include it here. When working with people's data, data cleaning quickly becomes a form of erasure. Removing humans from a dataset that is supposed to represent humans can be completely counterproductive, yet it is considered the norm and is done regularly. Who gets to say who is an outlier among us, especially when many of us are outliers by comparison with the biocentric Man?

The fifth substage is human domain expert collaboration. In this substage, the feature engineer works collaboratively with a human domain expert to create features. When it comes to manual feature engineering, domain plays an important role in feature generation because you cannot properly interpret the data without knowledge of the context behind it. The term expert is malleable because a single domain can have multiple experts. But at the core, the human domain expert is there to help the feature engineer contextualize the components of the dataset and make sense of what rules or risks there may be when the data is analyzed. For example, a feature engineer working with X-ray data may be paired with a radiologist as a human domain expert. This choice makes room for the biocentric Man's entrance because choosing which domain expert to rely on can affect the outcome of the data analysis. We see more of this impact in the policing context. In this context, who gets to be the human domain expert: a police officer, a sociologist, an incarcerated person, an individual living in an overpoliced neighborhood, or someone who lives in a wealthy neighborhood? This choice can easily steer us toward including some more than others. In addition, not all AI projects will use human domain experts. In projects without an expert, the feature engineer will rely on their own understanding, leaving room for misinterpretation.

The sixth substage is statistical assignment. In this substage, the feature engineer converts facts about the dataset and the people represented by it into statistical representations. This can be done separately or in tandem with the human domain expert, especially considering that not every AI project will use a domain expert. An interesting example of statistical assignments in feature engineering was provided in a paper by Jakub Adamczyk and Filip Malawski.[17] A feature engineer worked with a dataset containing motor activity for schizophrenic and depressed people. After being informed that schizophrenic people have more chaotic motor activity throughout the day, the engineer decided to represent chaotic motor activity through statistic "entropy." Fortunately, this representation was accurate. Unfortunately, many decisions made at this level can be inaccurate or otherwise ill contextualized. As the theme of this chapter shows, inaccurate or ill-contextualized decisions can devalue people not represented by the biocentric Man.

The seventh and eighth substages are feature extraction and feature generation. These substages share many similarities, but we feel necessary to name them separately because of their differences. In our model, the main difference is that feature extraction takes from what is there, while feature generation produces from what is there. The former covers features that do not appear from anywhere but directly descend from the attributes already drawn out in the dataset. In contrast, features whose ideas have been generated elsewhere but apply to the current dataset belong to feature

[17] Jakub Adamczyk & Filip Malawski, *Comparison of Manual and Automated Feature Engineering for Daily Activity Classification in Mental Disorder Diagnosis*, 40 Computing & Informatics 850 (2021).

generation. For example, if the dataset has an attribute "date" and from that you create a feature "weekday," that will be feature extraction. But if a dataset contains text strings of tweets, and the engineer creates a feature that counts those words, that will be feature generation.

The ninth substage is feature selection. In this substage, the feature engineer decides which features to include or reject. Several features may have been produced at this point in addition to those features that may have already come with the data. Because some features may seem too alike or irrelevant to the task at hand, the engineer will decide which features to cut and which to keep for model development down the line.

The tenth and final substage is feature evaluation. In this substage, the feature engineer evaluates whether the features they have chosen to include play an adequate part in the predictive aspect of the eventual AI model. There are numerous ways by which a feature engineer could evaluate the performance of these features, including but not limited to correlation, variance, and regression by comparison to target variables.

As we enter the later substages of feature engineering, the risk for centering on the biocentric Man looks increasingly similar between substages because the risk becomes increasingly abstract but not less threatening. We find very few, if any, reports directly citing feature engineering as the cause for unforeseen AI consequences—not because it is not happening but because the consequences are widely referred to as being the result of "data processing" and are often unspecified. Feature engineering and many other components belong to data processing, and they intermingle in inseparable ways. Such intermingling is why we feel that feature engineering and the quantification of people will always be at risk for serving the biocentric Man.

Nevertheless, it would serve our argument if we talked more specifically about data development pitfalls. We also believe that such discussion has not become the norm because we, as a computing society, view data development as grunt work.[18] Very few people refer to themselves or their colleagues as feature engineers because they consider it a small part of what they do. Data scientists and other engineers often do not feel that their identities are tied strongly and specifically to feature engineering. This is not the fault of those individuals but rather that of the low value placed on data processing. AI cannot exist without data processing, yet such processing is considered tedious and unworthy of the spotlight. So, we must find more ways to prove

[18] Gebru et al., *supra* note 12.

our argument that the biocentric Man is in these spaces. Hence our proposal for the mixed-method study presented later, despite knowing that Man exists in all places where humankind is truncated.

Model Development

The model development subprocess applies machine learning to the dataset created previously to identify patterns and insights within it. We have broken this subprocess down into seven stages: performance metric creation, model training, data augmentation, algorithm selection, parameter selection, model validation, and model evaluation. Performance metrics are established both as something for the model to optimize for and as something to judge when comparing the performance of multiple models. Optimization and the biocentric Man are closely related because model developers may inadvertently decide on whom to optimize for when choosing what to consider or develop as a performance metric. These choices often come back to who is represented in the dataset used to train the data, which is highly related to the model training stage. Performance metrics can also indicate what inputs do or do not fit properly into the model.

Choosing a performance metric is often regarded as a straightforward process, but it can have unexpected consequences, sometimes referred to as the Cobra effect.[19] Viewed through the perspective of the biocentric Man, a model that can achieve a high level of accuracy by accurately evaluating 90 percent of a dataset despite continuously inaccurately evaluating the remaining 10 percent is still often seen as accurate according to a performance metric that looks at the totality of accuracy. Many performance metrics focus on total accuracy, but few metrics would be developed to account for the fact that everyone in the 10 percent has the same or similar relations to existing systems of oppression (and thus the biocentric Man) and that these relations have resulted in the model behaving unexpectedly. The performance metric on its own, as this type of metric is currently and typically created, does not guarantee thorough feedback on who the 10 percent is. It only shows that the model has a 90-percent accuracy. The metric reports as though the accuracy is random, but it becomes clear that this is not the case when model

[19] TREVEIL ET AL., *supra* note 9.

developers eventually realize that the 10 percent had a racial differentiation from the remaining 90 percent.

An additional layer to this problem arises when one considers the comparative aspect of the performance metric. As performance metrics are interpreted now, when comparing two models that have been developed using a dataset, it can be misleading to use a performance metric that only considers total or summarized accuracy. If the first model correctly identifies 100 percent of the larger subset but none of the smaller subset, and the second model correctly identifies 90 percent of the larger subset as well as 50 percent of the smaller subset, the first model would still be considered more accurate even though it could not accurately assess anyone in the smaller subset. This is an extremely simplified version of what is happening in the real model development subprocess for the sake of explanation, but the concerns are the same. While the performance metric creation substage is highly regarded as straightforward, there is enough evidence that it perhaps should not be regarded as such.

Another notable stage in the model development subprocess is data augmentation, which employs statistical methods to produce additional data for model training. Such augmentation can take the form of bootstrapping, which will be the focus here. While data augmentation is a necessary step in model development, and while bypassing this step may be neither reasonable nor possible, it remains important to at least acknowledge the residuals of the bootstrapping process to contemplate further how we might be able to counter or rectify them. Bootstrapping replicates what it sees in the initial model training dataset. When this initial dataset replicates existing white supremacist relations and racialized content, the environment produced by this bootstrapping process also turns out to be racist. This is no surprise, but regardless of expectation, this is still incredibly harmful, especially considering that the output will be racist at a greater magnitude due to the numerosity of replicants.

Concluding the Development Process

As we near the later stages of the AI development process, it may or may not become less clear how the biocentric Man is being centered in this process. Still, each of the steps present—including those responsible not for the creation of the model but rather for its movement into an accessible environment with which users will interact—plays a role in facilitating the rest of the process. The deployment and risk assessment subprocess addresses the risks of the evaluated AI model and then moves the chosen model to the production environment. Risk assessment varies by strategy, but most procedures share similar principles while differing in iteration and concurrency. The stages in this subprocess are environment adaptation, risk evaluation, quality assurance, and deployment. The extent of environment adaptation depends on the cooperation between the development and production environments, but in any case, this stage is where such adaptation takes place. This type of transformation could also be risky to the validation process if the change was not prepared for during model development.

In considering the preparation for environment adaptation, it is important to consider the performance factors behind such adaptation. These factors may include latency (depending on languages used), power, server advancements, and data access. All of these factors can result in a reified biocentric Man as the acceptable environment, and data access is connected to what is seen as important for a production-ready AI system. Power and server advancement choices can have disproportional effects on communities composed of individuals not considered the biocentric Man, and accessed data is too often only representative of Man—or the relations to antiblackness seen in certain, easily accessible, online environments.[20] Furthermore, data access can have a more obvious impact on the AI model since it introduces the decisions of data updates, decisions that are impacted by antiblackness and the biocentric Man. AI models can be directly connected to either a stagnant form of data or a database that can be updated as needed. The former poses a risk to the model's relevancy after a period of time.

This discussion brings us to consider the remaining risks associated with the movement of the AI model into the production environment. These risks most often appear in the form of bugs, poor training data, high error rates, dissimilar training and production environments, and misuse of the model. Quality assurance throughout the other stages of the AI development process can reduce both the intensity of the quality assurance at this point and should be done at more points than one. Additional statistics surrounding the AI model's accuracy and efficiency are collected, and model developers can use

[20] Emily M. Bender, Timnit Gebru, Angelina McMillan-Major & Shmargaret Shmitchell, *On the Dangers of Stochastic Parrots*, *in* FAccT '21: Proceedings of the 2021 ACM Conference on Fairness, Accountability, and Transparency 610 (2021).

this information to decide whether the model is ready to be deployed. This same information can be used at a later point in time to compare the current model with a future, newer version of that model.[21]

In our representation of the integration and monitoring subprocess, the AI model has already been deployed in the production environment. This subprocess regards the maintenance and upkeep of the model throughout its life and consists of two stages: establishing feedback loops and model updates. Feedback loops typically include first forming a logging system for the feedback loop to store information in. This information will include some of the same statistics that we have seen up to this point. The data is then used in review to reevaluate the AI model to see if it needs to be retrained based on a decrease in accuracy rates, called drift. When creating new models to replace a model that has drifted, model developers will typically employ either shadow or A/B testing to compare the different models and update the production environment with the highest performing new model. The feedback loop and model update stages are quite intertwined, as the actual model update process itself resembles the deployment process, but the contents of the update are dependent upon the feedback generated from the feedback loop.

Racialized Artifacts and Creating Solutions

The majority of this chapter is meant to analyze the potential sources of antiblackness in the AI development process, but this analysis needs to be applicable in order for us to see any real movement away from the default catering to the biocentric Man. It is likely that this change will not arise from any single approach or framework, but rather from a foundational reconstruction that will more strongly encourage the consideration of the results of our decision-making and whom those results will impact. There is also great merit to understanding each of the concerns we presented and developing artifacts to address them individually. There is progress being made among many organizational inlets of the biocentric Man. While the initial stages of our research are dedicated more to understanding the structure we are deconstructing and seeing where the cracks are in that formation, we have begun to explore possible future solutions.

21 Alexandra Mateescu & Madeleine Clare Elish, AI in Context (2019).

Beginning with what was discussed in the problem identification subprocess, we found that inlets of the biocentric Man were majorly rooted in historical discrimination. The long-term effects of systematic racism of which Black Americans have been the victim for decades has caused an inherent vulnerability to exploitation, as those racialized as Black have been socially, economically, and politically marketed as such, and this fact does not stop at the border of technology. The disproportionate consequences inflicted upon Black Americans are not treated with the same concern or urgency of that of White Americans, and thus these consequences continue to multiply. Harmful technologies continue to be produced so long as it is only at the expense of Black people. Systems continue to be produced without considering how they will affect Black communities.

Moving toward a solution means encouraging (or mandating and demanding) that people with the power to bring these technologies into existence become aware of the social implications of their work. *Creation*, perhaps, needs to be reclaimed as a term reserved for new artifacts that do not cause additional destruction. With that, one needs to see and understand that not every invention or application is a form of technological progression. Progress is defined by movement forward, and we argue that technological progress for some only with the exploitation of others is not real progress at all. This argument, in turn, will bring one to consider action in the face of this exploitation. AI ethics principles often highlight data and algorithmic bias as high-risk, and they are correct in doing so. But we would like to draw attention to the fact that organizational inlets of the biocentric Man are found as early on as the decision to begin the AI development process. Introducing reforms at such an early stage is unpopular, but we need to become comfortable asking why some things are being made at all.

Conclusion

In this chapter, we have dissected the AI development process and paid particular attention to the dataset development and data processing subprocess, including at the feature engineering stage. We analyze what the common practices in this subprocess are and discuss further how the subprocess serves the biocentric Man. To promote inclusive innovation, we must consider how we include certain people while excluding others and how to avoid forms of predatory inclusion. The different stages of dataset development and data processing are full of opportunities to do both, and we should continue to explore and understand the engineering processes in these stages and their vulnerabilities.

11

Taking Stock

What Statistics Can and Cannot Do

David R. Hunter

Introduction

An old joke goes like this: Three statisticians sight a deer while on a hunting trip. One of them fires and misses to the left. Another fires and misses to the right. The third exclaims, "We hit it!"

One point of the joke, of course, is that statistical misinterpretation is so culturally salient that the mere mention that the hunters are statisticians implies a context where any sort of violation of common sense must be possible. More broadly, a popular misconception is that any data are capable of supporting whatever conclusion one might want. The Nobel Prize–winning economist Ronald Coase is quoted as saying "If you torture the data long enough, nature will confess."[1] Obviously, statistics alone cannot retroactively improve one's aim nor change nature. Yet statistical misperceptions persist and, in our modern world where artificial intelligence employs increasingly sophisticated—and often, therefore, impenetrable—statistical algorithms, one could argue that they are more prevalent now than ever before. This chapter addresses the theme of statistical misinterpretation by exploring how statistics can be used or misused in the context of inclusivity and bias.

In my view, a large fraction of the subject of basic statistics is what many would consider common sense. Supporting this claim is the vast range of statistical ideas in Carl Bergstrom and Jevin West's book, *Calling Bullshit: The Art of Skepticism in a Data-Driven World*.[2] The book arose from a course of the same title that these two authors teach at the University of Washington.

[1] T. Dudley Wallace, *Pretest Estimation in Regression: A Survey*, 59 Am. J. Agric. Econ. 431 (1977).
[2] Carl T. Bergstrom & Jevin D. West, Calling Bullshit: The Art of Skepticism in a Data-Driven World (2021).

David R. Hunter, *Taking Stock* In: *Inclusive Innovation in the Age of AI and Big Data*. Edited by: Daryl Lim and Peter K. Yu, Oxford University Press. © Oxford University Press 2026. DOI: 10.1093/9780197799444.003.0015

Some years ago, I noticed that their online syllabus overlapped substantially with my introductory-level statistics course, which ultimately led to a collaboration with a colleague from the Department of Philosophy at Penn State University, Paula Droege, in developing our version of a course on bullshit. Drs. Bergstrom and West were incredibly generous in sharing their course materials with Dr. Droege and me. In the end, we were able to offer our course, modified considerably from but still based on theirs, to a large group of first-year undergraduate students with no prerequisite training in mathematics, statistics, or logic.

One of the themes of our course on bullshit, or any basic statistics course that emphasizes quantitative literacy, is that common sense is still common sense, even in a statistical context. This chapter attempts to illustrate this notion using three separate vignettes that could be (and, in two cases, were) presented in our course, each involving inclusivity and bias in some way. The first argues in favor of interpretable statistical models—a particularly relevant point of view amid the increasing prominence of AI—from the point of view of a statistical consultant who worked on a formula used by the undergraduate admissions office of a major university that was ultimately disallowed by the United States Supreme Court. The second vignette retells a well-known cautionary tale involving the study of blinded orchestra auditions, among other things. This vignette illustrates the basic statistical concept that association and causation are not the same. The third reflects on a recent debate in view of the data on academic hiring might or might not reveal in view of the lingering presence of sexism in academic science.

The Importance of Interpretable Models: Admissions at the University of Michigan

My first foray into applying statistics to promote inclusivity was purely by happenstance. During my graduate studies at the University of Michigan in the late 1990s, I spent several semesters earning my tuition waiver and stipend as a research assistant for the university's Center for Statistical Consulting and Research (CSCAR). (The name of the Center has since changed—to Consulting for Statistics, Computing and Analytics Research—but the acronym has not.) Generally, important consulting projects from across the university were handled by CSCAR's staff of professional consultants, not graduate research assistants. But for some reason, the Center's director asked me one day in 1996 to help with a query from the Office of Undergraduate Admissions.

To wit, Michigan Admissions wanted to steel itself against a potential legal problem: In 1996, the U.S. Court of Appeals for the Fifth Circuit ruled in *Hopwood v. Texas* in favor of Cheryl Hopwood, who had been rejected by the University of Texas School of Law in 1992 despite having a higher combined Law School Admission Test score and undergraduate grade point average (GPA) than some applicants from underrepresented minority groups who had been admitted.[3] Referring to Justice Lewis Powell's opinion in *Regents of the University of California v. Bakke*, which was joined in different parts by different majorities,[4] the Fifth Circuit wrote: "Under [Justice Powell's] conception of the Fourteenth Amendment, a program that considered a host of factors that include race would be constitutional, even if an applicant's race 'tipped the scales' among qualified applicants. What a school could not do is to refuse to compare applicants of different races or establish a strict quota on the basis of race."[5] The Fifth Circuit rejected Powell's reasoning, writing that "the use of race per se is proscribed."[6] Moreover, the U.S. Supreme Court declined to review the Fifth Circuit's decision. The School of Law had discontinued its 1992 admissions policy, and the only issue was, therefore, whether race could be used in admissions decisions at all, not whether the ruling against the University of Texas should be reviewed.[7]

In short, the University of Michigan wanted to ensure that its admissions program could pass the standard articulated in 1978 by Justice Powell since the U.S. Supreme Court had yet to weigh in on a program that "considered a host of factors that include race."[8] As a statistical consultant, my task was to work with the Admissions Office to help develop a system for transforming all of the data from an individual student's record—including race—into a single statistical model that could aid in admissions decisions. Lacking relevant experience in college admissions, I would, of course, rely entirely on data from past decisions and help from the Office in determining what sorts of applicant data were available and relevant. (I remain grateful to my primary point of contact with that office, whose exceptional professionalism and kindness I recall to this day.)

[3] Hopwood v. Texas, 78 F.3d 932 (5th Cir. 1996).
[4] 438 U.S. 265 (1978).
[5] *Hopwood*, 78 F.3d at 943.
[6] *Id.* at 946.
[7] Hopwood v. Texas, 518 U.S. 1033 (1996).
[8] *Hopwood*, 78 F.3d at 943.

The statistical modeling task involves deriving a mathematical formula that relates data on a particular student to the yes-or-no decision on whether that student was admitted. Information to be considered included high school GPA, scores on standardized tests such as the Scholastic Aptitude Test (SAT), class rank, and various indicators such as in-state status and, importantly, whether the applicant is from an underrepresented minority group. This derivation utilized data from a sample of past students, including the ultimate decision on whether they were admitted, which, by design, included hundreds of applicants.

Using complicated mathematical formulas, modern statistical methods often seek to maximize the proportion of "correct" classifications—that is, those in which the actual admission decision matches the decision predicted by the method based on all of a student's data excluding the actual decision. Such methods drive the recent advances in artificial intelligence, which, for example, have produced formulas that are amazingly adept at predicting, when given a sequence of words or a photographic image, the most likely next word in the sequence or the most likely interpretation of the photo. These advances are only possible using massive datasets, many orders of magnitude larger than the hundreds of students in the Michigan Admissions dataset. Known as "training" data because they are used to train the model that will later be used to predict data outcomes as yet unobserved, these data result in very complicated formulas that require immense computing power in the training phase.

Even for the Michigan Admissions dataset, which is tiny by current standards, it would be possible to use modern machine learning methods to train a complicated model that would perfectly reproduce the previous admissions decisions. There are some technical reasons why this approach might not be ideal, but the approach, in any case, was practically impossible, as these methods were not widely known in the late 1990s, certainly not to a PhD student like me. More importantly, this approach would be inappropriate for the desired use case, since higher accuracy generally involves more complicated models and thus sacrifices interpretability, which was of vital importance in admissions decisions. In other words, a transparent formula for weighing the strength of applicants was essential for instilling in many professional staff members confidence in employing the formula as a decision-making tool to aid them in their jobs. As the story unfolded, interpretability turned out to be even more important than we appreciated.

Before arguing for the central thesis that interpretable models have value even if they sacrifice accuracy relative to more opaque models, it is necessary to describe some rudimentary statistical ideas that informed my work on the Michigan Admissions data. For each student in the sample, the data includes a single indicator of whether that student was admitted, which we denote by I_{Admit}. In this notation, the letter "I" stands for the indicator—that is, a value of zero or one, where one indicates the presence of some condition (in this case, a decision to grant admission). In addition to the admission indicator, which is the object of our statistical prediction, there are multiple other variables such as high school GPA, SAT scores, an indicator for in-state (as opposed to out-of-state) residency, and, importantly, an indicator for underrepresented racial minority (URM) group status.

Using all of these data on each student, I used a specific statistical method called logistic regression. This method is suitable for a dataset in which we observe a single yes-or-no variable for each individual, along with multiple additional variables, and we wish to systematically predict the former from the latter. The "training" of a logistic regression model involves "learning" the values of $\beta_1, \ldots, \beta_p$ in the following formula:

$$f(\text{Admit Probability}) = \beta_1(\text{GPA}) + \beta_2(I_{\text{SAT}>1200}) + \beta_3(I_{\text{SAT}>1300}) + \cdots + \beta_p(I_{\text{URM}}),$$

where the quantity on the left side is a particular function of the probability that the student is admitted, and each of the β_i values, for i ranging from 1 to p, may be interpreted as the "weight" associated with its corresponding data value. For example, the rightmost beta value, β_p, is multiplied in the formula above by the data value I_{URM}, which is the indicator of URM status. Since this indicator is either zero or one, the value of β_p is present for URM students and absent for non-URM students. Thus, this "weight," which we see below equals 20, is the additional value accorded by the logistic regression formula to a URM student, as compared with a hypothetical non-URM student who matches each of the other data values in the formula. The value of "Admit Probability" is never observed for any student; we merely see the value of I_{Admit}, which is either zero or one. Furthermore, the function $f(\text{Admit Probability})$ is unimportant here, except that larger values of the formula on the right side of the equals sign correspond to larger probabilities of admission.

The decision regarding which variables to include on the right side of the logistic regression formula above is a combination of art and science.

I cannot recall exactly the process I used in 1996 since the work I did became part of a court case, and I turned all of the work over to the lawyers involved. That case eventually made its way to the U.S. Supreme Court as *Gratz v. Bollinger.*[9] A key aspect of the analysis is that I used terms on the right side that result in positive estimates of the β_i values. Since the quantity on the left side is essentially arbitrary except to the extent that larger values are associated with larger probabilities of admittance, the formula above is not changed in any essential way if both sides are multiplied by some positive constant, which allowed me to scale all the learned beta values so that each could be easily rounded to a positive integer.

Ultimately, my logistic regression analysis provided to the Michigan Admissions office a formula consisting of a set of variables with corresponding positive integer multipliers. Since larger values of the formula correspond to greater predicted probabilities of admission, it was also possible to establish cutoffs, such as formula values above which students were nearly certain to be admitted and below which they were nearly certain not to be. The reality is that this formula did not neatly separate the admits from the non-admits in the dataset used to train the model. If memory serves, something like 5 percent of the admissions decisions in the training dataset ended up being misclassified—in the sense that non-admits scored higher than some admits, or vice versa. Such misclassification is not necessarily a negative feature in a process as nuanced as college admissions, where all cases, particularly those students whose scores landed them between the low and high cutoff values, could be subject to careful holistic reviews by admissions experts.

Although decades have passed since I surrendered all my legally defined "work product," there is ample information in *Gratz* from which I recognize my work from the late 1990s even today. I easily recall the value of 20 for the multiplier of I_{URM}—cited multiple times in *Gratz*—which signifies the 20 "points" awarded to applicants from underrepresented groups. I also remember upper and lower cutoffs of 100 and 90 points, signifying, respectively, nearly certain admission and nearly certain rejection, though these cutoffs had evidently evolved. According to *Gratz*, "This ['selection index'] was divided linearly into ranges generally calling for admissions dispositions as follows: 100–150 (admit); 95–99 (admit or postpone); 90–94 (postpone or admit); 75–89 (delay or postpone); 74 and below (delay or reject)." Owing

[9] 539 U.S. 244 (2003).

to the simplicity of this selection index, the Court was able to address the essential legal question as follows: Are the 20 points assigned to URM students excessive, given that 100 points guaranteed admission to the University?

Quite a bit has been written about *Gratz*, and I will certainly not attempt to argue the case's merits here. However, in a purely statistical manner, it is clear that the formula produced by logistic regression back in 1996, due to its simplicity, enabled a deep and nuanced discussion of the University of Michigan's undergraduate admissions policies that might not have been possible if a more opaque statistical model had been used. Indeed, in the parallel case of *Grutter v. Bollinger*, decided at the same time as *Gratz*, the Court came to a rather different conclusion.[10] In view of both *Gratz* and *Grutter*, the specific 20-point value of the I_{URM} variable, not the use of race per se, seems to have been the deciding factor in the Court's decision to declare the undergraduate admissions formula used by the University of Michigan unconstitutional.

While I am not happy about the outcome of *Gratz*, the case tells a compelling story about the potential impact of interpretability in a statistical model. While there are certainly applications where maximizing predictive power is the only goal, such as times when automatic decisions might impact people's health or safety, the *Gratz* story illustrates why the choice of a statistical modeling framework sometimes involves a tradeoff between better prediction and greater transparency.

The Difficulty of Inferring Causation: Blind Auditions

If the Michigan Admissions case illustrates what a statistical model *can* do, another statistics vignette has a more cautionary moral. Long after I left graduate school and joined the faculty of Penn State's Department of Statistics, my dean asked me to chair a committee in our College of Science to help improve our recruitment and retention of excellent diverse faculty members. The impetus for forming a committee with this aim had come partly from a recent contentious workshop put on slightly earlier by an outside group to achieve the same apparent purpose.

One controversial moment during the workshop involved a PowerPoint slide explaining a paper by Claudia Goldin and Cecilia Rouse about screened

[10] 539 U.S. 306 (2003).

auditions in orchestras.[11] The paper's basic premise is this: From the 1940s through the 1990s, the proportion of females in major U.S. symphony orchestras increased steadily and unambiguously. In addition to various factors discussed by the authors that could have produced this trend—such as changing societal attitudes and female music school graduates—the particular practice of blind auditions, where an applicant for an orchestra job auditions behind a screen that hides the applicant's identity from the reviewers, is of particular interest. The hypothesis is that blind auditions *caused* at least some portion of the increase in the female makeup of U.S. orchestras in the latter half of the twentieth century.

Unfortunately, such a conclusion simply cannot be supported by any statistical study. Even if we can use observational data to establish beyond a reasonable doubt that percent P is larger when effect E is true than when E is untrue, observational data alone do not allow an inference that E caused the increase in P. In this case, P is the percentage of females in U.S. orchestras, and E is blind auditions. Although the association between E and an increase in P is real and unmistakable, causation does not follow because we cannot know which other factors, known as confounding factors, might have been responsible for an increase in P while also related to E. The most obvious confounder here is the passage of time: Later years see a marked increase in P—perhaps for myriad reasons that might include blind auditions—and also a higher proportion of orchestras employing E. Statistical techniques do exist to correct for any such confounders, if they also happen to have been observed. Indeed, Goldin and Rouse attempted to provide such correction.[12] Still, it is never possible to rule out the presence of unmeasured confounders unless all experimental conditions are controlled by the experiment, and any statistical study based on data collected by observing uncontrolled phenomena should point out the possible presence of unmeasured confounders.

In the workshop, by contrast, the PowerPoint slide presenting the result of Goldin and Rouse displayed a time-series plot showing the changes in time of female proportion for the "big five" U.S. orchestras, with this accompanying text: "Data from 14,000 applicants show that the use of a screen increased the probability that a woman would advance preliminary rounds by 50%." All nuance regarding the problematic conflation of association and causation is

[11] Claudia Goldin & Cecilia Rouse, *Orchestrating Impartiality: The Impact of "Blind" Auditions on Female Musicians*, 90 Am. Econ. Rev. 715 (2000).
[12] *Id.*

lost in this language. Worse still, I recollect that the presenters became defensive when asked about the slide.

Much has been written about Goldin and Rouse's paper, and quite a bit of this writing gets into the statistical details of their analysis. Jonas Pallesen dives deeply into the statistical analyses,[13] and his conclusions are reinforced by Andrew Gelman.[14] These two blog posts present what I consider to be convincing critiques of some statistical methods employed and some conclusions drawn by Goldin and Rouse. To their credit, Goldin and Rouse do attempt to correct for confounding variables in their analysis, yet in describing their findings, they also invent the phrase "economically significant"—which has no statistical meaning—and write the following in their concluding paragraph: "we find that the screen increases—by 50 percent—the probability that a woman will be advanced from certain preliminary rounds and increases by severalfold the likelihood that a woman will be selected in the final round."[15] This language is, at best, nebulous regarding the question of causation, and it appears to invite the reader to infer a cause-and-effect relationship where the statistical analysis suggests none.

In the years following the publication of Goldin and Rouse's article, I have seen the work referred to on multiple occasions as providing evidence that using screens in orchestra auditions leads to more positive results for females than would be expected otherwise. The work was even cited in a dissenting opinion by Justice Ruth Bader Ginsburg in *Wal-Mart Stores, Inc. v. Dukes*.[16] Setting aside the fact that the statistical analyses may not be sound (a fact that requires considerable statistical expertise to assess), the simple commonsense facts remain that association is not the same thing as causation and that observational data (data gleaned from observing results outside of a randomized experiment where confounding variables can be controlled) cannot be used to infer the latter.

No statistical or logical objections demonstrate that blind auditions do *not* help women, as Gelman is careful to point out. If I were to advise an orchestra from a statistical perspective, I would recommend blind auditions wherever practicable on the theory that they cannot hurt and might help.

[13] Jonas Pallesen, *Blind Auditions and Gender Discrimination*, JSMP (May 12, 2019), https://jsmp.dk/posts/2019-05-12-blindauditions/blindauditions.html.

[14] Andrew Gelman, *Did Blind Orchestra Auditions Really Benefit Women?*, STAT MODELING, CAUSAL INFERENCE & SOC. SCI. (May 11, 2019), https://statmodeling.stat.columbia.edu/2019/05/11/did-blind-orchestra-auditions-really-benefit-women.

[15] Goldin & Rouse, *supra* note 11, at 738.

[16] 564 U.S. 338, 373 n.6 (2011).

Overselling statistical findings, on the other hand, can produce a backlash. Indeed, in a *Wall Street Journal* editorial, Christina Sommers concludes the following after summarizing the statistical objections raised by Gelman:

> Truth matters. Overhyped claims of scientific certainty create confusion, undermine public trust and send scarce resources in the wrong direction. Most of all, they don't solve problems. Sex discrimination in the workplace is a serious matter. But improvements require solid data, replicable research and careful evaluations of causation. As the scholar Alice Dreger says, "Evidence is an ethical issue." If blind auditions aren't helpful to women, it's important we know.[17]

While Sommers's conclusion may sound reasonable, the impossibly high standard of "solid data, replicable research and careful evaluations of causation" in the context of orchestra auditions over the last half of the twentieth century betrays either a failure to recognize that establishing causation is simply impossible—one of the same faults found in the original article—or a disingenuous argument that pretends "careful evaluations of causation" are simply a choice researchers decide whether to make. At the very least, a cautious approach to interpreting the role that screens may have played in helping U.S. orchestras increase their female membership reflects statistical, and common-sense, best practices.

The Streetlight Effect: The Paradox of Sexism in Academic Science

Since the abovementioned college committee was formed in 2018, we have presented our versions of workshops on what we consider best hiring practices. A question we sometimes get from the audience is, "Where is the evidence that we are making a difference vis-à-vis the diversity of our science faculty?" There is, after all, a common perception that, if what we are doing has value, there must be a way to measure that value. After all, the slogan "show me the data" generally signifies a desire to make informed decisions based on evidence. Yet a recent debate in the scientific community illustrates

[17] Christina Hoff Sommers, *Blind Spots in the "Blind Audition" Study*, Wall St. J. (Oct. 20, 2019), https://www.wsj.com/articles/blind-spots-in-the-blind-audition-study-11571599303.

that an overreliance on data can be problematic when available data are not informative regarding the question of interest.

Suppose we focus merely on the issue of female underrepresentation in certain science fields. Then again, perhaps there is no issue in the first place. In the *New York Times* op-ed entitled "Academic Science Isn't Sexist," Wendy Williams and Stephen Ceci argue that while "until recently, universities deserved their reputations as bastions of male privilege and outright sexism," times have changed.[18] They cite an earlier article, also published in 2014, that presents a detailed analysis of many possible factors in which bias against women might arise. That article concludes that, "although in the past, gender discrimination was an important cause of women's underrepresentation in scientific academic careers, this claim has continued to be invoked after it has ceased being a valid cause of women's underrepresentation in math-intensive fields."[19]

I had been unaware of this work until nearly a decade later, when these authors published another set of analyses. In particular, Stephen Ceci, Shulamit Kahn, and Wendy Williams state in another article: "[T]enure-track women are at parity with tenure-track men in three domains (grant funding, journal acceptances, and recommendation letters) and are advantaged over men in a fourth domain (hiring). For teaching ratings and salaries, we found evidence of bias against women."[20] This work has prompted debate in the scientific community. To cite just one example, Mara Kropinski rebuts some of the article's claims while taking *Inside Higher Ed* to task for its misleadingly titled synopsis, "Research Finds No Gender Bias in Academic Science."[21]

So who is right? Are women advantaged over men in hiring, or does sexism persist? Of course, both can be true. The findings of Ceci and his coauthors are completely unsurprising, even if I find the title of the Williams and Ceci op-ed misleading. For example, data that show a hiring advantage

[18] Wendy M. Williams & Stephen J. Ceci, *Academic Science Isn't Sexist*, N.Y. Times (Oct. 31, 2014), https://www.nytimes.com/2014/11/02/opinion/sunday/academic-science-isnt-sexist.html.

[19] Stephen J. Ceci, Donna K. Ginther, Shulamit Kahn & Wendy M. Williams, *Women in Academic Science: A Changing Landscape*, 15 Psych. Sci. Pub. Int. 75 (2014).

[20] Stephen J. Ceci, Shulamit Kahn & Wendy M. Williams, *Exploring Gender Bias in Six Key Domains of Academic Science: An Adversarial Collaboration*, 24 Psych. Sci. Pub. Int. 15, 15 (2023).

[21] Mara C. Kropinski, *A Misleading Portrayal of Women's Equality in Science*, Inside Higher Ed (May 13, 2023), https://www.insidehighered.com/opinion/letters/2023/05/13/misleading-portrayal-womens-equality-science; *see also* Kelly Knott, *Research Finds No Gender Bias in Academic Science*, Inside Higher Ed (Apr. 27, 2023), https://www.insidehighered.com/news/faculty-issues/diversity-equity/2023/04/27/research-finds-no-gender-bias-academic-science.

for women do not contradict a claim that sexism persists in academic science. Let us suppose that in academic hiring, excellent female candidates—not to mention candidates from other underrepresented groups—are very high in demand. It would be unsurprising to learn that they enjoy an advantage compared with men in the mean number of job offers per person. Ironically, it is partly the underrepresented status of women, in which sexism probably plays some role, that drives their competitiveness on the job market. Ceci and his coauthors admit: "Even in the four domains in which we failed to find evidence of sexism disadvantaging women, we nevertheless acknowledge that broad societal structural factors may still impede women's advancement in academic science."[22]

In the end, the failure to turn up evidence of sexism in science may be an instance of the "streetlight effect." In explaining this effect, Yohan John quotes Noam Chomsky in *A Life of Dissent*: "Science is a bit like the joke about the drunk who is looking under a lamppost for a key that he has lost on the other side of the street, because that's where the light is. It has no other choice."[23] In other words, when we use whatever data we have, we may sometimes overlook that these data do not measure exactly the effect we have in mind. Whether Chomsky is correct that this logical fallacy pervades all of science, rather than scattered instances such as the recent debate over whether sexism exists in academic science, is a topic far beyond the scope of this chapter.

Conclusion

Is there something about the introduction of statistics or data that makes the logical fallacy of the streetlight effect easier to overlook? Returning to the beginning of this chapter, the joke about the three hunters is funny because the attempt to obfuscate is so blatantly obvious; the deer is clearly not harmed by two shots that miss on either side. Yet obfuscation using statistics is not always so obvious. Furthermore, the fact that statistical methods are somewhat mysterious to many people lends these methods credulity even when some of the details of their usage may be dubious. Statistical practitioners should behave ethically, and there exist comprehensive guidelines for such ethical

[22] Ceci et al., *supra* note 20.

[23] Yohan J. John, *The "Streetlight Effect": A Metaphor for Knowledge and Ignorance*, 3 Quarks Daily (Mar. 14, 2016), https://3quarksdaily.com/3quarksdaily/2016/03/the-streetlight-effect-a-metaphor-for-knowledge-and-ignorance.html.

practice that call for, among other things, integrity of data and methods.[24] That said, there are varying degrees of understanding of this ethical obligation, just as there are varying degrees of understanding statistical methods themselves.

One lesson from the three vignettes presented here, regardless of one's level of statistical knowledge, is that statistics is a tool that can be used to either clarify or complicate. The most sophisticated statistical models could, in the case of the college admissions formula, achieve nearly perfect agreement with previous human-based decisions. Yet the need for interpretability in that context is so great that simplicity is worth a small sacrifice in accuracy, and in the end, this interpretability ended up enabling a vital societal debate. No level of statistical sophistication in analyzing the results of blinded orchestra auditions can overcome the fact that data alone cannot enable definitive conclusions about the causes of greater female representation over time when the possibility of confounding factors exists. And bringing data to bear on a question like sexism in academic science does not answer questions about phenomena that are not directly measured. I would argue that these are all common-sense arguments. Statistical methods, used properly, merely provide a quantitative extension of basic logic.

[24] Am. Stat. Ass'n, *Ethical Guidelines for Statistical Practice*, https://www.amstat.org/your-career/ethical-guidelines-for-statistical-practice (last visited July 29, 2025).

12
Equitable Progress and the Regulation of AI

Daryl Lim

Introduction

Artificial intelligence (AI) is reshaping the modern world, redefining industries, transforming the labor market, and challenging existing legal frameworks.[1] From generative AI systems like ChatGPT to groundbreaking scientific tools like AlphaFold, AI applications brought immense benefits, including enhanced productivity, novel problem-solving approaches, and democratized access to services like healthcare and education.[2] For many, however, today's conversation about AI's greatest capabilities remains premised on tomorrow's aspirations—a slick sales pitch glossing over its disparate impact on marginalized communities.[3] For them, AI's aspirations are an article of faith that ignores gaping digital divides, hard-coded biases, and workforce displacement, which callously affect lives and livelihoods.[4] As AI's influence grows, the lack of comprehensive governance frameworks risks widening societal disparities and undermining public trust in technological progress.

This chapter confronts these concerns over AI's impact on societal inequities and distills equity-based principles to guide AI advancement. The section "Measuring Equitable Progress" introduces key indicators of progress, such as social justice, participatory governance, autonomy,

[1] Daryl Lim, *AI & IP Innovation & Creativity in an Age of Accelerated Change*, 52 Akron L. Rev. 813 (2019).

[2] John Jumper et al., *Highly Accurate Protein Structure Prediction with AlphaFold*, 596 Nature 583 (2021).

[3] Charlie Warzel, *Sam Altman and Arianna Huffington Told Me That They Believe Generative AI Can Help Millions of Suffering People. I'm Not So Sure.*, Atlantic (July 12, 2024), https://www.theatlantic.com/technology/archive/2024/07/thrive-ai-health-huffington-altman-faith/678984/.

[4] Laura Bratton, *ChatGPT Is Stealing Jobs from Online Freelancers, Study Shows*, Quartz (June 24, 2024), https://qz.com/chatgpt-ai-steals-jobs-freelancers-1851557134.

Daryl Lim, *Equitable Progress and the Regulation of AI* In: *Inclusive Innovation in the Age of AI and Big Data*. Edited by: Daryl Lim and Peter K. Yu, Oxford University Press. © Oxford University Press 2026.
DOI: 10.1093/9780197799444.003.0016

and dignity, drawing inspiration from John Rawls, Jürgen Habermas, Amartya Sen, Martin Heidegger, and others. The section "Squaring Trade-offs: Innovation and the Imperative of Equity" highlights the challenges of balancing innovation with equity, transparency with performance, accountability with liability, and AI's economic benefits with its drawbacks. Internationally, efforts to regulate AI remain fragmented and vary widely across jurisdictions. These distinct frameworks reflect each region's cultural, political, and economic values but complicate the prospect of global harmonization. The section "Equity as the Foundation for Global AI Governance" proposes steps the international community can take toward global cooperation. It explains how generative AI is reshaping creativity, presenting both unprecedented opportunities for collaboration between humans and machines and profound challenges to the value, authenticity, and future of human artistic and intellectual expression while addressing the legal, economic, and ethical frameworks necessary to sustain a vibrant creative ecosystem.

Measuring Equitable Progress

Just as we need speedometers to measure how fast cars go, we need yardsticks to measure equitable progress.[5] Are AI rules collectively decided or subject to the hegemony of particular groups? Do they empower society's least advantaged individuals, mitigating gaps in access to healthcare, education, and work? Simon Chesterman observes, "Technology can change exponentially, while legal, social, and economic systems change incrementally."[6] He notes further that "[t]he tragedy of AI governance is that those with the greatest leverage to regulate AI have the least interest in doing so, while those with the greatest interest have the least leverage."[7] This rapid technological advancement poses a fundamental challenge to regulators, who often struggle to keep pace with innovations that reshape the boundaries of accountability and fairness.

[5] Michael Walzer, Spheres of Justice: A Defense of Pluralism and Equality 91 (1983).

[6] Simon Chesterman, *The Tragedy of AI Governance*, Just Security (Oct. 18, 2023), https://www.justsecurity.org/89432/the-tragedy-of-ai-governance/.

[7] *Id.*

Rawlsian Justice

John Rawls's difference principle posits that progress is measured by how it benefits society's least advantaged members.[8] He imagined a society where decisions are made in an environment where "no one knows his place in society, his class position or social status, nor does anyone know his fortune in the distribution of natural assets and abilities, his intelligence, strength, and the like."[9] He argued that reaching agreement behind this veil of ignorance would mean that the rules "are just only if they result in compensating benefits for everyone, particularly for the least advantaged members of society."[10]

Rawlsian equity directs AI system design to benefit all, especially marginalized communities. Operationalizing Rawlsian justice in AI governance requires metrics evaluating immediate technological benefits and their distributional effects across socioeconomic strata. A regulatory framework grounded in equity must also require that AI models be tested and audited for fairness, with robust mechanisms for redress when harm occurs.[11]

Unfortunately, algorithmic systems often use biased datasets, at the risk of perpetuating stereotypes and further marginalizing vulnerable groups.[12] These biases reflect historical inequities embedded in the training data and disproportionately affect groups based on race, gender, socioeconomic status, and other characteristics.[13] For instance, facial recognition systems have been found to disproportionately misidentify individuals from minority groups, leading to wrongful arrests and reinforcing systemic inequities.[14] Moreover, liability issues in AI systems present unique challenges, as these systems operate with a degree of autonomy that complicates traditional notions of legal responsibility.[15]

Regulators can ensure that AI systems do not perpetuate societal biases by drawing on concepts like fairness through awareness and counterfactual

[8] John Rawls, A Theory of Justice 53 (1971) ("Justice as fairness begins with the idea that the principles of justice are agreed to in an initial situation that is fair.").

[9] *Id.* at 12.

[10] *Id.* at 14–15.

[11] Bryant Walker Smith, *Automated Driving and Product Liability*, 2017 Mich. St. L. Rev. 1.

[12] Daryl Lim, *AI, Equity, and the IP Gap*, 75 SMU L. Rev. 815, 830 (2022).

[13] *Id.* at 853.

[14] *See, e.g.*, Thaddeus L. Johnson & Natasha N. Johnson, *Police Facial Recognition Technology Can't Tell Black People Apart*, Sci. Am. (May 18, 2023), https://www.scientificamerican.com/article/police-facial-recognition-technology-cant-tell-black-people-apart/.

[15] Harry Surden, *Artificial Intelligence and Law: An Overview*, 35 Ga. L. Rev. 1305, 1329 (2001).

fairness.[16] The burgeoning field of algorithmic fairness provides a theoretical foundation for addressing bias and discrimination in AI systems.[17] One widely accepted solution is to prioritize transparency and accountability.[18] This can involve creating specialized tribunals or regulatory bodies to handle AI-related grievances. Requiring systems to explain their decision-making processes empowers users to contest unfair outcomes. I will explore these themes further in the next section.

By integrating ethical guidelines into their operational practices, AI developers can help mitigate the risks of AI while fostering public trust in the technology. Equity-based governance means laws should ensure that AI developers design their technologies to align with fairness, transparency, and inclusivity principles at every stage—from data collection to model training to deployment.[19] It also means considering long-term societal benefits, rather than merely short-term profit maximization.

Participatory Governance

Equity in AI regulation requires inclusive dialogue and participatory governance. Here, Jürgen Habermas's discourse ethics offers a yardstick for how societies can collectively engage in democratic deliberation about the ethical use of technology.[20] His framework emphasizes that all stakeholders, particularly those from marginalized communities, must be included in shaping the technologies that affect their lives. This vision calls for transparent regulatory processes that actively engage diverse voices and ensure meaningful participation in decision-making.[21]

Habermas's participatory approach ensures that regulatory frameworks reflect diverse perspectives, fostering trust and legitimacy in AI systems. Participatory governance models have shown promise in contexts like urban planning, where inclusive approaches have led to equitable outcomes.

[16] *Id.* at 1316; *see also* Matt Kusner, Joshua Loftus, Chris Russell & Ricardo Silva, *Counterfactual Fairness*, 31 ADVANCES IN NEURAL INFO. PROCESSING SYS. 4066, 4066 (2017).

[17] Moritz Hardt, Eric Price & Nathan Srebro, *Equality of Opportunity in Supervised Learning*, 30 ADVANCES IN NEURAL INFO. PROCESSING SYS. 3315 (2016).

[18] Lim, *supra* note 12, at 834–35.

[19] *Id.* at 855.

[20] JÜRGEN HABERMAS, MORAL CONSCIOUSNESS AND COMMUNICATIVE ACTION 93 (1990).

[21] JÜRGEN HABERMAS, BETWEEN FACTS AND NORMS: CONTRIBUTIONS TO A DISCOURSE THEORY OF LAW AND DEMOCRACY 448 (1996).

Similar methodologies can be adapted for AI regulation on a global scale.[22] Including marginalized voices in AI policy helps ensure that technologies resonate with diverse societal needs, fostering greater trust and adoption.

Another way to operationalize the participatory approach is to provide marginalized groups with AI access and equip them to use those tools. Greater participation by marginalized groups in law, the arts, and public policy fosters a more inclusive society and enriches the cultural landscape.[23] By introducing new genres and styles rooted in diverse lived experiences, these contributions help bridge cultural divides and elevate underrepresented voices. To support this progress, AI developers and companies have an ethical duty to involve these communities in designing and deploying AI systems, particularly by engaging them in curating training datasets to reduce bias and ensure more representative outcomes.[24]

Habermas's framework also promotes awareness of risks. The influence of the private sector—particularly large technology companies like Google, Meta, and OpenAI—further complicates governance efforts, as they are primarily driven by profitability, rather than the public interest.[25] Moreover, the concentration of power in a few large corporations raises concerns about the risks of regulatory capture and the difficulty of enforcing meaningful standards. In the United States, for example, the laissez-faire approach has allowed private actors to dominate AI research and deployment, leading to rapid technological advancement at the cost of oversight. This approach risks an imbalance between public accountability and private control and underscores the need for international governance structures to regulate AI development effectively while ensuring that private interests do not overwhelm public concerns.

Finally, educating citizens about AI's capabilities and limitations can demystify the technology and mitigate fears. Similarly, encouraging open dialogue by creating forums for public consultation on AI-related policies can ensure that diverse perspectives inform regulatory decisions. Public participation in these processes is critical to ensuring that regulatory responses reflect societal values and concerns. AI can democratize access to critical services and be deployed with inclusivity as a central goal.

[22] Hari Srinivas, *Better Cities, Better Livability* (Glob. Dev. Rsch. Ctr., Concept Note Series No. E-202, 2023), https://www.gdrc.org/u-gov/part-gov/index.html.

[23] David Gunkel, Of Remixology: Ethics and Aesthetics After Remix (2016).

[24] Lim, *supra* note 12, at 827–28.

[25] Kate Crawford, The Atlas of AI: Power, Politics, and the Planetary Costs of Artificial Intelligence (2021).

In sum, equitable AI regulation demands a participatory approach grounded in transparency, inclusivity, and accountability. Drawing from Habermas's discourse ethics, inclusive dialogue must guide the development and oversight of AI technologies, ensuring that marginalized voices shape systems that profoundly impact society. By integrating diverse perspectives, fostering public trust, and mitigating systemic biases, participatory governance can lay the foundation for ethical and representative AI frameworks. At the same time, addressing the concentration of power in the private sector and educating citizens about AI's risks and benefits are crucial to balancing innovation with accountability. A commitment to inclusive AI policies not only bridges cultural divides but also strengthens the legitimacy and societal value of emerging technologies. These participatory governance mechanisms are not only tools for legitimacy but also vehicles for equitable progress. By centering marginalized voices in decision-making and design, such frameworks promote access, representation, and responsiveness, ensuring that the benefits of AI innovation are more widely and justly distributed.

Autonomy and Dignity

Amartya Sen's capability approach directs regulation to expand individuals' capabilities to lead fulfilling lives.[26] Regulators can incorporate this approach by designing policies that ensure access to digital tools, enabling individuals to participate fully in the digital economy. Under this lens, equitable progress can be measured by how much AI increases agency in decision-making and helps people enjoy lives with dignity. For example, AI-powered assistive technologies can enable individuals with disabilities to navigate physical and digital spaces more independently, exemplifying autonomy-enhancing design.[27] In doing so, regulators can ensure that AI systems enhance, rather than undermine, human dignity and self-determination.

Similarly, humanity in technology was central to Martin Heidegger's work. He warned against technological systems that reduce humans to

[26] Amartya Sen, Development as Freedom xii (1999).

[27] Maram Fahaad Almufareh, Sumaira Kausar, Mamoona Humayun & Samabia Tehsin, *A Conceptual Model for Inclusive Technology: Advancing Disability Inclusion Through Artificial Intelligence*, J. Disability Rsch. (Jan. 4, 2024), https://www.scienceopen.com/hosted-document?doi=10.57197%2FJDR-2023-0060.

mere resources, a phenomenon he called *Gestell* or enframing.[28] AI regulation should amplify human creativity and decision-making, rather than erode individual autonomy and dignity, a theme I explore further in the section "Equity as the Foundation for Global AI Governance." This means incentivizing AI-driven roles that complement human expertise and integrating AI tools into creative industries to enhance productivity without diminishing the value of human contributions or AI-generated ones.

Key to facilitating successful transition of groups, despite the risk of workforce displacement, is to adopt a mindset emphasizing collaboration between humans and AI, rather than viewing them as competitors. By enhancing human expertise, AI can help bridge the gap between individuals with varying skill levels, offering less-skilled workers opportunities to excel in specialized fields and reducing disparities. For instance, 85 percent of generative AI users report that the technology enables them to concentrate on their most critical tasks, while 83 percent find greater enjoyment in their work.[29]

AI could also broaden access to elite professional roles and address inequities. For small and medium-sized enterprises—which often face cost constraints, skill shortages, and competing demands more intensely than larger organizations—generative AI tools offer a way to compete more effectively.[30] Additionally, these tools empower creators from diverse backgrounds, enabling them to level the playing field by producing high-quality content without extensive resources.

In short, AI regulation must have the hallmarks of benefiting the vulnerable, participative decision-making, and empowering human dignity and autonomy. Establishing the ethical imperatives necessary for equitable governance by grounding AI regulation in these principles provides the much-needed foundation to navigate the complex trade-offs between innovation and equity, which I explore in the next section.

[28] Martin Heidegger, The Question Concerning Technology 23 (1977).

[29] Maria Greaves, *How Generative AI Is Leveling the Business Playing Field for Everyone*, Drum (May 22, 2024), https://www.thedrum.com/news/2024/05/22/how-generative-ai-leveling-the-business-playing-field-everyone.

[30] McKinsey & Co., The Economic Potential of Generative AI: The Next Productivity Frontier (2023), https://www.mckinsey.com/featured-insights/generative-ai/the-economic-potential-of-generative-ai-the-next-productivity-frontier.

Squaring Trade-offs: Innovation and the Imperative of Equity

Equitable progress is usually a mixed bag. AI's transformative potential offers opportunities for economic growth, creative expansion, and societal advancement but also risks exacerbating inequities and creating new vulnerabilities.[31] The net result can be indeterminate. Policymakers know they must decide, and those decisions will ripple through their societies for good or ill, usually both. This section explores four key trade-offs: the tension between innovation and equity, transparency and performance, accountability and liability, and economic benefits and workforce displacement.

Innovation and Equity

Healthcare is a powerful indicator of societal equity.[32] AI-powered diagnostic tools can help democratize access to expert medical advice, especially in regions that lack adequate healthcare resources.[33] AI can also speed up the development of lifesaving drugs. The process of creating a new drug currently spans an average of 10–15 years, with lead identification often taking several months.[34] Lead identification is a critical phase where researchers pinpoint the most promising molecule to address a drug's target. AI revolutionizes the drug development process, reducing the time required for this phase to just a few weeks.

Beyond healthcare innovation, OpenAI's Codex generates software programs from simple instructions.[35] In the legal industry, LexisNexis empowers legal professionals to automate document review, legal research,

[31] Daryl Lim, *Determinants of Socially Responsible AI Governance*, 25 Duke L. & Tech. Rev. 183 (2025).

[32] Div. of Health Pros. Healthcare, *What Is Health Equity and Why Is It Important?*, Univ. of Providence (July 8, 2024), https://www.uprovidence.edu/about/news/health-equity/.

[33] Robin Buller, *Harnessing AI's Potential to Lift Up Underserved Communities*, Cal. Health Care Found. (Sept. 17, 2024), https://www.chcf.org/blog/harnessing-ais-potential-lift-up-underserved-communities/.

[34] Cancer Rsch. UK, *How Long a New Drug Takes to Go Through Clinical Trials*, https://www.cancerresearchuk.org/about-cancer/find-a-clinical-trial/how-clinical-trials-are-planned-and-organised/how-long-it-takes-for-a-new-drug-to-go-through-clinical-trials; *see also Hit-to-Lead*, Oncodesign Servs., https://www.oncodesign-services.com/drive-idds/hit-to-lead/ (last visited May 17, 2025).

[35] Cade Metz, *A.I. Can Now Write Its Own Computer Code. That's Good News for Humans.*, N.Y. Times (Sept. 9, 2021), https://www.nytimes.com/2021/09/09/technology/codex-artificial-intelligence-coding.html.

and case analysis.[36] Such automation scales up the capabilities of small law firms serving marginalized communities and frees lawyers in large firms to do more pro bono work.[37] The shift in how legal work is performed mirrors AI's broader capacity to democratize other creative and professional fields, reducing the barriers to entry for individuals and traditionally underrepresented communities.

Innovation thrives in regulatory environments that minimize constraints, allowing rapid experimentation and deployment. The United States has historically favored an innovation-first approach to AI regulation, underpinned by a laissez-faire market philosophy.[38] The regulatory landscape is fragmented, with no comprehensive AI-specific legislation at the federal level.[39] Instead, regulatory efforts have been decentralized, with various agencies, such as the Federal Trade Commission, the National Institute of Standards and Technology, the United States Copyright Office, and the United States Patent and Trademark Office (USPTO) and other agencies within the U.S. Department of Commerce. These agencies issue guidelines and frameworks addressing specific aspects of AI, such as privacy, consumer protection, and industry standards.[40]

The United States' hands-off regulatory environment encourages rapid technological development and entrepreneurship, positioning the country as a leader in AI research and commercialization.[41] Companies like

[36] *Lexis+ AI: Transform Your Legal Work*, LexisNexis, https://www.lexisnexis.com/en-us?srsltid=AfmBOooGaxM2hkd4lXh64Yxa0g3qKiT6nk9pteFJHTbGSz4GAIuWxFyo (last visited May 17, 2025).

[37] Florin Amariei, *Lawyers Turn to AI to Expand Pro Bono Work*, Autoevolution (Sept. 15, 2024), https://www.autoevolution.com/news/same-ride-different-pay-algorithmic-wage-discrimination-might-be-real-at-uber-and-lyft-239827.html; Jeremy Glaser & Sharzaad Borna, *AI: The New Legal Powerhouse—Why Lawyers Should Befriend the Machine to Stay Ahead*, Reuters (Oct. 24, 2024), https://www.reuters.com/legal/legalindustry/ai-new-legal-powerhouse-why-lawyers-should-befriend-machine-stay-ahead-2024-10-24/; *see also* Lim, *supra* note 31.

[38] Anu Bradford, Digital Empires: The Global Battle to Regulate Technology (2023).

[39] Exec. Order No. 14110, 88 Fed. Reg. 75191 (Oct. 30, 2023); Exec. Order No. 14179, 90 Fed. Reg. 8741 (Jan. 23, 2025).

[40] *See, e.g.*, *Copyright Registration Guidance: Works Containing Material Generated by Artificial Intelligence*, 88 Fed. Reg. 16190 (Mar. 15, 2023); Nat'l Inst. of Standards & Tech., AI Risk Management Framework (2024), https://www.nist.gov/itl/ai-risk-management-framework; U.S. Dep't of Com., Nat'l AI Initiative Off., Advancing Responsible AI Innovation (2023), https://www.ai.gov/; U.S. Pat. & Trademark Off., Public Views on Artificial Intelligence and Intellectual Property Policy (2020), https://www.uspto.gov/about-us/news-updates/uspto-releases-report-artificial-intelligence-and-intellectual-property; Press Release, Fed. Trade Comm'n, FTC Report Warns About Using Artificial Intelligence to Combat Online Problems (June 16, 2023), https://www.ftc.gov/news-events/news/press-releases/2022/06/ftc-report-warns-about-using-artificial-intelligence-combat-online-problems.

[41] Betsy Vereckey, *Does Regulation Hurt Innovation? This Study Says Yes*, Ideas Made to Matter (June 7, 2023), https://mitsloan.mit.edu/ideas-made-to-matter/does-regulation-hurt-innovation-study-says-yes.

OpenAI, Google, Meta, and Microsoft thrive in this environment, driving advancements that benefit industries worldwide. Proponents of a more laissez-faire approach suggest that market forces and self-regulation are better suited to address AI technology's dynamic and evolving nature.[42] Stringent regulations risk curbing the innovation that has positioned the United States as a leader in AI development.[43]

While these concerns are valid, they must be weighed against the potential long-term costs of failing to address equity and accountability concerns early in the development of AI technologies. For example, the absence of robust federal data protection laws leaves significant room for exploitation of personal data in AI training processes.[44] Moreover, existing regulatory frameworks inadequately address issues such as algorithmic bias and lack of transparency.[45] While legislation such as the Algorithmic Accountability Act has been introduced, it remains insufficient to mitigate the risks associated with unchecked AI development.[46]

Balancing innovation with equity requires carefully calibrated regulation that incentivizes inclusive development while holding developers accountable for harmful impacts. If not carefully designed and monitored, algorithmic decision-making systems are prone to creating inequities. Experiences from ridesharing companies like Uber and Lyft illustrate how algorithms can be used to exploit workers through wage discrimination. The pricing algorithms of these companies adjust driver wages based on location, time of day, and demographic factors.[47] Drivers on these platforms are often paid different amounts for providing the same rides. One analysis revealed that more than 60 percent of drivers with identical rides were offered different pay rates.[48] This practice disproportionately affects those already disadvantaged within the gig economy. It highlights the need for robust

[42] Daryl Lim, *Notification and Permission-Based Approaches for Generative AI Platforms*, Competition Pol'y Int'l TechReg Chronicles (Nov. 1, 2024), https://www.pymnts.com/cpi-posts/notification-and-permission-based-approaches-for-generative-ai-platforms/.

[43] *Id.*

[44] Woodrow Hartzog, *The Inadequate, Invaluable Fair Information Practices*, 76 Md. L. Rev. 952 (2017).

[45] Lim, *supra* note 12, at 837.

[46] H.R. 6580, 117th Cong. (2022); *see also* Jakob Mökander, Prathm Juneja, David S. Watson & Luciano Floridi, *The US Algorithmic Accountability Act of 2022 vs. The EU Artificial Intelligence Act: What Can They Learn from Each Other?*, 32 Minds & Machines 751 (2022).

[47] Veena Dubal, *On Algorithmic Wage Discrimination*, 123 Colum. L. Rev. 1929, 1935 (2023).

[48] Florin Amariei, *Same Ride, Different Pay: Algorithmic Wage Discrimination Might Be Real at Uber and Lyft*, Autoevolution (Sept. 15, 2024), https://www.autoevolution.com/news/same-ride-different-pay-algorithmic-wage-discrimination-might-be-real-at-uber-and-lyft-239827.html.

regulatory frameworks that ensure algorithmic transparency and fairness, preventing companies from perpetuating inequalities under the guise of automated efficiency.

Policymakers also face the challenge of ensuring the broad distribution of AI's benefits. For example, AI-driven healthcare tools can democratize access to diagnostics and treatment, but their deployment often favors wealthier regions with robust infrastructure.[49] Bridging this gap requires targeted interventions, such as subsidies for deploying AI in underserved areas and mandating inclusive design principles during development. These efforts can help ensure that innovation does not come at the expense of societal fairness.

Regulatory bodies are beginning to develop frameworks prioritizing inclusivity and fairness to address the risks of bias and discrimination in AI-driven hiring processes. The U.S. Department of Labor's newly released AI and Inclusive Hiring Framework, published in collaboration with the Partnership on Employment and Accessible Technology, aims to help employers navigate the ethical implementation of AI in hiring.[50] This framework emphasizes the importance of ensuring that AI systems used in recruitment are transparent, explainable, and inclusive, particularly for disabled job seekers.[51] Its key recommendations enable human oversight of AI decisions, providing accommodations and complying with legal requirements under federal laws such as the Americans with Disabilities Act.[52]

Balancing innovation with equity in AI requires a nuanced regulatory approach that fosters technological advancement while addressing systemic biases and societal disparities. While America's laissez-faire philosophy has driven rapid innovation, targeted interventions and inclusive frameworks are essential to prevent exploitation and ensure fair distribution of AI's benefits. By prioritizing transparency, accountability, and accessibility, policymakers can create an environment where AI serves as a force for both innovation and equity.

[49] Leigh McCormack, *Improving Health Equity Through AI*, FED'N AM. SCIENTISTS (June 27, 2024), https://fas.org/publication/improving-health-equity-through-ai/.

[50] Press Release, U.S. Dep't of Lab., US Department of Labor Announces Framework to Help Employers Promote Inclusive Hiring as AI-Powered Recruitment Tools' Use Grows (Sept. 24, 2024), https://www.dol.gov/newsroom/releases/odep/odep20240924.

[51] *Id.*

[52] Bradford J. Kelley, *DOL Issues "AI & Inclusive Hiring Framework" Through Non-Governmental Organization*, MONDAQ (Sept. 30, 2024), https://www.mondaq.com/unitedstates/employee-rights-labour-relations/1523060/dol-issues-ai-inclusive-hiring-framework-through-non-governmental-organization.

Transparency and Performance

Public perception plays a crucial role in shaping how trade-offs are managed. Building trust requires policymakers to address concerns through rigorous regulation and proactive community outreach by governments and AI developers.[53] Fostering a norm of transparency will help the public leverage AI's performance-enhancing benefits. Mandatory algorithmic audits and public reporting help build trust by demystifying AI systems and ensuring their fair and ethical operation.[54]

In response to concerns about algorithmic opacity, the European Union's General Data Protection Regulation includes a "right to explanation," which grants individuals the right to understand how automated decisions affecting them are made.[55] While this right has been interpreted narrowly thus far, it represents an important step toward greater transparency in AI systems.[56] Similar measures could be adopted in other jurisdictions to provide individuals with access to meaningful explanations of AI decisions, particularly in high-stakes contexts like employment, healthcare, and criminal justice.[57] To address these problems, a small subfield of AI research known as "mechanistic interpretability" has spent years trying to peer inside the guts of AI language models.[58] The work has been slow, and progress has been incremental.[59]

At the same time, efforts to increase explainability may come at the cost of reducing AI's effectiveness, creating a trade-off between transparency and performance, similar to the tension between innovation and equity.[60] Deep-learning models, which underpin many generative AI systems, often seem

[53] Yeong Zee Kin, *Singapore's Model Framework Balances Innovation and Trust in AI*, OECD. AI (June 24, 2020), https://oecd.ai/en/wonk/singapores-model-framework-to-balance-innovation-and-trust-in-ai.

[54] Lim, *supra* note 12, at 846.

[55] Regulation 2016/679, art. 22, 2016 O.J. (L 119) 1 (EU).

[56] Sandra Wachter, Brent Mittelstadt & Luciano Floridi, *Why a Right to Explanation of Automated Decision-Making Does Not Exist in the General Data Protection Regulation*, 7 Int'l Data Privacy L. 76 (2017).

[57] Ben Chester Cheong, *Transparency and Accountability in AI Systems: Safeguarding Wellbeing in the Age of Algorithmic Decision-Making*, 6 Frontiers Hum. Dynamics (July 2, 2024), https://www.frontiersin.org/journals/human-dynamics/articles/10.3389/fhumd.2024.1421273/full.

[58] Kevin Roose, *A.I.'s Black Boxes Just Got a Little Less Mysterious*, N.Y. Times (May 21, 2024), https://www.nytimes.com/2024/05/21/technology/ai-language-models-anthropic.html?smid=nytcore-android-share.

[59] *Id.*

[60] Barnaby Crook, Maximilian Schlüter & Timo Speith, *Revisiting the Performance-Explainability Trade-Off in Explainable Artificial Intelligence (XAI)* (July 26, 2023), https://arxiv.org/abs/2307.14239.

like "black boxes" due to their complexity and opacity.[61] Demanding greater transparency can enhance trust and accountability but may reduce the performance of these models. For example, in predictive policing, greater transparency might reduce algorithmic efficacy by revealing decision-making processes to bad actors, creating a direct trade-off between security and accountability.

Distrust in AI systems, particularly when perceived as opaque or biased, can exacerbate societal resistance and hinder the adoption of otherwise beneficial technology.[62] For instance, the public has resisted using AI in law enforcement over concerns about racial bias and the lack of transparency in decision-making.[63] Facial recognition technologies are also significantly less accurate for people of color, leading to wrongful arrests and discriminatory outcomes.[64] Building public trust requires engaging with communities, implementing transparency measures, and demonstrating a commitment to equity. This trust is essential for navigating contentious trade-offs and fostering acceptance of AI's broader societal role.

Algorithmic bias is a key eroder of trust,[65] yet AI models struggle to differentiate between when they should reflect historical realities or aim for an idealized representation of society.[66] When generating content, AI models can overrepresent dominant societal narrative structures based on race, gender, or other characteristics.[67] The very design of these systems then risks embedding inequalities that might further solidify them, rather than challenging existing social structures. For instance, Tonja Jacobi and Matthew Sag note that, when AI models overrepresent dominant narratives, particularly those of white men, they perpetuate historical power dynamics.[68] They explain that "historically, men have dominated, women and minorities have been sidelined and given lower status, and representations of women have been highly sexualized."[69]

[61] FRANK PASQUALE, THE BLACK BOX SOCIETY: THE SECRET ALGORITHMS THAT CONTROL MONEY AND INFORMATION (2016).
[62] Cynthia Dwork & Martha Minow, *Distrust of Artificial Intelligence: Sources & Responses from Computer Science & Law*, 151 DAEDALUS 309 (2022).
[63] *Statement of Concern About Predictive Policing by ACLU and 16 Civil Rights Privacy, Racial Justice, and Technology Organizations*, AM. CIV. LIBERTIES UNION (Aug. 31, 2016), https://www.aclu.org/documents/statement-concern-about-predictive-policing-aclu-and-16-civil-rights-privacy-racial-justice.
[64] *Id.*
[65] Lim, *supra* note 12, at 829.
[66] Tonja Jacobi & Matthew Sag, *We Are the AI Problem*, 74 EMORY L.J. ONLINE 1, 5 (2024).
[67] *Id.*
[68] *Id.* at 5.
[69] *Id.*

However, AI models trained to be "neutral" may produce outputs that distort reality. An example of AI's difficulty in aligning with societal aspirations is the so-called "Black Nazi" problem, where overcorrections for bias in image generation can result in historically or socially inappropriate depictions, such as AI-generated images of Black Nazi soldiers.[70]

AI systems thus expose our ongoing, present-day inequalities, rather than aspirations for a more equitable future. Unlike how AI models detect cancer in radiology scans, there is no ground truth to what equity objectively looks like.[71] As Jacobi and Sag put it, "there simply is no ground truth for Generative AI, only layers of subjectivity all the way down."[72] They further observe that "[c]ulture and cultural representation are inherently subjective, so representations can be popular or unpopular, they can be provocative, certainly, but they can't be wrong."[73] Moreover, "[a] text-to-image model trained on billions of images does not reflect the truth: on one level, its output is merely a convergence of billions of subjective human judgments. In addition to all of the subjectivity in the individual works in the training data, there are layers of subjectivity in how that data is assembled, filtered, and processed."[74] Thus, "[u]nderstanding those aspects of the AI creation process reveals that AI's foibles are a symptom of our ongoing struggle with the ramifications of past inequality and the difficulty of balancing inherently conflicting goals, such as aspirational diversity and historical accuracy."[75]

Jacobi and Sag note that "intervening in how a model responds to user queries is not a disruption of some preordained neutral output or a departure from objectivity. All data selection and fine-tuning are normative. It is impossible to avoid human aspiration and subjectivity because both are built into every AI model."[76] They reach the following sobering conclusion:

> Every AI system reflects human values and is significantly shaped by the choices made by its developers, whether they perceive themselves as making choices or not. It is natural—and efficient—for companies to self-consciously make AI systems that reflect their values and the values of the users they hope to attract. Google's mistake was not in attempting to impose

[70] *Id.* at 4.
[71] *Id.* at 16.
[72] *Id.*
[73] *Id.* at 22.
[74] *Id.* at 17.
[75] *Id.* at 5.
[76] *Id.* at 19.

> a set of values of the market, but in leaving users with too little control or notice, they create unrealistic expectations. If users better understood how biases in the training data are prone to manifest in AI platforms' outputs, if they appreciated that this is as much a problem with society and not a result of malevolent coding, if they saw model outputs not as truth claims but as offering different possibilities and interpretations, they might take the occasional surprise encounter with a Black Nazi in stride.[77]

Regulators must, therefore, decide where and when to prioritize transparency. Striking this balance requires sector-specific approaches that weigh the societal impact of AI systems against their operational constraints. In high-risk, high-stakes applications like healthcare or criminal justice, transparency is critical to ensuring fairness and public trust. However, in less sensitive domains, such as digital advertising, a degree of opacity may be acceptable to preserve efficiency. AI ethics boards could ensure that the deployment of generative AI is consistent with broader societal goals of fairness and equity.[78] Boards within organizations that develop or deploy AI technologies, modeled after institutional review boards used in medical research, can evaluate the ethical implications of AI systems before they are introduced to the market.

When algorithms act autonomously, assigning responsibility for harm becomes complex, challenging traditional legal frameworks designed for human actors. Transparency must, therefore, be paired with effective avenues for redress, ensuring that those affected by biased AI can seek justice. The next subsection addresses this issue.

Accountability and Liability

Accountability is central to building trust in AI systems. Traditional liability models, such as negligence or strict liability, presume a human actor whose conduct can be evaluated based on the harm caused. However, in the case of AI systems, the line between human and machine-based decision-making

[77] *Id.* at 21.

[78] Avi Perera, *The Role of Ethics Review Boards in AI Research and Development*, Avi Perera Blog (Oct. 26, 2024), https://aviperera.com/the-role-of-ethics-review-boards-in-ai-research-and-development/.

is often blurred. Moreover, most AI systems operate autonomously, thereby complicating who should be liable when harm occurs.[79]

One option is to apply strict liability to AI developers or deployers. Those introducing AI systems into the market would be held liable for any harm caused by the AI, regardless of fault. This approach parallels product liability law, where manufacturers can be held strictly liable for defective products that cause harm even if the manufacturer has exercised reasonable care in designing and producing the product.[80] Strict liability is most appropriate for high-risk AI applications, such as autonomous vehicles, medical diagnostics, and surveillance systems. Such liability would incentivize AI developers to take extra precautions in designing safe and reliable systems. For instance, strict liability frameworks can streamline compensation processes in autonomous vehicle incidents, ensuring that victims are not burdened with proving negligence.[81]

Emerging case law is already testing the practical application of this idea. For instance, plaintiffs alleged a defect in Tesla's autopilot system caused a fatal crash.[82] The court had to consider whether liability rested with the vehicle manufacturer, the AI software developer, or the vehicle user.[83] Ultimately, the jury found in favor of Tesla, determining that there was no manufacturing defect.[84] This decision underscores the complexities courts face in assigning responsibility among manufacturers, software developers, and users when AI-driven systems are involved. Adopting strict liability in high-risk applications would offer a clearer path to compensation for victims while incentivizing companies to prioritize safety in AI development.

Another option is to introduce insurance schemes that cover AI-related risks. Given the difficulty in predicting when and how AI systems might cause harm, mandatory insurance for AI developers and users could be a buffer against the financial consequences of AI-related accidents. This would

[79] Iria Giuffrida, *Liability for AI Decision-Making: Some Legal and Ethical Considerations*, 88 Fordham L. Rev. 439 (2019).

[80] Michael Franklin, *Product Liability vs. Strict Liability: Understanding the Differences*, Values L. Blog (Aug. 30, 2024), https://www.valueslaw.com/product-liability-vs-strict-liability-understanding-the-differences/.

[81] Mark A. Geistfeld, *A Roadmap for Autonomous Vehicles: State Tort Liability, Automobile Insurance, and Federal Safety Regulation*, 105 Calif. L. Rev. 1611, 1615 (2017) (discussing strict liability regimes in the context of audiovisual technologies).

[82] Andrew J. Hawkins, *Tesla Wins Again as Lawsuit Challenging Autopilot Claims Is Dismissed*, Verge (Oct. 1, 2024), https://www.theverge.com/2024/10/1/24259588/tesla-lawsuit-autopilot-dismissed-elon-musk-self-driving.

[83] *Id.*

[84] *Id.*

provide additional protection for individuals and organizations relying on AI technologies while ensuring that companies are financially accountable for unintended consequences. This approach is particularly relevant in sectors like healthcare, where AI systems are integrated into critical decision-making processes. Governments could play a role in regulating these insurance markets, ensuring that coverage is adequate and affordable.

AI companies also offer indemnity programs to shield users from infringement claims from AI-generated outputs. These programs provide financial and legal support in disputes over alleged intellectual property infringements, which can occur when generative AI systems inadvertently replicate protected material from training datasets. Some pledge to cover legal costs or damages for users who act in good faith and use the AI outputs within prescribed guidelines.[85] These measures aim to foster user trust and reduce the perceived legal risks of adopting generative AI.[86]

The EU approach to AI regulation offers a useful case study of trade-offs. The European Union has embraced a precautionary stance, emphasizing transparency, accountability, and the protection of fundamental rights. The EU AI Act embodies this approach by categorizing AI systems based on their associated risks and enforcing stringent requirements for high-risk applications.[87] This risk-based regulatory framework divides AI systems into four categories—minimal, limited, high, and unacceptable risk—imposing rigorous standards on high-risk systems, particularly those deployed in critical areas such as healthcare, transportation, and law enforcement.[88] These systems must adhere to transparency, accountability, and explainability principles, aligning with the European Union's commitment to safeguarding human dignity, privacy, and nondiscrimination. A significant aspect of this regulation is its emphasis on algorithmic transparency and human oversight, designed to address the potential harms of automated decision-making on vulnerable populations.

[85] Camilla Hodgson, *AI Firms' Pledges to Defend Customers from IP Issues Have Real Limits: Indemnities Offered by Amazon, Google, and Microsoft Are Narrow*, Ars Technica (Jan. 8, 2024), https://arstechnica.com/ai/2024/01/ai-firms-pledges-to-defend-customers-from-ip-issues-have-real-limits/.

[86] *Id.*

[87] Regulation 2024/1689, 2024 O.J. (L 144) (EU) [hereinafter EU AI Act]. The Act became part of the EU legal system on August 1, 2024. It is legally binding and applicable, with provisions "applying" at various milestones. The EU AI Act | Updates, Compliance, https://www.artificial-intelligence-act.com/ (last visited May 17, 2023).

[88] EU AI Act, *supra* note 87 (describing its risk-based framework and regulatory approach).

The AI Act also introduces a new transparency obligation to enable rightsholders to police AI training processes.[89] AI developers must offer a summary containing sufficient detail to allow copyright enforcement. It is intended "to facilitate parties with legitimate interests, including copyright holders, to exercise and enforce their rights."[90] Martin Senftleben notes, "The adoption of specific transparency rules in the area of generative AI systems confirms the existence of transparency and trust issues."[91]

However, the EU AI Act's stringent requirements may stifle innovation by creating significant compliance burdens, particularly for smaller enterprises. Its requirements for rights clearance in AI training, including the opt-out provisions, present significant obstacles for AI startups and investors.[92] Senftleben warns:

> The AI Act package may lead to a situation where the spectrum of generative AI systems on the EU market is smaller than in other regions, and where the generative AI systems that do become available in the EU are less sophisticated and powerful than in other regions. Perhaps even more importantly, the various obstacles posed in the AI Act may marginalize the role and availability of EU cultural productions and EU cultural heritage in generative AI systems. This implies that EU culture will be less visible in EU output.[93]

Senftleben observes that "the transparency obligation—and the submission of detailed summaries of copyrighted training resources—are a substantial administrative burden."[94] There will be difficult issues to address, such as measuring value and setting licensing prices. Would all works be valued the same? If not, on what criterion could differential value and payments be assessed? Would there be a one-time or regular payment? Would payments depend on who has registered with a governmental entity administering the licensing regime? What would the administrator do with orphan works or works with disputed ownership rights?

[89] Lim, *supra* note 42.

[90] EU AI Act, *supra* note 87, recital 60k, art. 52(c).

[91] Martin Senftleben, *AI Act and Author Remuneration—A Model for Other Regions?* (Mar. 19, 2024), https://ssrn.com/abstract=4740268.

[92] Lim, *supra* note 42.

[93] Senftleben, *supra* note 91, at 13–14.

[94] *Id.* at 12.

Because collective licensing regimes aim to collect significant sums to support authors and artists, a proliferation of collective licensing regimes might make the development of generative AI too expensive to be feasible.[95] One solution is a remuneration model that compensates human creators for their contributions to AI training datasets. This model could involve royalties for creators whose works are used to train generative AI systems or other funding mechanisms to support human-driven artistic innovation. Other solutions include a hybrid model where AI-generated works could be co-owned by the human programmer or the human user who contributed to the AI's training or introducing new categories of copyright specifically tailored to AI-generated content.

While the European Union aims to protect creators, its rigid framework may inadvertently stifle innovation, driving AI companies to train their models in jurisdictions with more permissive laws, such an outcome risks limiting the global competitiveness of European AI developers.[96] Worse still, Senftleben warns that "schemes ensuring direct payments to individual artists are not at the negotiation table, the results of the new remuneration infrastructure may disappoint individual creators."[97] Moreover, Jacobi and Sag warn:

> [I]f we are concerned that unrepresentative training data lead to unrepresentative models, legal rules that limit the availability of training data may be undesirable. Judicial rulings narrowing the scope of fair use for nonexpressive uses or legislative interventions to that effect, may simply push AI development offshore; but even if not, the result may be models that are more reliant on more biased, low-friction training data that exacerbates problems in Generative AI representation.[98]

Whether the training has occurred in the European Union or elsewhere, it imposes a market ban on AI systems not trained according to EU requirements, including the obligation to observe opt-outs.[99] Its

[95] Pamela Samuelson, *Fair Use Defenses in Disruptive Technology Cases*, 71 UCLA L. Rev. 1484 (2024).

[96] Pascale Davies, *Could the New EU AI Act Stifle GenAI Innovation in Europe? A New Study Says It Could*, Euronews (Mar. 22, 2024), https://www.euronews.com/next/2024/03/22/could-the-new-eu-ai-act-stifle-genai-innovation-in-europe-a-new-study-says-it-could.

[97] Senftleben, *supra* note 91, at 12.

[98] Jacobi & Sag, *supra* note 66, at 21.

[99] EU AI Act, *supra* note 87, recital 60j.

extraterritorial provisions could also lead to tensions with jurisdictions that adopt more permissive regulatory models, complicating international cooperation, which I address in the section "Equity as the Foundation for Global AI Governance."[100] In contrast, countries like Japan and Singapore have adopted broader exceptions for text and data mining or computational data analysis, facilitating more flexible innovation.[101]

In sum, crafting liability frameworks for AI systems requires balancing innovation, accountability, and victim protection. Strict liability can streamline compensation and incentivize safer AI design, but it must be carefully calibrated to avoid stifling innovation. International approaches, such as the European Union's transparency-focused AI Act, highlight trade-offs that policymakers must navigate to foster trust while supporting technological advancement.

Economic Benefits and Workforce Displacement

AI advancements will lead to workforce displacement, and not just in repetitive roles. The International Monetary Fund (IMF) cautioned that AI "raises profound concerns about massive labor disruptions and rising inequality."[102] EY-Parthenon estimated that two-thirds of U.S. employment—more than 100 million jobs—is highly or moderately exposed to generative AI.[103] Customer service roles, administrative positions, and even information and professional services, which include graphic design, accounting, and legal services, are increasingly automated, raising concerns about job security.[104]

On the one hand, workforce displacement is old news. Samanth Subramanian notes, "The twentieth century is cluttered with the vacated chairs and discarded uniforms of workers whose jobs have been automated. Human hands once stuffed sausages, riveted cars together, and transferred

[100] Lim, *supra* note 31.

[101] Matthew Sag & Peter K. Yu, *The Globalization of Copyright Exceptions for AI Training*, 74 Emory L.J. 1163 (2025).

[102] Fernanda Brollo, Era Dabla-Norris, Ruud de Mooij, Daniel Garcia-Macia, Tibor Hanappi, Liu Li & Anh D. M. Nguyen, *Broadening the Gains from Generative AI: The Role of Fiscal Policies* (Int'l Monetary Fund, Staff Discussion Note No. 2024/002, 2024), https://www.imf.org/en/Publications/Staff-Discussion-Notes/Issues/2024/06/11/Broadening-the-Gains-from-Generative-AI-The-Role-of-Fiscal-Policies-549639.

[103] Sydney Ember, *Can A.I. Answer the Needs of Smaller Businesses? Some Push to Find Out*, N.Y. Times (June 17, 2024), https://www.nytimes.com/2024/06/17/business/economy/artificial-intelligence-small-business.html.

[104] *Id.*

calls in telephone exchanges."[105] Innovation makes previously valuable skills or knowledge irrelevant. For example, knowledge of the roads used to be the most valuable part of London cab drivers' skills, but global positioning systems rendered this knowledge redundant, and self-driving vehicles may soon displace what remains of the job.

At the same time, AI will create new tasks. David Autor estimates that 60 percent of U.S. workers today are employed in occupations that did not exist in 1940.[106] Just as there will not be drivers without cars or social media professionals without the internet, many future jobs will owe their existence to generative AI. As he notes further: "by leveling up human expertise, AI can potentially reduce the gap between the least and most proficient people in a given domain of expertise."[107] As a result, "[s]kills that complement AI, such as critical thinking, creativity, and emotional intelligence, may become more valuable and in demand."[108]

There is already roaring demand in the technology labor market for those with the technical knowledge or experience with large-language models that fuel chatbots. Thousands elsewhere have faced layoffs amidst reorganizations and micro-cuts as companies leverage AI.[109] Savvy workers reskill by taking AI courses. LinkedIn figures show terms like Copilot and ChatGPT appearing over 1,400 percent more frequently year-on-year, with posts mentioning AI receiving 17 percent more applications than non-AI roles.[110]

Proactive policies can support workers transitioning to new roles. Countries like Germany, Switzerland, and the United Kingdom have demonstrated the effectiveness of apprenticeship programs in equipping workers with skills that align with emerging technological demands, offering a blueprint for AI-era reskilling initiatives.[111] Unemployment insurance tied to reskilling and upskilling can help displaced workers adapt to evolving labor markets without encouraging sloth. For instance, the IMF

[105] Samanth Subramanian, *AI and the End of the Human Writer*, New Republic (Apr. 22, 2024), https://newrepublic.com/article/180395/ai-artifical-intelligence-writing-human-creativity.

[106] Terence Ho, *AI Could Be a Basic Job Skill Soon*, Straits Times (June 3, 2024), https://www.straitstimes.com/opinion/ai-could-be-a-basic-job-skill-soon.

[107] *Id.*

[108] Laura Bratton, *ChatGPT Is Stealing Jobs from Online Freelancers, Study Shows*, Quartz (June 24, 2024), https://qz.com/chatgpt-ai-steals-jobs-freelancers-1851557134.

[109] Katherine Bindley, *Tech Workers Retool for Artificial-Intelligence Boom*, Wall St. J. (May 26, 2024), https://www.wsj.com/tech/ai/ai-skills-tech-workers-job-market-1d58b2dd.

[110] *Id.*

[111] *Advancing AI Skills Through the Apprenticeship Model*, Google Pub. Pol'y Blog (Nov. 13, 2023), https://publicpolicy.google/article/advancing-AI-skills-through-apprenticeship/.

recommended offering lifelong learning through sector-based training and apprenticeship to help workers transition to new tasks and sectors.[112] To stay relevant, workers in affected jobs must focus on tasks where they continue to outperform automation or AI while leveraging technology to perform other parts of their work more efficiently.

On the other hand, the IMF recommended against implementing specific taxes on AI to mitigate its negative impacts, warning that such measures might hinder productivity growth.[113] Instead, the organization suggested increasing taxes on capital gains, profits, and corporate income—areas where tax rates have significantly declined in recent decades—to address growing wealth inequality.[114] Additionally, it is worth noting that regulatory measures that raise operational costs for businesses, such as the EU AI Act's permission-based model for using copyrighted works, function in practice as a form of taxation.[115]

In sum, while AI advancements will inevitably disrupt the workforce, they also present opportunities for innovation, new job creation, and enhanced productivity. Proactive policies—such as apprenticeship programs, reskilling initiatives, and lifelong learning—can help mitigate the impact of displacement by equipping workers with the skills necessary to thrive in an AI-driven economy. Equitable progress in this context means designing labor and innovation policies that reduce participation gaps across class, geography, and identity. It also means democratizing the ability to create with and shape AI tools, not just adapt to them. This requires long-term investments in inclusive education, infrastructure, and governance. By fostering adaptability, incentivizing upskilling, and addressing inequality through thoughtful fiscal measures, societies can harness the potential of AI to create a more dynamic and equitable labor market, ensuring that the benefits of technological progress are broadly shared.

Rapid AI technology advancements present unparalleled opportunities and significant challenges, demanding thoughtful governance that reflects diverse global values and advances equitable participation in innovation. Nations have responded to these challenges in markedly different ways, shaped by their political, cultural, and economic contexts. However, AI's

[112] Ho, *supra* note 106.
[113] Valentina Romei, *IMF Warns of "Profound Concerns" over Rising Inequality from AI*, Fin. Times (June 17, 2024), https://www.ft.com/content/b238e630-93df-4a0c-80d0-fbfd2f13658f.
[114] *Id.*
[115] Lim, *supra* note 42.

borderless nature necessitates a cohesive global approach to governance that balances innovation with ethical responsibility. By examining the strategies of key players like the United States, Europe, China, and Singapore, this chapter identifies the obstacles to and potential avenues for international collaboration.

Equity as the Foundation for Global AI Governance

While America favors a market-driven model for governing AI, Europe has adopted a precautionary rights-based stance.[116] Meanwhile, China prioritizes state sovereignty, economic development, and social harmony over individual autonomy.[117] The political, economic, and cultural values of these countries shape these diverse regulatory frameworks, yet AI's cross-border impact necessitates international collaboration to create cohesive regulatory standards. For instance, developing international liability standards would help ensure that those harmed by AI systems can seek redress, regardless of where the AI system was developed or deployed.

Fragmentation

The global response to AI's rapid growth has been uneven, with only a handful of countries enacting comprehensive laws.[118] Despite numerous guidelines, frameworks, and principles, there is a lack of coherent, collective governance that serves the public interest.[119] The United States, the European Union, and China all seek AI dominance through different routes: America leverages its free market policies,[120] Europe advances prescriptive market regulation,[121] and China promotes rapid scaling and pro-AI

[116] Daryl Lim, *Governing Generative AI*, 57 Akron L. Rev. 209 (2024).
[117] *Id.*
[118] *Global AI Law and Policy Tracker*, Int'l Ass'n Priv. Pros. (Nov. 2024), https://iapp.org/resources/article/global-ai-legislation-tracker.
[119] Natasha Lomas, *AI Governance Can't Be Left to the Vested Interests*, TechCrunch (Sept. 19, 2024), https://techcrunch.com/2024/09/19/ai-governance-cant-be-left-to-the-vested-interests/.
[120] Christiaan Hetzner, *Former Google CEO Eric Schmidt Tells Government to Leave A.I. Regulation to Big Tech*, Fortune (May 15, 2023), https://fortune.com/2023/05/15/former-google-ceo-eric-schmidt-tells-government-to-leave-regulation-of-ai-to-big-tech-openai-chatgpt-bardai-midjourney/.
[121] Danny Friedmann, *Creation and Generation Copyright Standards*, 14 N.Y.U. J. Intell. Prop. & Ent. L. 51 (2024).

laws, facial recognition technology, and mass application of Western technology.[122] Catherine Thorbecke provides an incisive analysis of the differing U.S. and Chinese approaches:

> The US innovation ecosystem, driven by entrepreneurship, has spurred decades of rapid economic growth and consumer benefits. But after startups became the biggest companies in the world, the incentive to experiment and invent something truly new became obfuscated. It's no longer innovate or die, but create shareholder value or perish. This has encouraged the brightest minds in Silicon Valley to focus on short-term returns rather than novel breakthroughs. It has turned once-exciting product launch events into boring updates.
>
> China's use of national interests as an incentive for innovation isn't as far off from an all-too-American playbook that predated the US tech revolution. Like the space race during the US-Soviet Union Cold War that paved the way for Silicon Valley, many of these developments may end up having a dual use, providing downstream benefits to consumers.[123]

Chesterman points out that current efforts to impose global AI governance often limit access to critical technology, as seen in America's controls on exports of high-performance computing chips to China.[124] Such measures underscore the difficulty of achieving meaningful global coordination when AI technologies and their geopolitical implications are deeply intertwined. I have contrasted the American and European approaches earlier and elsewhere, warning against stifling innovation with overly burdensome regulations.[125]

A fourth model worth studying is Singapore, an approach to AI regulation that seeks to balance innovation with ethical governance.[126] Singapore has positioned itself as a leader in ethical AI governance by adopting a balanced approach that fosters innovation while prioritizing societal well-being.[127] Its Model Artificial Intelligence Governance Framework provides

[122] ANU BRADFORD, THE BRUSSELS EFFECT: HOW THE EUROPEAN UNION RULES THE WORLD (2020); *see also* Friedmann, *supra* note 121, at 9–10, 29–57.
[123] Catherine Thorbecke, *China Has Sharpened Its Tech Sector, Not Destroyed It*, STRAITS TIMES (Oct. 2, 2024), https://www.straitstimes.com/opinion/china-has-sharpened-its-tech-sector-not-destroyed-it.
[124] Chesterman, *supra* note 6, at 10.
[125] Lim, *supra* note 42.
[126] Lim, *supra* note 31.
[127] *Id.*

voluntary guidelines for companies to implement responsible AI practices, emphasizing transparency, fairness, and accountability while promoting flexibility to accommodate the rapid pace of technological advancement.[128]

Moreover, Singapore's emphasis on international collaboration and standard-setting positions the country as a potential bridge between divergent regulatory models, fostering dialogue and cooperation. The government's proactive engagement with international stakeholders, such as the Organisation for Economic Co-Operation and Development (OECD) and the World Economic Forum, ensures that Singapore's AI regulatory framework aligns with global best practices.[129] As a small, highly connected nation, Singapore's ability to adapt its regulatory framework to emerging technologies ensures its continued relevance in the global AI landscape.

However, Singapore's reliance on voluntary guidelines may limit the enforceability of ethical standards, particularly in the absence of mandatory regulations. While the Model AI Governance Framework provides a strong foundation for responsible AI development, whether companies fully adhere to its principles without legal compulsion remains to be seen. Moreover, as AI systems become more integrated into critical sectors, stronger regulatory mechanisms may be needed to address potential risks.

In sum, the fragmented global approach to AI governance highlights the challenges of balancing innovation with ethical oversight and the public interest. While the United States, Europe, and China pursue distinct strategies rooted in their political and economic priorities, Singapore offers a promising middle ground by fostering innovation alongside ethical governance through voluntary frameworks and international collaboration. Nevertheless, achieving cohesive global governance will require bridging these divergent models, strengthening enforceable standards, and ensuring that ethical principles are upheld across jurisdictions to address the risks and opportunities posed by AI.

Cooperation

The report of the UN Secretary-General's High-Level Advisory Body on Artificial Intelligence (UN High-Level Advisory Body) on AI governance

[128] SING. PERS. DATA PROT. COMM'N, MODEL ARTIFICIAL INTELLIGENCE GOVERNANCE FRAMEWORK (2d ed. 2020).

[129] Yeong, *supra* note 53.

highlights a "global governance deficit" concerning AI.[130] Cooperation makes sense because laws are national in scope, but the development and impact of data and AI transcends borders.[131] Moreover, regulatory coherence is crucial to preventing regulatory arbitrage, where companies exploit the gaps between different jurisdictions to avoid stricter regulations. A collaborative model would also help ensure that competing national interests do not undermine AI regulation.

Recent bilateral efforts underscore the importance of cross-border cooperation in AI governance. For example, Singapore has been actively working with the United States to standardize AI risk management frameworks.[132] Singapore's Minister for Digital Development and Information likened the process to developing aviation safety standards, noting that AI safety is still nascent but rapidly progressing toward consensus.[133] She emphasized that such cooperation will make it easier for businesses to comply with regulations without having to start from scratch in different jurisdictions.[134] This collaboration also includes joint initiatives on privacy-enhancing technologies and trusted data flows, further reinforcing Singapore's role in shaping a global AI governance structure that balances innovation with ethical oversight.[135]

A cohesive global governance framework is essential for addressing cross-border challenges like algorithmic bias and data privacy and fostering trust and equity. This chapter advances three proposals to strengthen global cooperation. These initiatives could serve as a foundation for a global framework that respects local values while promoting common standards, including a right to explanation for individuals affected by AI-driven decisions, particularly as the development of AI remains largely in the hands of a few powerful multinational corporations.[136]

The first proposal is to establish a transnational AI governance body that can serve as a platform for international dialogue, coordinate cross-border

[130] U.N. Sec'y-Gen.'s High-Level Advisory Body on A.I., *Governing AI for Humanity: Final Report* (Sept. 2024) [hereinafter *Governing AI for Humanity*].

[131] Trisha Ray, *Can AI Be Creative? Global Copyright Laws Need an Answer*, New Atlanticist (Dec. 18, 2023), https://www.atlanticcouncil.org/blogs/new-atlanticist/can-ai-be-creative-global-copyright-laws-need-an-answer/.

[132] Yong Jun Yuan, *Singapore Working with US to Standardise AI Risk Frameworks*, Bus. Times (July 31, 2024), https://www.businesstimes.com.sg/singapore/economy-policy/singapore-working-us-standardise-ai-risk-frameworks (discussing the U.S.-Singapore collaboration on standardizing AI risk management frameworks and their implications for global AI governance).

[133] *Id.*

[134] *Id.*

[135] *Id.*

[136] *Id.*

policies, and oversee the implementation of global standards. This entity could facilitate dialogue among nations, coordinate cross-border policies, and oversee the implementation of global standards. International agreements like the OECD AI Principles offer a foundation for harmonizing global standards, providing a baseline for ethical AI practices across borders.[137] By participating in such global collaborations, countries can create interoperable AI regulations that reduce the risk of fragmentation and ensure equitable access to AI technologies. Furthermore, developing international standards through organizations such as the International Organization for Standardization (ISO) will help harmonize AI governance and promote inclusive innovation across different legal systems. A cooperative global framework should not merely manage risk or promote efficiency. It must advance equity. Embedding inclusive governance structures across jurisdictions enables more equitable participation in and enjoyment of AI's benefits, especially for those historically excluded from technological innovation.

Global certification programs help foster common standards for ethical AI practices, incentivizing compliance with international standards. One ethical standard could be whether regulations prioritize inclusivity by addressing barriers to access and empowering underrepresented groups. This could be financial incentives for deploying AI technologies in regions with limited access to healthcare, education, and legal resources. Consistent with the yardsticks discussed in the section "Measuring Equitable Progress," these programs could equip disadvantaged populations with the skills to engage with and benefit from AI technologies.

The second proposal is to promote transparency and accountability. The UN High-Level Advisory Body recently proposed seven key recommendations to address AI-related risks.[138] A big red flag raised by this body is that a handful of technology giants dominate AI development.[139] This concentration of power creates an imbalance in which the rest of society—governments, smaller firms, and individuals—has little say in how the technology is applied. To combat this, the advisory body recommended the creation of a global AI data framework that ensures transparency and accountability, giving the public more control over how AI impacts their

[137] Org. for Econ. Co-op. & Dev., OECD AI Principles (2019), https://www.oecd.org/en/topics/ai-principles.html.

[138] *Governing AI for Humanity*, *supra* note 130.

[139] *Id.*

lives.[140] Data-sharing agreements should be international agreements that ensure secure and ethical data sharing, enabling AI systems to access diverse and representative datasets. A related initiative could involve marginalized communities in decision-making processes related to AI development and deployment, ensuring that their needs and perspectives are represented.

The third proposal is to focus on capacity building. Recent research highlights that AI adoption remains limited in developing countries due to inadequate infrastructure and technical expertise.[141] In contrast, high-income and upper-middle-income countries are better positioned to leverage AI's economic potential, thanks to a robust digital infrastructure, extensive resources for AI development, and advanced data systems.

Philip Schellekens and David Skilling observe that, while high-income countries may face greater labor market disruptions, due to their larger share of skill-intensive jobs susceptible to AI automation, they are significantly better equipped to handle these changes.[142] Their well-established social safety nets and active labor market policies, such as Germany's retraining programs, can mitigate the impacts, facilitate worker transitions, and foster job creation.[143]

Conversely, poorer nations encounter more severe challenges. Limited financial and institutional resources, coupled with underdeveloped social protection systems, leave them ill-prepared to manage the economic and social upheavals driven by AI.[144] Many low-income and lower-middle-income countries already struggle with high levels of informal employment and fragile labor markets, which make workers particularly vulnerable to sudden shifts.[145] The lack of fiscal capacity further constrains their ability to invest in essential measures, such as reskilling programs, infrastructure development, or targeted welfare initiatives, to support affected communities.[146] Without these safeguards, job losses linked to AI could intensify unemployment and exacerbate poverty.[147]

[140] *Id.*

[141] Giovanni Melina, *Mapping the World's Readiness for Artificial Intelligence Shows Prospects Diverge*, IMF Blog (June 25, 2024), https://www.imf.org/en/Blogs/Articles/2024/06/25/mapping-the-worlds-readiness-for-artificial-intelligence-shows-prospects-diverge. *See also* Peter Yu's chapter in this volume.

[142] Philip Schellekens & David Skilling, *Three Reasons Why AI May Widen Global Inequality*, World Bank (Oct. 17, 2024), https://www.worldbank.org/en/news/press-release/2024/03/05/accelerated-by-covid-and-ai-global-digital-landscape-remains-uneven.

[143] *Id.*

[144] *Id.*

[145] *Id.*

[146] *Id.*

[147] *Id.*

Schellekens and Skilling identify two further concerning trends. First, AI is likely to cement the dominance of wealthier nations in high-value industries like finance, pharmaceuticals, advanced manufacturing, and defense.[148] By using AI to boost productivity and innovation, these countries make it increasingly difficult for poorer nations to compete in these sectors.[149] Second, while AI will most likely threaten skill-intensive jobs in advanced economies, automation could disrupt low-cost labor markets in developing countries.[150] Advances in AI-enabled manufacturing, logistics, and quality control may allow wealthier nations to produce goods more efficiently, reducing reliance on low-wage foreign labor.[151] With predictive analytics and enhanced customization, richer countries could outcompete their developing counterparts in cost, speed, and product appeal.[152]

A global regulatory framework should ensure that generative AI's benefits are equitably distributed. Without targeted interventions, there is a risk that AI development will primarily benefit wealthy nations and large corporations, deepening global inequalities. Policies that promote access to AI technologies for developing countries, small businesses, and underrepresented communities can alleviate this risk.

One recommendation is to implement technology transfer agreements that facilitate the sharing of AI innovations with developing countries.[153] These agreements would ensure that nations with limited resources can still participate in the AI economy and benefit from its advancements. Additionally, capacity-building initiatives should be established to provide training and resources to underrepresented groups, enabling them to contribute to and benefit from AI development.

The UN High-Level Advisory Body proposed a global AI capacity development network to boost governance capabilities, especially in regions without the infrastructure to manage AI risks effectively.[154] With the suggestion for a Global AI Fund, this initiative could help countries get the resources they need to develop responsible AI systems, ensuring that no one gets left behind in the AI race. Governments and international organizations could also invest in "AI for Social Good" programs that use AI technologies

[148] *Id.*
[149] *Id.*
[150] *Id.*
[151] *Id.*
[152] *Id.*
[153] See Peter Yu's chapter in this volume.
[154] *Governing AI for Humanity*, *supra* note 130.

to address critical global challenges, such as climate change, public health, and poverty alleviation. These programs would demonstrate AI's potential to improve global welfare and ensure that its benefits reach those who need them most.

Reframing

Generative AI offers both opportunities and existential challenges for artists, authors, and other creators, fundamentally reshaping how creative content is produced, distributed, utilized, and experienced. AI tools gradually encroach on tasks that previously required human creativity, whether in film editing, scriptwriting, or music composition.[155] By rapidly producing content based on human-created works, AI systems threaten to displace the very creators whose intellectual labor fuels these models.

As a result, human authors may find themselves increasingly unable to compete with AI-generated content that is faster and cheaper to produce. As these tools become more sophisticated, critics warn that the creative process risks being hollowed out, turning skilled professionals into electronic gig workers.[156] Photographers, for example, see demand for their work plummet as AI-generated images become more accessible and cost-effective.[157]

For some, generative AI may serve as a synthetic echo of the past, unable to contribute meaningfully to building the future.[158] It can only mimic human literary and artistic expression because it relies on analyzing existing human creations. As a technology that makes statistical predictions based on previously encountered data, its outputs reproduce what has already been done. Society risks losing these transformative elements if human authors lose the incentive to write and publish works that inspire, foster empathy, transport

[155] Vuk Dukic, *AI in Creative Industries: Revolutionizing Art, Music, and Content Creation*, ANABLOCK BLOG (Sept. 9, 2024), https://www.anablock.com/blog/ai-in-creative-industries-revolutionizing-art-music-and-content-creation.

[156] Noam Scheiber, *Will A.I. Upend White-Collar Work? Consider the Hollywood Editor.*, N.Y. TIMES (July 30, 2024), https://www.nytimes.com/2024/07/30/business/economy/artificial-intelligence-hollywood-unions.html.

[157] Katie Deighton, *The Last Stock Photographers Await Their Fate Under Generative AI*, WALL ST. J. (May 1, 2024), https://www.wsj.com/articles/the-last-stock-photographers-await-their-fate-under-generative-ai-822d1e6a.

[158] David Karpf, *Generative AI Is Challenging a 234-Year-Old Law*, ATLANTIC (Feb. 5, 2024), https://www.theatlantic.com/technology/archive/2024/02/generative-ai-lawsuits-copyright-fair-use/677595/.

us to imaginative worlds, or offer fresh perspectives. If generative AI becomes the primary driver of creativity, it could stagnate cultural progress.

Moreover, supporting human creativity is crucial for the arts and the continued development of generative AI itself. Without a continuous influx of fresh human-created content, AI systems will become stuck in a loop of recombining existing material, leading to stagnation. To avoid a future dominated by recycled creativity, it is essential to ensure that human artistic projects are enabled to push boundaries in ways that AI cannot. By investing in human creativity, the AI industry benefits from a richer, more diverse set of training materials, which enables more innovative outputs.

The reality is more nuanced. First, art has always evolved through borrowing and adapting techniques and themes from earlier works, punctuated by rare bursts of profound originality. As Dennis Yi Tenen observes, "We create new art by imitating and riffing off each other."[159] While writers may draw inspiration from the books they have absorbed in a more intuitive way than AI, those influences still play a crucial role in shaping their identity as creators.

Moreover, art transcends technical proficiency; it is a reflection of human experience, emotion, and thought. While AI systems can replicate styles and produce visually appealing content, they lack the lived experiences and emotional depth to infuse human-created art with profound meaning. Although AI can contribute to artistic projects, its creations are inherently constrained by the absence of human consciousness, a core element of the artistic process. The value we place on the authenticity of a painting—such as questioning whether it is a genuine da Vinci—is tied to its origin as the unique work of a historical individual.[160] In the digital age, mechanisms like nonfungible tokens have emerged to replicate a sense of scarcity and uniqueness, echoing this traditional notion of specialness.

Second, the law has long adapted to embrace new technology. When photography debuted in the nineteenth century, it was described as "the pencil of nature."[161] Until *Burrow-Giles Lithographic Co. v. Sarony*, it remained unclear whether they merged idea with expression so closely that they were uncopyrightable.[162] There, the U.S. Supreme Court categorically recognized

[159] Subramanian, *supra* note 105.

[160] Kwame Anthony Appiah, *Should You Be Allowed to Profit from A.I.-Generated Art?*, N.Y. TIMES (Sept. 27, 2024), https://www.nytimes.com/2024/09/27/magazine/ai-generated-art-profit.html.

[161] Christine Haight Farley, *The Lingering Effects of Copyright's Response to the Invention of Photography*, 65 U. PITT. L. REV 385, 396 (2004).

[162] Burrow-Giles Lithographic Co. v. Sarony, 111 U.S. 53, 60 (1884).

photographers as authors of creative works when they engage in "posting, selecting and arranging of costumes and accessories, in the arranging of light and shadows, and in the suggestion and evoking of expressions."[163] Jane Ginsburg explains that "even though a machine was involved in the creation of the work, the work showed the ideas in the mind of the author that are given visible expression, so it's not just an idea, it's also how you put it down."[164]

Third, many industries have embraced AI and moved beyond those esoteric copyright questions. Advertisers must contend with the reality of fragmented channels to advertise across multiple devices and formats. AI enables multichannel campaigns across search and shopping. Hybrid models, where AI assists human creators in brainstorming or prototyping, can amplify creativity while preserving human contributions' unique insights and emotional depth.[165]

As forms of AI grow increasingly widespread, we need to get used to so-called "centaur" models—collaborations between human and machine cognition. As James Thomas, global chief technology officer at dentsu Creative, explains: "Generative AI makes you more creative in an agency—it doesn't replace creativity. It's another tool in your tool kit. We can leverage AI to visualize ideas and concepts with lightning speed while the clients are in the room. That would have taken weeks and months to do previously."[166] Similarly, Boston Consulting Group uses AI that could create local advertisements in different languages and formats. With the push of a button, the system can turn a commercial about Finnish dishwashing detergent from English into Spanish.[167]

In sum, generative AI presents an interplay of challenges and opportunities for the creative industries. While it threatens to displace traditional creators by producing faster and cheaper content, it also has the potential to amplify human creativity through collaborative "centaur" models that combine

[163] *Id.*

[164] Jane C. Ginsburg, *Intellectual Property Expert: "We Are Not Ready to Accept the Idea of the Machine Being the Author,"* El País (Apr. 2, 2024), https://english.elpais.com/technology/2024-04-02/jane-c-ginsburg-intellectual-property-expert-we-are-not-ready-to-accept-the-idea-of-the-machine-being-the-author.html.

[165] Jodie Rhodes, *Balancing AI and Human Creativity in Media: A Synergistic Approach*, Firemind (Apr. 12, 2024), https://www.firemind.com/insights/balancing-ai-and-human-creativity-in-media-a-synergistic-approach/.

[166] Greaves, *supra* note 29.

[167] Tripp Mickle, *The A.I. Boom Has an Unlikely Early Winner: Wonky Consultants*, N.Y. Times (June 26, 2024), https://www.nytimes.com/2024/06/26/technology/ai-boom-business-consultants.html.

machine efficiency with human ingenuity. To preserve cultural progress, supporting human creativity as a vital source of innovation and emotional depth is essential, while recognizing AI as a tool, rather than a replacement. By fostering a balance between technological advancements and human contributions, society can ensure that the arts continue to evolve in ways that inspire, challenge, and reflect the richness of human experience.

Conclusion

AI presents transformative opportunities alongside profound ethical and societal challenges. This chapter explains why equitable progress must underpin AI regulation, emphasizing fairness, inclusivity, and accountability to bridge systemic inequities and empower marginalized communities. By balancing innovation with equity and fostering international cooperation, policymakers can harmonize global standards and ensure that AI's benefits are broadly shared. Embedding principles of justice and human dignity into AI governance is a technical and moral imperative. Decisions made today will shape the trajectory of innovation and societal well-being for generations, making it vital to harness AI's potential for a more inclusive, just, and prosperous future. Realizing this future requires sound governance and a conscious effort to democratize innovation. Equitable progress depends on empowering all communities, particularly those on the margins, to help shape, use, and benefit from AI. By doing so, governance becomes not just a constraint on innovation but a catalyst for inclusive transformation.

Future research should focus on measuring AI's social and economic impact, particularly on marginalized communities, by developing robust metrics to evaluate the efficacy of equity-focused governance models. Comparative studies are essential to identify best practices and transferable lessons by examining the successes and challenges of regulatory frameworks in diverse jurisdictions. Additionally, research must address the ethical, legal, and societal implications of emerging AI technologies, such as generative AI and autonomous systems, exploring their effects on human creativity, agency, and employment. Yet equity must not be an afterthought or an incidental benefit of innovation. It should be a deliberate objective of governance. Centering on equitable progress ensures that marginalized communities are not merely passive recipients but active participants in shaping AI's development and its distributional outcomes. Ultimately, AI governance must serve not just innovation or protection, but justice, dignity, and inclusive progress for all, ensuring that the ability to shape and benefit from AI is not reserved for the few but extended meaningfully to the many. By prioritizing these research areas, policymakers, technologists, and scholars can ensure that AI evolves as a tool for equitable progress, fostering shared prosperity and safeguarding humanity's future.

13

Responsibility, Transparency, and Accountability in AI Patents

W. Keith Robinson

Introduction

Recent discussions about artificial intelligence (AI) have centered on responsibility, transparency, and accountability (RTA) of AI systems.[1] Responsibility focuses on the actions of AI developers. This chapter defines responsibility as the inventor's obligation to perform and fulfill their expected duties during prosecution of their patent application. Transparency provides public access to AI-related processes and decisions. In the patent context, this is accomplished by the patent applicant describing their invention in a patent application. Finally, accountability means that developers and patent holders are answerable for how their inventions are used, including any resulting negative consequences. It reflects the principle that the individual or entity that owns or licenses a patent bears responsibility for the invention's deployment and its impacts.

Inclusive innovation is not just about who participates in the inventive process; it is also about who benefits from the outcomes. While it is essential to ensure that diverse teams and inventors contribute to technological development, it is equally important to consider the impact of those inventions on underserved and marginalized communities. From this perspective, assessing the impact of deploying new technologies is a crucial aspect of inclusive innovation. Incorporating RTA principles into discussions about AI

[1] Cary Coglianese & Erik Lampmann, *Contracting for Algorithmic Accountability*, 6 Admin. L. Rev. Accord 175, 176 (2021); Sonia K. Katyal, *Private Accountability in the Age of Artificial Intelligence*, 66 UCLA L. Rev. 54, 108 (2019); Peter K. Yu, *Beyond Transparency and Accountability: Three Additional Features Algorithm Designers Should Build into Intelligent Platforms*, 13 Ne. U. L. Rev. 263, 276 (2021).

W. Keith Robinson, *Responsibility, Transparency, and Accountability in AI Patents* In: *Inclusive Innovation in the Age of AI and Big Data*. Edited by: Daryl Lim and Peter K. Yu, Oxford University Press. © Oxford University Press 2026.
DOI: 10.1093/9780197799444.003.0017

inventions can help ensure that these technologies serve all sectors of society, not just the privileged few.

Promoting RTA in the development and implementation of AI can help mitigate the biases that are often embedded in these technologies. When trained on unrepresentative or skewed data, AI systems risk perpetuating discrimination and inequities. By embedding RTA into innovation pathways, developers and policymakers can better anticipate unintended consequences and design interventions that proactively address the needs of historically marginalized populations.

These principles are important due to the pronounced biases sometimes exhibited in AI systems, particularly those impacting marginalized communities such as women and underrepresented minorities.[2] This issue is especially pressing when we consider the role of AI-related patents as proxies for innovation. In light of the recent enthusiasm for AI, evaluating AI-related inventions through the RTA lens provides useful principles for addressing the potential societal impact of AI innovations.

Despite the recent excitement, AI-related inventions have existed for decades. The release of the AI patent dataset by the United States Patent and Trademark Office (USPTO) in 2019 highlights the significance of this field for the future of innovation in the United States.[3] This chapter explores the current landscape of AI patenting in the country. Through this exploration, it seeks to understand how the RTA principles are reflected in current patent law and practice. In the patenting context, the concept of responsibility primarily focuses on the actions and representations of the inventor and the consequences that follow from those actions. The patent system accomplishes transparency by providing the public with access to information related to innovations.[4] Finally, accountability is tied to the concept of patent ownership. Specifically, the patent owner is accountable for the invention's use and the outcomes flowing from its use.

Using the RTA concepts, this chapter explains how the USPTO can respond to the societal and technological challenges posed by AI while also acknowledging the potential limitations of patent office interventions. Despite some limitations, the Office will be critical in advancing these

[2] Aram A. Gavoor & Raffi Teperdijan, *A Structural Solution to Mitigating Artificial Intelligence Bias in Administrative Agencies*, 89 Geo. Wash. L. Rev. Arguendo 71, 80 (2021).

[3] Alexander V. Giczy, Nicholas A. Pairolero & Andrew A. Toole, *Identifying Artificial Intelligence (AI) Invention: A Novel AI Patent Dataset*, 47 J. Tech. Transfer 476 (2022).

[4] Pfaff v. Wells Elecs., Inc., 525 U.S. 55, 57 (1998) (emphasizing the public disclosure function of the patent system).

efforts, ensuring that the United States remains a leader in innovation and principled AI practices.

The section "AI-Related Patents" provides some useful background on AI-related patents. The next three sections explain how the RTA concepts are incorporated into AI-related patents. For each principle, this chapter offers suggestions on how the patenting process can be used to ensure that these principles are consistently reflected in future AI patents, thereby encouraging the safe development and use of AI by innovators. This chapter concludes by underscoring the importance of fostering the development of AI systems that align with the RTA principles.

AI-Related Patents

This section introduces the concept of AI patents and explains why they matter. AI is a term used to encompass a broad set of technologies and techniques to allow machines to mimic human cognitive behavior.[5] Signaling the importance of these technologies, the USPTO developed a dataset consisting of patent documents related to AI technologies.[6] This section briefly describes AI patents as defined by this dataset and explains why AI patents provide an important signal of whether advancements in AI technology align with legal, ethical, and regulatory considerations.

In the United States, patents are legal grants provided by the government that give inventors the right to exclude others from making, using, selling, or importing their patented invention in exchange for the full disclosure of that invention.[7] Thus, "AI-related patents" is a broad term used to identify patents that have been granted on a broad range of technologies used in developing and implementing AI applications. In 2021, the USPTO created a publicly available dataset that included patents granted on AI technology from 1976 to 2020.[8] This dataset categorizes the patents based on technology, such as

[5] Nesma Mohammed Abd El-Maksoud & Eman Badawy Ahmed, *Artificial Intelligence Applications in Green Architecture*, 7 Fayoum Univ. J. Eng'g 317, 324 (2024) (discussing how AI, designed to simulate human intelligence, aids in repetitive tasks, error detection, and proposing time-saving design solutions).

[6] Giczy et al., *supra* note 3, at 477.

[7] Markman v. Westview Instruments, Inc., 517 U.S. 370, 373 (1996) (discussing Congress's constitutional authority to promote progress by granting inventors exclusive rights to their discoveries and referencing the 1790 Patent Act, which established the issuance of patents in exchange for full disclosure).

[8] Giczy et al., *supra* note 3, at 477.

knowledge processing, speech, AI hardware, evolutionary computation, natural language processing, machine learning, computer vision, and planning or control.[9] By collecting AI patents granted over almost half a century and organizing them by category, the USPTO has signaled the importance of understanding these technologies and their development over time. Various entities are actively using this dataset to study and shape AI development. A number of academic papers illustrate how the data is being applied across disciplines.[10] For example, some studies trace the diffusion of AI through U.S. patent records, while others examine the role of geographic tech clusters and population centers in the spatial transformation of U.S. inventions. The data has also been used to develop an index measuring occupational exposure to AI, to explore the direct role of government agencies in driving AI innovation, and to assess women's participation in both university-based and commercial AI invention. These diverse applications underscore the dataset's value as a tool for empirical research and policy analysis.

While the public at large is fascinated by how AI works, many also focus on its potential societal impact across various domains. Several commentators have warned that techno-optimism and enthusiasm for AI have cloaked many problems with the implementation and use of AI systems.[11] Two particularly relevant issues related to the RTA principles mentioned above are the "black box" problem and bias.

In the past decade, AI's "black box" problem has received increased attention. This problem centers around researchers' inability to explain how a particular AI system works.[12] The problem may occur in systems that use deep learning and neural networks because the decision-making employed by these systems is hard to understand at greater levels of complexity.[13] The black box problem is a significant hurdle for stakeholders wishing to assess the effectiveness and impacts of AI systems. Automated decision-making is far from perfect; in many cases, it has led to drastic outcomes

[9] *Id.*

[10] Nicholas A. Pairolero, Alexander V. Giczy, Gerard Torres, Tisa Islam Erana, Mark A. Finlayson & Andrew A. Toole, *The Artificial Intelligence Patent Dataset (AIPD) 2023 Update*, 50 J. Tech. Transfer 2587 (2025).

[11] Cathy O'Neil, Weapons of Math Destruction (2016).

[12] Dawood Ali MoDastoni, *Exploring Methods to Make AI Decisions More Transparent and Understandable for Humans*, 3 Advances Eng'g Innovation 32–33 (2023) (discussing the challenges posed by the opacity of advanced AI models, particularly deep learning networks, and their implications for end-users, developers, regulators, and stakeholders).

[13] *Id.* Also note that companies may withhold this information and attempt to protect it as a trade secret.

that perpetuate bias and lead to undesirable discriminatory outcomes.[14] When affected parties attempt to challenge or question the decisions made by these flawed AI systems, they encounter a second roadblock: The opacity of these systems prevents them from being interrogated so that the harm can be remedied and the decision-making process corrected.[15] Accordingly, commentators have called for greater insight into AI models to promote ethical use of the technology and minimize any unnecessary harm these systems might cause.[16]

AI systems also struggle with bias. For example, bias may be present in the training data selected for use by the AI system.[17] The data itself may also be embedded with social bias.[18] Furthermore, AI systems fall short in that they are only statistical models of the real world at a discrete moment in time. These models encounter difficulty when dealing with exceptions or boundary cases that commonly occur in daily life. Accordingly, deploying AI models in sensitive domains where life-altering decisions are being made about people requires close supervision to ensure that societal biases are not perpetuated under the guise of a "neutral" AI system.

The patent system can be an essential policy lever to encourage RTA in future AI systems. Some of these principles are already incorporated into the statutory rules used to evaluate whether an inventor can obtain a patent. For example, the written description and enablement requirements demand that a patent applicant sufficiently disclose their claimed invention so that (1) the public is put on notice of the subject matter the applicant is claiming to have invented;[19] and (2) other practitioners in the field can make or use the

[14] Xavier Ferrer, Tom van Nuenen, Jose M. Such, Mark Coté & Natalia Criado, *Bias and Discrimination in AI: A Cross-Disciplinary Perspective*, 40 IEEE Tech. & Soc'y Mag. 72, 72–74 (2021) (discussing how automated systems can make consequential decisions that sometimes lead to systematic discrimination, particularly affecting individuals based on characteristics like income, education, gender, or ethnicity).

[15] Sylvia Lu, *Algorithmic Opacity, Private Accountability, and Corporate Social Disclosure in the Age of Artificial Intelligence*, 23 Vand. J. Ent. & Tech. L. 99, 103 (2020).

[16] Vibhuti Choubisa & Divyansh Choubisa, *Towards Trustworthy AI: An Analysis of the Relationship Between Explainability and Trust in AI Systems*, 11 Int'l J. Sci. & Rsch. Archive 2219, 2221 (2024) (discussing the multifaceted challenges of building trustworthy AI, including issues related to data privacy, bias, fairness, and explainability).

[17] Raub McKenzie, *Bots, Bias and Big Data: Artificial Intelligence, Algorithmic Bias and Disparate Impact Liability in Hiring Practices*, 71 Ark. L. Rev. 529, 537 (2018).

[18] *Id.* at 542 ("Research shows that applying machine learning to everyday human language reproduces existing societal bias.").

[19] Nuvo Pharms. (Ir.) Designated Activity Co. v. Dr. Reddy's Lab'ys. Inc., 923 F.3d 1368, 1382 (Fed. Cir. 2019) (emphasizing that the written description requirement is distinct from enablement and focuses on whether the specification sufficiently discloses the boundaries and scope of the claimed invention and shows possession of the invention).

invention.[20] In short, the patent system already serves as a filter for concerns about RTA in AI systems.

This focus on the patent system is important as more funding is funneled toward new research and development of AI technologies.[21] We can already observe the proliferation of AI tools being used across many industries in the United States.[22] The increased funding will also likely lead to increased patenting activity from both new and incumbent inventors. By identifying which aspects of the patent system align with RTA principles, we can determine how to monitor and, where appropriate, modify the patenting process to further promote these principles in future AI systems. The next three sections define the RTA concepts in the patent context.

Responsibility

This section examines how the principle of responsibility operates within the patent system, particularly in relation to inventors. Understanding the concept of responsibility is crucial for maintaining and developing a robust and effective patent system. In the patent context, this chapter defines responsibility as the inventor's obligation to perform and fulfill their expected duties during the prosecution of their patent application. The concept of responsibility primarily focuses on the inventor's actions and representations and the consequences that follow from those actions.

The U.S. patent system incorporates the principle of responsibility in several ways. A hallmark of the patent system is that patents are generally granted to person(s); the inventor's name is included on the front page of a patent.[23] Many scholars have written about the reputational benefits of inventorship.[24] In return, the patent system imposes several obligations on a patent applicant or inventor that embody the principle of responsibility.

[20] *Id.* (clarifying that the enablement requirement focuses on teaching how to make and use the claimed invention without undue experimentation).

[21] *Artificial Intelligence*, NAT'L SCI. FOUND., https://new.nsf.gov/focus-areas/artificial-intelligence (last visited Sept. 27, 2024) (noting that the U.S. National Science Foundation has funded foundational AI research since the 1960s).

[22] *What Industries Are Using AI?*, N.C. DEP'T OF COM., https://www.commerce.nc.gov/news/the-lead-feed/what-industries-are-using-ai (last visited Sept. 27, 2024) (reporting that businesses project increased AI use across all sectors within the next six months).

[23] 35 U.S.C. § 115(a) (requiring that a patent application include the name of the inventor and that each inventor execute an oath or declaration in connection with the application).

[24] Jason Rantanen & Sarah E. Jack, *Patents as Credentials*, 76 WASH. & LEE L. REV. 311, 311 (2019) (discussing the role of patents as indicators of expertise and credibility in various fields).

First, the patent inventor must sign an oath or declaration attesting that they invented the subject matter claimed in the patent application.[25] The purpose of that oath or declaration is to ensure that the inventor(s) was the first and true inventor(s) of the invention. If this information is incorrect or falsified, it could jeopardize the patent's validity.[26] Thus, the inventor's obligations and responsibilities are tied directly to the legal efficacy of the patent.

Second, as a patent applicant, the inventor owes a duty of candor to the USPTO.[27] Patent examination is a long and sometimes difficult process in which information asymmetry typically exists. Because the inventor may be in a position to know much more about their invention and its surrounding field than the patent examiner, the duty of candor levels this playing field by obligating the inventor to disclose information that may be relevant to the examination of the patent.[28] This information may include prior art that could negatively impact the prosecution of the inventor's patent.[29] When an inventor upholds the duty of candor, their conduct can lead to more positive outcomes for the patent system, such as better examination and screening of patent applications.[30] On the contrary, neglecting the duty of candor can lead to negative outcomes, such as granting low-quality patents or having the patent invalidated.[31]

Finally, new challenges have emerged with rapid AI development—in particular, how the patent system treats potential inventions created wholly or partly by AI. At the time of publication of this volume, AI cannot be named as an inventor on a patent in the United States.[32] However, there is the possibility of patenting an invention created with the assistance of AI.[33] In early

[25] 35 U.S.C. § 115(a).

[26] *Id.*

[27] 37 C.F.R. § 1.56 (2024) (imposing a duty of candor and good faith on individuals associated with the filing and prosecution of a patent application, including the obligation to disclose all information known to be material to patentability).

[28] *Id.*

[29] *Id.*

[30] Daniel L. Parr IV, Christopher J. Jannuzzi, E. Jennings Taylor & Johna Leddy, *Journal Patent Citations—A New Paradigm for Journal Quality?*, 30 Electrochemical Soc'y Interface 12, 12–13 (2021) (noting that the USPTO relies on printed documents, such as journal publications, as prior art to assess novelty and nonobviousness during patent examination).

[31] 37 C.F.R. § 1.56 (stating that no patent will be granted if the duty of disclosure was violated through bad faith or intentional misconduct).

[32] Thaler v. Vidal, 43 F.4th 1207, 1210 (Fed. Cir. 2022) (holding that the Patent Act unambiguously requires inventors to be natural persons, that is, human beings).

[33] Requirement of Naming the Inventor in Patent Applications, 89 Fed. Reg. 10043, 10046 (Feb. 16, 2024) (clarifying that natural persons who significantly contributed to AI-assisted inventions must be named as inventors, in accordance with statutory and case law).

2024, the USPTO issued guidance concerning AI-assisted inventions.[34] Such inventions consist of patentable subject matter developed by a human with the assistance of an AI system.[35] Thus, applicants using AI in the innovation process are now responsible for ensuring that humans create, at least in part, the subject matter of their inventions. The recent decision by the U.S. Court of Appeals for the Federal Circuit on AI inventions and the recent USPTO guidance signal that the U.S. patent system, for now, will continue to incentivize human invention.[36] This requirement signals that the patent system ultimately holds humans responsible for their inventions. Recent developments in AI have also made it more important than ever to ensure that the principle of responsibility remains central to AI innovation.

The patent system is uniquely positioned to incorporate an ethos of responsibility among AI innovators. First, lawmakers must resist calls to change the law so that inventions created by AI alone are eligible for patenting.[37] For example, some commentators argue that humans are ultimately responsible for the outcomes of AI models.[38] Therefore, one way to incorporate this principle would be not to consider AI as an inventor.

Second, since legal disputes will inevitably arise concerning AI inventorship, the judicial arm of the patent system should deliberately develop how the law responds to the disputes. The number of AI patents currently in existence demonstrates that the patent system has facilitated significant innovation in the field. Because that activity signals AI's importance to U.S. innovation, there may be a temptation to modify legal rules to accommodate further innovation.[39] However, the law should develop slowly, especially around issues related to inventorship. A gradual approach allows for adaptation, and the deliberate development of legal doctrines will preserve the principle of responsibility within the patent system.

Finally, responsibility must begin and end with the inventor. One way to preserve responsibility in AI patents is to impose additional obligations on

[34] Inventorship Guidance for AI-Assisted Inventions, 89 Fed. Reg. 10043 (Feb. 13, 2024).

[35] *Id.*

[36] *Thaler*, 43 F.4th 1207.

[37] *Id.* at 1212 (rejecting the argument that "inventor" under the Patent Act includes AI software, emphasizing that the statute uses "individual" to refer to human inventors and noting that nonhumans may infringe patents but cannot be inventors).

[38] David De Cremer & Dishan Narayanan, *How AI Tools Can—and Cannot—Help Organizations Become More Ethical*, 6 FRONTIERS A.I. 1093712 (2023) (cautioning against relying solely on AI tools for ethical decisions and emphasizing the essential role of humans in ethical decision-making).

[39] Request for Comments on Patenting Artificial Intelligence Inventions, 84 Fed. Reg. 44889 (Aug. 27, 2019) (asking questions about changes in legal rules in view of AI).

the inventor. For example, the USPTO could modify the current oath or declaration statement to include a responsibility clause where the inventor agrees that they will take responsibility for potentially negative outcomes that might arise from their AI invention if the risk was reasonably foreseeable at the time the oath or declaration was signed.[40] In addition, the patent system could require those inventors to undergo mandatory training on AI ethics and other responsible development practices.

While responsible development practices are commendable, some may argue that the benefits could unduly burden innovation. Refusing to recognize AI as a sole inventor could stifle innovation.[41] In addition, AI is so unique and fast-developing that the law must change to provide certainty and support for AI innovation. Finally, imposing additional obligations on inventors may discourage these inventors from patenting, thus depriving the public of the benefits derived from the disclosure of their AI invention.

One way to respond to these objections is to monitor carefully how the patent system is attempting to address these issues. For example, the current USPTO guidance on AI-assisted inventions, while not law, provides a testing ground for inventors to use AI to help them invent. It represents how our understanding of the law can adapt to facilitate AI innovation.[42] Finally, although it may be burdensome to place additional obligations on inventors, at this stage in AI development, the additional burden is warranted to ensure ethical development and deployment of AI systems. In sum, requiring human invention, moving slowly, and imposing additional obligations on inventors are ways in which the principle of responsibility can be incorporated into the AI patenting process.

Transparency

This section explores how the principle of transparency is understood and implemented within the patent system. Similar to responsibility, the idea of transparency as it exists in the legal system has been analyzed by several scholars.[43] A primary theme emerging from this literature is that access

[40] O'Neil, *supra* note 11, at 205 (suggesting data scientist take a pledge recognizing the potential misuse of their models and taking responsibility).

[41] *Thaler*, 43 F.4th at 1213 (arguing that AI-generated inventions should be patentable to encourage innovation and public disclosure).

[42] Inventorship Guidance for AI-Assisted Inventions, 89 Fed. Reg. 10043 (Feb. 13, 2024).

[43] *See, e.g.*, Ida Koivisto, The Transparency Paradox ch. 6 (2022).

to information is central to the idea of transparency.[44] The patent system accomplishes transparency by providing the public with access to information about inventions.[45]

In the context of AI patents, one way transparency manifests is as the information contained in the patent. For example, a patent applicant must meet the statutory disclosure requirements to obtain a patent.[46] The written description requirement prohibits an applicant from obtaining a patent on subject matter beyond what they have disclosed in the patent.[47] In other words, an applicant's patented invention is limited in its scope to what they describe in the specification of the patent. Thus, the written description requirement mandates the applicant's full disclosure of what they claim as their invention.

A second statutory lever of transparency is the enablement requirement. This requirement states that the patent applicant must disclose their invention in enough detail to enable a person of ordinary skill in the art to make or use the invention without undue experimentation.[48] The requirement prevents patent applicants from hiding the ball. In exchange for the patent right, the requirement ensures that the inventor publicly and sufficiently disclose how their invention works.[49] The enablement requirement is fundamentally at odds with "black box" AI systems, whose inner workings may be opaque even to their inventors. In some cases, meeting the requirement compels applicants to disclose additional technical details to explain how the system functions. In others, it may altogether preclude patent protection for AI systems that cannot be meaningfully explained.

The patenting process is also transparent because the correspondence produced during the examination process is generally publicly available.[50]

[44] Robert H. Sloan & Richard Warner, *Beyond Bias: Artificial Intelligence and Social Justice*, 24 Va. J.L. & Tech. 1, 21 (2020).

[45] Pfaff v. Wells Elecs., Inc., 525 U.S. 55, 57 (1998).

[46] Alfred Früh, *Transparency in the Patent System: Artificial Intelligence and the Disclosure Requirement*, *in* Patents as an Incentive for Innovation 235 (Rafał Sikorski & Žaneta Zemła-Pacud eds., 2021).

[47] Ariad Pharms., Inc. v. Eli Lilly & Co., 598 F.3d 1336, 1353–54 (Fed. Cir. 2010) (explaining that the written description requirement ensures the claims do not exceed the inventor's contribution, serving as part of the quid pro quo by providing meaningful public disclosure in exchange for patent rights).

[48] Phillips Petroleum Co. v. U.S. Steel Corp., 673 F. Supp. 1278, 1291 (D. Del. 1987) (explaining that, to satisfy the enablement requirement, a patent application must describe the invention sufficiently for a person skilled in the art to make and use it, and minor experimentation is permissible as long as it is not unduly extensive).

[49] *Id.*

[50] Changes to Implement Electronic Maintenance of Official Patent Application Records, 68 Fed. Reg. 38611, 38611 (July 1, 2003) (highlighting the advantages of the electronic Patent Application Information Retrieval (PAIR) system, including public access to patent records).

This allows interested parties to monitor the progress of a patent application and understand the reason why that application is successful. Usually, a patent application is published eighteen months after filing.[51] Providing the application to the public allows for scrutiny of the application and enables interested parties to participate in procedures, such as third-party submissions that may aid the patent examiner.[52] The public record is also vital if the patent is litigated. Because the patent prosecution process is transparent, accused infringers have access to information about the patent, which may help with their defense.

In sum, transparency in the patent system operates to inform the public of what the invention is, how it works, and why it is worthy of a patent. Several benefits flow from such disclosure. For example, the disclosure may prevent researchers from wasting effort on already-developed technologies.[53] It also encourages follow-on innovation by building on the existing body of knowledge captured in patents.[54] Finally, transparency provides a window into why the USPTO decided to grant a patent to an inventor.

As the existing body of knowledge surrounding AI patents increases, it is important to consider the impact these innovations will have on the public. The patent system is uniquely positioned to ensure that the principle of transparency remains a central tenet of AI innovation. Specifically, the patent system can make several interventions at various stages of the patent lifecycle to encourage transparency. These interventions could be implemented by themselves or in combination.

A primary intervention aimed at solving the "black box" problem mentioned above would be to increase the amount and quality of information disclosed in a patent application. Using a stick-and-carrot approach, the USPTO could first implement enhanced disclosure requirements similar to what is done now for particular patents in the anti-body field.[55]

[51] 35 U.S.C. § 122(b)(1)(A) (requiring patent applications to be published eighteen months after the earliest filing date).

[52] 35 U.S.C. § 122(e)(1) (allowing third parties to submit relevant patents or publications for consideration in a patent application before the notice of allowance or within certain timeframes after the application's publication or rejection).

[53] Luisa Magazzini, Fabio Pammolli, Massimo Riccaboni & Maria Rossi, *Patent Disclosure and R&D Competition in Pharmaceuticals*, 18 Econ. Innovation & New Tech. 467, 475 (2009).

[54] Stefano Baruffaldi & Markus Simeth, *Patent Disclosure and the Diffusion of Knowledge*, 49 Rsch. Pol'y 103927 (2020) (noting that knowledge disclosure, particularly through the patent system, is a key factor in fostering cumulative innovation by building on existing research and findings).

[55] Tabrez Y. Ebrahim, *Artificial Intelligence Inventions & Patent Disclosure*, 125 Penn St. L. Rev. 147, 211 (2020).

Second, the USPTO could incentivize enhanced disclosure during the prosecution process by offering applicants several advantages. For example, the Office might pilot an enhanced disclosure program where participants meeting higher disclosure procedures receive priority examination. The type of disclosure requested could include more details about the AI model, information about the data used to train the model, and the weights or bias procedures used to tune that model.

Despite the potential benefits, heightened disclosure requirements have some disadvantages. First, inventors may resist heightened disclosure requirements to avoid disclosing trade secret subject matter. Undisclosed information related to a patented invention may still qualify for trade secret protection. Furthermore, refinements developed after a patent's issuance may also be protected as a trade secret.[56] Therefore, it is possible that the proposed requirements may discourage patenting. Ultimately, the decision to patent AI inventions will likely be based on the need of AI innovators to recoup their research investment. Several billions of dollars continue to be invested in AI.[57] Therefore, it is likely that in many instances the need to profit directly from a patented invention will outweigh the benefits of secrecy.

Second, these standards would likely result in increased upfront costs and time-investments for inventors because of the additional informational burden.[58] Similarly, taking time to review additional information provided by the inventor would place a greater administrative burden on the patent examiner.[59] Thus, while enhanced disclosure for AI patents could improve transparency and foster innovation, it also introduces significant challenges that must be carefully managed.

Historically, the USPTO has managed similar challenges by piloting programs to incentivize the public's actions that align with its policy goals.[60]

[56] SCR-Tech LLC v. Evonik Energy Servs. No. 08 CVS 16632, 2014 WL 7534071 (N.C. Super. Ct. Dec. 31, 2014).

[57] Zachary Arnold, Ilya Rahkovsky & Tina Huang, Tracking AI Investment Initial Findings: From the Private Markets (2020), https://cset.georgetown.edu/publication/tracking-ai-investment/.

[58] Enzo Biochem, Inc. v. Gen-Probe Inc., 323 F.3d 956, 983 (Fed. Cir. 2002) (Rader, J., dissenting) (noting that the *Lilly/Enzo* rule may prejudice university and small inventors who lack resources to process biotechnological inventions and may chill development in the field).

[59] Regents of the Univ. of Minn. v. LSI Corp., 926 F.3d 1327, 1331–32 (Fed. Cir. 2019) (noting that patent examiners often report insufficient time to conduct thorough examinations, given that they are allocated only about twenty-two hours per application).

[60] *See, e.g.*, 4 Lester Horwitz, Ethan Horwitz & Lisa Hershman, Patent Office Rules and Practice § 36A[C] (2024).

Transparency in AI patents is a worthy policy goal, and the patent system can implement and carefully manage changes that would achieve this goal.

Accountability

The third RTA principle is accountability, which is tied to concepts of ownership. This section examines the principle of accountability and its role in the governance of AI-related inventions within the patent system. It is the idea that the person or entity that owns or licenses the patent is accountable for the invention's use and the outcomes flowing from its use. In most commercial contexts, the accountable entity is a third party assigned or licensed rights to the invention. The patent's assignee or licensee may seek to commercialize the subject matter described. Thus, the invention may exist and operate in the public marketplace. Once an AI invention enters the public sphere, we must ask who will answer for any negative outcomes flowing from the use and existence of the invention.

The patent system holds inventors, owners, and licensees accountable for actions that stifle innovation. Patents give owners the right to exclude others from making, using, or selling the invention.[61] One way to ensure that this right to exclude does not impede innovation is to require patent owners to pay periodic maintenance fees that increase over time.[62] The escalating nature of maintenance fees forces patent owners to evaluate whether their patent is commercially viable. If the patent is not commercially viable, they can allow it to expire and enter the public domain.[63] Accordingly, maintenance fees can discourage patent owners from maintaining unused patents, which would otherwise impede the ability of other actors to commercialize the patent subject matter.

When a patent owner or licensee commercializes a product covered by a patent, they may indicate such coverage.[64] This provision, referred to as patent marking, is another way the patent system holds patent owners and licensees accountable. Patent marking informs the public that a specific

[61] Markman v. Westview Instruments, Inc., 517 U.S. 370, 373 (1996).

[62] 35 U.S.C. § 41(b)(1) (outlining the maintenance fees for patents, including $980 at three years and six months, $2,480 at seven years and six months, and $4,110 at eleven years and six months after grant).

[63] *Id.*

[64] 35 U.S.C. § 287 (stating that failure to mark a patented article prevents recovery of damages in an infringement action unless the infringer was notified and continued infringing thereafter).

patent covers the product at issue.[65] In turn, members of the public can research the patent and obtain any relevant information contained therein, including the name of the inventor and the patent's original assignee.

One last way patent owners are held accountable for their behavior is through enforcement during the patent lifecycle. A common defense to patent infringement is patent misuse. This defense prevents a patent holder from asserting rights beyond the patent's permissible scope.[66] For example, patent owners are not allowed to charge royalties for using a patent after its expiration.[67] Courts may also hold patent owners accountable for their conduct during litigation if the conduct is exceptional.[68] For example, a court may award attorney fees to a prevailing defendant if such conduct is unreasonable.[69] Thus, the judicial arm of the patent system holds patent owners accountable by discouraging them from asserting rights outside the patent scope and participating in weak or abusive patent litigation.

While the patent system encourages accountability to prevent patent owners from stifling innovation, the nature of AI patents may call for additional accountability. There is little to say about existing mechanisms that will ensure that patents are used in ways that will not harm the public.

To help integrate the principle of accountability into AI patenting, several suggestions are included below. As mentioned above, patent marking indicates to the public that a commercial product is patented. Generally, inventions directed to processes or methods are not marked.[70] However, in the case of AI patents, the law should require patent marking for patented AI processes, models, and methods. Marking these AI inventions would put the public on notice that they are patented. It would also allow the public to

[65] Arctic Cat Inc. v. Bombardier Recreational Prods. Inc., 876 F.3d 1350, 1366 (Fed. Cir. 2017) (explaining that the marking statute serves to avoid innocent infringement, encourage patentees to give public notice of patent status, and help the public identify whether an article is patented).

[66] Mallinckrodt, Inc. v. Medipart, Inc., 976 F.2d 700, 704 (Fed. Cir. 1992) (noting that the concept of patent misuse arose to restrain practices that, while not illegal, drew anticompetitive strength from the patent right, contrary to public policy).

[67] Brulotte v. Thys Co., 379 U.S. 29, 33–34 (1964) (holding that the exaction of royalties for the use of a machine after the patent has expired is unenforceable).

[68] Standard Oil Co. v. Am. Cyanamid Co., 774 F.2d 448, 455 (Fed. Cir. 1985) (discussing the circumstances in which a district court may award attorney fees in "exceptional" cases under 35 U.S.C. § 285, including willful infringement, misconduct during litigation, and vexatious or unjustified litigation).

[69] *Id.*

[70] Arctic Cat Inc. v. Bombardier Recreational Prods. Inc., 950 F.3d 860, 864 (Fed. Cir. 2020) (holding that the notice provisions of 35 U.S.C. § 287 do not apply to patents directed to processes or methods).

identify the inventor, original assignee, and possible patent owner—actors that may be held accountable for the AI invention.

Accountability for an AI invention begins with the inventor and, if existed, the original assignee. In addition to requiring the patent marking of all relevant AI models, patent owners should also be required to understand the impact of their AI systems before commercial deployment. An algorithmic impact assessment (AIA) determines the potential impact of an algorithm before it is deployed.[71] The USPTO could require AI patent applicants to submit an AIA as a condition for granting the patent. While it is unlikely that the USPTO has the resources needed to conduct a qualitative assessment, requiring an AIA would ensure (1) that the future patent owner is aware of the algorithm's impact; and (2) that the public has been put on notice of the patented AI system's impact. In sum, requiring an AI patent owner to complete an assessment injects another layer of accountability into the system.

Accountability best practices also suggest the use of algorithmic audits.[72] Algorithmic audits are processes designed to evaluate algorithms at different stages in the algorithm's lifecycle. In lieu of or in addition to AIAs, the USPTO should require that patented AI systems undergo algorithmic audits after the grant of the patents and upon their deployment. In contrast to the AIA, an algorithmic audit would provide critical information about the algorithms' impact in the real world. An ideal time for patent owners to undergo further algorithmic audits and submit their audit results would be in concert with the payment of regular maintenance fees. These periodic assessments would ensure that patent owners continue to monitor the AI inventions' commercial impact. Furthermore, the cost of conducting an AIA may ensure that patents on AI inventions not being used are allowed to expire before their full term. Thus, an algorithmic audit is another way to ensure that AI patent owners practice the principle of accountability.

Some may argue that patent owners should not be held accountable for the societal impact of their inventions. Generally, morally objectionable inventions are not prohibited from being patented.[73] Therefore, one could conclude that patent law is not the preferred tool for controlling the societal

[71] Jodi Daniels, *AI Assessments: How and When to Conduct Them*, Int'l Ass'n Privacy Pros. (Aug. 7, 2024), https://iapp.org/news/a/ai-assessments-how-and-when-to-conduct-them.

[72] Ellen P. Goodman & Julia Trehu, *Algorithmic Auditing: Chasing AI Accountability*, 39 Santa Clara High Tech. L.J. 289, 330 (2023).

[73] Juicy Whip, Inc. v. Orange Bang, Inc., 185 F.3d 1364, 1368 (Fed. Cir. 1999) (explaining that the utility requirement in patent law does not involve determining deceptive trade practices).

impact of patents. Furthermore, their burden may outweigh the benefit provided by the accountability tools proposed in this section. For example, suppose the USPTO does not have the bandwidth to carefully review impact assessments or algorithmic audits. In that case, requiring assessments and audits will impose a heavy burden on patent owners without benefit. However, since the patenting process is open to the public, that requirement can inform third parties of potentially harmful AI models in advance. In addition, AI inventions arguably have the potential to impact people who may not even be aware of an AI model's existence. The accountability measures proposed above would allow the public to avoid the commercial product or pressure the AI model's owner to change their operation to minimize the model's harmful effects.

In sum, the owners of AI patents should be accountable for the use and societal impact of their inventions. The patent system encourages accountability through various mechanisms, such as patent maintenance fees, marking, and disincentivizing unreasonable and abusive patent enforcement practices. Despite these existing mechanisms, the nature of AI inventions may require additional steps to make AI patent holders accountable. This section recommends patent marking for AI method patents and the institution of impact assessments and algorithmic audits to ensure the accountability of patent owners of AI inventions. Ultimately, the potential power and societal impact of AI inventions call for enhanced accountability.

Why the Patent System?

An overarching objection to the proposals in this chapter is that the patent system is ill-suited to implement policy goals. Specifically, fostering the development of AI systems that align with the RTA principles is beyond the USPTO's capabilities. Instead, a purist might argue that the patent system's primary role is to encourage and reward inventive activity.[74] Thus, interventions grounded in patent policy will have limited societal impact

[74] Aronson v. Quick Point Pencil Co., 440 U.S. 257, 262 (1979) (discussing the three purposes of the federal patent system: fostering invention, promoting disclosure to stimulate further innovation, and ensuring public domain ideas remain accessible).

beyond the innovation ecosystem. This section defends the idea that the patent system can be used to promote RTA principles in AI innovation.

While the purist view underscores the essential function of patents in promoting invention, it ignores the larger societal context in which the patent system exists. This chapter illustrates that the patent system already incorporates mechanisms that incentivize RTA. These mechanisms have affected how patents are obtained and used after they are granted. Furthermore, the USPTO is uniquely situated as an agency that can implement many of the proposals discussed in this chapter.

Historically, the USPTO has managed similar challenges by implementing different programs to incentivize alignment of the public's actions with its policy goals. For example, the Green Technology Pilot Program sought to encourage inventive activity in green technology by incentivizing patent applicants.[75] Introduced as a pilot in 2009, that program was sunset in 2012.[76] In addition, the USPTO uses several current rules to incentivize patenting behavior. It lowers filing fees for small businesses and micro-entities to reduce the barrier to entry for smaller firms.[77] It also incentivizes first-time applicants by expediting the examination of their inventions.[78] The USPTO could pursue similar initiatives to advance goals aligned with the RTA principles. For instance, it might establish an AI patent pilot program requiring applicants to meet defined RTA criteria proposed in this chapter. In return, qualifying applications could receive expedited examination or other procedural benefits. In short, there are several ways in which the USPTO can use small interventions to accomplish its policy objectives.

[75] Amanda Patton, *When Patent Offices Become Captain Planet: Green Technology and Accelerated Patent Examination Programs in the United States and Abroad*, 3 Am. U. Intell. Prop. Brief 30, 31 (2011) (discussing the USPTO's 2009 pilot program to accelerate green technology patent applications, launched just before the United Nations Climate Change Conference in Copenhagen, and its procedural requirements, including claim limitations and environmental enhancement statements).

[76] Sunset of the Patent Application Backlog Reduction Stimulus Plan and a Limited Extension of the Green Technology Pilot Program, 76 Fed. Reg. 77978, 77980 (Dec. 15, 2011) (announcing that the USPTO Green Technology Pilot Program would not be extended beyond March 30, 2012, or once 3,500 applications had been given special status, due to the availability of prioritized examination under Track I procedures).

[77] 35 U.S.C. § 41(b) (mandating a 60-percent reduction in patent fees for small entities and an 80-percent reduction for micro-entities, as defined in 35 U.S.C. § 123).

[78] U.S. Pat. & Trademark Off., *Certification and Petition for the First-Time Filer Expedited Examination Pilot Program*, Form PTO/SB/464 (Mar. 2023).

Conclusion

This chapter has explored the current landscape of AI patenting in the United States and identified how the RTA principles are reflected in patent law and practice. It has further discussed how the patent system can leverage these principles to incentivize the safe and responsible deployment of AI systems in society.

In the last decade, interest in AI has risen dramatically. Recognizing this growth area, the USPTO created a unique dataset of AI patents, signaling the importance of tracing innovation in this field.[79] Because certain AI models have had negative societal impacts upon deployment, there is an outsized interest in ensuring that future AI systems operate more safely and fairly.[80]

The RTA principles offer a robust method for ensuring the responsible deployment of future AI models. Fortunately, these principles are reflected in the current patent system in various ways. That system holds inventors responsible for their inventions, incentivizes transparency in the disclosure of inventions, and includes mechanisms to hold patent owners accountable for their inventions. In addition, this chapter has suggested additional ways in which the patent system can continue to encourage development based on the RTA principles, especially in relation to AI-related patents.

The effectiveness of the U.S. patent system will depend in part on how it responds to international issues. Future challenges will likely include efforts toward the global harmonization of AI patent laws, which are currently fragmented and risk creating significant uncertainty for inventors and businesses operating internationally. In addition, as AI becomes a critical strategy for international competitiveness, tensions around intellectual property rights in AI innovations may intensify, raising complex geopolitical issues. Moreover, the continued development of AI technology will continue to raise philosophical and ethical questions that will inevitably shape the evolving legal and commercial landscape of AI patenting.

Further attention needs to be directed toward refining the patent system so that AI inventions align with societal values, which will incentivize inventors to be more proactive in responsible AI development. Additional investigation could examine how post-grant mechanisms, such as *inter partes* review,

[79] Giczy et al., *supra* note 3, at 477.
[80] O'Neil, *supra* note 11, at 3.

can be used to ensure that AI-related patents are imbued with the RTA principles throughout the patent's pendency.[81]

Beyond the patent system, the RTA principles have important implications for other regulatory frameworks encouraging ethical innovation. By extending these principles, regulators could better address the challenges posed by AI in fields such as healthcare, finance, and autonomous technology. Looking toward the future, the USPTO will play a critical role in refining regulatory processes to ensure that the United States remains a hub for innovation and a model for the world regarding the responsible deployment of AI technology.

[81] *Inter partes* review is an administrative procedure designed to be distinct from and more efficient than district court litigation that allows a third party, who is not the patent owner, to challenge the validity of one or more claims of an issued patent. 35 U.S.C. § 311.

V.

AI-DRIVEN INNOVATION AND GLOBAL CHALLENGES

14

Navigating Turbulence

The Challenge of Inclusive Innovation in the U.S.–China AI Race

Jyh-An Lee and Jingwen Liu

Introduction

Artificial intelligence (AI) has not only transformed the global economy but also redefined the international power hierarchy. The current "AI arms race" is often likened to the space race of the 1960s or the nuclear arms race from the 1950s to the 1980s.[1] Consequently, it is hardly surprising that some assert that the dominant force in AI technology may ultimately govern global leadership.[2] Although AI development is making breakthroughs around the world, many believe that global AI competition ultimately boils down to a contest between the United States and China.[3]

The AI market in the United States continues to drive significant venture capital investment. According to data from Crunchbase, AI startups secured US$18.9 billion in the third quarter of 2024, accounting for 28 percent of all venture funding during that period.[4] The strong culture of entrepreneurship and a well-established practice in technology investment have provided U.S. AI firms with an unparalleled advantage in the global arena. OpenAI's launch of ChatGPT in November 2022 has further showcased to the world the extraordinary potential of generative AI. Beyond ChatGPT, American companies have developed most of the world's advanced large-language

[1] Lee Kai-Fu, AI Superpowers China, Silicon Valley and the New World Order (2018).

[2] Radina Gigova, *Who Vladimir Putin Thinks Will Rule the World*, CNN (Sept. 1, 2017), https://edition.cnn.com/2017/09/01/world/putin-artificial-intelligence-will-rule-world/index.html.

[3] *See, e.g.*, Neil Savage, *The Race to the Top Among the World's Leaders in Artificial Intelligence*, Nature Index (Dec. 9, 2020), https://www.nature.com/articles/d41586-020-03409-8.

[4] Gené Teare, *Global Funding Slowed in Q3, Even as AI Continued to Lead*, Crunchbase News (Oct. 3, 2024), https://news.crunchbase.com/venture/global-startup-funding-recap-q3-2024/.

Jyh-An Lee and Jingwen Liu, *Navigating Turbulence* In: *Inclusive Innovation in the Age of AI and Big Data*. Edited by: Daryl Lim and Peter K. Yu, Oxford University Press.
DOI: 10.1093/9780197799444.003.0019

models (LLMs), including Claude from Anthropic, BERT, Gemini, and Gemma from Google, Llama from Meta, and Grok from xAI.

However, AI companies in Silicon Valley are now encountering fierce competition from their counterparts on the other side of the globe. In recent years, China's AI industry has witnessed rapid growth. According to the China Center for Information Industry Development, the country's core AI industry has grown to an approximate scale of US$69.48 billion in 2023, encompassing over 4,400 enterprises.[5] The market scale for AI large models is projected to reach US$2.1 billion, marking a 110-percent year-on-year increase.[6] On March 16, 2023, Chinese technology giant Baidu launched its ERNIE Bot, a new-generation knowledge-enhanced LLM. The latest iteration, released on June 21, 2023, was reported to have surpassed ChatGPT-4 in several Chinese-language capabilities.[7]

The introduction of DeepSeek in early 2025 has shed further light on the current capabilities of Chinese AI technology.[8] Despite the United States' heightened export controls on semiconductor chips to constrain China's AI advancements, DeepSeek-R1 has demonstrated performance metrics in mathematics, coding, and complex reasoning that are on par with OpenAI's leading models. For instance, in the realm of mathematics, DeepSeek-R1 achieved a score of 79.8 percent on the AIME (Artificial Intelligence Math Evaluation) 2024 benchmark, slightly surpassing OpenAI o1's 79.2 percent. Similarly, in coding proficiency, DeepSeek-R1 excelled at the 96.3rd percentile on Codeforces, closely trailing OpenAI o1's 96.6th percentile.[9]

In the midst of a fervent global arms race in technology, governments have played pivotal roles in fostering AI innovation. Strategic plans on the use and deployment of AI can be found across various nations.[10] In the United States, strategic AI policies started with the Obama administration's publication

[5] *China to Launch AI Plus Initiative: Government Work Report*, GLOB. TIMES (Mar. 5, 2024), https://www.globaltimes.cn/page/202403/1308210.shtml.

[6] *Id.*

[7] *Introducing ERNIE 3.5: Baidu's Knowledge-Enhanced Foundation Model Takes a Giant Leap Forward*, BAIDU RSCH. (June 27, 2023), https://research.baidu.com/Blog/index-view?id=185.

[8] Wang Fan & João da Silva, *DeepSeek: How China's "AI Heroes" Overcame US Curbs to Stun Silicon Valley*, BBC (Jan. 28, 2025), https://www.bbc.com/news/articles/czepw096wy4o.

[9] Craig S. Smith, *DeepSeek: How China's AI Innovators Are Challenging the Status Quo*, FORBES (Jan. 22, 2025), https://www.forbes.com/sites/craigsmith/2025/01/22/deepseek-how-chinas-ai-innovators-are-challenging-the-status-quo/.

[10] *See, e.g.*, DEPARTMENT FOR SCIENCE, INNOVATION & TECHNOLOGY, A PRO-INNOVATION APPROACH TO AI REGULATION, 2023, Cm. 815 (UK); INNOVATION, SCI. & ECON. DEV. CAN., THE PAN-CANADIAN AI STRATEGY (2017); SMART NATION SING., NAIS 2.0: SINGAPORE NATIONAL AI STRATEGY (2023).

of the report on "Preparing for the Future of Artificial Intelligence" and the National Artificial Intelligence Research and Development Plan in 2016.[11] This trajectory continued under President Trump, who launched the American AI Initiative to preserve U.S. leadership in AI in his first administration.[12] Further advancing these efforts, the Biden administration, in May 2023, revised the National Artificial Intelligence Research and Development Strategic Plan, building upon its predecessors from 2016 and 2019.[13] This update introduced a principled, coordinated strategy for international collaboration in AI research, enhancing eight strategic directions.[14]

The strategic significance of AI also resonated within Congress. For instance, the National Artificial Intelligence Initiative Act was proposed in the House of Representatives in December 2020, aiming to secure ongoing U.S. supremacy in AI research and development (R&D).[15] In June 2023, Senators Michael Bennet (D-Colo.), Todd Young (R-Ind.), and Mark Warner (D-Va.) introduced the bipartisan Global Technology Leadership Act.[16] This act was designed to bolster American competitiveness in crucial emerging technologies, including AI. Its need was underscored by the Senators' explicit reference to the technological rivalry with China in these strategic domains.[17]

Reflecting similar concerns, the Chinese government has demonstrated significant ambition in both advancing AI innovation and sculpting its regulatory landscape. As early as 2017, the State Council articulated its aspiration to achieve global leadership in AI by 2030 through its Next-Generation Artificial Intelligence Development Plan.[18] In March 2024, Premier Li

[11] EXEC. OFF. OF THE PRESIDENT, NAT'L SCI. & TECH. COUNCIL COMM. ON TECH., PREPARING FOR THE FUTURE OF ARTIFICIAL INTELLIGENCE (2016), https://obamawhitehouse.archives.gov/sites/default/files/whitehouse_files/microsites/ostp/NSTC/preparing_for_the_future_of_ai.pdf; NAT'L SCI. & TECH. COUNCIL NETWORKING & INFO. TECH. RSCH. & DEV. SUBCOMM., NATIONAL ARTIFICIAL INTELLIGENCE RESEARCH AND DEVELOPMENT PLAN (2016), https://www.nitrd.gov/PUBS/national_ai_rd_strategic_plan.pdf.

[12] Exec. Order No. 13859, 84 Fed. Reg. 3967 (Feb. 11, 2019).

[13] NAT'L SCI. & TECH. COUNCIL, SELECT COMM. ON A.I., NATIONAL ARTIFICIAL INTELLIGENCE RESEARCH AND DEVELOPMENT STRATEGIC PLAN: 2023 UPDATE (May 2023), https://bidenwhitehouse.archives.gov/wp-content/uploads/2023/05/National-Artificial-Intelligence-Research-and-Development-Strategic-Plan-2023-Update.pdf.

[14] *Id.*

[15] National Artificial Intelligence Initiative Act, H.R. 6216, 116th Cong. (2020).

[16] Global Technology Leadership Act, S. 1873, 118th Cong. (2023).

[17] Michael Bennet, *Bennet, Young, Warner Introduce Bill to Strengthen U.S. Technology Competitiveness*, U.S. SENATORS FOR COLO. (June 8, 2023), https://www.bennet.senate.gov/public/index.cfm/2023/6/bennet-young-warner-introduce-bill-to-strengthen-u-s-technology-competitiveness.

[18] Next-Generation Artificial Intelligence Development Plan (新一代人工智能发展规划) (promulgated by the State Council, July 20, 2017, effective July 20, 2017) (China).

Qiang unveiled the "AI Plus" initiative, which aims to harness AI's potential within traditional industries to fuel economic growth and foster technological progress.[19] Additionally, local governments, such as those in Shanghai and Shenzhen, have enacted and implemented regulations to form AI ethics committees. These committees are responsible for overseeing AI development, conducting audits and assessments, and facilitating the creation of industrial parks designed for the easy and lawful exchange of input and training data. Although Chinese legislators are still crafting a comprehensive AI law, a framework of interim regulations is already operational at both the national and local levels.[20]

Despite the exponential growth in AI regulations in both the United States and China, a closer examination of their regulatory frameworks reveals distinct ideological differences between these two global powerhouses. For instance, as depicted in Table 14.1, the AI industry in the United States remains driven by the market and is rather decentralized,[21] while private investors in China tend to depend more on government-guided funds to navigate market trends, a practice influenced by heightened policy uncertainty. On the other

[19] Government Work Report of March 5, 2024 at the Second Session of the 14th National People's Congress (政府工作报告—2024年3月5日在第十四届全国人民代表大会第二次会议上), State Council Gazette No. 9 [2024]; Ben Jiang, *"Two Sessions" 2024: China's Lawmakers Call for More AI Development to Catch Up with US, While Keeping It Under Regulatory Control*, S. China Morning Post (Mar. 11, 2024), https://www.scmp.com/tech/policy/article/3254851/two-sessions-2024-chinas-lawmakers-call-more-ai-development-catch-us-while-keeping-it-under.

[20] *See, e.g.*, Interim Measures for Administration of Generative Artificial Intelligence Services (生成式人工智能服务管理暂行办法) (promulgated by the Cyberspace Admin. of China, Nat'l Dev. & Reform Comm'n, Ministry of Educ., Ministry of Sci. & Tech., Ministry of Indus. & Info. Tech., Ministry of Pub. Sec. & Nat'l Radio & Television Admin., July 10, 2023, effective Aug. 15, 2023) St. Council Gaz., Aug. 30, 2023 (China) [hereinafter Interim Measures for Administration of Generative AI Services]; Provisions on the Administration of Algorithm-Generated Recommendations for Internet Information Services (互联网信息服务算法推荐管理规定) (promulgated by the Cyberspace Admin. of China, Ministry of Indus. & Info. Tech., Ministry of Pub. Sec. & State Admin. for Market Reg., Dec. 31, 2021, effective Mar. 1, 2022) St. Council Gaz., Mar. 30, 2022 (China) [hereinafter Provisions on Algorithm-Generated Recommendations]; Provisions on Administration of Deep Synthesis of Internet-Based Information Services (互联网信息服务深度合成管理规定) (promulgated by the Cyberspace Admin. of China, Ministry of Indus. & Info. Tech. & Ministry of Pub. Sec., Nov. 25, 2022, effective Jan. 10, 2023) St. Council Gaz., Feb. 10, 2023 (China) [hereinafter Provisions on Deep Synthesis].

[21] *See, e.g.*, Anu Bradford, Digital Empires: The Global Battle to Regulate Technology (2023); Alex Engler, *The EU and U.S. Diverge on AI Regulation: A Transatlantic Comparison and Steps to Alignment*, Brookings, (Apr. 25, 2023), https://www.brookings.edu/articles/the-eu-and-us-diverge-on-ai-regulation-a-transatlantic-comparison-and-steps-to-alignment/; Emma Klein & Stewart Patrick, *Envisioning a Global Regime Complex to Govern Artificial Intelligence*, Carnegie Endowment for Int'l Peace (Mar. 21, 2024), https://carnegieendowment.org/research/2024/03/envisioning-a-global-regime-complex-to-govern-artificial-intelligence?lang=en; Stewart Patrick, *Rules of Order: Assessing the State of Global Governance*, Carnegie Endowment for Int'l Peace (Sept. 12, 2023), https://carnegieendowment.org/research/2023/09/rules-of-order-assessing-the-state-of-global-governance?lang=en.

Table 14.1. Comparison between key performance indicators of the AI industry in the United States and China in 2023

	United States	China
AI patent filings[a]	32%	*34.7%*
Top publications on AI[a]	22.6%	*36.7%*
Number of newly funded AI start-ups[b]	897	122
Private investment in AI[b]	US$67.2 billion	US$7.8 billion
Public investment in AI[c]	US$1.8 billion	Not available
Notable AI models[b]	61	15
World's top 50 AI hubs[d]	10	2

[a] Inst. of Sci. & Tech. Info. of China & Peking Univ., Global AI Innovation Index 2023 [2023全球人工智能创新指数报告] (2023).

[b] Stanford Univ., Inst. for Human-Centered A.I., Artificial Intelligence Index Report 2024 (2024).

[c] Networking & Info. Tech. R&D Prog. & Nat'l A.I. Initiative Off., Supplement to the President's FY 2024 Budget (2023), https://www.nitrd.gov/pubs/FY2024-NITRD-NAIIO-Supplement.pdf.

[d] Bhaskar Chakravorti, Ajay Bhalla, Ravi Shankar Chaturvedi & Christina Filipovic, *50 Global Hubs for Top AI Talent*, Harv. Bus. Rev. (Dec. 21, 2021), https://hbr.org/2021/12/50-global-hubs-for-top-ai-talent.

hand, some commentators believe that, while the United States views AI competition as a sprint (focusing on exclusivity and short-term victories), China approaches it as a marathon (emphasizing inclusivity and sustained outcomes).[22]

These differences could shape each country's strengths and weaknesses in the ongoing AI arms race, either enhancing or hindering innovation in AI technologies. More importantly, the escalating technological rivalry has led to exclusionary policymaking, prioritizing national interest over inclusive innovation. With both parties increasingly regulating the flow of technology, capital, and personnel in response to the AI race, ensuring inclusive and sustainable development, as well as equal access to the benefits of AI research, has become more challenging than ever.

In this chapter, we explore three critical aspects of the American and Chinese legal infrastructures that significantly impact AI innovation: data

[22] Tariq Malik, *The Philosophies Behind the US-China Tech War*, LSE Bus. Rev. (Feb. 5, 2025), https://blogs.lse.ac.uk/businessreview/2025/02/05/the-philosophies-behind-the-us-china-tech-war/.

privacy, intellectual property (IP) rights, and export restrictions. Through this comparative analysis, we argue that, while China's legal environment may offer certain advantages in terms of access to training data and IP protection, the United States maintains superior resources by enforcing strict export controls on semiconductor chips, AI models, as well as outbound investments in these areas. This nuanced examination helps illuminate how each country's legal framework could influence the ultimate trajectory of the AI race and how the technological rivalry has led to exclusionary rulemaking on a global scale.

Data Privacy

AI technologies and individual privacy intersect primarily in three areas: the training of AI algorithms, automated decision-making (ADM), and government surveillance. Training AI requires very large datasets. It is estimated that computer scientists at OpenAI initially used a 175-billion-parameter model to train ChatGPT-3 in 2019.[23] However, using extensive personal data heightens the risk of privacy breaches.[24] Privacy safeguards in data collection typically hinge on two practices: obtaining informed consent from data subjects and implementing data anonymization by processors. Yet, the widespread adoption of AI could exacerbate privacy risks by increasing the likelihood of data de-anonymization,[25] particularly as larger datasets tend to facilitate this process.[26]

Privacy concerns also emerge during the implementation phase in both ADM and surveillance analytics.[27] For instance, a bank using AI tools in the ADM process to evaluate an applicant's personal data for a loan decision might face issues if the data is incomplete, potentially leading to compromised, biased, or even discriminatory decisions that could severely

[23] Caitlin Chin-Rothmann, *Protecting Data Privacy as a Baseline for Responsible AI*, Ctr. for Strategic & Int'l Stud. (July 18, 2024), https://www.csis.org/analysis/protecting-data-privacy-baseline-responsible-ai.

[24] Shlomit Yanisky-Ravid & Sean K. Hallisey, *"Equality and Privacy by Design": A New Model of Artificial Intelligence Data Transparency via Auditing, Certification, and Safe Harbor Regimes*, 46 Fordham Urb. L.J. 428, 458 (2019).

[25] *Id.* at 471.

[26] *Id.*

[27] Katerina Demetzou, Gabriela Zanfir-Fortuna & Sebastião Barros Vale, *The Thin Red Line: Refocusing Data Protection Law on ADM, A Global Perspective with Lessons from Case-Law*, 49 Comput. L. & Sec. Rev 1, 2 (2023).

impact an individual's legal rights or interests.[28] Moreover, integrating AI with surveillance technologies—such as facial recognition systems that identify or verify individuals by their facial features—has intensified privacy intrusions, a longstanding issue in institutional governance.[29] These potential misuses underscore the urgent need for heightened vigilance and proactive measures from AI developers, users, and regulators to safeguard privacy and prevent abuses.

United States

Statutory protections for privacy in the United States vary across sectors and states. Without federal legislation, state laws, sector-specific federal laws, and agency regulations have emerged to address privacy concerns through fragmented and piecemeal solutions.[30] By the end of 2024, twenty states have enacted their own consumer privacy regulations, with the California Privacy Rights Act of 2020 (CPRA), building upon the California Consumer Privacy Act of 2018, being one of the most comprehensive privacy statutes.[31] Introducing the first data minimization rule in the United States, the CPRA emphasized that businesses should only collect consumers' personal information to the extent necessary for the intended purposes. It also mandated an opt-out mechanism for individuals to decline certain forms of ADM systems, including those leveraging AI technologies.[32]

At the federal level, the regulation is fragmented across sectors. Laws such as the Children's Online Privacy Protection Act (COPPA) and the Health Insurance Portability and Accountability Act (HIPAA) hold the potential to

[28] *See, e.g.*, Lee Jyh-An, *Algorithmic Bias and the New Chicago School*, 14 L. Innovation & Tech. 95, 98 (2022); Cameron F. Kerry, *Protecting Privacy in an AI-Driven World*, Brookings (Feb. 10, 2020), https://www.brookings.edu/articles/protecting-privacy-in-an-ai-driven-world/.

[29] Peter Mantello, Manh-Tung Ho, Minh-Hoang Nguyen & Quan-Hoang Vuong, *Machines That Feel: Behavioral Determinants of Attitude Towards Affect Recognition Technology—Upgrading Technology Acceptance Theory with the Mindsponge Model*, 10 Humans. & Soc. Sci. Commc'ns 430 (2023); Wang Xukang, Wu Ying Cheng, Zhou Mengjie & Fu Hongpeng, *Beyond Surveillance: Privacy, Ethics, and Regulations in Face Recognition Technology*, 7 Frontiers Big Data 1, 1 (2024).

[30] Jennifer King & Caroline Meinhardt, *Rethinking Privacy in the AI Era: Policy Provocations for a Data-Centric World* (Stanford Univ., Inst. for Human-Centered A.I., White Paper, Feb. 2024), https://hai.stanford.edu/sites/default/files/2024-02/White-Paper-Rethinking-Privacy-AI-Era.pdf.

[31] Cal. Civ. Code § 1798 (West 2025).

[32] *A New Landmark for Consumer Control Over Their Personal Information: CPPA Proposes Regulatory Framework for Automated Decisionmaking Technology*, Cal. Privacy Prot. Agency (Nov. 27, 2023), https://cppa.ca.gov/announcements/2023/20231127.html.

regulate certain aspects of AI privacy issues.[33] Yet recent surveys and poll reveal a call from U.S. consumers for a comprehensive federal privacy law in the style of the European Union's General Data Protection Regulation (GDPR).[34] The American Privacy Rights Act was introduced to the U.S. House of Representatives in April 2024, incorporating similar data minimization and opt-out rules.[35] However, the revised draft in June omitted civil rights protection measures that required large data holders, including AI developers, to assess the impact of data usage for model training.[36]

Despite the absence of a comprehensive federal privacy act, AI developers' data misuse could violate existing antitrust and consumer protection laws, subject to enforcement by the Federal Trade Commission (FTC), if such actions undermine fair competition.[37] Section 5 of the Federal Trade Commission Act prohibits "unfair methods of competition in or affecting commerce,"[38] which, as interpreted by the Supreme Court, extends beyond the conducts specified in the Sherman and Clayton Acts to encompass other unfair practices that negatively affect competition.[39] The FTC has explicitly acknowledged that these unfair methods of competition could include instances where "powerful firms unfairly use AI technologies in a manner that tends to harm competitive conditions."[40] Violations of these regulations may lead to enforcement actions by the FTC. For example, in February 2023,

[33] Dennis Crouch, *Using Intellectual Property to Regulate Artificial Intelligence*, 89 Mo. L. Rev. 781, 802 (2024); Karl Manheim & Lyric Kaplan, *Artificial Intelligence: Risks to Privacy and Democracy*, 21 Yale J.L. & Tech. 106, 162 (2019).

[34] Tony Bradley, *Privacy and Trust in the AI Age*, Forbes (Oct. 30, 2024), https://www.forbes.com/sites/tonybradley/2024/10/30/privacy-and-trust-in-the-ai-age/.

[35] American Privacy Rights Act, H.R.8818, 118th Cong. §§ 102, 106 (2024).

[36] *Committee Chairs Cantwell, McMorris Rodgers Unveil Historic Draft Comprehensive Data Privacy Legislation*, U.S. Senate Comm. on Com., Sci. & Transp. (Apr. 7, 2024), https://www.commerce.senate.gov/2024/4/committee-chairs-cantwell-mcmorris-rodgers-unveil-historic-draft-comprehensive-data-privacy-legislation.

[37] Fed. Trade Comm'n, Off. of Tech., *AI Companies: Uphold Your Privacy and Confidentiality Commitments*, Fed. Trade Comm'n (Jan. 9, 2024), https://www.ftc.gov/policy/advocacy-research/tech-at-ftc/2024/01/ai-companies-uphold-your-privacy-confidentiality-commitments.

[38] 15 U.S.C. § 45(a)(1).

[39] *See, e.g.*, Fed. Trade Comm'n v. Ind. Fed'n of Dentists, 476 U.S. 447, 454 (1986); Fed. Trade Comm'n v. Sperry & Hutchinson Co., 405 U.S. 233, 242 (1972); Fed. Trade Comm'n v. Texaco, 393 U.S. 223, 262 (1968); Fed. Trade Comm'n v. Brown Shoe, 384 U.S. 316, 321 (1966); Atlantic Refin. Co. v. Fed. Trade Comm'n, 381 U.S. 357, 369 (1965); Fed. Trade Comm'n v. Colgate-Palmolive Co., 380 U.S. 374, 384–85 (1965); PAN AM v. United States, 371 U.S. 296, 306–08 (1963); Fed. Trade Comm'n v. Nat'l Lead Co., 352 U.S. 419, 428–29 (1957); Am. Airlines, Inc. v. N. Am. Airlines, Inc., 351 U.S. 79, 85 (1956); Fed. Trade Comm'n v. Motion Picture Advert. Serv. Co., 344 U.S. 392, 394–95 (1953); Fed. Trade Comm'n v. Cement Inst., 333 U.S. 683, 708 (1948); Fed. Trade Comm'n v. R.F. Keppel & Bro., Inc., 291 U.S. 304, 310 (1934).

[40] *Comment of the United States Federal Trade Commission*, Fed. Trade Comm'n (Oct. 30, 2023), https://www.ftc.gov/system/files/ftc_gov/pdf/p241200_ftc_comment_to_copyright_office.pdf.

the agency filed a complaint in the Northern District of California against a company that breached its commitment by sharing users' personal information with unauthorized third-party advertising platforms, thereby violating the Federal Trade Commission Act.[41] In July 2023, the FTC imposed a US$7.8 million fine on another company and prohibited it from sharing consumers' health data for advertising purposes.[42]

The fragmented, laissez-faire approach to data regulation may inadvertently help maintain the competitiveness of American AI firms, as generalized privacy regulations could stifle digital innovation nationwide.[43] Since AI training inherently involves a trade-off between data availability and privacy safeguards,[44] a more flexible privacy regime ostensibly promises better access to data. Ironically, however, this advantage has gradually been compromised by the overpopulation of such sectoral acts—instead of falling into the gap between regulations, many companies are now facing multiple, overlapping regulations, which makes compliance more complicated.[45]

Meanwhile, there is a growing demand for enhanced privacy safeguards in the AI development process,[46] a factor that could impede the pace of AI innovation in the United States. In October 2022, the Biden administration unveiled the Blueprint for an AI Bill of Rights (Blueprint), encompassing key principles for regulating AI.[47] The Blueprint envisaged that data collection by AI developers should conform to reasonable expectations, to the strictly necessary extent, and with the data subject's consent. It also underscored the importance of safeguarding civil liberties from unwarranted surveillance, advocating for increased oversight of surveillance technologies.[48]

41 Complaint, U.S. v. GoodRx Holdings, Inc., No. 23-cv-460 (N.D. Cal. Feb. 2, 2023).

42 BetterHelp, Inc., FTC Docket No. C-4796 (Fed. Trade Comm'n July 7, 2023).

43 Anu Bradford, *The False Choice Between Digital Regulation and Innovation*, 119 Nw. U. L. Rev. 377, 397 (2024).

44 Ajay Agrawal, Joshua Gans & Avi Goldfarb, Prediction Machines: The Simple Economics of Artificial Intelligence 163 (2018); Peter K. Yu, *Beyond Transparency and Accountability: Three Additional Features Algorithm Designers Should Build into Intelligent Platforms*, 13 Ne. U. L. Rev. 263, 293 (2021).

45 Daniel J. Solove, *The Growing Problems with the Sectoral Approach to Privacy Law*, TeachPrivacy (Nov. 13, 2015), https://teachprivacy.com/problems-sectoral-approach-privacy-law/.

46 *See, e.g.*, Tate Ryan-Mosley & Melissa Heikkilä, *Three Things to Know About the White House's Executive Order on AI*, MIT Tech. Rev. (Oct. 30, 2023), https://www.technologyreview.com/2023/10/30/1082678/three-things-to-know-about-the-white-houses-executive-order-on-ai/.

47 *Blueprint for an AI Bill of Rights Making Automated Systems Work for the American People*, White House (Oct. 2022), https://bidenwhitehouse.archives.gov/ostp/ai-bill-of-rights/.

48 *Id.*

While the Blueprint advocates for self-regulation within the industry, its nonbinding nature has raised concerns, particularly regarding its exclusion of law enforcement matters. Such exclusion has prompted calls for congressional action to all law enforcement to the proposed regulations.[49] Despite challenges in enforcement, the Blueprint inspired subsequent policymaking and regulatory efforts. In October 2023, the White House issued the Executive Order on the Safe, Secure, and Trustworthy Development and Use of Artificial Intelligence, emphasizing the protection of privacy and civil liberties amidst the rapid advancement of AI technology and highlighting the legal and societal risks posed by improper data collection and use, including the chilling of First Amendment protections.[50] Following these two pivotal initiatives, several federal agencies—such as the FTC, the Department of Defense, the National Institute of Standards and Technology (NIST), the National Telecommunications and Information Administration, the Cybersecurity and Infrastructure Security Agency, and the Securities and Exchange Commission—have integrated AI consideration into their regulatory frameworks.[51]

Following the 2024 Presidential election, the arrival of the Trump administration has profound implications for U.S. AI policy. Notably, Trump repealed Biden administration's executive order, which the new president considered dangerous and potentially stifling to AI innovation.[52] Some commentators anticipate that, with President Trump's re-election, policy priorities will shift toward leveraging AI as a geopolitical advantage, rather than safeguarding individual rights, including privacy.[53] Private stakeholders support this approach. In a Congressional hearing on social media privacy and data abuse, Meta CEO Mark Zuckerberg emphasized the

[49] Nicol Turner Lee & Jack Malamud, *Opportunities and Blind Spots in the White House's Blueprint for an AI Bill of Rights*, Brookings (Dec. 19, 2022), https://www.brookings.edu/articles/opportunities-and-blind-spots-in-the-white-houses-blueprint-for-an-ai-bill-of-rights/.

[50] Exec. Order No. 14110, 88 Fed. Reg. 75191 (Oct. 30, 2023).

[51] *Landmark Actions Coming: The AI Act and Growing US Regulations*, KPMG Insight (Dec. 2023), https://kpmg.com/us/en/articles/2023/landmark-actions-coming-the-ai-act-and-growing-us-regulations-reg-alert.html. Key outputs include the *AI Accountability Policy Report* issued in March 2024 by the National Telecommunications and Information Administration, the Artificial Intelligence Risk Management Framework issued in June 2024 by the National Institute of Standards and Technology, the Risk Management Profile for Artificial Intelligence and Human Rights issued in July 2024 by the Department of State, and the Artificial Intelligence Roadmap issued in March 2024 by the Department of Homeland Security.

[52] Exec. Order No. 14179, 90 Fed. Reg. 8741 (Jan. 23, 2025); Philipp Hacker, Ramayya Krishnan & Marco Mauer, *Global AI Governance—Part 3: A Fragmented Future and a Trump Twist*, Oxford Bus. L. Blog (Dec. 11, 2024), https://blogs.law.ox.ac.uk/oblb/blog-post/2024/12/global-ai-governance-part-3-fragmented-future-and-trump-twist.

[53] Hacker et al., *supra* note 52.

importance of "enabling innovation" when regulating sensitive technologies, such as facial recognition. He specifically referenced threats from Chinese firms that could gain competitive advantages if the extensive regulation hampers the U.S. companies' ability to innovate.[54] Overall, although the lack of an overreaching privacy act appears to favor AI innovation, multiple complications have made this effect less evident.

China

Since 2021, China has put in place the Personal Information Protection Law (PIPL), the country's first comprehensive personal data protection law.[55] Before the statute's promulgation, privacy protection law in China was as fragmented as in the United States. For example, the Cybersecurity Law of 2016 contains principles of data minimization and informed consent,[56] the E-Commerce Law of 2018 restricts certain ADM practices such as targeted advertising,[57] and the Data Security Law of 2021 mandates certain data processors to employ risk-management measures and conduct periodical risk assessment.[58] In 2020, the National People's Congress passed the new Civil Code, which became effective on January 1, 2021.[59] The Code added privacy and personal information interests to the scope of recognized civil rights, bolstering the enactment and implementation of the PIPL later that year.[60] Multiple guidelines and standards were gradually put in place in the following two years, setting out the specific measures to effectuate the mechanisms pinned down by the PIPL.[61] The legal

[54] *Facebook, Social Media Privacy, and the Use and Abuse of Data: Joint Hearing Before the S. Comm. on Com., Sci. & Transp. and the S. Comm. on the Judiciary*, 115th Cong. 22 (2018) (statement of Mark Zuckerberg, Chairman and CEO, Facebook), https://www.congress.gov/event/115th-congress/senate-event/LC64510/text.

[55] Personal Information Protection Law (个人信息保护法) (promulgated by the Standing Comm. Nat'l People's Cong., Aug. 20, 2021, effective Nov. 1, 2021), art. 1 (China).

[56] Cybersecurity Law (网络安全法) (promulgated by the Standing Comm. Nat'l People's Cong., Nov. 7, 2016, effective June 1, 2017), art. 41 (China).

[57] E-Commerce Law (电子商务法) (promulgated by the Standing Comm. Nat'l People's Cong., Aug. 31, 2018, effective Jan. 1, 2019), art. 18 (China).

[58] Data Security Law (数据安全法) (promulgated by the Standing Comm. Nat'l People's Cong., June 10, 2021, effective Sept. 1, 2021), arts. 27, 29, 30 (China).

[59] Civil Code (民法典) (promulgated by the Nat'l People's Cong., May 28, 2020, effective Jan. 1, 2021) (China).

[60] *Id.* arts. 1032, 1034.

[61] *See, e.g.*, Regulations on the Security Protection of Critical Information Infrastructure (关键信息基础设施安全保护条例) (promulgated by the State Council, Apr. 27, 2021, effective Sept. 1,

framework governing personal data protection in China is a comprehensive and vertically integrated regime, with the PIPL at its core. The PIPL grants individuals various rights, including the right to be informed, decide, restrict, or refuse the processing of their personal information, as well as the right to access, copy, transfer, rectify, supplement, or erase their personal data. Moreover, individuals have the right to request that personal information processors clarify their data processing practices.[62] The PIPL also imposes obligations on data processors concerning authorization, notification, consent, security measures, impact assessments, and sharing data with third parties.[63] AI developers and operators are obligated to comply with these legal provisions if they fall under the category of "personal information processors" and "data processors" as defined by the PIPL and the Data Security Law, respectively.[64]

The government's regulation of AI technologies also extends to issues related to data and privacy. In 2022 and early 2023, regulations on certain subcategories of AI technologies such as algorithm-generated recommendations and deep synthesis were released, setting out obligations and liabilities for algorithm operators and deep synthesis service providers.[65] In July 2023, seven state agencies jointly issued the Interim Measures for the Management of Generative Artificial Intelligence Services, the first

2021) St. Council Gaz., Sept. 10, 2021 (China); Measures for the Administration of Data Security in the Field of Industry and Information Technology (for Trial Implementation) (工业和信息化领域数据安全管理办法（试行）), Notice of the Ministry of Indus. & Info. Tech. No. 166 [2022] (promulgated by the Ministry of Indus. & Info. Tech., Dec. 8, 2022, effective Jan. 1, 2023) (China); Opinions on Building Basic Systems for Data to Give Full Play to the Role of Data Resources (关于构建数据基础制度更好发挥数据要素作用的意见) (promulgated by the Cent. Comm'n & State Council, Dec. 2, 2022, effective Dec. 2, 2022) St. Council Gaz., Jan. 10, 2023 (China); Information Security Technology—Guidance for Personal Information Security Impact Assessment (信息安全技术个人信息安全影响评估指南), GB/T 39335-2020 (issued by the Standardization Admin. of China, Nov. 19, 2020, effective June 1, 2021) (China); Information Security Technology—Implementation Guidelines for Notices and Consent in Personal Information Processing (信息安全技术个人信息处理中告知和同意的实施指南), GB/T 42574-2023 (promulgated by the Standardization Admin. of China, May 23, 2023, effective Dec. 1, 2023) (China); Information Security Technology—Personal Information Security Testing and Evaluation Specification in Mobile Internet Applications (App) (信息安全技术移动互联网应用程序（App）个人信息安全测评规范), GB/T 42582-2023 (issued by the Standardization Admin. of China, May 23, 2023, effective Dec. 1, 2023) (China).

[62] Personal Information Protection Law, *supra* note 55, arts. 44–48.

[63] *Id.* arts. 13, 14, 17, 51–57.

[64] Shen Weixing & Liu Yun, *China's Normative Systems for Responsible AI: From Soft Law to Hard Law*, *in* The Cambridge Handbook of Responsible Artificial Intelligence: Interdisciplinary Perspectives 150, 157 (2022).

[65] Provisions on Algorithm-Generated Recommendations, *supra* note 20, art. 7; Provisions on Deep Synthesis, *supra* note 20, art. 14.

comprehensive AI regulation in China.[66] The Interim Measures contain rules safeguarding AI users' rights to their personal information, as well as requirements on data minimization, anonymization, and prohibition against unauthorized sharing.[67] Furthermore, it sets forth requirements regarding training data of machine learning models, including those requiring these training data to have a legitimate source with respect to IP and personal information.[68]

Under the general rule in the PIPL, state agencies are held to the same data protection standards as private data processors. However, the statute provides certain exceptions—for instance, the waiver of the notification requirement if providing notice would impede the state agency's ability to fulfill its legal obligations.[69] These exceptional provisions may permit the deployment of surveillance technologies, including image capture and personal identification systems, in public spaces to enhance public security,[70] even though biometric data is classified as "sensitive personal information" and requires a higher level of protection.[71] As a result, the notion of "public security" is often perceived as a manipulable tool, as governments could broadly interpret this concept to bypass necessary procedures.[72] Consequently, many of the envisioned mechanisms for safeguarding personal data outlined in laws and regulations may not function as effectively in practice.[73] Some critics go as far as to characterize privacy legislation in China as granting the state a near-exclusive authority over the permissible use of personal information, rather than primarily focusing on the protection of individuals' data privacy.[74]

Given that government-collected data typically surpasses private-sector data in both volume and breadth, AI companies that can tap into government-controlled data gain a significant edge in training their language models.[75] A key avenue for private firms to secure such data access is

[66] Interim Measures for Administration of Generative AI Services, *supra* note 20.
[67] *Id.* art. 11.
[68] *Id.* art. 7.
[69] Personal Information Protection Law, *supra* note 55, art. 35.
[70] *Id.* art. 26.
[71] *Id.* art. 28.
[72] Lee Jyh-An & Zhou Peng, *FRT Regulation in China*, *in* The Cambridge Handbook of Facial Recognition in the Modern State 242, 246 (Rita Matulionyte ed., 2024).
[73] *Id.* at 247.
[74] Karman Lucero, *Artificial Intelligence Regulation and China's Future*, 33 Colum. J. Asian L. 94, 142 (2019).
[75] Martin Beraja, David Y. Yang & Noam Yuchtman, *Data-Intensive Innovation and the State: Evidence from AI Firms in China*, 90 Rev. Econ. Stud. 1701, 1701 (2023).

by offering services to governmental entities.[76] In China, prominent technology firms foster cooperative ties with government bodies by engaging in government-driven initiatives, while regulatory oversight and standardization mechanisms empower the government to steer the industry.

Collaboration between public and private sectors manifests across various AI applications, spanning from crime detection to hotel check-ins to hospital registrations. Facial recognition stands out as a prime example among these applications, as the PIPL authorizes Chinese public security agencies to capture facial data through surveillance systems. Subsequently, by partnering with public security units, AI companies can gain access to government surveillance data, leveraging them to enhance and innovate their algorithms.[77]

Empirical evidence underscores the significant impact of government data on commercial AI advancement, highlighting how furnishing government data to AI companies serving state interests has propelled Chinese entities to the forefront of global facial recognition technology.[78] China hosts leading facial recognition enterprises like Megvii and SenseTime, based in Beijing and Hong Kong, respectively. The existence of these technology firms and their success underscore the potential of readily available government data as an innovation catalyst that can drive AI progress within a nation.[79] In contrast, major U.S. technology firms, such as Microsoft, Amazon, and IBM, have refrained from supplying facial recognition solutions to U.S. law enforcement following instances of police misconduct that sparked widespread protests.[80] Such actions may impede the evolution of AI technologies in these spheres, signaling a divergence in approaches between the United States and China regarding the utilization of facial recognition technologies.

Copyright

The intersection of AI and copyright primarily revolves around two aspects: (1) at the input stage, whether the use of copyright-protected

[76] *Id.* at 1702.
[77] *Id.*
[78] *Id.* at 1720.
[79] *Id.* at 1721.
[80] Rebecca Heilweil, *Big Tech Companies Back Away from Selling Facial Recognition to Police. That's Progress*, Vox (June 12, 2020), https://www.vox.com/recode/2020/6/10/21287194/amazon-microsoft-ibm-facial-recognition-moratorium-police; Karen Weise & Natasha Singer, *Amazon Pauses Police Use of Its Facial Recognition Software*, N.Y. Times (June 10, 2020), https://www.nytimes.com/2020/06/10/technology/amazon-facial-recognition-backlash.html.

content in AI training constitutes copyright infringement; and (2) at the output stage, whether AI-generated content is copyrightable.

Using Copyrighted Work as Training Data

Potential copyright infringement may arise during the training phase,[81] with AI developers ordinarily defending their use of other's copyrighted works based on limitations or exceptions in copyright law. If AI developers and users are forced to abandon their projects due to the threat of widespread copyright infringement, this uncertainty could adversely impact the growth of the AI industry. Consequently, the extent to which AI developers face copyright infringement risks will significantly influence the pace of AI development.

In the United States, fair use, the primary form of copyright limitation and exception, requires the determination of four key factors: the purpose and character of the use, the nature of the copyrighted work, the amount and substantiality of the portion used in relation to the whole work, and the effect of the use on the potential market for or value of the copyrighted work.[82] The introduction of the transformative use under the first factor has been pivotal in many fair use cases.[83]

A fair use analysis can yield conclusions on both sides of the debate. Some scholars argue that AI models do not undergo significant enough transformation to qualify as fair use, as many of these models do not produce a creative output that is distinctly different in nature or purpose from the original work.[84] Additionally, the third and fourth factors can present obstacles for AI training to qualify as fair use. Copyright owners may contend that courts should rule in favor of the third factor, as machine learning often involves replicating the entire work.[85] Moreover, given the possibility for copyrighted works used for AI training to represent a lucrative licensing market, which enables copyright owners to generate significant revenues, AI developers

[81] *See, e.g.*, Christina Han, *Parasites or Boosters of Human Creativity?: A Model to Solve Copyright Issues of Training Dataset of Artificial Intelligence Before AlphaArt Defeats Human Artists*, 49 AIPLA Q.J. 281, 296 (2021) (stating that extracting training dataset from scrapped content from the Internet could potentially amount to copyright infringement if the content is copied without authorization).

[82] 17 U.S.C. § 107.

[83] Pierre N. Leval, *Toward a Fair Use Standard*, 103 Harv. L. Rev. 1105, 1111 (1990).

[84] Mark A. Lemley & Bryan Casey, *Fair Learning*, 99 Tex. L. Rev. 743, 764 (2021).

[85] *Id.* at 763–65.

may find it challenging to make a compelling argument concerning the fourth factor.[86]

Conversely, others argue that using copyrighted materials to train generative AI models should be considered fair use due to its transformative nature.[87] Furthermore, although the works in the training data are usually copied in their entirety, such complete copying is merely an intermediate technical step in the analytical process, unrelated to communicating the underlying original expression. As long as this use remains nonexpressive, it will not have a cognizable effect on the potential market for or value of the copyrighted work.[88]

While arguments can be made for both sides, it is indisputable that determining fair use under U.S. law is a highly fact-specific exercise. This inherent legal uncertainty can induce substantial infringement risks, potentially discouraging AI development within the country. In *Andersen v. Stability AI Ltd.*, a group of artists filed a class action lawsuit against several AI companies, including Stability AI, the developer of AI image generator Stable Diffusion. They alleged, inter alia, copyright infringement for the AI's generation of works substantially similar to the artists' composition style.[89] In response to the defendants' motion to dismiss, the court allowed the plaintiffs' copyright infringement claim to go forward even though it dismissed several claims based on breach of contract, unjust enrichment, and the Digital Millennium Copyright Act.[90] Denying the defendants' motion, the court ruled that "whether a fair use defense applies are issues that must be tested on an evidentiary basis."[91]

While all cases regarding the unauthorized utilization of copyrighted works as training data are currently pending in the United States, it is evident that the ability of AI companies to effectively defend such use as fair use will have a crucial impact on their operational expenses and the pace of technological advancement in the AI field moving forward.

86 *Id.* at 765–66.
87 *See, e.g.*, Elizabeth Spica, *Public Interest, the True Soul: Copyright's Fair Use Doctrine and the Use of Copyrighted Works to Train Generative AI Tools*, 33 Tex. Intell. Prop. L.J. 67, 80–87 (2024).
88 Matthew Sag & Peter K. Yu, *The Globalization of Copyright Exceptions for AI Training*, 74 Emory L.J. 1163 (2025).
89 Andersen v. Stability AI Ltd., No. 23-cv-00201-WHO, 2024 WL 3823234, at *1 (N.D. Cal. Aug. 12, 2024).
90 *Id.*
91 *Id.*

The Chinese Copyright Law specifies thirteen distinct limitations and exceptions.[92] To be deemed noninfringing in China, a use must fall into one of the thirteen categories enumerated in Article 24 of the Copyright Law—such as teaching, research, or news reporting. At first glance, this enumerative approach may seemingly disadvantage AI developers seeking to invoke fair use to mitigate liability, as AI does not fall squarely within the specified categories of Article 24. While the exceptions for "private research" and "education and public-school research" might encompass certain uses of training data, both exceptions explicitly exclude commercial exploitation and impose limitations on the scale of use, which AI training is likely to surpass.[93]

Nevertheless, Article 24 includes at the end a catch-all provision, stipulating that "other circumstances provided in laws and administrative regulations" may be exempted from copyright infringement liabilities.[94] This miscellaneous provision has partially shifted the closed-list approach toward an open-ended one in copyright law by providing more flexibility for copyright authorities to decide new copyright limitations and exceptions via administrative rules.[95] Therefore, the copyright authorities may play a pivotal role in fostering the advancement of AI through the expansion of copyright limitations and exceptions.

Such flexibility is not currently the reality in China. In 2023, the Guangzhou Internet Court found an AI company liable for generating images that were substantially similar to the Japanese anime figure Ultraman, owned by Tsuburaya Productions.[96] There was a high likelihood that the AI company used Tsuburaya's Ultraman characters to train its AI model. The case revealed the significant legal risks associated with copyright infringement for AI companies operating in China.

Presently, both U.S. and Chinese AI companies face the risk of copyright infringement arising from the unauthorized use of copyrighted works as

[92] Copyright Law (著作权法) (promulgated by the Standing Comm. Nat'l People's Cong., Sept. 7, 1990, rev'd Nov. 11, 2020, effective Nov. 11, 2020), art. 24 (China).

[93] He Tianxiang, *Copyright Exceptions Reform and AI Data Analysis in China: A Modest Proposal*, *in* Artificial Intelligence and Intellectual Property 196, 205 (Lee Jyh-An, Reto Hilty & Liu Kung-Chung eds., 2021) [hereinafter AI and Intellectual Property].

[94] Copyright Law, *supra* note 92, art. 24(13).

[95] Lee Jyh-An & Li Yangzi, *The Pathway Towards Digital Superpower: Copyright Reform in China*, 70 GRUR Int'l 861, 867 (2021).

[96] Shanghai Xinchuanghua Cultural Dev. Co. v. Guangzhou XX Network Tech. Co. (上海新创华文化发展有限公司诉广州XX网络科技有限公司著作权侵权纠纷案), (2024) Yue 0192 Min Chu No. 113 ((2024)粤0192民初113号) (Guangzhou Internet Ct. Feb. 8, 2024) (China).

training data. However, further clarifications from U.S. and Chinese courts and copyright authorities could mitigate this risk. In essence, these decisions will influence the AI race between the two nations.

Copyrightability of AI-Generated Content

The eligibility of AI-generated works for copyright protection significantly impacts the incentives for AI development.[97] Currently, in most jurisdictions, AI-generated works are not subject to copyright protection due to their lack of human creativity, which is essential for originality—a fundamental requirement for copyright protection.[98] This principle was affirmed in the United States when the U.S. District Court for the District of Columbia—and, later, also the U.S. Court of Appeals for the District of Columbia Circuit—ruled that a work of art created solely by AI, without any human input, could not be copyrighted.[99] This decision upheld the Copyright Office's rejection of an application filed by computer scientist Stephen Thaler for an artwork entitled "A Recent Entrance to Paradise" created by a computer algorithm. In his application, Thaler identified the authorship as "autonomously created by a computer algorithm running on a machine" and claimed copyright himself under the work-made-for-hire doctrine, given his ownership of the computer algorithm.[100]

In rejecting Thaler's claim, the district court reasoned that, under the 1976 Copyright Act, copyright subsists in "original works of authorship fixed in any tangible medium of expression, now known or later developed, from which they can be perceived, reproduced, or otherwise communicated,

[97] *See, e.g.*, Jeremy A. Cubert & Richard G.A. Bone, *The Law of Intellectual Property Created by Artificial Intelligence*, *in* RESEARCH HANDBOOK ON THE LAW OF ARTIFICIAL INTELLIGENCE 411, 425 (Woodrow Barfield & Ugo Pagallo eds., 1st ed. 2018); Jane C. Ginsburg & Luke A. Budiardjo, *Authors and Machines*, 34 BERKELEY TECH. L.J. 343 (2019); Shlomit Yanisky-Ravid & Luis Antonio Velez-Hernandez, *Copyrightability of Artworks Produced by Creative Robots, Driven by Artificial Intelligence Systems and the Originality Requirement: The Formality-Objective Model*, 19 MINN. J.L. SCI. & TECH. 1 (2018).

[98] *See, e.g.*, Lee Jyh-An, *Computer-Generated Works Under the CDPA 1988*, *in* AI AND INTELLECTUAL PROPERTY, *supra* note 93, at 177, 183; Jani Ihalainen, *Computer Creativity: Artificial Intelligence and Copyright*, 13 J. INTELL. PROP. L. & PRAC. 724, 726–27 (2018); Paul Lambert, *Computer-Generated Works and Copyright: Selfies, Traps, Robots, AI and Machine Learning* 39 EUR. INTELL. PROP. REV. 12, 14 (2017); Mark Perry & Thomas Marhoni, *From Music Tracks to Google Maps: Who Owns Computer-Generated Works?* 26 COMPUT. L. SEC. REV 621, 624–25 (2010).

[99] Thaler v. Perlmutter, 687 F. Supp. 3d 140 (D.D.C. Aug. 18, 2023), *aff'd*, 130 F.4th 1039 (D.C. Cir. 2025).

[100] *Id.* at 143.

either directly or with the aid of a machine or device."[101] The statute requires that the work be fixed "by or under the authority of the author."[102] The court pointed out that while the Copyright Act does not explicitly define the term "author," the term's linguistic meaning denotes an originator with the capacity for intellectual, creative, or artistic labor. This originator must be a human being, as "human authorship is a bedrock requirement of copyright."[103] Thus, the court rejected Thaler's claim for copyright.[104]

Notably, the United States Copyright Office has previously denied applications from AI users for creations generated with AI tools.[105] The Office explained that creators using AI text-to-image generators cannot meet the human authorship requirement if the work was produced through a process involving random noise, where the creator did not dictate the specific results.[106] This stance was further affirmed in its "Copyright and Artificial Intelligence" report, which concluded that even an extremely detailed or complex prompt does not confer copyright ownership over an AI-generated output.[107]

Nevertheless, human users can still secure copyright over a compilation of AI-generated works if they infuse it with originality. In February 2025, the United States Copyright Office for the first time granted copyright to an AI-generated image, "A Single Piece of American Cheese."[108] Initially, the copyright registration was rejected, but the decision was subsequently reversed. The Office recognized that the work "contains a sufficient amount of human original authorship in the selection, arrangement, and coordination of the AI-generated material that may be regarded as copyrightable."[109] Notably,

[101] 17 U.S.C. § 102(a).

[102] *Thaler*, 687 F. Supp. 3d at 147.

[103] *Id.* at 146.

[104] *Id.* at 150.

[105] *See, e.g.*, Letter from the Copyright Rev. Bd. to Tamara Pester, Esq., Tamara S. Pester, LLC (Sept. 5, 2023), https://www.copyright.gov/rulings-filings/review-board/docs/Theatre-Dopera-Spatial.pdf [hereinafter Copyright Review Board Letter to Tamara Pester]; Letter from the U.S. Copyright Off. to Van Lindberg, Taylor English Duma LLP (Feb. 21, 2023), https://www.copyright.gov/docs/zarya-of-the-dawn.pdf [hereinafter USCO Letter to Van Lindberg].

[106] Edward Lee, *Prompting Progress: Authorship in the Age of AI*, 76 Fla. L. Rev. 1445, 1454 (2024).

[107] U.S. Copyright Off., Copyright and Artificial Intelligence: Part 2: Copyrightability 18–20 (2025).

[108] Kent Keirsey, *Invoke Secures Copyright in Landmark Ruling for AI-Assisted Artwork*, Invoke Blog (Feb. 10, 2025), https://www.invoke.com/post/invoke-receives-copyright-in-landmark-ruling-for-ai-assisted-artwork.

[109] *How We Received the First Copyright for a Single Image Created Entirely with AI-Generated Material*, Invoke Blog (Feb. 10, 2025), https://44037860.fs1.hubspotusercontent-na1.net/hubfs/44037860/Invoke-First-Copyright-Image-AI-Generated-Material-Report.pdf.

although the initial image was produced by an AI program named Invoke, the user added original expression by repeatedly selecting, modifying, and regenerating parts of the image. This process transformed the initial prompt-based AI-generated outputs into an "original work guided by human creativity," and the user has recorded every step of the transformation.[110] Following this landmark registration, Assistant General Counsel Jalyce Mangum revealed in an April 2025 interview that the Office "has registered more than a thousand works where applicants have followed our guidance to disclose and disclaim AI-generated material."[111] Therefore, this decision from the Copyright Office sends a positive signal to artists across the United States who incorporate AI into their creative processes.

In contrast to the United States, China has adopted a more lenient approach by recognizing the copyrightability of AI-generated works. In *Shenzhen Tencent Computer System Co. v. Shanghai Yingxun Technology Co.*, Tencent successfully argued that human originality was present in the AI-generated work, thereby making it eligible for copyright protection.[112] This case involved a commentary on the stock market composed by AI software developed by Tencent. Unlike the view taken by the *Thaler* court in the United States, the Chinese court in *Tencent* held that human originality could be identified in various phases of the AI software's process of creating the article.[113] The court ruled that, although the AI system took only two minutes to produce the disputed article without any human participation, its automatic operation did not occur in a vacuum. The software was not self-aware; rather, its autonomous operation reflected the developers' personalized selection and arrangement of data types, data formats, the conditions triggering the writing of the article, the templates for article structure, the setting of the corpus, and the training of the intelligent verification algorithm model.[114]

[110] *Id.*

[111] Miriam Lord, *US Copyright Office on AI: Human Creativity Still Matters, Legally*, WIPO Mag. (Apr. 24, 2025), https://www.wipo.int/web/wipo-magazine/articles/us-copyright-office-on-ai-human-creativity-still-matters-legally-73696.

[112] Shenzhen Tencent Comput. Sys. Co. v. Shanghai Yingxun Tech. Co. (深圳腾讯诉上海盈讯著作权侵权案), (2019) Yue 0305 Min Chu No. 14010 ((2019)粤0305民初14010号) (Shenzhen Nanshan Dist. Ct. Dec. 24, 2019) (China).

[113] *Id.*

[114] *Id.*; *see also* Rita Matulionyte & Lee Jyh-An, *Copyright in AI-Generated Works: Lessons from Recent Developments in Patent Law*, 19 SCRIPTed 5, 16–18 (2022) (providing more details of the case).

In another case, *Li v. Liu*, the plaintiff created an image by entering specific prompts into the AI system Stable Diffusion and subsequently shared this image on his social media platform.[115] It later came to the plaintiff's attention that the defendant had utilized this image in her own article on a different social media site without obtaining permission. In assessing the originality of the contested image, the Beijing Internet Court aligned its reasoning with that of the *Tencent* court. The Beijing court noted that "the plaintiff employed prompt words to influence elements of the image such as the character portrayal and its presentation, and adjusted parameters to refine the layout and composition of the image . . . Such modifications and personalization indicate the plaintiff's aesthetic sensibility and individual judgment."[116] Accordingly, the court recognized the originality in the AI-generated image and the plaintiff as the copyright owner.[117]

However, in another case, *Feng v. Zhu*, the Suzhou Intermediate People's Court rejected the plaintiff's copyright claim over images generated by Midjourney, a text-to-image AI application, on the grounds that she failed to provide sufficient evidence of her own creative input during the creation process.[118] The plaintiff herself conceded that it was impossible to reproduce the exact same AI-generated images, even when using identical prompts, due to the inherent randomness in Midjourney's generative process. The court further elaborated that works primarily generated automatically by AI are unlikely to qualify for copyright protection, as it is AI—not the user—that ultimately determines the output. Conversely, if the user employs AI merely as a tool and exercises original intellectual input throughout the creative process, the resulting AI-assisted content may be copyrightable.

The perspectives on originality in AI-generated works vary significantly between the United States and China, a disparity that could potentially influence the competitive dynamics of AI development between these two nations. In this context, several American scholars have criticized the stance taken by the United States Copyright Office and federal courts in relation

[115] Li v. Liu (李某某诉刘某某侵害作品署名权、信息网络传播权纠纷案), (2023) Jing 0491 Min Chu No. 11279 ((2023)京0491民初11279号) (Beijing Internet Ct. Nov. 27, 2023) (China).

[116] *Id.*

[117] *Id.*

[118] Feng v. Zhu (丰某诉朱某等著作权侵权、不正当竞争纠纷案), (2025) Su 05 Min Zhong No. 4840 ((2025)苏05民终4840号) (Suzhou Interm. People's Ct., Apr. 17, 2025) (China) .

to the copyright registration applications in cases such as those involving Stephen Thaler,[119] *Zarya of the Dawn*,[120] Jason Allen,[121] and *Suryast*.[122] They argue that these decisions hinder the advancement of AI technologies, which enable new and more accessible modes of creative production.[123] These critics contend that the stringent criteria for AI originality in the United States may place domestic creators and businesses at a considerable competitive disadvantage.[124] Conversely, Chinese courts have taken proactive steps to encourage AI innovation by recognizing copyright in AI-generated works. Despite the United States Copyright Office's acknowledgment of the originality of human users in the selection, coordination, and arrangement of AI-generated works, the AI-generated content itself remains uncopyrightable under the U.S. perspective. Therefore, it can be reasonably argued that China has created a more conducive environment for the copyright protection of AI-generated works.

Export Restrictions

As the AI race intensifies, a country's policy aims not only to promote the development of its own AI sector but also to hinder that of its competitors. This regulatory approach extends beyond AI algorithms and models to encompass the entire upstream and downstream infrastructure. This strategy is evident in the countries' efforts to dominate control over capital, knowledge, resources, raw materials, and personnel in the relevant fields.

One of the primary battlegrounds between the United States and China centers on semiconductor chips, which are crucial to the AI industry. An AI chip consists of graphics processing units (GPUs), field-programmable gate arrays (FPGAs), and application-specific integrated circuits (ASICs) specialized for AI. As AI advances, general-purpose chips such as central processing units (CPUs) are becoming less favorable, since AI chips are tens or thousands of times faster, more efficient, and more cost-effective than CPUs

[119] *Thaler v. Perlmutter*, 687 F. Supp. 3d 140 (D.D.C. Aug. 18, 2023), *aff'd*, 130 F.4th 1039 (D.C. Cir. 2025).

[120] USCO Letter to Van Lindberg, *supra* note 105.

[121] Copyright Review Board Letter to Tamara Pester, *supra* note 105.

[122] Letter from the Copyright Rev. Bd. to Alex P. Garens, Esq., Day Pitney, LLP (Dec. 11, 2023), https://www.copyright.gov/rulings-filings/review-board/docs/SURYAST.pdf.

[123] Lee, *supra* note 106, at 1517.

[124] *Id.* at 1563–64.

for training AI algorithms.[125] Furthermore, older AI chips with larger, slower, and more energy-consuming transistors incur more costs, which will quickly rise to unaffordable levels, making it virtually impossible to develop cutting-edge AI algorithms without highly advanced AI chips.[126] These challenges led to countries' determination to develop the most advanced AI chips amid the AI war.

Notably, both the United States and China have provided substantial fiscal support to the development of advanced AI and semiconductor chips. According to the National Science and Technology Council's report, U.S. government agencies allocated US$1.8 billion to AI R&D in the fiscal year 2023, with a larger budget of US$1.9 billion requested for the fiscal year 2024.[127] In addition to direct funding for AI firms, subsidies are also provided to upstream manufacturers of semiconductor chips to "bring cutting-edge artificial-intelligence chip development and manufacturing to American soil."[128] This funding was allocated under the CHIPS and Science Act of 2022, which requires recipients to "demonstrate significant worker and community investments" and prohibits them from "build[ing] certain facilities in China and other countries of concern."[129] Recipients of subsidies under this act include domestic chip makers such as Intel and foreign manufacturers like Taiwan Semiconductor Manufacturing Co. (TSMC) and Samsung as an effort to entice them to build factories and bring the most advanced technology to the United States.[130]

In addition, the government has concurrently implemented measures to restrict access to these critical resources for China. Since 2018, the

[125] Saif M. Khan & Alexander Mann, *AI Chips: What They Are and Why They Matter*, Ctr. for Sec. & Emerging Tech. (Apr. 2020), https://cset.georgetown.edu/publication/ai-chips-what-they-are-and-why-they-matter/.

[126] *Id.*

[127] Networking & Info. Tech. R&D Prog. & Nat'l A.I. Initiative Off., Supplement to the President's FY 2024 Budget (2023), https://www.nitrd.gov/pubs/FY2024-NITRD-NAIIO-Supplement.pdf.

[128] Yuka Hayashi, *Eager for Economic Wins, Biden to Announce Billions for Advanced Chips*, Wall St. J. (Jan. 27, 2024), https://www.wsj.com/politics/policy/eager-for-economic-wins-biden-to-announce-billions-for-advanced-chips-7e341e30; Stephen Nellis & Max A. Cherney, *AI Chip Manufacturing Subsidy Leaves US Officials with Tough Choices*, Reuters (Mar. 6, 2024), https://www.reuters.com/world/us/us-officials-face-tough-choices-subsidizing-ai-chip-manufacturing-2024-03-06/.

[129] *FACT SHEET: CHIPS and Science Act Will Lower Costs, Create Jobs, Strengthen Supply Chains, and Counter China*, White House (Aug. 9, 2022), https://www.bidenwhitehouse.archives.gov/briefing-room/statements-releases/2022/08/09/fact-sheet-chips-and-science-act-will-lower-costs-create-jobs-strengthen-supply-chains-and-counter-china/.

[130] Hayashi, *supra* note 128.

U.S. government has employed export controls that impact the AI sector, affecting everything from semiconductor chip production to AI modeling and financial investment. In 2022, the Department of Commerce's Bureau of Industry and Security (BIS) introduced export controls on specific advanced computing chips and semiconductor chip manufacturing equipment, as well as transactions involving supercomputers and certain integrated circuit applications.[131] These restrictions were further expanded in 2023 to include less advanced chips previously not covered by the bans.[132]

This strategic move aligns with the U.S. response to China's ambitious goal to become a global AI leader by 2030. The BIS articulated that these restrictions are designed to safeguard U.S. national security and uphold foreign policy interests, while also emphasizing that U.S. technological supremacy is rooted in both values and innovation.[133] Under these regulations, advanced chips such as Nvidia's A100 and H100 data center chips and their subsequent models tailored for Chinese markets post-2022 ban, the A800 and H800 GPUs, are prohibited from being sold to China.[134] Reports indicate that the Department of Commerce has also mandated foreign firms like TSMC to cease supplying China with seven-nanometer or more advanced chips.[135] These measures are poised to significantly impact major Chinese technology firms, including Tencent, ByteDance, and Alibaba.[136]

Officials have expressed that the objective of these export limitations is to curtail China's access to advanced semiconductor chips, which are pivotal to AI advancements, and sophisticated computing systems crucial for military

[131] *Commerce Implements New Export Controls on Advanced Computing and Semiconductor Manufacturing Items to the People's Republic of China* (PRC), BUREAU OF INDUS. & SEC. (Oct. 7, 2022), https://www.bis.doc.gov/index.php/documents/about-bis/newsroom/press-releases/3158-2022-10-07-bis-press-release-advanced-computing-and-semiconductor-manufacturing-controls-final/file [hereinafter *Commerce Implements New Export Controls*].

[132] *Implementation of Additional Export Controls: Certain Advanced Computing Items; Supercomputer and Semiconductor End Use; Updates and Corrections*, BUREAU OF INDUS. & SEC. (Oct. 16, 2023), https://www.bis.doc.gov/index.php/documents/federal-register-notices-1/3353-2023-10-16-advanced-computing-supercomputing-ifr/file.

[133] *Commerce Implements New Export Controls*, *supra* note 131.

[134] Che Pan & Ann Cao, *How the Latest US Chip Export Controls Exposed China's Weak Link in the Semiconductor Supply Chain*, S. CHINA MORNING POST (Nov. 4, 2023), https://www.scmp.com/tech/tech-war/article/3239803/how-latest-us-chip-export-controls-exposed-chinas-weak-link-semiconductor-supply-chain.

[135] Karen Freifeld & Fanny Potkin, *Exclusive: US Ordered TSMC to Halt Shipments to China of Chips Used in AI Applications*, REUTERS (Nov. 10, 2024), https://www.reuters.com/technology/us-ordered-tsmc-halt-shipments-china-chips-used-ai-applications-source-says-2024-11-10/.

[136] Pan & Cao, *supra* note 134.

applications in China.[137] The regulations were further intensified in April and December 2024, with the December update incorporating twenty-four types of semiconductor chip manufacturing equipment and three types of software tools essential for the development or production of semiconductor chips, thereby bolstering the efficacy of existing controls.[138] Furthermore, international allies such as Japan and the Netherlands have joined the United States in imposing similar controls on semiconductor chip equipment, effectively preventing China from acquiring chip-making technology from alternative sources, including industry giants like ASML, Nikon, and Tokyo Electron.[139]

In the future, the scope of export control will likely be broadened to include downstream AI models.[140] The proposed Enhancing National Frameworks for Overseas Restriction of Critical Exports (ENFORCE) Act, pending approval by both the House of Representatives and the Senate, seeks to amend the Export Control Act of 2018. This amendment would empower the BIS and the White House to require U.S. companies to secure licenses for exporting AI models to China that could threaten U.S. national security.[141]

The U.S. government has also imposed restrictions on domestic companies' investments in foreign chip and AI industries. In August 2023, the Biden administration issued an executive order prohibiting U.S. investments in China's advanced chip and AI sectors.[142] The White House explained that, while the United States generally supports international investment, it must align with national security interests. The administration expressed concerns that certain investments could potentially enhance the development of

[137] Ana Swanson, *U.S. Tightens China's Access to Advanced Chips for Artificial Intelligence*, N.Y. Times (Oct. 17, 2023), https://www.nytimes.com/2023/10/17/business/economy/ai-chips-china-restrictions.html.

[138] *Commerce Strengthens Export Controls to Restrict China's Capability to Produce Advanced Semiconductors for Military Applications*, Bureau of Indus. & Sec. (Dec. 2, 2024), https://www.bis.gov/press-release/commerce-strengthens-export-controls-restrict-chinas-capability-produce-advanced-semiconductors-military; *see also* Liu Jingwen & Lee Jyh-An, *Strategic Stalemates: The Paradox of Export Controls in the U.S.-China AI Race*, 35 J. Transnat'l L. & Pol'y (forthcoming 2026).

[139] Tim Kelly & Miho Uranaka, *Japan Restricts Chipmaking Equipment Exports as It Aligns with US China Curbs*, Reuters (Mar. 31, 2023), https://www.reuters.com/technology/japan-restrict-chipmaking-equipment-exports-aligning-it-with-us-china-curbs-2023-03-31/.

[140] Enhancing National Frameworks for Overseas Restriction of Critical Exports Act (ENFORCE Act), H.R. 8315, 118th Cong. (2024).

[141] Tobias Mann, *Lawmakers Advance Bill to Tighten White House Grip on AI Model Exports*, Register (May 23, 2024), https://www.theregister.com/2024/05/23/us_lawmakers_advance_bill_to.

[142] Exec. Order No. 14105, 88 Fed. Reg. 54867 (Aug. 9, 2023).

sensitive technologies in nations that might use them to undermine U.S. and allied capabilities.[143] Consequently, foreign investment in China's semiconductor sector plummeted to US$600 million in 2023, marking its lowest level since 2020.[144]

In response to the escalating export controls imposed by the United States, particularly concerning semiconductor chips, China has implemented retaliatory measures that include restricting exports of essential raw materials for semiconductor chip production and substantially financing its domestic chipmaker. In July 2023, the Chinese Ministry of Commerce announced export controls on critical rare earth materials such as gallium and germanium.[145] In October 2023, China tightened existing export restrictions on graphite by applying more stringent standards.[146] A similar ban on antimony and superhard materials was introduced in August 2024.[147] Four months later, China further strengthened these restrictions, just a day after the United States announced its latest comprehensive export controls.[148] Unlike previous measures, which the Ministry stated did not target any specific country or region,[149] this latest action was explicitly retaliatory against the United States. According to the U.S. Geological Survey, China accounts for 98 percent of the world's gallium production and supplied more than half of the U.S. germanium imports from 2019 to 2022.[150] These raw materials are

[143] *Id.*

[144] The market decline occurred even before the policy's promulgation in August, right after its announcement. Che Chang & John Liu, *"De-Americanize": How China Is Remaking Its Chip Business*, N.Y. Times (May 11, 2023), https://www.nytimes.com/2023/05/11/technology/china-us-chip-controls.html.

[145] Notice on Implementing Export Control on Gallium- and Germanium-Related Substance (关于对镓、锗相关物项实施出口管制的公告), Notice of the Gen. Admin. of Customs No. 3 [2023] (issued by the General Admin. of Customs of the Ministry of Com., July 3, 2023, effective Aug. 1, 2023) (China).

[146] Notice on Improving and Adjusting the Provisional Export Control Measures on Graphite (关于优化调整石墨物项临时出口管制措施的公告), Notice of the Gen. Admin. of Customs No. 39 [2023] (promulgated by the Gen. Admin. of Customs of the Ministry of Com., Oct. 20, 2023, effective Dec. 1, 2023) (China).

[147] Notice on Implementing Export Control on Antimony and Other Related Substance (关于对锑等相关物项实施出口管制的公告), Notice of the Gen. Admin. of Customs No. 33 [2024] (promulgated by the Gen. Admin. of Customs of the Ministry of Com., Aug. 15, 2024, effective Sept. 15, 2024) (China).

[148] Notice on Strengthening Export Control of Dual-Use Substance to the United States (关于加强相关两用物质对美国出口管制的公告), Notice of the Gen. Admin. of Customs No. 46 [2024] (promulgated by the Gen, Admin. of Customs of the Ministry of Com., Dec. 3, 2024, effective Dec. 3, 2024) (China).

[149] *Press Conference of the Spokesperson of the Ministry of Commerce on the Export Control Policy for Antimony and Other Related Substance* (商务部新闻发言人就锑等物项出口管制政策应询答记者问), Ministry of Com. (Aug. 15, 2024).

[150] U.S. Dep't of the Interior, U.S. Geological Surv., Mineral Commodities Summary 2024, at 75, 80 (2024), https://pubs.usgs.gov/periodicals/mcs2024/mcs2024.pdf.

essential to the manufacture of high-frequency computer chips, electronic vehicle batteries, and national defense systems.

In response to China's export control, the U.S. Department of Defense acknowledges that, while there may be short-term consequences, the government is actively enhancing domestic mining operations and diversifying supply chains.[151] Potential alternative sources include resource-rich nations such as Australia and Canada, although the cost of materials from these countries is anticipated to rise.[152] Despite these challenges, in recognition of the risks associated with excessive dependence on foreign critical minerals, President Trump signed an executive order in April 2025 amid the ongoing tariff war, directing the Secretary of Commerce to initiate a Section 232 investigation and make relevant recommendations. Industry observers suggest that these export restrictions imposed by China may ultimately encourage U.S. lawmakers to augment investments in critical minerals.[153]

In addition to implementing retaliatory export controls, the Chinese government has been actively cultivating its domestic chipmaking industry. In 2014, the State Council issued the Guidelines on Promoting National Integrated Circuit Development, leading to the creation of the China Integrated Circuit Industry Investment Fund, commonly known as "the Big Fund." This initiative aimed to bolster integrated circuit manufacturing within the nation, drawing initial investments from several of the largest state-owned enterprises in the communications and finance sectors. Notable beneficiaries have included leading domestic chipmakers such as Semiconductor Manufacturing International Corporation (SMIC), a state-owned entity, and Hua Hong, a key supplier to Huawei. In May 2024, the Big Fund entered its third phase, amassing a registered capital of RMB 344 billion (approximately US$47.09 billion), with all six major commercial banks participating as investors.[154] This state-backed fund has compensated

[151] Idrees Ali, Phil Stewart, Valerie Insinna & Rami Ayyub, *Pentagon Has Strategic Germanium Stockpile but No Gallium Reserves*, REUTERS (July 6, 2023), https://www.reuters.com/markets/commodities/pentagon-has-strategic-germanium-stockpile-no-gallium-reserves-2023-07-06/.

[152] Annabelle Liang & Nick Marsh, *Gallium and Germanium: What China's New Move in Microchip War Means for World*, BBC (Aug. 2, 2023), https://www.bbc.com/news/business-66118831; Ayeshea Perera, *Why China Curbing Rare Earth Exports Is a Blow to the US*, BBC (Apr. 15, 2025), https://www.bbc.com/news/articles/c1drqeev36qo.

[153] Ali et al., *supra* note 151.

[154] *With 344 Billion Yuan Registered Capital, Here Comes Phase Three of the Big Fund! Or It May Invest in These Key Projects* (注册资本3440亿，国家大基金三期来了！或将投资这些重点项目), CCTV.COM (May 28, 2024), https://finance.cctv.com/2024/05/28/ARTIhM6N831KrZyhRYMQziH8240528.shtml.

for the withdrawal of foreign capital. In 2023, China surpassed the United States in investment into semiconductor startups by a significant margin.[155] Highlighting this progress, Huawei, in August 2023, introduced its Mate 60 Pro, which features a seven-nanometer processor from SMIC, developed amidst stringent U.S. export controls. With this fresh influx of capital, SMIC is now fervently advancing its R&D toward more sophisticated five-nanometer chips, positioning itself just one generation behind the forefront of three-nanometer technology.[156]

Commentators have pointed out that China's substantial investment in semiconductor R&D may place the United States in a challenging predicament. While easing export controls could grant China access to state-of-the-art chips, maintaining these restrictions could unintentionally motivate China's technological advancements.[157] This scenario is exemplified by the launch of DeepSeek, which claims to achieve results comparable to leading U.S. models with significantly higher efficiency and lower costs. This development has sparked debate over the resource-heavy training methods employed by American AI firms like OpenAI, contributing to a staggering US$1 trillion decline in U.S. technology stocks. Meanwhile, there are suspicions that DeepSeek might have circumvented stringent U.S. export controls by using intermediaries in Singapore to acquire advanced Nvidia chips for training its model, prompting an investigation by the U.S. Department of Commerce.[158] Both Nvidia and Singapore's Ministry of Trade and Industry have refuted these allegations.[159]

As the AI race intensifies, the foreign trade policies of both countries increasingly target each other, leading to unpredictable outcomes. The most likely consequence is that these external constraints will decelerate AI development in both nations. However, such mutual exclusion might also compel each country toward greater self-reliance. For instance, U.S. export

[155] Jacob Robbins, *China Outpaces US in Backing Chip Startups*, PitchBook (Jan. 25, 2024), https://pitchbook.com/news/articles/china-semiconductors-startups-vc.

[156] Liu Qianer, *China on Cusp of Next-Generation Chip Production Despite US Curbs*, Fin. Times (Feb. 6, 2024), https://www.ft.com/content/b5e0dba3-689f-4d0e-88f6-673ff4452977.

[157] Ariel Cohen, *China's Massive Barrage in the Chip Battle*, Forbes (May 31, 2024), https://www.forbes.com/sites/arielcohen/2024/05/31/chinas-massive-barrage-in-the-chip-battle/.

[158] Karen Freifeld, *US Looking into Whether DeepSeek Used Restricted AI Chips, Source Says*, Reuters (Feb. 1, 2025), https://www.reuters.com/technology/us-looking-into-whether-deepseek-used-restricted-ai-chips-source-says-2025-01-31/.

[159] *Press Statement on Whether DeepSeek Gained Access to US Export-Controlled Chips Through Intermediaries in Singapore*, Ministry of Trade & Indus. Sing. (Feb. 1, 2025), https://www.mti.gov.sg/Newsroom/Press-Releases/2025/02/Press-Statement-on-whether-DeepSeek-gained-access-to-US-export-controlled-chips.

controls on semiconductor chips have catalyzed the advancement of China's domestic chipmaking, while Chinese export controls on raw materials have stimulated U.S. investments in critical minerals. Ultimately, whether these export restrictions will foster or hinder AI innovation in the long run remains an open question.

Conclusion

The legal framework for fostering technological innovation and economic growth presents a complex challenge. This chapter delves into a comparative analysis of the legal infrastructures in the United States and China, assessing their impacts on the AI competition between these two countries, particularly through the lenses of data privacy, copyright, and export restrictions.

In the realm of data privacy, Chinese companies collaborating with government agencies for surveillance purposes may benefit from unparalleled access to vast amounts of personal data. This access facilitates the training of their AI models, providing a significant competitive edge. In contrast, privacy reforms in the United States could potentially restrict similar data access for American AI firms, impacting their model training capabilities.

Regarding copyright issues, while the United States Copyright Office has recently acknowledged the copyrightability of human compilations of AI-generated contents, China has adopted a more favorable stance toward AI innovation. Unlike the United States, where courts and the Copyright Office have declined to grant copyright protection to AI-generated works, Chinese courts have recognized the intellectual contributions of programmers who develop algorithms and users who configure prompts. This progressive approach grants copyright protection to AI-generated works, potentially accelerating AI innovation in China.

Lastly, the United States has implemented export restrictions targeting China's semiconductor industry, aiming to block access to advanced semiconductor chips and thus impede China's AI development. The long-term effects of these restrictions on China's technological progress in semiconductor chip technologies remain uncertain. This strategic move highlights the intense rivalry and strategic maneuvering prevalent in the global AI race.

Overall, the legal, financial, and institutional landscapes in the United States and China reflect a distinct ideological divergence between the two countries. China's model of public-guided private investment offers notable benefits in terms of capital deployment, infrastructure development, and strategic development. In contrast, the United States boasts a more fluid capital market and a more agile commercialization mechanism, which together foster AI entrepreneurship. Additionally, the United States continues to hold an edge in attracting global AI talents. However, increasing restrictive policies within the United States[160] are gradually eroding these advantages. Ultimately, this geopolitical rift is likely to impede the critical goal of fostering inclusive innovation in the AI sector.

Acknowledgments

This study was made possible by the Direct Research Grant (Project No. 4059076) at the Chinese University of Hong Kong Faculty of Law.

[160] An increasing number of restrictive measures are being introduced, spanning from exportation to investment to overseas students. Anniek Bao, *U.S. Blacklists over 50 Chinese Companies in Bid to Curb Beijing's AI, Chip Capabilities*, CNBC (Mar. 26, 2025), https://www.cnbc.com/2025/03/26/us-blacklists-50-chinese-companies-in-bid-to-curb-beijings-ai-chip-capabilities.html; Fu Ting, *Republican Legislation Seeks to Ban Chinese Nationals from Studying in the US*, AP NEWS (Mar. 15, 2025), https://apnews.com/article/chinese-student-republican-visa-ban-946e613a8dace3b0092580fa6fe4e50b.

15

Bridging the Global Artificial Intelligence Divide

Peter K. Yu

Introduction

In the past few years, policymakers, commentators, and the mass media have paid growing attention to the intersection of intellectual property and artificial intelligence (AI). Noted challenges at this intersection include the eligibility of AI-generated creations for intellectual property protection, the unauthorized use of protected works and inventions to train AI models, and the deployment of AI to support the examination, protection, enforcement, or licensing of intellectual property rights.[1] Although the ongoing debate seems to capture well the complicated law and policy questions involved, it has been frequently overlooked that these questions and their answers focus primarily on developed and large emerging countries,[2] as opposed to the Global South.[3]

[1] For the author's discussion of these issues, see Peter K. Yu, *Artificial Intelligence, Autonomous Creation, and the Future Path of Copyright Law*, 50 BYU L. Rev. 753 (2025); Peter K. Yu, *Artificial Intelligence, the Law–Machine Interface, and Fair Use Automation*, 72 Ala. L. Rev. 187 (2020); Peter K. Yu, *Can Algorithms Promote Fair Use?*, 14 FIU L. Rev. 329 (2020); Peter K. Yu, *The Law–Machine Interface and the Changing Interplay Between Artificial Intelligence and the Law*, *in* Research Handbook on the Law of Artificial Intelligence: Current and Future Directions 194 (Woodrow Barfield & Ugo Pagallo eds., 2d ed. 2025).

[2] Chinmayi Arun, *AI and the Global South: Designing for Other Worlds*, *in* The Oxford Handbook of Ethics of AI 589 (Markus D. Dubber, Frank Pasquale & Sunit Das eds., 2020); Peter K. Yu, *Artificial Intelligence, Intellectual Property, and Sustainable Development*, *in* Intellectual Property, Ethical Innovation and Sustainability: Towards a New Social Contract for the Digital Economy? (Christophe Geiger ed., forthcoming 2026).

[3] To highlight the AI divide as an inequitable gap between the haves and have-nots, this chapter uses the term "Global South," notwithstanding its much-criticized negative connotations. At times, the chapter uses this term interchangeably with "developing countries," another problematic term. Where the level of economic development is relevant or sufficiently distinct, the chapter mentions high-, middle-, and low-income countries. While all labels face inherent linguistic and rhetorical challenges, it is worth noting that some intergovernmental bodies and commentators have used alternative terms, such as the "majority world" or the "Global Majority." *See, e.g.*, U.N. Sec'y-Gen.'s

Peter K. Yu, *Bridging the Global Artificial Intelligence Divide* In: *Inclusive Innovation in the Age of AI and Big Data*. Edited by: Daryl Lim and Peter K. Yu, Oxford University Press.
DOI: 10.1093/9780197799444.003.0020

In the developing world, AI-related technological challenges tend to be drastically different, even though some of these challenges are also present in the Global North. Even when the challenges are identical, the legal, policy, institutional, and technological responses to these challenges may be quite different in developing countries. As Chinmayi Arun reminds us, individuals in these countries harbor very different concerns about AI-driven products and technologies than those in the developed world:

> [T]hey may be thinking of web-based AI designed by people who live in worlds that rarely see power cuts or internet shutdowns and then deployed to the rural hinterlands of countries with poor internet connectivity and only a few hours of electricity a day. They may worry about the resources diverted from education and healthcare budgets to technology-centric solutions from the companies that are building these systems. They may be concerned about the surveillance of Southern children through AI for Education, built by people whose own children go to private school and have restricted access to screens. In authoritarian countries, they may lose sleep over AI that uses facial recognition, drones, and other forms of surveillance to oppress vulnerable populations. They may worry about the loss of jobs and the impact on economies as AI replaces low-skilled workers.[4]

Moreover, because many AI-driven products and technologies used in the Global South are created in the Global North,[5] these products and technologies may be "design[ed] in a manner that is at best an uneasy fit, and at worst amplifies existing systemic harm and oppression to horrifying proportions."[6] While AI has presented unique challenges in the Global South, these challenges go beyond AI technology to cover other areas, such as training data. As World Bank President David Malpass reminds us in *World Development Report 2021*, "the perspective of lower-income countries

High-Level Advisory Body on A.I. [UN Advisory Body], *Governing AI for Humanity: Interim Report* 5 (Dec. 2023); Shahidul Alam, *Majority World: Challenging the West's Rhetoric of Democracy*, 34 AMERASIA J. 88 (2008).

[4] Arun, *supra* note 2, at 591.

[5] Ralph Hamann, *Developing Countries Need to Wake Up to the Risks of New Technologies*, CONVERSATION (Jan. 4, 2018), https://theconversation.com/developing-countries-need-to-wake-up-to-the-risks-of-new-technologies-87213.

[6] Arun, *supra* note 2, at 591.

has so far been largely absent from th[e] global debates [on data governance] and urgently needs to be heard."[7]

In the debate on global AI law and policy, one area that deserves greater scrutiny and intervention is what commentators have described as the "AI divide,"[8] the "algorithmic divide,"[9] or the "new digital divide."[10] Although there are distinctions between these terms, they collectively refer to the proverbial "gap between those who have access to, or proficiency in, algorithmically enhanced or AI-driven technological products and services and those who do not."[11] Without successful efforts tackling this inequitable gap, those on the less inclusive side of the AI divide are unlikely to be able to fully realize the promise of machine learning and AI, including generative AI and other latest AI-powered technologies.

This chapter explores the different policy options available to developing countries to boost local AI adoption and development and, in turn, to bridge the global AI divide. Through these options, countries will be able to maximize the benefits provided by AI technology while increasing their participation in AI-driven innovation. At the global level, active participation in AI development, on both the production and consumption ends, will make the innovation environment more inclusive, thereby fostering the development of globally inclusive AI.

This chapter begins by outlining the challenges confronting AI development in the Global South. It then identifies six policy options that developing countries could embrace to boost local AI adoption and development: (1) intellectual property reforms, (2) international technology transfer obligations, (3) the Global Fund for AI, (4) AI resource pools, (5) open innovation and datasets, and (6) indigenous innovation. This chapter concludes by offering

[7] David R. Malpass, *Foreword* to WORLD BANK, WORLD DEVELOPMENT REPORT 2021: DATA FOR BETTER LIVES, at xi, xi (2021).

[8] U.N. CONF. ON TRADE & DEV. [UNCTAD], TECHNOLOGY AND INNOVATION REPORT 2025: INCLUSIVE ARTIFICIAL INTELLIGENCE FOR DEVELOPMENT 21–23 (2025); UN Advisory Body, *Governing AI for Humanity: Final Report* 14 (Sept. 2024).

[9] Peter K. Yu, *The Algorithmic Divide and Equality in the Age of Artificial Intelligence*, 72 FLA. L. REV. 331 (2020) [hereinafter Yu, *Algorithmic Divide*]; Peter K. Yu, *The Algorithmic Divide in China and an Emerging Comparative Research Agenda*, *in* AUTOMATING GOVERNANCE IN CHINA? DATA-DRIVEN SYSTEMS IN THE SCORING SOCIETY 211 (Yu Haiqing & Rogier Creemers eds., 2025) [hereinafter Yu, *Research Agenda*].

[10] Cosette Jarrett, *AI Could Be Driving a New Digital Divide*, VENTUREBEAT (Oct. 5, 2017), https://venturebeat.com/2017/10/05/ai-could-be-driving-a-new-digital-divide/; Anjana Susarla, *The New Digital Divide Is Between People Who Opt Out of Algorithms and People Who Don't*, CONVERSATION (Apr. 17, 2019), https://theconversation.com/the-new-digital-divide-is-between-people-who-opt-out-of-algorithms-and-people-who-dont-114719.

[11] Yu, *Research Agenda*, *supra* note 9, at 211.

three key takeaways from the discussion of national, regional, and international efforts to bridge the global AI divide.

Challenges

The Global South faces many challenges in the AI arena. The overarching challenge is a lack of economic resources, which will impact the developing countries' ability to obtain AI-relevant resources, such as computing power and technological infrastructure, human talents, and training data.[12] The United Nations Conference on Trade and Development (UNCTAD) has referred to these three types of resources collectively as the "[t]hree critical leverage points for AI adoption and development."[13] Although this overarching challenge covers a wide array of resources, this section identifies the challenge up front to highlight its tendency to go beyond the three leverage points mentioned above to impact the overall enabling environment for AI adoption and development in the Global South.

Developing AI technology is very costly. As the Institute for Human-Centered Artificial Intelligence at Stanford University observes in *Artificial Intelligence Index Report 2025*:

> While AI companies rarely disclose exact figures, costs are widely estimated to reach into the millions of dollars—and continue to rise. OpenAI CEO Sam Altman, for instance, indicated that training GPT-4 exceeded $100 million. In July 2024, Anthropic CEO Dario Amodei noted that model training runs costing around $1 billion were already underway. Even more recent models, such as DeepSeek-V3, reportedly cost less—about $6 million—but overall, training remains extremely expensive.[14]

To be sure, the arrival of DeepSeek (and other low- or lower-cost foundation models) has suggested cost savings through the use of open-source or open-weight AI models and the potential for increased efficiency in AI training (using processes different from those currently deployed by Google, Meta, OpenAI, and other dominant AI firms). Nevertheless, it is still doubtful that

[12] UN Advisory Body, *supra* note 8, at 16.
[13] UNCTAD, *supra* note 8, at 79.
[14] STANFORD UNIV., INST. FOR HUMAN-CENTERED A.I., ARTIFICIAL INTELLIGENCE INDEX REPORT 2025, at 65 (2025).

low-income and lower-middle-income countries[15] will have ready access to the economic resources needed to develop capital-intensive AI foundation models. To complicate matters further, many low-income countries are still struggling to "meet basic needs, such as the provision of clean drinking water, food, shelter, electricity, schools and basic health care."[16] Developing AI training models is simply not a priority for many countries in the Global South.

The next three types of challenges are more granular and AI-specific. The first AI-specific challenge pertains to computational power, or what AI experts have called "compute." As the UN Secretary-General's High-Level Advisory Body on Artificial Intelligence (UN Advisory Body) declares in its final report: "Of the top 100 high-performance computing clusters in the world capable of training large AI models, none is hosted in a developing country. There is only one African country among the top 300. Two countries account for half of the world's hyperscale data centres."[17] Likewise, UNCTAD observes: "Most developing countries have limited capacities in AI hardware and infrastructure, which hinder their adoption and development of AI."[18]

The linguistically awkward term "compute," in general, is defined broadly to cover various types of technological resources used to develop AI, including "digital connectivity and computing power, and the associated networks, architecture and resources necessary to create, train and use AI solutions."[19] To promote AI development, firms and governments will need to devote considerable resources to "storage, network connectivity, security and backup systems."[20] Apart from a lack of compute, many developing countries lack reliable access to critical energy supply needed to support high volumes of computation, including electricity and water (important for cooling down computing equipment).[21]

[15] Based on the World Bank, low-income and lower-middle-income countries have a gross national income per capita of less than US$4,495 (calculated using the World Bank Atlas method). *World Bank Country and Lending Groups*, World Bank, https://datahelpdesk.worldbank.org/knowledgebase/articles/906519-world-bank-country-and-lending-groups (last visited May 24, 2025).

[16] Peter K. Yu, *Enforcement, Economics and Estimates*, 2 WIPO J. 1, 2 (2010).

[17] UN Advisory Body, *supra* note 8, at 62.

[18] UNCTAD, *supra* note 8, at 21.

[19] *Id.* at 79.

[20] *Id.* at 16.

[21] UN Advisory Body, *supra* note 8, at 61.

The second AI-specific challenge relates to human talents. The lack of human capital in the high-tech area remains a common problem for developing countries, not to mention that "[e]xperts from the Global South are often invisible at global conferences on AI."[22] As the UN Advisory Body observes: "[N]ot every society needs cadres of computer scientists for building their own models. However, whether technology is bought, borrowed or built, a baseline socio-technical capacity is needed to understand the capabilities and limitations of AI, and harness AI-enabled use cases appropriately while addressing context specific risks."[23] To a large extent, the lack of human capital to promote AI development recalls the widely documented brain drain problem in developing countries.[24] While many locals from these countries do not return home after studying AI development abroad, foreign AI firms also actively recruit local talents away, offering them more remunerative positions, better working conditions, and more promising careers. Even when these local talents choose to stay behind, many of them may be using "their skills [to] benefit the development of technology outside their home countries," thus creating what commentators have termed "virtual brain drain."[25]

The third AI-specific challenge involves training data. Successful AI technology requires the presence of large volumes of high-quality, diverse data.[26] Yet many developing countries lack adequate training data—about themselves and other parts of the world.[27] To the extent that training data have to be licensed from intellectual property rights holders—a current and contentious law and policy debate at both the national and international levels[28]—those data will become costly and, therefore, unaffordable to firms and governments in the Global South. Even if these firms and governments manage to obtain open or donated datasets, they may not have the data representative of, and meaningful to, local users. In the healthcare area, for example, "around half of the leading data sets can be traced to a

[22] UN Advisory Body, *supra* note 3, at 20.
[23] UN Advisory Body, *supra* note 8, at 14.
[24] U.N. Off. of the Sec'y-Gen.'s Envoy on Tech. [ODET] & Int'l Lab. Org., Mind the AI Divide: Shaping a Global Perspective on the Future of Work 13 (2024).
[25] *Id.* at 13–14.
[26] Daryl Lim & Peter K. Yu, *The Antitrust–Copyright Interface in the Age of Generative Artificial Intelligence*, 74 Emory L.J. 847, 862–64 (2025).
[27] UN Advisory Body, *supra* note 8, at 14; Yu, *Algorithmic Divide*, *supra* note 9, at 359–61.
[28] U.S. Copyright Off., Copyright and Artificial Intelligence: Part 3: Generative AI Training (2025); Matthew Sag & Peter K. Yu, *The Globalization of Copyright Exceptions for AI Training*, 74 Emory L.J. 1163, 1212–22 (2025); Martin Senftleben, *Generative AI and Author Remuneration*, 54 Int'l Rev. Intell. Prop. & Competition L. 1535 (2023).

dozen organizations, with one in Europe, one in Asia and the rest in North America."[29]

Finally, AI development has sparked some indirect and less frequently mentioned challenges in the Global South. Although the limited scope of this chapter does not allow for a more in-depth discussion of these challenges, it will be helpful to identify two distinct indirect challenges: ecological damage and lack of correction mechanisms. Ecological damage should come as no surprise to scholars writing about cutting-edge technology, such as cloud computing, big data analytics, and crypto currency. As Kate Crawford observes in the AI context:

> Minerals are the backbone of AI, but its lifeblood is still electrical energy. Advanced computation is rarely considered in terms of carbon footprints, fossil fuels, and pollution; metaphors like "the cloud" imply something floating and delicate, within a natural, green industry. Servers are hidden in nondescript data centers, and their polluting qualities are far less visible than the billowing smokestacks of coal-fired power stations. The tech sector heavily publicizes its environmental policies, sustainability initiatives, and plans to address climate-related problems using AI as a problem-solving tool. It is all part of a highly produced public image of a sustainable tech industry with no carbon emissions. In reality, it takes a gargantuan amount of energy to run the computational infrastructures of Amazon Web Services or Microsoft's Azure, and the carbon footprint of the AI systems that run on those platforms is growing.[30]

Likewise, the UN Inter-Agency Working Group on Artificial Intelligence, co-led by the United Nations Educational, Scientific and Cultural Organization (UNESCO) and the International Telecommunication Union, laments the "gap in global accountability regarding the overall carbon footprint of the AI value chain."[31]

The second indirect challenge concerns the developing countries' inability to provide quick legal and policy responses to address new technological challenges. The challenges posed by AI are no exception. The

[29] UN Advisory Body, *supra* note 8, at 62.

[30] KATE CRAWFORD, ATLAS OF AI: POWER, POLITICS, AND THE PLANETARY COSTS OF ARTIFICIAL INTELLIGENCE 41 (2022).

[31] U.N. Inter-Agency Working Grp. on A.I., *United Nations System White Paper on AI Governance: An Analysis of the UN System's Institutional Models, Functions, and Existing International Normative Frameworks Applicable to AI Governance* 8 (Apr. 16, 2024).

widely documented problems in this area include algorithmic bias and resulting injustice, inadequate protection of personal data, and widespread job displacement.[32] Because many developing countries fail to introduce the needed safeguards or correction mechanisms, they will struggle to integrate into the new AI-driven technological environment.[33] Even worse, the lack of these mechanisms could pose significant risks to the international community, leading the UN Advisory Body to call for the creation of "capabilities . . . at a global level to monitor, report, and rapidly respond to systemic vulnerabilities and disruptions to international stability."[34]

In sum, developing countries face a wide array of challenges impeding local AI adoption and development—both direct and indirect. If these countries are to succeed in bridging the global AI divide, they will need to devise solutions to tackle these challenges. They should also do so quickly before they fall too far behind the Global North in AI development.

Six Policy Options

Garnering wide public attention since the mid-1990s, the digital divide refers to the proverbial gap between those who have access to the Internet, information technology, and digital content from those who do not.[35] In the age of AI and big data, this divide logically extends to "access to, or proficiency in, algorithmically enhanced or AI-driven technological products and services."[36] As the UN Advisory Body declares in its final report:

> Left ungoverned, . . . AI's opportunities may not manifest or be distributed equitably. Widening digital divides could limit the benefits of AI to a handful of States, companies and individuals. Missed uses—failing to

[32] Kate Crawford & Jason Schultz, *Big Data and Due Process: Toward a Framework to Redress Predictive Privacy Harms*, 55 B.C. L. REV. 93 (2014); Yu, *Algorithmic Divide*, *supra* note 9, at 354–59, 364.

[33] Although the development of these safeguards and correction mechanisms lies outside the scope of this chapter, intergovernmental bodies, nongovernmental organizations, policymakers, commentators, and consumer advocates have provided many helpful proposals and recommendations. Yu, *Algorithmic Divide*, *supra* note 9, at 368–82. See also Daryl Lim's and Keith Robinson's chapters in this volume.

[34] UN Advisory Body, *supra* note 3, at 20–21.

[35] Peter K. Yu, *Bridging the Digital Divide: Equality in the Information Age*, 20 CARDOZO ARTS & ENT. L.J. 1, 2 (2002).

[36] Yu, *Research Agenda*, *supra* note 9, at 211.

> take advantage of and share AI-related benefits because of lack of trust or missing enablers such as capacity gaps and ineffective governance—could limit the opportunity envelope.[37]

In its interim report, this UN body also warns: "There is a real danger, even if humanity harnesses only the positive aspects of AI, that those will be limited to a club of the rich."[38]

In 2024, the UN General Assembly adopted two resolutions expressing the UN members' resolve to bridge "the artificial intelligence and other digital divides between and within countries."[39] In its "Recommendation on the Ethics of Artificial Intelligence," UNESCO also states:

> [D]igital and knowledge divides within and between countries need to be addressed throughout an AI system life cycle, including in terms of access and quality of access to technology and data, in accordance with relevant national, regional and international legal frameworks, as well as in terms of connectivity, knowledge and skills and meaningful participation of the affected communities, such that every person is treated equitably.[40]

The statements made by these various UN bodies recall Target 9.C of the UN Sustainable Development Goals (SDGs), which underscores the need for efforts to "[s]ignificantly increase access to information and communications technology and strive to provide universal and affordable access to the Internet in least developed countries by 2020."[41] Although efforts to advance these SDGs have been around for a decade now, the goal of providing universal and affordable access to the Internet in least developed countries has yet to be realized.[42] In the age of AI and big data, Target 9.C should be logically expanded to cover access to different types of AI technology, at least those that will affect one's ability to function in today's AI-driven world.

[37] UN Advisory Body, *supra* note 8, at 7.
[38] UN Advisory Body, *supra* note 3, at 2.
[39] G.A. Res. 78/265, Seizing the Opportunities of Safe, Secure and Trustworthy Artificial Intelligence Systems for Sustainable Development, ¶ 1 (Mar. 21, 2024); G.A. Res. 78/311, Enhancing International Cooperation on Capacity-Building of Artificial Intelligence, ¶ 1 (July 1, 2024).
[40] U.N. Educ., Sci. & Cultural Org. [UNESCO], *Recommendation on the Ethics of Artificial Intelligence*, ¶ 30 (Nov. 23, 2021).
[41] G.A. Res. 70/1, Transforming Our World: The 2030 Agenda for Sustainable Development, at 21 (Sept. 25, 2015).
[42] UN Advisory Body, *supra* note 3, at 8.

Such an AI-oriented upgrade is consistent with the positions taken by international intergovernmental bodies in the past few years. For instance, the Global Digital Compact, which was adopted at the UN Summit of the Future in September 2024, recognized the "commit[ment] to advance equitable and inclusive approaches to harnessing artificial intelligence benefits and mitigating risks in full respect of international law."[43] In its report on Artificial Intelligence for Sustainable Development, UNESCO declares: "To prevent the replication or exacerbation of inequities and divides, it will be key to define access to the internet and AI technologies as twenty-first-century fundamental human rights."[44] In the education context, Special Rapporteur on the Right to Education Farida Shaheed writes: "Closing digital divides in education entails not only addressing access, including Internet connectivity and device availability, but also instructional design and how students use AI tools."[45]

To help bridge the global AI divide, this section identifies six policy options developing countries could embrace to boost local AI adoption and development and, in turn, to bridge the global AI divide. Because these options are intended to be both nonexhaustive and complementary, policymakers and commentators are encouraged to use them—alone or in combination—while also searching for new alternatives.

Intellectual Property Reforms

The close interrelationship between AI and intellectual property makes it logical to explore how to harness the intellectual property system to bridge the global AI divide. For example, developing countries could introduce robust copyright exceptions to support AI training. It does not matter whether these exceptions take the form of an open-ended regime (such as fair use in Israel and the United States) or a closed regime governed by carefully stipulated copyright exceptions (similar to those found in Japan, the European Union, Singapore, and the United Kingdom).[46]

[43] G.A. Res. 79/1 annex, Global Digital Compact, ¶ 52 (Sept. 22, 2024).

[44] UNESCO, Artificial Intelligence for Sustainable Development: Synthesis Report 26 (2019).

[45] Special Rapporteur on the Right to Education (Farida Shaheed), *Right to Education*, U.N. Doc. A/79/520, ¶ 82 (Oct. 16, 2024).

[46] Sag & Yu, *supra* note 28, at 1177–92.

As Matthew Sag and I observe in a recent work, countries around the world, especially those in the Global North, are eager to facilitate the use of copyrighted works to train AI models.[47] Their eagerness has resulted in an emerging international equilibrium for establishing copyright exceptions for AI training. It remains to be seen whether developing countries feel comfortable following their counterparts in the developed world to introduce AI-friendly exceptions. These exceptions are important to the Global South, as they will lower training and transaction costs, reduce uncertainty in the innovation environment, and provide freedom of operation in the AI space.

While the study Professor Sag and I conducted focuses on copyright law developments, its findings regarding the developed countries' eagerness to introduce exceptions to support AI development can be extended to other areas of intellectual property rights, including patents and trade secrets. Drawing lessons from this study, developing countries should adopt exceptions for AI development in different bodies of intellectual property law. They could introduce new exceptions, expand existing ones, or formulate tailored exceptions to cover specific areas, such as education[48] and public health.[49] To reduce barriers to AI development, they should also carefully review the existing scope of intellectual property rights, including the protection of trade secrets (which has become increasingly important in the AI context).[50] In addition, for technologies essential to AI development, developing countries could embrace FRAND licensing—licensing on "fair, reasonable, and non-discriminatory" terms—similar to what is already widely used in the context of standards-essential patents.[51]

Finally, developing countries could consider licensing arrangements that suit their weaker economic and technological conditions, including the use of compulsory or statutory licenses.[52] Provided by major

[47] *Id.* at 1223.

[48] Peter K. Yu, *Rethinking Education Theft Through the Lens of Intellectual Property and Human Rights*, 123 Colum. L. Rev. 1449, 1465–66 (2023).

[49] Peter K. Yu, *Deferring Intellectual Property Rights in Pandemic Times*, 74 Hastings L.J. 489, 496–99 (2023); Peter K. Yu, *The International Enclosure Movement*, 82 Ind. L.J. 827, 864–65 (2007).

[50] See Keith Robinson's chapter in this volume.

[51] On FRAND licensing, see Jorge L. Contreras, *A Market Reliance Theory for FRAND Commitments and Other Patent Pledges*, 2015 Utah L. Rev. 479; Thomas F. Cotter, *Comparative Law and Economics of Standard-Essential Patents and FRAND Royalties*, 22 Tex. Intell. Prop. L.J. 311 (2014); Jay P. Kesan & Carol M. Hayes, *FRAND's Forever: Standards, Patent Transfers, and Licensing Commitments*, 89 Ind. L.J. 231 (2014); Srividhya Ragavan, Brendan Murphy & Raj Davé, *FRAND v. Compulsory Licensing: The Lesser of the Two Evils*, 14 Duke L. & Tech. Rev. 83 (2015).

[52] Some commentators, especially those in continental Europe, have distinguished between compulsory and statutory licenses by noting that the former "refer[s] to a particular species of mandatory

international intellectual property agreements, these licenses enable countries to use protected creations and inventions at a reduced, and often significantly reduced, rate. In the copyright area, an oft-cited—though at times criticized—internationally accepted arrangement is the issuance of compulsory licenses by qualified developing countries under the appendix to the Berne Convention for the Protection of Literary and Artistic Works.[53] In the patent area, an equally widely accepted arrangement is the issuance of compulsory licenses to patented products and technologies under Articles 31 and 31*bis* of the Agreement on Trade-Related Aspects of Intellectual Property Rights (TRIPS Agreement).[54] Along with limitations and exceptions in intellectual property law, the availability of compulsory or statutory licenses will help developing countries devise tailored solutions to boost local AI development.[55]

International Technology Transfer Obligations

Relating to intellectual property law and policy are the international obligations concerning transfer of technology, usually from the Global

license under which the payment is subject to negotiation, rather than established *a priori*." John T. Cross & Peter K. Yu, *The Copyright Holdout Problem and New Internet-Based Services*, *in* REMUNERATION OF COPYRIGHT OWNERS: REGULATORY CHALLENGES OF NEW BUSINESS MODELS 241, 249 (Liu Kung-Chung & Reto M. Hilty eds., 2017).

[53] On the Berne Appendix, see INTERNATIONAL COPYRIGHT AND NEIGHBORING RIGHTS: THE BERNE CONVENTION AND BEYOND 960–63 (Sam Ricketson & Jane C. Ginsburg, 2d ed. 2005); Peter K. Yu, *A Tale of Two Development Agendas*, 35 OHIO N.U. L. REV. 465, 481–84 (2009); Ruth L. Okediji, *The International Copyright System: Limitations, Exceptions and Public Interest Considerations for Developing Countries* (UNCTAD–ICTSD Project on IPRs and Sustainable Development, Issue Paper No. 15, 2006).

[54] Agreement on Trade-Related Aspects of Intellectual Property Rights arts. 31 and 31*bis*, Apr. 15, 1994, Marrakesh Agreement Establishing the World Trade Organization, Annex 1C, 1869 U.N.T.S. 299 [hereinafter TRIPS Agreement]. For the author's discussion of Article 31*bis*, see Peter K. Yu, *The International Enclosure Movement*, 82 IND. L.J. 827 (2007).

[55] Although policymakers and commentators have expressed concerns about how issuing compulsory licenses could reduce incentives to develop new technologies, these licenses tend to focus on foreign technologies needed by developing countries, because they are either unaffordable or inaccessible (even if affordable). Whether the issuance of these licenses would reduce foreign direct investment is likely to depend on many other location factors beyond intellectual property protection. Keith E. Maskus, *The Role of Intellectual Property Rights in Encouraging Foreign Direct Investment and Technology Transfer*, 9 DUKE J. COMPAR. & INT'L L. 109, 130–31 (1998); Carlos A. Primo Braga & Carsten Fink, *The Relationship Between Intellectual Property Rights and Foreign Direct Investment*, 9 DUKE J. COMPAR. & INT'L L. 163, 164 (1998); Peter K. Yu, *Intellectual Property, Economic Development, and the China Puzzle*, *in* INTELLECTUAL PROPERTY, TRADE AND DEVELOPMENT: STRATEGIES TO OPTIMIZE ECONOMIC DEVELOPMENT IN A TRIPS-PLUS ERA 173, 176–180 (Daniel J. Gervais ed., 1st ed. 2007).

North to the Global South but more recently also from large emerging countries[56]—such as from China to the Global South.[57] Article 66.2 of the TRIPS Agreement requires developed country members of the World Trade Organization to "provide incentives to enterprises and institutions in their territories for the purpose of promoting and encouraging technology transfer to least-developed country Members in order to enable them to create a sound and viable technological base."[58] Paragraph 11.2 of the Ministerial Decision on Implementation-Related Issues and Concerns confirmed that "the provisions of Article 66.2 of the TRIPS Agreement are mandatory."[59]

While the provisions in the TRIPS Agreement provide oft-cited examples, similar technology transfer obligations have been introduced in other contexts. For instance, the Conference of the Parties to the United Nations Framework Convention on Climate Change established the Technology Mechanism at its sixteenth session in Cancún, Mexico in 2010.[60] Serving as the implementation body of this mechanism and hosted at the UN Environmental Programme, the Climate Technology Centre and Network "accelerates the development and transfer of technologies through three services": (1) "[p]roviding technical assistance at the request of developing countries on technology issues"; (2) "[c]reating access to information and knowledge on climate technologies"; and (3) "[f]ostering collaboration among climate technology stakeholders via its network of regional and sectoral experts."[61] Likewise, at the World Health Organization (WHO), both the Pandemic Influenza Preparedness Framework for the Sharing of Influenza Viruses and Access to Vaccines and Other Benefits[62] and the newly

[56] For the author's discussion of intellectual property developments in the BRICS countries (Brazil, Russia, India, China, and South Africa) or other emerging countries, see Peter K. Yu, *Access to Medicines, BRICS Alliances, and Collective Action*, 34 AM. J.L. & MED. 345 (2008); Peter K. Yu, *Intellectual Property Negotiations, the BRICS Factor and the Changing North–South Debate*, *in* THE BRICS-LAWYERS' GUIDE TO GLOBAL COOPERATION 148 (Rostam J. Neuwirth, Alexandr Svetlicinii & Denis De Castro Halis eds., 2017); Peter K. Yu, *The Middle Intellectual Property Powers*, *in* LAW AND DEVELOPMENT OF MIDDLE-INCOME COUNTRIES: AVOIDING THE MIDDLE-INCOME TRAP 84 (Randall Peerenboom & Tom Ginsburg eds., 2014) [hereinafter Yu, *Middle Intellectual Property Powers*].

[57] Peter K. Yu, *Building Intellectual Property Infrastructure Along China's Belt and Road*, 14 U. PA. ASIAN L. REV. 275, 316–21 (2019).

[58] TRIPS Agreement, *supra* note 54, art. 66.2.

[59] World Trade Organization, *Implementation-Related Issues and Concerns: Decision of 14 November 2001*, ¶ 11.2, WTO Doc. WT/MIN(01)/17 (Nov. 20, 2001).

[60] *Technology Mechanism*, U.N. FRAMEWORK CONVENTION ON CLIMATE CHANGE, https://unfccc.int/ttclear/support/technology-mechanism.html (last visited July 11, 2025).

[61] *Id.*

[62] WORLD HEALTH ORG., PANDEMIC INFLUENZA PREPAREDNESS FRAMEWORK FOR THE SHARING OF INFLUENZA VIRUSES AND ACCESS TO VACCINES AND OTHER BENEFITS ¶ 6.13 (2d ed. 2021).

adopted WHO Pandemic Agreement contain provisions supporting technology transfer in the public health arena.[63]

To the extent that countries find ineffective the technology transfer obligations in existing multilateral, regional, and plurilateral agreements, they should actively strengthen these obligations through renegotiations. Working in tandem with intergovernmental bodies, developing countries may also establish technology transfer hubs to boost AI development in the Global South. Examples in the non-AI areas include the hub established by the WHO's mRNA Vaccine Technology Transfer Programme in Cape Town, South Africa[64] and the Technology Mechanism implemented by the Climate Technology Centre and Network mentioned above.[65]

Notwithstanding the strong theoretical appeal of international technology transfer obligations, putting them in practice has been historically challenging.[66] Thus far, the international community has not been able to achieve consensus on the specificities of these obligations, including what technologies are to be covered.[67] In addition, because of the enormous technological disparities between the Global North and the Global South, the latter have a tough time articulating concrete demands for technology transfer (beyond the usual general requests).[68] To the extent that developing countries consider technology transfer key to AI development, they should explore strategies to formulate concrete requests for technology transfer both as a general matter and more specifically in the AI context. Creating these

[63] World Health Assembly Res. WHA78.1, WHO Pandemic Agreement, art. 11 (May 20, 2025).

[64] *The mRNA Vaccine Technology Transfer Programme*, WORLD HEALTH ORG., https://www.who.int/initiatives/mrna-technology-transfer-(mrna-tt)-programme (last visited July 11, 2025); Sven J.R. Bostyn, *Access to Drugs, Patents, and Pandemic Crisis: A Tale of (Non-)inclusivity*, *in* RESEARCH HANDBOOK ON INTELLECTUAL PROPERTY RIGHTS AND INCLUSIVITY 266, 295–98 (Cristiana Sappa ed., 2024) [hereinafter IPRs AND INCLUSIVITY].

[65] UNCTAD, *supra* note 8, at 163.

[66] On the challenges of facilitating technology transfer at the international level, including through the development of the International Code of Conduct on the Transfer of Technology, see MICHAEL BLAKENEY, LEGAL ASPECTS OF THE TRANSFER OF TECHNOLOGY TO DEVELOPING COUNTRIES (1989); INTERNATIONAL TECHNOLOGY TRANSFER: THE ORIGINS AND AFTERMATH OF THE UNITED NATIONS NEGOTIATIONS ON A DRAFT CODE OF CONDUCT (Surendra J. Patel, Pedro Roffe & Abdulqawi Yusuf eds., 2001); SUSAN K. SELL, POWER AND IDEAS: NORTH–SOUTH POLITICS OF INTELLECTUAL PROPERTY AND ANTITRUST 79–106 (1998); Yu, *supra* note 53, at 493–505; Peter K. Yu, *International Technology Contracts, Restrictive Covenants and the UNCTAD Code*, *in* EMPLOYEES, TRADE SECRETS AND RESTRICTIVE COVENANTS 41 (Christopher Heath & Anselm Kamperman Sanders eds., 2017); Padmashree Gehl Sampath & Pedro Roffe, *Unpacking the International Technology Transfer Debate: Fifty Years and Beyond* (ICTSD Programme on Innovation, Tech. & Intell. Prop., Issue Paper No. 36, 2012).

[67] Peter K. Yu, *The U.S.-China Forced Technology Transfer Dispute*, 52 SETON HALL L. REV. 1003, 1038 (2022).

[68] *Id.*

strategies is particularly important considering that much of the technical assistance provided to developing countries thus far has focused primarily on the protection of intellectual property rights, as opposed to the different available options for strengthening indigenous innovation.[69]

Global Fund for AI

In its final report, the UN Advisory Body calls for the establishment of a "global fund for AI."[70] This fund aims to "address the underlying capacity and collaboration gaps for those unable to access requisite [AI] enablers," which includes compute, human talents, and training data (the "[t]hree critical leverage points for AI adoption and development" mentioned above).[71] In advancing the proposal, the UN body took note of the fact that developing countries need support in different areas of AI development. Instead of specifying which specific enablers the fund would support, the report aims to "put a floor under the AI divide for those unable to secure needed enablers via other means."[72]

While it is urgent and important to develop a funding mechanism to boost AI adoption and development in the Global South, past international intergovernmental efforts to develop similar funding mechanisms remain disappointing. A case in point is the Digital Solidarity Fund, which was proposed as an international voluntary fund to help bridge the global digital divide during the Geneva phase of the World Summit on Information Society in 2003.[73] Established eventually at the Tunis phase in 2005, that fund was dissolved after slightly more than three years.[74] Despite this failure, some international funding mechanisms have been quite successful. Listed among

[69] On technical assistance, see Duncan Matthews & Viviana Munoz-Tellez, *Bilateral Technical Assistance and TRIPS: The United States, Japan and the European Communities in Comparative Perspective*, 9 J. World Intell. Prop. 629 (2006); Christopher May, *Capacity Building and the (Re)production of Intellectual Property Rights*, 25 Third World Q. 821 (2004).

[70] UN Advisory Body, *supra* note 8, at 16–17.

[71] *Id.* at 16; UNCTAD, *supra* note 8, at 79.

[72] UN Advisory Body, *supra* note 8, at 14.

[73] World Summit on the Information Society, Dec. 10–12, 2003, Declaration of Principles, ¶ 61, U.N. Doc. WSIS-03/GENEVA/DOC/4-E (Dec. 12, 2003); World Summit on the Information Society, Nov. 16–18, 2005, Tunis Agenda for the Information Society, ¶ 28, U.N. Doc. WSIS-05/TUNIS/DOC/6(Rev. 1)-E (Nov. 18, 2005).

[74] *The Status of the Global Digital Solidarity Fund (DSF)*, S. Ctr., https://www.southcentre.int/wp-content/uploads/2017/09/Ev_170925_SC-Workshop-on-E-Commerce-and-Domestic-Regulation_Presentation-The-Status-of-the-Global-Digital-Fund-David-Kapya-and-Lameck-Jaston.pdf (last visited June 21, 2025).

the UN Advisory Body's recommendations are the European Organization for Nuclear Research (CERN), Gavi, the Vaccine Alliance, the Global Fund (to Fight AIDS, Tuberculosis and Malaria), and the Complex Risk Analytics Fund.[75] It remains to be seen whether the new UN proposal for the Global Fund for AI will achieve greater success than the earlier effort to create an international voluntary fund to bridge the global digital divide.

AI Resource Pools

Resource pools are effective vehicles for aggregating the funds, knowledge, technology, and other resources needed to boost AI adoption and development in the Global South. As the UN Advisory Body observes, "detailed strategies should be outlined to pool global resources together to build capacity, catalyse collective action towards equitable sharing of opportunities and close the digital divide."[76] Given the different types of resources needed to support AI adoption and development, developing countries should actively establish resource pools. These pools could be modeled after the Medicines Patent Pool (MPP) or the COVID-19 Technology Access Pool (C-TAP). Other potential models mentioned in the UN Advisory Body's interim report include CERN, the European Molecular Biology Laboratory, and the International Thermonuclear Experimental Reactor.[77]

Established in 2010 as a spinoff from UNITAID (a global health initiative financed by levies on plane tickets), the MPP aimed to "increase access to quality, appropriate, affordable medicines for people living with HIV in developing countries."[78] Functioning more as a clearing house than a traditional patent pool,[79] the MPP has since expanded its coverage to other types of medicines, including COVID-19 vaccines. During the pandemic, Costa Rica submitted a proposal to the WHO to establish what eventually became C-TAP.[80] Building on the MPP, this technology access pool "provides a single global platform for the developers of COVID-19 therapeutics,

[75] UN Advisory Body, *supra* note 8, at 67; UN Advisory Body, *supra* note 3, at 9.
[76] UN Advisory Body, *supra* note 8, at 63.
[77] UN Advisory Body, *supra* note 3, at 9, 20.
[78] Peter K. Yu, *Virotech Patents, Viropiracy, and Viral Sovereignty*, 45 Ariz. St. L.J. 1563, 1602 (2013).
[79] Jorge L. Contreras, *The Open COVID Pledge: Design, Implementation and Preliminary Assessment of an Intellectual Property Commons*, 2021 Utah L. Rev. 833, 853.
[80] Peter K. Yu, *Modalities, Challenges, and Possibilities: An Introduction to the Pharmaceutical Innovation Symposium*, 7 Tex. A&M J. Prop. L. 1, 32–34 (2021).

diagnostics, vaccines and other health products to share their intellectual property, knowledge, and data with quality-assured manufacturers through public health-driven, transparent, voluntary, non-exclusive and transparent licences."[81] Unfortunately, even though the MPP has been quite successful, C-TAP has not achieved the success many intergovernmental bodies, policymakers, and commentators hoped that it would have.[82]

Apart from these international initiatives, commentators, in the past two decades, have proposed the use of pooled procurement to improve access to essential medicines in developing countries. A notable proposal was advanced by Frederick Abbott and Jerome Reichman, who called for establishing pooled procurement strategies and regional pharmaceutical supply centers.[83] As they explained:

> [A] group of developing countries interested in price regulation of pharmaceuticals could harmonize and coordinate their policies in this regard. With or without price regulation, a pooled procurement strategy would provide incentives to the originator pharmaceutical companies themselves to become "low bidders" under supply contracts offered by a centralized procurement authority.[84]

During the COVID-19 pandemic, Professors Abbott and Reichman updated their proposal to include the development of licensing facilities and joint manufacturing arrangements at the regional and plurilateral levels.[85]

Although most of the abovementioned examples aim to promote public health, resource pools can be developed easily in the AI context. For example, governments and intergovernmental bodies can utilize open licenses, pledges,[86] or other commons-based arrangements to establish AI resource pools. In addition to resources in the Global South, such pools can solicit

[81] *WHO COVID-19 Technology Access Pool*, World Health Org., https://www.who.int/initiatives/covid-19-technology-access-pool (last visited July 11, 2025).

[82] Bostyn, *supra* note 64, at 276.

[83] Frederick M. Abbott & Jerome H. Reichman, *The Doha Round's Public Health Legacy: Strategies for the Production and Diffusion of Patented Medicines Under the Amended TRIPS Provisions*, 10 J. Int'l Econ. L. 921, 973–77 (2007).

[84] *Id.* at 973.

[85] Frederick M. Abbott & Jerome H. Reichman, *Facilitating Access to Cross-Border Supplies of Patented Pharmaceuticals: The Case of the COVID-19 Pandemic*, 23 J. Int'l Econ. L. 535, 543–50 (2020).

[86] On pledges, see Patent Pledges: Global Perspectives on Patent Law's Private Ordering Frontier (Jorge L. Contreras & Meredith Jacob eds., 2017); Jorge L. Contreras, *Patent Pledges*, 47 Ariz. St. L.J. 543 (2015); Contreras, *supra* note 79.

contributions from the Global North, intergovernmental bodies, and donor organizations. Whether at the regional or global level, greater cooperation will expedite and strengthen the development of resource pools.

Recognizing this potential, the UN General Assembly adopted a resolution on "Enhancing International Cooperation on Capacity-Building of Artificial Intelligence."[87] The UN Advisory Body also "recommend[ed] the creation of an AI capacity development network to link up a set of collaborating, United Nations–affiliated capacity development centres making available expertise, compute and AI training data to key actors."[88] Building such a network is important because it will "ensure that all nations benefit from the latest advancements, bridging the gap between developed and developing countries by providing equal access to critical AI knowledge."[89] Increased multinational research-and-development collaborations may also "lead to significant advancements in AI technologies, benefiting all participating countries and driving global progress in the field."[90]

Open Innovation and Datasets

Open innovation is highly beneficial, especially in areas such as education and public health.[91] As Henry Chesbrough reminds us: "Opening up mobilizes knowledge from many different places, causing our learning to advance and our progress against the disease to accelerate. Openness unleashes a volunteer army of researchers, working in their own facilities, across different time zones, and different countries."[92] Promoting open innovation

[87] G.A. Res. 78/311, *supra* note 39.

[88] UN Advisory Body, *supra* note 8, at 15.

[89] ODET & INT'L LAB. ORG., *supra* note 24, at 18.

[90] *Id.*

[91] On open innovation, including in the pharmaceutical context, see HENRY CHESBROUGH, OPEN INNOVATION: THE NEW IMPERATIVE FOR CREATING AND PROFITING FROM TECHNOLOGY (2003); GENE PATENTS AND COLLABORATIVE LICENSING MODELS: PATENT POOLS, CLEARINGHOUSES, OPEN SOURCE MODELS AND LIABILITY REGIMES 169–244 (Geertrui Van Overwalle ed., 2009); Dasgupta Partha & Paul A. David, *Toward a New Economics of Science*, 23 RSCH. POL'Y 487 (1994); Amy Kapczynski, *Order Without Intellectual Property Law: Open Science in Influenza*, 102 CORNELL L. REV. 1539 (2017); Amy Kapczynski, Samantha Chaifetz, Zachary Katz & Yochai Benkler, *Addressing Global Health Inequities: An Open Licensing Approach for University Innovations*, 20 BERKELEY TECH. L.J. 1031 (2005); Krishna Ravi Srinivas, *Open Source Drug Discovery: A Revolutionary Paradigm or a Utopian Model?*, *in* INCENTIVES FOR GLOBAL PUBLIC HEALTH: PATENT LAW AND ACCESS TO ESSENTIAL MEDICINES 263 (Thomas Pogge, Matthew Rimmer & Kim Rubenstein eds., 2010).

[92] Henry Chesbrough, *To Recover Faster from Covid-19, Open Up: Managerial Implications from an Open Innovation Perspective*, 88 INDUS. MKTG. MGMT. 410, 410 (2020).

makes good policy sense considering the substantial funding governments, intergovernmental bodies, and donor organizations have already provided to research and development.[93]

During the COVID-19 pandemic, intergovernmental bodies, nongovernmental organizations, commentators, and public health activists advocated the use of open innovation to develop vaccines, therapeutic treatments, diagnostic kits, medical devices, and other health technologies.[94] For instance, WHO Director General Tedros Ghebreyesus asked "all countries, companies and research institutions to support open data, open science and open collaboration so that all people can enjoy the benefits of science and research."[95] In addition, government agencies, private firms, and not-for-profit organizations proactively launched open licensing initiatives to facilitate domestic and international cooperation.[96] An international coalition of legal experts, scientists, and technologists also released the Open COVID Pledge, which "calls on organizations around the world to make their patents and copyrights freely available in the fight against the COVID-19 pandemic."[97]

Inspiring these wide-ranging open innovation initiatives is the longstanding use of free and open source software,[98] which dates back more than half a century and pioneered today's open innovation movement.[99] To the Global South, this type of software provides several important benefits:

> [Free and open source software] provides users with the ability to experiment with software development at no cost. It gives them freedom to modify the program code to suit local needs. It also helps develop "a learning environment," in which technology is transferred through "a massive apprentice-teacher network." Through participation in free and open source software communities, users not only learn computer and

[93] Pedro Roffe with Christoph Spennemann & Johanna von Braun, *From Paris to Doha: The WTO Doha Declaration on the TRIPS Agreement and Public Health*, *in* NEGOTIATING HEALTH: INTELLECTUAL PROPERTY AND ACCESS TO MEDICINES 9, 13 (Pedro Roffe, Geoff Tansey & David Vivas-Eugui eds., 2006); Yu, *supra* note 54, at 837.

[94] Yu, *supra* note 80, at 23–25.

[95] *WHO Director-General's Opening Remarks at the Media Briefing on COVID-19—6 April 2020*, WORLD HEALTH ORG. (Apr. 6, 2020), https://www.who.int/dg/speeches/detail/who-director-general-s-opening-remarks-at-the-media-briefing-on-covid-19---6-april-2020.

[96] Yu, *supra* note 80, at 25.

[97] *About Us*, OPEN COVID PLEDGE, https://opencovidpledge.org/about/ (last visited July 24, 2025).

[98] STEVEN WEBER, THE SUCCESS OF OPEN SOURCE (2004).

[99] On insights provided by the pioneers in the open source movement, see OPEN SOURCES: VOICES FROM THE OPEN SOURCE REVOLUTION (Chris DiBona, Sam Ockman & Mark Stone eds., 1999).

programming skills, but also teamwork, team management, and coordination as well as copyright and licensing.[100]

In addition, the use of free and open source software has been praised for its ability to "democratiz[e] knowledge and resources, enabl[e] global collaboration and innovation and improv[e] transparency and trust."[101]

Like free and open source software, software using open or semi-open licenses, such as Creative Commons, can be highly beneficial to the Global South. To a large extent, introducing these licensing arrangements and other common-based production platforms would "foster a more inclusive approach to innovation by opening the innovation process to participation by members of the public at large and enabling any member of the public to share in the benefits of the innovation output."[102]

In the AI context, open innovation will be particularly important. As the UN Advisory Body declares, "[a] set of shared resources—including open models—is needed to support inclusive and effective participation by all Member States in the AI ecosystem."[103] Nevertheless, it reminds us that, when evaluating or implementing the different open innovation models, "it is important to recognize that openness in AI systems is more of a spectrum than a single attribute," with varying degrees of public access to data, code, model weights, and other resources needed for AI development.[104] It is also worth noting that this spectrum of options comes with different trade-offs, such as those between transparency and innovation on the one hand and control and safety on the other.[105]

As far as AI development is concerned, open innovation will be needed beyond the development of models and algorithms.[106] As noted above, AI firms will need large volumes of high-quality, diverse data. Given the limited resources in developing countries, the wide availability of open datasets in these countries will be key to AI development, whether the data are from the real world or artificially generated. Noted examples of open datasets

[100] Peter K. Yu, *The Trust and Distrust of Intellectual Property Rights*, 18 Revue quebecoise de droit Int'l 107, 122 (2005).
[101] UNCTAD, *supra* note 8, at 162.
[102] Sunimal Mendis, *Re-thinking Intellectual Property Law's Promise of Democratic Inclusion*, *in* IPRs and Inclusivity, *supra* note 64, at 10, 28.
[103] UN Advisory Body, *supra* note 8, at 14.
[104] *Id.* at 50.
[105] *Id.* at 50–51. See also Daryl Lim's chapter in this volume.
[106] UNCTAD, *supra* note 8, at 161–62; UN Advisory Body, *supra* note 3, at 8.

include the Human Genome Project, the COVID-19 Open Research Data Set, the Human Connectome Project, as well as the growing volume of data the private sector has made available in recent years.[107] Some UN bodies and the World Bank have also advocated for the development of data commons, open data policies, or a "digital public infrastructure for AI."[108]

Greater use of open data "can facilitate the training and testing of AI models and foster innovation by allowing researchers and developers to experiment with data and create new AI solutions."[109] Such use can also "allow a wide set of researchers to approach otherwise impossible or prohibitively expensive research questions."[110] In addition, the use of open data can "improve transparency and facilitate the assessment of new AI models and applications."[111] It is, therefore, no surprise that the UN Advisory Body lays down in its interim report the guiding principle that "AI governance should be built in step with data governance and the promotion of data commons."[112]

Indigenous Innovation

Thus far, the five options discussed in this chapter have called for either weaker intellectual property protection or the development of alternative innovation models—practices not commonly found in the Global North. Nevertheless, developing countries do have options that align more closely with the intellectual property and innovation policies in developed countries. After all, the appropriate level of protection and the preferred mode of innovation vary from country to country. The available choices often depend on the specific needs, interests, conditions, and priorities of the relevant country.

While many developing countries undoubtedly will benefit from greater use of limitations and exceptions in intellectual property law, such as those for AI training or development, other countries will need economic incentives provided by traditional intellectual property rights.[113] Thus, the

[107] UNCTAD, *supra* note 8, at 161.

[108] *Id.* at 158–61; UN Advisory Body, *supra* note 3, at 16; WORLD BANK, *supra* note 7, at 201–02.

[109] UNCTAD, *supra* note 8, at 161.

[110] U.S. AGENCY FOR INT'L DEV. & U.S. DEP'T OF STATE, GLOBAL AI RESEARCH AGENDA 16 (2024).

[111] UNCTAD, *supra* note 8, at 161.

[112] UN Advisory Body, *supra* note 3, at 16.

[113] Rochelle Cooper Dreyfuss, *Human Rights in a Technological Age: The Right to Participate in Science*, 55 N.Y.U. J. INT'L L. & POL. 581, 610–11 (2023); Ruth L. Okediji, *Does Intellectual Property Need Human Rights?*, 51 N.Y.U. J. INT'L L. & POL. 1, 58 (2018).

key to formulating satisfactory policies to boost AI adoption and development in developing countries is to enable these countries to determine for themselves based on local conditions.

To maximize self-determination and informed decision-making, individuals, firms, and government agencies in developing countries will need a higher level of algorithmic and AI literacy.[114] Such literacy will not only enable these actors to use a greater variety of AI technology, including off-the-shelf AI models and technology,[115] but it will also help them make better and more informed decisions. Although AI literacy is often mentioned alongside technical skills, it also covers ethical considerations,[116] such as "how to properly use [AI] systems in developing countries" and what safeguards, correction mechanisms, or other complementary measures these countries should introduce.[117]

As mentioned above, it will be cost-prohibitive for many developing countries to develop AI foundation models. Nevertheless, these countries could create customized offerings to promote indigenous AI development,[118] including through "context specific tuning of [AI] models."[119] Such offerings could facilitate the production of products or services that have a strong global appeal and high export potential. After all, there have already been some good examples of how researchers in developing and emerging countries can take advantage of cost-prohibitive technological models created in the Global North, such as Google Earth.[120]

Because technological needs vary from country to country, and because AI technology created in the Global North do not always meet the needs of the Global South, indigenous innovation can come in handy when developing countries need to play catch-up with their more developed counterparts. Even if AI technology imported from abroad is affordable—which is rarely the case—such technology may bring along problems such as

[114] Yu, *Algorithmic Divide*, *supra* note 9, at 362–65.

[115] As Justin Lin reminds us, "th[e] possibility of using off-the-shelf technology and entering existing industries is what has allowed some of the newly industrialized East Asian economies to sustain annual GDP growth rates of 8 percent, and even 10 percent, for several decades." JUSTIN YIFU LIN, THE QUEST FOR PROSPERITY: HOW DEVELOPING ECONOMIES CAN TAKE OFF 113–14 (2015).

[116] Special Rapporteur on the Right to Education, *supra* note 45, ¶¶ 103–08.

[117] ODET & INT'L LAB. ORG., *supra* note 24, at 14.

[118] UNCTAD, *supra* note 8, at 22; Yu, *supra* note 2.

[119] UN Advisory Body, *supra* note 3, at 20.

[120] Dylan Weyer, Joana Carlos Bezerra & Alta De Vos, *Participatory Mapping in a Developing Country Context: Lessons from South Africa*, 8 LAND, no. 134 (2019), https://doaj.org/article/a3a8343e6dbd46348be0f490b019c8a5.

biases, discrimination, a propensity to confabulate (or hallucinate), a lack of protection for personal data, and inadequate cybersecurity protection.

Moreover, one should not ignore what Alexander Gerschenkron, Justin Lin, and other commentators have referred to as the "advantage of backwardness."[121] As I elaborated in an earlier work: "The important takeaway from this seemingly paradoxical concept is that countries do not need to progress in a linear fashion or a locked-step manner to play economic and technological catch-up. Given the right conditions and support, countries could easily leapfrog from underdevelopment and backwardness to economic strength and technological proficiency."[122] As far as leapfrogging is concerned, a boost to indigenous innovation may be the best way to ensure the development of customized, context-specific AI technology that will benefit local communities.

Three Key Takeaways

After identifying six policy options available for developing countries to boost local AI adoption and development, this chapter turns to three key takeaways that can be drawn from the discussion of these options as well as other related national, regional, and international initiatives.

Inclusive Innovation

The global AI divide affects inclusive innovation on both the production and consumption ends, impacting large swarths of the world's population.[123] On the production end, this inequitable gap makes it difficult for individuals, firms, and governments to take advantage of the technological advances

[121] ALEXANDER GERSCHENKRON, ECONOMIC BACKWARDNESS IN HISTORICAL PERSPECTIVE 169 (1962); LIN, *supra* note 115, at 143.

[122] Yu, *Middle Intellectual Property Powers*, *supra* note 56, at 104–05.

[123] On inclusive innovation, see HANDBOOK OF INCLUSIVE INNOVATION: THE ROLE OF ORGANIZATIONS, MARKETS AND COMMUNITIES IN SOCIAL INNOVATION (Gerard George, Ted Baker, Paul Tracey & Havovi Joshi eds., 2020) [hereinafter HANDBOOK OF INCLUSIVE INNOVATION]; ROBYN KLINGLER-VIDRA, ALEX GLENNIE & COURTNEY SAVIE LAWRENCE, INCLUSIVE INNOVATION (2022); NEW MODELS OF INCLUSIVE INNOVATION FOR DEVELOPMENT (Richard Heeks, Christopher Foster & Yanuar Nugroho eds., 2017); THEO PAPAIOANNOU, INCLUSIVE INNOVATION FOR DEVELOPMENT: MEETING THE DEMANDS OF JUSTICE THROUGH PUBLIC ACTION (2018); IPRS AND INCLUSIVITY, *supra* note 64.

provided through AI-driven innovation. On the consumption end, the AI divide also deprives these individuals and entities of the opportunity or ability to realize the benefits provided by the AI revolution.

Given the critical role AI is now playing in promoting technological advancement, the global AI divide will harm the Global South on both the production and consumption ends, making developing countries less competitive, if not uncompetitive. To avoid falling too far behind their developed counterparts in AI development, these countries should adopt laws and policies to facilitate the development of globally inclusive AI. They should also cooperate with the Global North, intergovernmental bodies, and donor organizations to help bridge this inequitable gap.

Enabling Environment

The development of AI and other emerging technology depends on the construction of an enabling environment for such development.[124] Thus far, no "one size fits all" model has been found to support successful AI development across the world, nor is there any international consensus on what law and policy reforms would be ideal for boosting such development. Instead, the enabling environment needed for AI adoption and development has varied from region to region, country to country, and sector to sector.

Thus, when the UN Advisory Body recommended the establishment of the Global AI Fund, it refrained from specifying the requisite enablers for promoting AI development. As the final report states, "Our intention in proposing a fund is not to guarantee access to advanced compute resources and capabilities. The answer may not always be more compute. We also need better ways to connect talent, compute and data."[125] Similar to the approach taken by the UN body, this chapter identifies six nonexhaustive and complementary policy options that developing countries could embrace to boost local AI adoption and development. What options will work well in a country will largely depend on that country's specific needs, interests, conditions, and priorities. To the extent that the options discussed in this chapter are deployed in combination, their effectiveness and synergies will

[124] For the author's discussion of enabling environments in the intellectual property context, see Peter K. Yu, *Enforcement, Enforcement, What Enforcement?*, 52 IDEA 239, 265–68 (2012); Yu, *supra* note 55, at 213–16.

[125] UN Advisory Body, *supra* note 8, at 16.

also vary according to the choice of combination and the underlying local conditions.

Technological Change

Although this chapter explores efforts to bridge the global AI divide based on the current state of technology—including the need for big data analytics and large-language models to advance AI technology—it is important to keep in mind that AI technology will continue to evolve. So will the global AI divide and the legal, policy, and technological responses needed to bridge this inequitable gap.

At the technical level, commentators have already discussed the importance of exploring alternatives that rely on "lean data"[126] or "small-language models,"[127] even though many policymakers, commentators, and industry leaders continue to view large datasets as necessary for AI development. In addition, commentators have identified measures to boost AI development in the Global South, including a strengthened ability to handle small and messy datasets, the development of intelligent data-acquisition strategies and compression algorithms, the creation of transfer-learning models for low-resource languages, and the facilitation of machine learning with limited computational capabilities.[128]

Moreover, the past few years have seen a growing discussion of using synthetic data to train AI models.[129] Although artificially generated data come with significant limitations,[130] especially when used alone for AI training, synthetic data will be deployed more widely in the near future. It is, therefore, worthwhile to explore how this type of data can be used more effectively

[126] Matti Keltanen, *Why "Lean Data" Beats Big Data*, GUARDIAN (Apr. 16, 2013), https://www.theguardian.com/media-network/media-network-blog/2013/apr/16/big-data-lean-strategy-business; Daniel Newman, *Bigger Isn't Always Better: It's All About Lean Data*, FORBES (Dec. 4, 2019), https://www.forbes.com/sites/danielnewman/2019/12/04/bigger-isnt-always-better-its-all-about-lean-data/#7c84d0838940; *Separating Better Data from Big Data: Where Analytics Is Headed*, KNOWLEDGE@WHARTON (May 10, 2018), https://knowledge.wharton.upenn.edu/article/where-analytics-is-headed-next/.

[127] Nagesh Mashette, *Small Language Models (SLMs)*, MEDIUM (Dec. 12, 2023), https://medium.com/@nageshmashette32/small-language-models-slms-305597c9edf2.

[128] Maria De-Arteaga, William Herlands, Daniel B. Neill & Artur Dubrawski, *Machine Learning for the Developing World*, ACM TRANSACTIONS ON MGMT. INFO. SYS., Aug. 2018, at 9–10.

[129] Michal S. Gal & Orla Lynskey, *Synthetic Data: Legal Implications of the Data-Generation Revolution*, 109 IOWA L. REV. 1087 (2024); Peter Lee, *Synthetic Data and the Future of AI*, 110 CORNELL L. REV. 1 (2025).

[130] Gal & Lynskey, *supra* note 129, at 1109–10; Lee, *supra* note 129, at 35–37.

in developing countries to boost local AI development as well as what safeguards, correction mechanisms, and other complementary measures can be introduced to address the documented limitations.

Finally, to help boost AI adoption and development in the Global South, it will be important to assess periodically the strengths and weaknesses of the different policy options identified in this chapter as well as new alternatives. To the extent that new options become available to reduce the cost of training or developing AI models, they should be quickly and seriously considered, as the reduced costs will free up resources that can be used elsewhere to bridge the global AI divide. Just as intergovernmental bodies, policymakers, and commentators have highlighted the possibility of using bottom-up, frugal, grassroots, and rural innovation to foster inclusive innovation,[131] policymakers in developing countries and their supportive commentators should also evaluate the feasibility of using "frugal" AI innovation to bridge the global AI divide.

Conclusion

In the past few years, intergovernmental bodies, policymakers, and commentators have paid considerable attention to the potential risks, problems, and challenges brought by advances in AI technology. Notwithstanding these shortcomings, AI can greatly benefit the Global South—in education, public health, business development, and many other areas. If developing countries are to take full advantage of the AI revolution and realize the myriad opportunities the new technology now provides to individuals, firms, and governments, they will need to properly contextualize, based on local conditions, the debate on AI technology and related legal, policy, and technological responses. They should also undertake proactive efforts to bridge the global AI divide, including those identified in this chapter.

The Internet has provided many political, social, economic, cultural, educational, and career opportunities to individuals, firms, and governments

[131] Klingler-Vidra et al., *supra* note 123, at 4–5; Papaioannou, *supra* note 123, at 57–63; World Intell. Prop. Org., 2011 World Intellectual Property Report: The Changing Face of Innovation 40 (2011); Yasser Bhatti & Jaideep Prabhu, *Frugal Innovation and Social Innovation: Linked Paths to Achieving Inclusion Sustainably*, *in* Handbook of Inclusive Innovation, *supra* note 123, at 354.

in the Global South, yet the digital divide has held many developing countries back. Although it is late to redesign Internet policies to lift those on the unfortunate side of the digital divide, advances in AI technology, including generative AI, have presented us with new opportunities to make proactive policy adjustments to promote a more inclusive innovation environment that benefits the Global South. By identifying the wide array of challenges confronting developing countries on both the production and consumption ends and the policy options available to these countries to boost local AI adoption and development, this chapter aims to foster a dialogue on the global AI divide. The sooner the Global South—and, by extension, the entire world—can bridge this important yet oft-overlooked inequitable gap, the more inclusive AI-driven innovation will become, and the better off we will all be in the end.

Acknowledgments

A portion of this chapter expands from the research the author conducted for a book chapter entitled "Artificial Intelligence, Intellectual Property, and Sustainable Development," forthcoming from Edward Elgar Publishing.